NELL GWYNS LOOKING GLASS,

In the Collection of Sir Page Dicks of Port Hall

Charles Beauclerk

Nell Gwyn

A Biography

MACMILLAN

First published 2005 by Macmillan
an imprint of Pan Macmillan Ltd
Pan Macmillan, 20 New Wharf Road, London N1 9RR
Basingstoke and Oxford
Associated companies throughout the world
www.panmacmillan.com

ISBN 0 333 90471 0

1 3 5 7 9 8 6 4 2

A CIP catalogue record for this book is available from
the British Library.

Typeset by SetSystems Ltd, Saffron Walden, Essex
Printed and bound in Great Britain by
Mackays of Chatham plc, Chatham, Kent

For my father

Contents

Acknowledgements

JUST AS IT TAKES a village to raise a child, so it takes a broad community of souls to bring a book into being. Many of those who helped won't be conscious that they did, and even the author himself will be unaware of, and certainly unable to name, all of them. And that's just the living. Anyone who writes a biography of a long-dead person will be availing himself of the efforts and insights of generations of observers, researchers and scholars, many of them long gone, without being conscious of the enormity of his debt. Then, if he is lucky enough to finish, there are the editors who help refine the text, clarify the ideas, and in my case improve the writing. So many books are published today that we tend to take them for granted, but each one represents a miraculous cooperation of diverse interests.

I should like to thank my father, the Duke of St Albans, for giving me access to previously unresearched family papers. As titular head of the house of Nell Gwyn, his support has been highly significant, as has that of the family historian, Peter Beauclerk-Dewar, who has given me the benefit of his encyclopaedic knowledge of the Beauclerks as well as access to his research notes for *The House of Nell Gwyn* (1974).

Thanks are also due to my ex-wife, Louise Burford, for suggesting the book in the first place and for helping with the initial research. Our conversations about Nell Gwyn and the court of Charles II stimulated many ideas.

Help and encouragement were freely given by Sally Mosher and Vere descendant Lawrence David Moon, both of whom read and commented upon the early chapters, Derran Charlton who researched for me at the Brotherton Library, Leeds University, Aidan Hartley, who hectored me to good effect, and historians Brenda James and Stephanie Hughes. And a very special thank-you goes to my erstwhile employer and mentor, the poet and philosopher Nicholas Hagger.

Help with Nell's descendants was provided by Lord and Lady Wakehurst, Lord Cavendish of Furness, the Marquess of Waterford, Lieutenant-Colonel John Silcock, Lady Hagart-Alexander, my uncles Lords Peter and John Beauclerk, my aunt Lady Caroline ffrench-Blake, Geoffrey Meace, Catherine Merrick, Lisa Wingate, Charles Scott, and Ross Sillars, General Manager of the Bestwood Lodge Hotel.

In addition, I have received kind assistance from the staff at a number of libraries and other institutions. These have included my own local library at Hadleigh in Suffolk, at which Geoff Ross has been unfailingly efficient; the London Library, with its sure-fire crew of researchers; the British Library; Edinburgh University Library; the Beinecke Library at Yale University; the Monash University Library, Australia; the Royal Archives at Windsor and St James's Palace; the Victoria & Albert Museum; Lincolnshire County Archives; Northumberland County Archives; the RNLI; the Army & Navy Club; Child & Co.; and the London Metropolitan Archives. Sterling service has also been provided by Edward Priday at Coutts Bank; Louisa Stockdale at Sotheby's; Dr Richard Aspin, Director of Archives at the Wellcome Library; and Jayne Cottrell of the Priory, Ticehurst House.

Heartfelt thanks must go to my agent Natasha Fairweather, who navigated the book through many a tempest with calm and authority, and to the team at Macmillan: the book's commissioner Jeremy Trevathan; Georgina Morley, editorial director of non-fiction; my editor Jason Cooper, who transformed whole passages with the merest touch of his pencil and taught me a good deal about decent writing in the process; and Talya Baker, senior desk editor, for her countless improvements.

Last but by no means least, I should like to thank all my family and friends for their good-humoured encouragement.

prince's ball, there is something almost miraculous in the way that Nell Gwyn was able to capture the heart of the King. How was it possible for an oyster wench brought up in the slums of London to form a lasting relationship with the most powerful man in the land and to make herself at home in his court? After all, she must have been more like a hurricane than a breath of fresh air in the corridors and drawing rooms of Whitehall. Bishop Burnet, the outspoken critic of Charles II, described Nell as 'the indiscreetest and wildest creature that ever was in a Court'.

The answer lies to a large extent in the role she adopted, that of the fool, whose badge of innocence assured royal protection and a peculiarly intimate and inviolable place in the heart of the sovereign. In a sense Nell was merely continuing the comedic career she had begun in the theatre, but this time with the court as her stage. Mimic, prankster and general Lady of Misrule, she filled a very real gap at the post-medieval court of Charles II.

I write as a direct descendant of Nell Gwyn and King Charles II, and heir to the dukedom of St Albans, the title the King created for their son, which makes it as well to declare at the outset that this is very much a subjective portrait of my ancestress. By this I do not mean that my regard for the 'facts' is any less rigorous than that of my biographical predecessors, but rather that I intend to plug into that vital ancestral current which links me to my foremother. Ultimately, what I have attempted to present in this biography is an intimate portrait of Nell Gwyn, moving beyond the icon to the person and exploring the impact she had on the life of the court and the country at large.

By examining her role and significance in the life of the nation not only by means of the historical record but also through the myths and stories that informed her life, I hope I have been able to hint at Nell Gwyn's significance for her time and even for ours. Here was a woman who brought the monarchy to the people and the people to the monarchy, indeed symbolized the union of King and subject, and what wouldn't the present-day House of Windsor give for such a force to set to work in the nation's psyche?

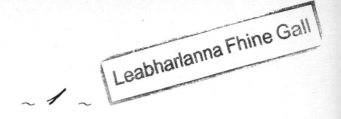

1

Humble Beginnings

REMARKABLY FOR ONE OF HER upbringing and lowly early station in life, we not only have an exact date of birth for Nell Gwyn, but a time too. We owe this piece of good fortune to the antiquarian and astrologer Elias Ashmole, who cast the horoscope bearing her name now preserved at the Bodleian Library in Oxford. According to Ashmole, who may have derived his information from the lady herself, Nell Gwyn was born on Saturday, 2 February 1650, at six o'clock in the morning. The place of her birth is left blank; nor do we know when or at whose behest the birth chart was calculated.

Astrologers, two of whom have been her biographers, seem agreed that the chart drawn up by Ashmole gives a true portrait of Nell Gwyn, which makes it more than likely that the birth data supplied were accurate. Unsurprisingly, Venus was on the horizon at the moment of her birth, bestowing beauty and charm as well as a love of pleasure and material comforts, while Jupiter at the top of the chart (in the charismatic sign of Scorpio) gave her star quality as well as protection from on high, ensuring that few obstacles would keep her from the limelight she craved. The chart is almost bereft of the earthy element that so many naturally associate with Nell; instead, wit and spontaneity emerge as her chief strengths.

Her birthday fell on the Celtic festival of Imbolc, which celebrated the return of the Sun. It was the feast day of the Celtic goddess Brigid, the light-bringer, whose temple at Kildare housed the eternal flame. Under the Catholic Church, Brigid became St Brigit and Imbolc was transformed into the Feast of Candlemas, or the Purification of the Blessed Virgin Mary, at which candles are lit at midnight to attend the first stirrings of spring.

Despite the associations with light implicit in her name and birthday, Nell Gwyn was born at one of the darkest hours in her nation's history. King Charles I had been executed almost exactly a year before, leaving the nation shocked and bewildered. The theatres were closed, the maypoles axed, public entertainments and holidays banned, dancing, singing and playing musical instruments proscribed. Even wrestling, leaping, running and 'unnecessary' walking (i.e., walking for pleasure) were denied the common people. Adultery was now a capital offence. The great iron giant of Puritanism thundered through the land, threatening to rip up the entire fabric of society.

There was a strong feeling that the end of the world was approaching and that Christ would return to begin his 1,000-year reign on earth. The execution of the King had fuelled this millennarian fervour. Messiahs, prophets and ranters of both sexes and every conceivable sect flooded into London from the countryside, as England suffered something in the nature of a nervous breakdown. Predictions were rife and could be used by the government to create a climate of opinion conducive to their aims, as with those that foretold the execution of the King as a necessary precondition for the rule of Christ. The London of Nell Gwyn's childhood was teeming with possessed souls.

Women of course were the main target of the Puritans' blind projection of humankind's darker nature, and their status in the new regime was little better than that of children. Gone were the days of Shakespeare's witty heroines. The Puritans strove relentlessly for the light, their instincts bound like squirming devils and shoved into some dark corner of the soul. Instead, they looked outside themselves for the objects of their torment. Women were the obvious scapegoat, and those whose independent spirits did not allow them to submit either ran mad or became prostitutes. Indeed, it is no surprise that prostitution was more widespread under the Commonwealth than in Charles I's reign. Such are the fruits of demonization.

Poetic justice, however, was served one famous morning in St Paul's Cathedral. A Puritan divine was preaching on the Resurrection when a lady in the congregation suddenly stripped herself naked in her pew and advanced on him with cries of 'Welcome the Resurrection!' One can only hope, for the minister's sake, that the members of the congregation that rose up in response did not include his own! Merry England may have gone underground, but it was certainly not dead.

Nothing perhaps gives a better flavour of the dreary theocracy that was Puritan England than the names with which devout Puritans saddled their children, names such as Abstinence, Forsaken, Tribulation, Ashes, Lamentation, Fear-not, Weep-not, Kill-sin and Fly-fornication. How delightfully bright and simple 'Nell Gwyn' sounds beside a name like 'Perseverance Middleton'. No wonder the *Encyclopaedia Britannica* describes her as 'the living antithesis of Puritanism'. Art too was forced underground, as were all expressions of joy, beauty, and panache. In the words of the poet, the lovers and the dancers were beaten into the clay.[1]

At the exact date of Nell Gwyn's birth, 2 February 1650, Cromwell was marching through rain-sodden Tipperary in the heat of his campaign of butchery in Ireland. The judgement of God was upon those 'barbarous wretches' and the privilege of wielding His righteous sword fell to the future Lord Protector of England. Cromwell's fierce star was in the ascendant. Meanwhile the nineteen-year-old King Charles II was in Jersey with his ragged ad hoc court, where he enjoyed sailing and long walks as distractions from the constant bickering of his followers and the sheer boredom of his permanently makeshift life. Money was scarce. The King himself ate sparingly; his clothes were conspicuously threadbare. Restoration seemed an impossible dream.

Appropriately enough, the royal seal designed for the accession of King Charles in Jersey showed St George on the obverse, for the King in exile was to endure another ten years as the wandering knight, though the dragons that he would vanquish were those reared in the bowels of his own being. Over the next decade he would learn to live as a man among men. Enduring frustrations and humiliations that would have broken others, he came to know himself as few monarchs ever have or ever could. The depth of Charles's self-transformation in exile has rarely been noted, possibly because he hugged this new man to himself in defiant secrecy. Having learnt to conceal himself for survival's sake, he later turned this necessity into an art.

Of all the misfits of Puritan England that took to the roads, Charles Stuart had the furthest to go. It was as if fate had prescribed that the future King of England should know the sorrows and afflictions of ordinary men, for he could have no better tutors for the life of kingship that awaited him. Nothing tested him more ferociously than the forty days and nights after the Battle of Worcester. Charles was disguised as a woodsman and given the name 'Will Jones', his long black locks lopped with a pair of shears, his face smeared with soot. In addition to his coarse peasant shirt and breeches, he wore a greasy, grey steeple-crowned hat and shoes so ill-fitting that his feet bled horribly. Some accounts say he carried a thorn-stick, others a bill-hook. If Nell Gwyn was ever baptized, it would most likely have been in the aftermath of Worcester, while her future lover was enduring his own second baptism, that of fire.

This teenage vagabond King had already become a father before Nell Gwyn was born. He had sired a son upon his first great love, another beauty of Welsh ancestry, Lucy Walter, who was quickly shunted out of the way by exiled courtiers loyal to the King. The boy, who was later to become the Duke of Monmouth, was only prised from his mother in 1658. Later that year, the same year that Cromwell passed away, Lucy lost her life to syphilis.

In a very real sense, Charles's experiences as an exile were an apprenticeship for his relationship with Nell Gwyn, for it was during his years of wandering that he came to identify with the underdog and the common man. Living off charity and in social limbo, despised by those in power, he knew what it was to wear dirty clothes and survive on one meal a day. Through hardship he came to appreciate the ordinary pleasures of life with an almost ritualistic enjoyment.

The parliamentary posters calling for Charles's capture referred to the King as 'a long dark man, above two yards tall'. (His great height, coming as he did from two such tiny parents, was as unexpected as his dark looks.) The language used is telling, for psychologically speaking Charles was indeed the shadow not only of Cromwell personally but of Puritan England itself. Here was a dark, shadowy figure moving across the country, hiding himself in trees and dark places like an animal, living off instinct and the land, dependent on the loyalty of the people. When Charles was finally restored, the oak tree in which he had hidden at Boscobel wood became the emblem of his kingship.[2] This was not to be the dogmatic crown of his father, but a living crown that could grow with the ages. Diarist John Evelyn in his dedication to Charles of *Sylva* (1664) wrote, 'You are our God of the forest-trees, King of the grove, as having once your Temple, and Court too under that Holy Oak which you consecrated with your Presence . . .'

The primary psychological task of Restoration England would be to reconnect the nation with the life of the instincts and spirit. In other words, to restore Merry England (in the Spenserian sense of 'high-hearted'), and so foster a society in which the nation's genius could flourish. And there could be no better catalyst for this restoration than that quintessentially merry soul, Nell Gwyn.

Three cities have been put forward as the birthplace of Nell Gwyn – London, Oxford and Hereford – but in each case the evidence is weak. There is no doubt that the Gwyns were of Welsh origin and that there were Gwyns or Gwynnes living in the Welsh Marches in the seventeenth century. The family, reputed to descend from the Welsh princes, came originally from Llansanor in the Vale of Glamorgan. And, indeed, when Nell came to have a coat of arms designed, towards the end of her life, the blue lion on a gold and silver shield was modelled closely on the armorial bearings of the Gwyns of Llansanor. With her red hair, greenish eyes and beautiful singing voice, it's not hard to discern the strong Celtic element coursing through Nell's veins.

Nevertheless the ancient origins of Nell's family have little bearing on her birthplace, and contemporary evidence for Hereford is lacking. It's true that one of her grandsons, Lord James Beauclerk, became Bishop of Hereford and that Charles II had the cathedral organ repaired, but what of that? *The Dictionary of National Biography* claims that there is a tradition among Hereford historians that she was born there in Pipe Well Lane, which was renamed Gwyn Street in the nineteenth century. The house itself was pulled down in 1859 to provide space for the enlargement of the Bishop's Palace gardens, and a memorial plaque on the outside face of the garden wall marks the spot today. Sadly, the seventeenth-century baptismal registers for the city are sketchy and offer no answers.

It may well be that Nell's father was born and brought up in Hereford, we simply don't know. But it is unlikely that Helena Smith (the future Mrs Gwyn), who was born in the parish of St Martin-in-the-Fields in London and seems to have lived most of her life there, should have found herself in Hereford in 1650. Indeed, London's claim rests largely on the fact that Nell's mother was born there and that she and her sister Rose were almost certainly brought up in one of the streets off Drury Lane. In his *Lives of the Court Beauties* (1715), Captain Alexander Smith gives Coal Yard Alley as her place of birth, and subsequent biographers have tended to follow his lead. Professor John Harold Wilson confidently opens his 1952 biography with a chapter entitled 'The Gwyns of Covent Garden' and states without demur, 'Nell Gwyn was born somewhere in or near the Covent Garden district'. But this is conjecture.

The reason why London's claim remains compelling in the face of very weak evidence has much to do with the demands of the romantic imagination, for the public seems determined to think of Nell Gwyn as the feisty little cockney girl who became mistress to a king. If one thinks in terms of accents, however, it is virtually inconceivable that Nell Gwyn could have survived and flourished at the court of Charles II with a cockney accent, which in those days was the tradesman's accent par excellence. According to H. C. Wyld in *A Short History of English*, 'To speak with the accent of a rural district, even at Court, was not derogatory to the character and prestige of a Gentleman – what was not tolerated was to speak like a tradesman . . .' In Shaw's *Pygmalion*, when Professor Higgins first hears the cockney Eliza Doolittle speak, he refers to 'this creature with her kerbstone English: the English that will keep her in the gutter to the end of her days', and that was in 1916. Even with her actor's training a cockney accent would have been one obstacle too far for Nell Gwyn, rendering her well nigh incomprehensible. Nor do contemporary accounts of her from snobbish courtiers satirize such an impediment.

Oxford, which has traditionally been the least valued of the three birthplaces, seems to me to hold the strongest claim. Whether or not he was born in Hereford, Nell's father, who by most accounts was a

Captain Thomas Gwyn in the Royalist army, certainly lived in Oxford and may well have ended his days there in a debtors' jail. And if Dr Edward Gwyn, a canon of Christ Church, Oxford, was – as the Oxford antiquary Anthony à Wood, among others, claimed – this Thomas's father, then we have a very strong connection.

After his marginal victory at Edgehill in October 1642 Charles I had made Oxford his military and political headquarters, and thus it remained until the summer of 1646. Space was at a premium as Royalists from all over the country flocked to the city and the sick and wounded from Edgehill were brought there. Supplies were short and tempers soon frayed. Despite the King's own sobriety and his efforts to maintain a dignified court, Oxford during the Civil War was like most garrison towns in wartime a wild and distinctly cavalier place, rife with dancing, duelling, drunkenness and debauchery. Men and women came together impulsively in the hectic shadow of war, not always caring to consecrate their union before the altar.

Interestingly, the playwright George Etherege in one of his lampoons, entitled 'The Lady of Pleasure: a Satyr', seems to refer to the idea that Nell was at least conceived in a garrison town. He writes,

> No man alive could ever call her daughter,
> For a battalion of arm'd men begot her.

And Wood tells us that Mrs Gwyn 'lived some time in Oxford' in the parish of St Thomas, so Nell and her sister may have been born there. Unfortunately, no seventeenth-century baptismal registers survive for St Thomas's.

Whether Nell's father was already living in Oxford at the outbreak of war, or whether he arrived from Hereford, we shall probably never know. Nor are we likely to discover what prompted Helena Smith to make her way to the King's new capital from her native London, though Royalist sympathies and the hope of catching some dashing cavalier on the hip are reasons enough. Nevertheless, there is something satisfying in the thought of Nell's parents making their separate ways, one from the east the other from the west of the country, to the heart of Royalist England to produce the child who would in due course come to symbolize a new, more integrated society.

Whether Captain Gwyn actually married Nell's mother is also a matter for conjecture, nor do we know how soon after the war he fell into debt, though the contemporary tradition that he died in prison, having lost his livelihood in the King's service, seems authentic enough. The anonymous author of *A Panegyrick* (1681) wrote,

> From Oxford Prisons many she [i.e., Nell] did free
> Their dy'd her Father and there glory'd shee
> In giving others Life and Libertye
> So pious a remembrance still she bore
> Ev'n to the Fetters which her Father wore . . .

Also, Nell's elder sister, Rose, in a petition for bail written from prison in 1663, mentioned that her father had 'lost all he had in service of the late king.' If we accept her word, then it's unlikely that Thomas Gwyn ever went to London with his wife and two young daughters. Rather it was probably his death in the early 1650s that prompted Madam Gwyn, as she came to be known, to return to her old stamping ground of Covent Garden with Rose and Nell in tow. It's easy to see too how as a single mother with two young daughters to support she quickly fell (back) into that most ancient of professions: prostitution.

All paths, then, seem to lead to Oxford. Maybe Ashmole left the place of birth blank on the horoscope because he was casting it in his home town of Oxford. We shall probably never know. What is certain, however, is that when Nell's eldest son, Charles, first came to be ennobled in 1676, the titles he was granted – Burford and Headington – were both in Oxfordshire. It's interesting too that Nell's future daughter-in-law would turn out to be the heiress of the last Earl of Oxford, Lady Diana de Vere, while her putative uncle Henry Gwyn was secretary to this same Earl.

Nell herself doesn't seem to have been forthcoming about her background and may have found it advantageous to cultivate a certain mystique. Many, though, must have wondered about her origins and even today a certain mystery surrounds her identity. There is a reference to her as 'Mrs. Margaret Symcott (i.e. Eleanor Gwyn)' in a list of charitable bequests to the Prisoners on the Common Side of King's Bench Prison, while Fairburn claims that she made many charitable donations 'as Lady Simcock' after the King's death.[3] More recently Arnold Hawker, a genealogist, came to the conclusion that Nell was born Elizabeth Fawconer, the daughter of a Wiltshire squire. No doubt her confident manner at court as well as her success in playing well-bred ladies on the stage encouraged the notion that she was well-born.

We know nothing of Mrs Gwyn's life before she arrived in (or returned to) London. Most biographers of Nell Gwyn have assumed that her mother was low-born, but this is conjecture derived from later reports of her squalid circumstances and degrading profession during the years of Nell's girlhood. Given that her husband died in a debtors' jail, misfortune and poverty, rather than low birth and depravity, are just as likely to have been the causes of her descent into London's bawdy underworld. There is no reason to suppose that she was not at one time the social equal of her husband, who if he wasn't a gentleman seems to have teetered on the brink of gentility.

The monument that Nell erected for her mother at St Martin-in-the-Fields placed her birth in 1624, the final year of King James I's reign. If this is accurate, then Madam Gwyn's coming of age would have coincided with the outbreak of the Civil War. Even taking into account the exaggerations of the satirists, it is clear from contemporary records that Nell's mother was a Falstaffian figure with the sort of mythic status acquired by her fellow heroines of the underworld, the notorious procuresses Madams Ross, Bennett and Cresswell, Mother Mosely, and Orange Moll.[4]

The picture the lampoons give us of Nell's mother is of a gargantuan brandy-swigging, pipe-smoking bawd, who drowned in a stream or ditch after an almighty binge. Sadly, there is no description of her character, yet certain recurring images used by the satirists unwittingly illuminate an important facet of her emotional life – her buried rage. As a young woman she may well have had much of the beauty, wit and sparkle of her younger daughter, enough at least to attract a captain's love. But the war intervened and after several difficult years in Oxford she found herself back in London, a single mother with two young daughters and, with the theatres closed, no outlet for her talents. A life of prostitution followed, and before long she was running her own bawdy house. One can easily imagine the resentment of this lively woman.

Indeed, one senses that she was all but engulfed by the frustrations of her unlived life. In one mock elegy on 'that never to be forgotten Matron, Old Madamm Gwinn', Nell's mother is compared with the monstrous dragon Typhon, which Zeus killed by dropping Mount Etna on it, yet whose wrath found expression, even after death, in the eruptions of the volcano. This is a good image for Mrs Gwyn's seething rage, which was fuelled by alcohol and would have strongly influenced the emotional life of her daughters.

In terms of Nell's early life, then, the absent father and the devouring mother are key archetypes, as, indeed, they were for her future lover, the young Charles Stuart. Her search for the gentlemanly father she lost in infancy would end with Charles himself (who was twenty years her senior), while the rage she inherited from her mother would find a creative outlet in her trenchant humour both at the theatre and at court, where she played the bittersweet fool.

Whatever the devices Nell found to convert her gyves to graces, growing up under the volcano cannot have been easy. Both she and her sister were completely uneducated – Nell never even learnt to sign her name – and they were set to work in their mother's establishment from a very early age. According to Samuel Pepys, Nell told fellow actress Beck Marshall that she was 'brought up in a bawdy house to fill strong waters to the gentlemen'.

A bawdy house in the seventeenth century wasn't a brothel; though it offered the same service it was a little more discreet. The heart of the establishment was more often than not simply a cellar or an upstairs room in someone's house, where drinks were served and which was presided over by a bawd who kept a stable of young girls to entertain male clients. The girls didn't live at the establishment, but were called in as and when they were required. There were separate rooms in the house to which they could retire with their 'guests', who might be anything from courtiers to pickpockets.

Nell's phrase 'brought up in a bawdy house' could mean that her mother worked from home or that she leased an establishment somewhere else, the latter being the more likely. It could also mean that she worked in another establishment altogether, such as Madam Ross's. Either way, the underworld was Nell's early home, and it's not difficult to imagine her serving 'Nantz' or brandy to the leery guests and cultivating the lightning repartee that would one day startle the court of Charles II. Just as she was to have three Charleses in her life, so she would have three stages: the bawdy house, the theatre and the court.

Even at the tender age of nine or ten, Nell would have found herself fending off the attentions of her mother's more lecherous clients. Nor is it inconceivable that she became a child prostitute along the way; we shall never know for sure. But with only an alcoholic mother for protection she would have been vulnerable to such exploitation and could easily have found a surrogate warmth in the attentions that her charm and quick wit won from the punters. The sketchy evidence suggests, too, that Nell's elder sister, Rose, became a prostitute in her early teens, making it harder for the younger girl to steer a different course. That said, it would be wrong to imagine that the bawdy house was a wholly unpleasant place for a little girl to grow up in. Alive with convivial humanity, it did at least provide fertile ground for Nell's budding humour and insight, as well as keeping the chill winds of Puritanism at bay.

The Covent Garden district of London was an area of lively contrasts. At its heart was the piazza itself, dominated by the Church of St Paul's and surrounded by fashionable town houses. Behind these were a maze of small streets and alleys with their more cramped lodging houses, shops and taverns, as well as the notorious bawdy houses and slum tenements. This was home territory for Nell, a dense city forest and she its brightest nymph. To the north lay open fields, to the south the palaces of the nobility, with their rich gardens sloping down to the river. The theatre that would make Nell Gwyn famous throughout the capital had yet to be built.

If Nell was brought up in Coal Yard Alley in the Parish of St Giles, then simply to have survived the slums of London was an achievement. Disease and vermin were rife, sanitation poor or non-existent, and even in the healthier sections of the city one out of two children died before their second birthday. The stench of refuse and decay on a hot summer's day must have been well nigh unbearable. And if Nell really did live in one of the slum tenements, then all there would have been downstairs were a couple of dingy, smoky rooms – no windows –

with dirt floors covered in straw and a cinder fire to cook over. She would have been lucky to retire upstairs at night to a wooden box bed with straw mattress. Baths and privy closets were out of the question.

Nevertheless, the street life of Drury Lane and its neighbourhood must have provided an exciting release from the wearisome duties of child labour. With its strong bohemian spirit it was one of the most colourful and entertaining districts in London. Street performers of every description and nationality drew crowds with their bizarre and daring acts. In the absence of toys or other games, the ragged street children had to invent their own amusements and were often responsible for making sure they got enough to eat, in which case filching from the market stalls was the order of the day. There were few restrictions on their movements or behaviour, but the price they paid for such freedoms was insecurity. They danced in the shadow of death, and slept 'among tygers wild'.[5] Little wonder then that strong bonds of camaraderie bound the urchins of a London street.

Nell relished having such a willing and appreciative audience among her fellow strays. Setting up her eager little court in one of the deserted dead-end alleys of St Giles, she could at least be a 'Queen in Imagination', as an anonymous biography of 1752 has it. And, remembering the tales of old King Charles's court that she'd heard from the customers in the bawdy house, the incorrigible imp would step forth, an old blanket serving as her jewelled train, and put on that royal look that so delighted her half-starving subjects that they dropped instantly to their knees with shouts of 'God save good Queen Nell!'. Like poor Tom Canty in Twain's *The Prince and the Pauper*, she filled her days with such imaginings; and, as with Tom, it seems likely that her 'speech and manners became curiously ceremonious and courtly, to the vast admiration and amusement of [her] intimates'.

One anecdote related in a note in John Downes's *Roscius Anglicanus* (1708) gives a vivid insight into the strong network of loyalties at work among the waifs of Drury Lane. We are told that Nell's first love was a link-boy (or torch-bearer) by the name of Poor Dick, a homeless lad who was convinced that Nell was the daughter of a lord, for that was the only way he could explain her uncommon beauty. Cut to the heart by the sight of her bare chilblained feet, he set aside his meagre wages to buy her a pair of worsted stockings. According to Nell, he put them on her feet himself, and as his tears fell on her chilblains he said that he would be the happiest creature on earth if the stockings did her some good.

Aprocryphal though the story may be, it is valuable in demonstrating that even as a young girl Nell's beauty and depth of character were thought to have inspired deep loyalty. We will find, too, as we progress with our story that much was made throughout her life of Nell's delicate and delightfully pretty feet. It's interesting to note that in China, where the story of Cinderella originated, a small, prettily shaped foot was seen as a mark of extraordinary virtue and beauty.

There are many references in the lampoons of the time to the young Nell Gwyn as 'Cinder Nell', no doubt because it was thought that raking the cinders was one of her duties in her mother's bawdy house. True or not, it shows that unconsciously her detractors associated her with the figure of Cinderella. In *A Panegyrick*, the author wrote,

> Ev'n while she cinders rak'd her swelling breast
> With thoughts of glorious whoredom was possess'd . . .

And the author of 'The Lady of Pleasure', thought to be Etherege, gives us a vivid picture of Nell, the street urchin:

> He that had seen her mudling in the street
> With face of potlid black, unshoo'd her feet
> And in a cloud of dust her cinders shaking
> Cou'd he have thought her fit for Monarch's taking . . . ?

Probably not. What is certain, however, is that young Nell had heard stories of the King over the water (London was abuzz with rumours of his adventurous life) and even now harboured certain wild thoughts against the day of his return.

And although an unnatural calm settled on England after the death of Cromwell in September 1658, it would not be long before the prince of Cinder Nell's dreams arrived back in his kingdom. The Republican movement had lost much of its zeal under the quasi-monarchic rule of the Lord Protector, and though it still wasn't safe to mention the King over the water in public, more and more people began to nurse a secret desire for his return. Thus when in May 1659 Oliver's son Richard let slip the reins of power and vanished across the Channel, the time-honoured formula of the King in Parliament reasserted its irresistible logic.

2

Restoration

CROMWELL HAD DIED ON THE seventh anniversary of the Battle of Worcester, at which he had defeated the twenty-one-year-old King Charles II. Because the stench of his rotting spleen defied both the embalmer's and the undertaker's art, Cromwell was buried privately a few days after his death. In accordance with royal custom, a wax effigy of the Lord Protector was made for his lying-in-state at Somerset House, and it was to this – as it lay on the candlelit bed of state – that the public paid their respects. Towards the end of the second week Old Noll's glass-eyed doll was raised like a patient into a sitting position and the imperial crown placed on its head. The kingship he had so coveted in life now mocked him in death. Then, on the day of the funeral itself, nearly two months after the Protector's death, his wax dummy, dressed in black velvet and with all the paraphernalia of royalty (crown, sceptre and orb), rode to Westminster Abbey in an open chariot. According to John Evelyn, 'it was the joyfullest funeral I ever saw, for there were none that cried but dogs, which the soldiers hooted away with a barbarous noise, drinking and taking tobacco in the streets as they went.'

Oliver was succeeded as Protector by his third son, Richard, popularly known as Tumbledown Dick, who had very little appetite for power and even less ability to exercise it. Bullied by the army, the Council of State and finally Parliament itself, he was dismissed in May 1659. Although he left office willingly enough, he dared not leave the Palace of Whitehall for fear of arrest for debt. Finally he managed to slip abroad at the time of the Restoration and lived in France under the name of John Clarke. In a bizarre parody of King Charles's exile, he spent nearly twenty years wandering obscurely on the Continent before being allowed to return to his homeland in 1680.[1]

When Charles landed at Dover on 25 May 1660 to shouts of 'God save the King!', his youngest brother, the Duke of Gloucester, was heard to cry, 'God save General Monk!' Without Monk, or 'old George' as his soldiers called him, the Restoration would have been a good deal longer in coming. After the failed Royalist uprising of August 1659 there was no clear power in the land. The army under General Lambert was menacing, yet disorganized, the Rump Parliament – as ever – utterly incredible. It was obvious that Monk, who was commander-in-chief of Scotland and who sided with the Rump, was the only man who could restore order. Even the King had made overtures to Monk after the failure of the second Protectorate, but the time had not been ripe and the general had declined to receive his letters.

Then Lambert dismissed the Rump, and Monk, prompted half by inclination, half by fate, began his march south from Edinburgh on 1 January 1660. His aim was to secure the freedom and rights of the three kingdoms 'from arbitrary and tyrannical usurpations'. On his way down to London Monk was besieged with petitions for a Free Parliament, but he refused to declare his hand. Charles, waiting nervously in Brussels, made contact through his agents and a tacit understanding grew between the two men. Monk's authority was such that people were not inclined to resist the momentum of his silent mission. The landscape was covered in snow, and the general stared into the silence as if caught up in a dream. ('He is a black Monk', wrote Lord Mordaunt, 'and I cannot see through him.')

Monk arrived in London in February 1660. The City fathers were refusing to pay taxes unless a Free Parliament was called. Monk seized his chance and, having convened a council of his principal officers, wrote a letter to the Rump demanding that writs be issued for the recall of those members of Parliament that had been excluded by Colonel Pride in his purge of 1648 and, further, that the first and only act of the newly reassembled Parliament should be to effect its own dissolution. Thus would the path be cleared for a Free Parliament.

And though nobody said anything for the moment, a Free Parliament almost certainly meant the return of the King.

As soon as news of Monk's letter was out, Londoners took to the streets to celebrate. Sides of beef were roasted in the streets on open fires and the city bells rang out. The tyranny of the army was at an end and the supremacy of the civil law once more established. Yet Parliament required the royal spark to make it fully sovereign. The Commonwealth had begun to establish the idea that Parliament derives its power from the people, yet for a nation reared on the Bible the ultimate source of Parliament's authority was divine: and this divinity was symbolized by the throne and its incumbent. During the Commonwealth there had been nothing to command the people's allegiance beyond abstract principles; now that allegiance could be given freely to the rightful King, symbol of the hopes, aspirations and unity of an entire people.

Deep in the psyche of the nation a new relationship had evolved between the sovereign and Parliament, and it was this golden thread that would finally lead to the true genius of the British system: constitutional monarchy.

Not until the end of March when he met the King's emissary, Sir John Grenville, did Monk fully reveal his hand. Now the two men whom fate had drawn silently together began that correspondence which was to lead to Charles's full and unconditional restoration. On Monk's advice, Charles left the Spanish Netherlands and travelled to Breda in Holland where, with the help of his Lord Chancellor Edward Hyde, later Earl of Clarendon, he drew up the justly celebrated Declaration of Breda. This eloquent document granted an amnesty to all those who had fought against his father (excepting only those who had contrived the execution itself) as well as declaring 'a liberty to tender consciences', so that 'no man shall be disquieted or called in question for differences of opinion in matters of religion, which do not disturb the peace of the kingdom'. In addition, he wrote letters to both Houses of Parliament.

As soon as the King's addresses were received by Parliament, he was invited unanimously on 1 May to return to England to be crowned. In addition, the sum of £50,000 was voted for his personal use. That month of May 1660 must have seemed like a dream to the King and his family and followers in exile, or at the very least like some fabulous masque. On 15 May, at the invitation of the States-General, who themselves voted him a sum of £30,000, Charles journeyed to The Hague, where delegations from the Lords and Commons awaited him. And while he was there a further delegation arrived from the City of London, bearing a chest containing £10,000 in gold. Charles and his brothers, the Dukes of York and Gloucester, long-time strangers to wealth, stood feasting their eyes on the money. There followed eight days of banquets and receptions in honour of the King, while suitors for his goodwill flocked to The Hague from every corner of Europe. Secretary of State Henry Coventry wrote from London to the Marquess of Ormonde in Holland, saying, 'I pray, my Lord, hasten his Majesty over as soon as may be, to prevent the town's running mad; for betwixt joy and expectation the people hardly sleep'.

It's not hard to imagine the excitement among Nell's ragged crew of urchins. Being born under the Commonwealth, the very word 'King' must have sounded in their ears with a special magic. As they watched the exiled Cavaliers streaming back into the capital in advance of Restoration Day, bringing with them the latest French fashions for their wives and daughters, they must have dreamed of a new world of colour, chivalry and adventure. I can see Nell badgering her mother for descriptions of the young Prince of Wales, as he had been in the years before his exile. If so, she would have heard how his dark looks had earned him the nickname of the 'Black Boy', which doubtless suited her fancies very well, being herself the Queen of Coal Yard Alley. And maybe Mrs Gwyn described the rather solemn young man with the black shoulder-length hair and large black eyes, who at the age of eleven had been sent to the House of Lords by his father to plead for the life of 'Black Tom', the ill-fated Earl of Strafford; and told how the capital had been abuzz with reports of the boy's courage and self-possession that day.

And just as the whole country was as nervous and excited as a bride on the eve of her wedding day, brim-full with thoughts of the mysterious groom, so little Nell herself – the Cinderella of the London slums – no doubt spent hours in front of her mother's cracked and grimy mirror, combing the dust and cinders from her hair in readiness for the King's return. Now was the time to put on Poor Dick's stockings and to pin that old chipped brooch she'd found in the street to her best serving-smock. Now was the time to gather her wild and faithful crew about her to pour out her dreams of future glory. Listening open-mouthed, they might have heard tell how one day she would marry the King and invite them all to the palace for a slap-up dinner.

On 23 May the royal party set sail in the *Naseby*, hastily renamed the *Royal Charles*, and the King's thoughts not unnaturally returned to his perilous escape after the Battle of Worcester, the last time he had walked his native soil. Samuel Pepys, the twenty-seven-year-old Secretary to the Navy, was on board and listened on the verge of tears to the King's account of his sufferings. Contrary to what he had been led to believe, Pepys was impressed by the King's energy and spirit and his habit of rising early, which had earned him the nickname 'Chanticleer'. More than that, the two men shared a love of music, and Samuel was put in charge of the King's guitar.

The royal party landed at Dover on 25 May at dawn. Even at that early hour a crowd of some 50,000 people had gathered on the dunes and cliffs to witness the King's arrival. They cheered themselves hoarse as Charles stepped ashore and fell to his knees to give thanks for his safe return. When he rose he was greeted by General Monk and the Mayor of Dover, who presented him with a Bible, which the King professed to love 'above all other things in the world'. After sojourns at Canterbury and Rochester, Charles, whose entire route had been lined with ecstatic well-wishers, arrived in London on 29 May, his thirtieth birthday. The fact that it was the King's birthday is highly significant: the day of the nation's restoration was the day of his rebirth.

It is hard to imagine the sheer wonder and, indeed, incredibility of the King's reappearance in his kingdom, which must to many have seemed like an apparition or the miraculous contrivance of providence. The bells of all the churches rang out, the streets were strewn with flowers, the houses draped with banners and tapestry, and the fountains filled with wine. According to Pepys, the shouting and joy expressed by all were 'past imagination', while Evelyn, the other great diarist of the age, wrote,

I stood in the Strand and beheld it, and bless'd God. And all this was done without one drop of blood shed, and by that very army which rebelled against him; but it was the Lord's doing, for such a Restoration was never mentioned in any history ancient or modern, since the return of the Jews from the Babylonish captivity; nor so joyful a day and so bright ever seen in this Nation, this happening when to expect or effect it was past all human policy.

Nell would have been in her element, as London became one huge street party. Working as she did either in her mother's bawdy house or in Madam Ross's, her shock of red hair and impudent wit would have been familiar to the many inhabitants and pleasure-seekers of Covent Garden. There was a plethora of quacks and street entertainers in her neighbourhood and had Nell wished to attract the King's attention from among the crowds of several hundred thousand, she would have had little difficulty in procuring herself a pair of stilts on which to teeter out to the Strand, where she could set herself up among the clowns and zanies and stand a lookout for her less cocksure comrades.

She would have heard the echoing shouts of 'God save the King!' long before she actually saw Charles approaching with his gorgeously attired retinue of nobles and aldermen, bearing their gilded pikestaffs. The King himself was seated on a magnificent white charger, while his followers thronged below on foot. His tall steeple-crowned black hat was decorated with golden plumes, and was doffed again and again in acknowledgment of the cheering crowds. The perfume from the crushed flowers that strewed his way mingled with the scent of the wine that gushed from the fountains to intoxicate even the most puritan disposition. And the little girl on stilts would have rejoiced to stand level with the man who would one day share the secrets of her soul.

The King's procession took seven hours to traverse the capital, arriving towards evening at Whitehall, where he received loyal addresses from both Houses of Parliament. Fatigued as he was, Charles must have been overcome by a wave of melancholy, for Whitehall was not only the scene of some of his fondest childhood memories: it was the place of his father's execution. In many ways he felt alienated from the land of his birth, like a man returning to a burgled house. There was the knowledge too that so many of those whom he must now govern and protect were complicit in his father's murder. Had he looked down at his hand, he would have seen the ring entrusted by his father to Bishop Juxon at the point of execution. It had been sent to him in France with the solitary injunction, 'Remember!' On the blood-red stone the old King had been exquisitely – and ironically – carved as the Emperor Augustus, a wreath of laurel upon his head. On the reverse the thorny leaves of the acanthus symbolized both his own sufferings and the wasteland to which war had reduced his kingdom. Twenty-five years later Charles would give this same ring to the 1st Duke of St Albans, his son by Nell Gwyn, an heirloom that remained in the ownership of the Dukes of St Albans until the twenty-first century.

It was doubtless here before the Banqueting Hall that Charles vowed never to go on his travels again; staying on his throne would be the best way to honour the memory of his murdered father. Looking round him at the unanimous adulation of his subjects, this shrewdest of politicians was heard to say, 'I doubt [i.e. suspect] it has been my own fault that I have been absent so long, for I see nobody that does not protest he has ever wished for my return.' There was certainly irony in his voice, maybe even a little bitterness, though Charles was a master at disguising his feelings. The execution of his father and his own sufferings in exile were bound to have taken their toll. Charles never really trusted the English again, and though unfailingly courteous to all who approached him, he maintained to the end of his days a curious detachment from the people he governed.

Nor, on the whole, did the King lose an opportunity to cock a snook at his fellow countrymen, albeit unconsciously, for his natural desire for revenge could not but out. In Charles's case, his actions from the start made it plain that he would not be bound by English social conventions. For instance, it is the stuff of legend that Charles spent his first night back in Whitehall in the arms of nineteen-year-old Barbara Palmer (née Villiers), and that he declined the service of thanksgiving that had been planned in the Abbey for that evening, the quicker to reach her embrace. (Their first child, a daughter, was born exactly nine months later on 25 February 1661.)

gentleman'.) Like his maternal grandfather, Henri IV of France, who famously quipped that Paris was worth a Mass, Charles was unable to take religious dogma seriously. As historian Hesketh Pearson remarks, 'He was tolerant of all beliefs, and indifferent to all, preferring personal honesty to any profession of faith.'[4] Charles's one-time chaplain Bishop Burnet noted that the King possessed his own faith or religious philosophy, which strikes us today as peculiarly modern. He believed that God would never condemn man's sensual enjoyment of life as long as it did no harm to others, for 'to be wicked and to design mischief is the only thing God hates'.[5] The King, noted Burnet half admiringly, had a strange command of himself.

Given his early experiences, it's little wonder that Charles grew cynical about man's constancy and the durability of his allegiance, or that he developed a steely determination to serve his own turn before other men's, especially if such a stance contributed to the health of the kingdom. He had learnt too that men only respect a king who exercises his power and authority. The deluge of gold and good wishes at the Restoration from men who had spurned him in his hour of need can only have confirmed the King in his sceptical resolve to trust no one.

Charles's own virtues of patience, fortitude and impartiality, as well as his refusal to succumb to despair, were as much responsible for the Restoration as events in England, which were beyond his control. What strikes one about his years in exile is not the King's profligacy and debauchery, which were largely a figment of Puritan imagination and propaganda, but rather his remarkable self-control and moderation. It could be said that Charles's genius lay both in his detachment from and his acceptance of people and events. He had developed the knack of navigating the political current without being swept away by it, while his sufferings had taught him to be a truer democrat than his Republican opponents. He had learnt not to judge a man by his birth or standing; nobility, he knew, was a quality of character.

In contrast to his father, Charles I, and his grandfather, James I, who both held a rigidly theoretical view of kingship, Charles II cared not a fig for political abstractions and theorizing, for he knew too well how ephemeral such mental constructions are. He saw his political task very clearly: to stay on the throne and act the part of a king. His was the old Elizabethan certainty, unencumbered by self-doubting dogma. If he had a political philosophy, it was to be found in his famous paraphrase of Solomon, 'I would have every man live under his own vine and fig tree'. In other words, he believed in economic prosperity and liberty of conscience for all. His was a temperament ideally suited to constitutional monarchy and the creation of a post-medieval state. Indeed, in the battles he would have to fight with Parliament over religious toleration, his was, in the words of Churchill, 'the only modern and merciful voice that spoke'.

Though soon to be dubbed the 'merry monarch', the King who entered London on that bright summer's day seemed more grave than merry. Pepys, who first saw the King at The Hague on 17 May 1660, described him in his *Diary* as 'a very sober man'. Though his features were too lean and dark to be characterized as either handsome or merry, he had long cultivated a debonair demeanour to conceal the profound vein of melancholy that traversed his nature. Charles was in full control of his emotions, and was happy to be thought of as merry or even slightly frivolous if that helped to wrong-foot his opponents. Indeed, it was only natural that a good many myths should have grown up around a figure who had been in the nature of a fictional character to his compatriots for the better part of a generation. Those that knew him well, however, recognized him for what he was: self-possessed, quick-witted, courteous to all regardless of their birth and quietly determined.

As Shakespeare makes plain in the case of Henry V, who sowed his wild oats as Prince Hal, self-knowledge in a ruler is vital to the health of a nation. The King must govern himself before he can govern others. Charles II acquired this self-knowledge through his sufferings in exile, as he himself makes plain in his first letter as King to the Speaker of the Commons, which ends, 'And we hope that we have made that right Christian use of our afflictions, and that the obser-vations and experience we have had in other countries hath been such as that we, and we hope all our subjects, shall be the better for what we have seen and suffered.' As with all the Stuart monarchs, tragedy brought out the best in Charles and he had an uncanny ability to rise to the big occasions. Yet he always suffered from a fatal sense of rootlessness, which, according to Cecil Chesterton, caused him to steer clear of any absolute loyalty, even to the country he ruled.[6]

There was and still is a gulf between Charles as he was and Charles as he has been reported. His impatience with the bureaucracy of government has been called laziness, which couldn't be further from the truth. If anything, the King possessed a superabundance of energy that made it very hard for him to relax. He rose before dawn to take his exercise (riding, swimming or tennis) and had dispatched a good deal of official business before any of his ministers arrived at the council table. He walked so fast that officials and petitioners had to run to keep up with him. Even Cromwell had marvelled at Charles's energy and skill in raising troops in Scotland in 1651.

And when he wasn't engaged in state business, he was receiving people at all hours of the day, patronizing the arts and sciences and even performing chemical experiments in his private laboratory. His grasp of mathematics, astronomy and navigation are justly famous. Architecture was also a passion, and Charles was a talented draughtsman. John Evelyn, himself a polymath, records the following encounter with the King on 27 October 1664:

> He [the King] then caus'd me to follow him alone to one of the windows, and ask'd me if I had any paper about me unwritten, and a crayon; I presented him with both, and then laying it on the window-stool, he with his own hands design'd to me the plot for the future building of White-hall, together with the roomes of state, and other particulars. After this he talk'd with me of severall matters . . . in which I find his Majesty had an extraordinary talent becoming a magnificent prince.

His intelligence and love of witty conversation were remarked upon again and again by admirers and detractors alike. This mercurial quality made him quick to understand commercial opportunities, and being of Medici stock on his mother's side there was a calculating, mercantile streak to his nature which was well suited to take advantage of the changing world in which he found himself. Indeed, it was because he was so alive to new ideas that his reign looked forward to the modern age in almost every particular. Even his commitment to leisure has a modern feel to it. When it comes down to it, Charles was more radical and more truly meritocratic than Cromwell, who slyly hankered after the throne and was intolerant of divergent views. The King, on the other hand, tutored by his long and wearisome exile, was both realistic and unprejudiced. He understood the importance of the free market and cultivated science as the basis of a new and more civilized society.

Despite the numerous affairs he had abroad and their resulting off-spring (he was the father of five by 1660), Charles's womanizing in exile has been exaggerated. And though he was to take a number of mistresses as King, it was no more than his Tudor predecessors. Charles's sensual enjoyment of women was vividly apparent. Halifax wrote that the King's 'inclinations to love were the effects of health and a good constitution, with as little mixture of the seraphic part as ever man had'. But if there were no seraphs, there were certainly demons. Even as a boy Charles had been enthralled by the sexual power of women. Seduced by his old wet nurse, Christabella Wyndham, sex became his comforter, a substitute for real care.

Important too for Charles was the feeling of power that came with the conquest, especially if, as seems likely, he was unable to relax sufficiently to enjoy sex. Besides, it was one of the badges of a king to create a harem, even out of the wives of his associates; it was a demonstration of his power and had little to do with physical pleasure. The flavour of this sort of prowess is well captured in the opening of Dryden's *Absalom and Achitophel*, where Charles is portrayed as David, King of Israel, and the Restoration as the beginning of a new golden age of primitive content:

> In pious times, e'er Priest-craft did begin,
> Before *Polygamy* was made a Sin;
> When Man on many multipli'd his kind,
> E'r one to one was cursedly confin'd,
> When Nature prompted and no Law deni'd
> Promiscuous Use of Concubine and Bride;
> Then *Israel's* Monarch, after Heaven's own heart,
> His vigorous warmth did variously impart
> To Wives and Slaves: And, wide as his Command,
> Scatter'd his Maker's Image through the Land.

On the level of myth, the body of the nation was purged of Puritanism through the love life of Charles II. As Clarendon pointed out, Charles's love nature owed much to his maternal grandfather, Henri IV of France.

He, like Charles, gave his mistresses official positions at court and insisted that his Queen accept them. Henri was also famed for his sexual prowess (he is credited with fifty-four mistresses) and was dubbed 'Le Vert Galant' (the lusty gallant) by an admiring public, just as Charles was given the nickname 'Old Rowley' after one of his stallions.

On the whole, Charles's passion for women was in healthy contrast to the anaemic love life of his immediate predecessors. On his father's side, at least, he came from a long line of men who had repressed their sexuality. His great-grandfather Henry Stuart, Lord Darnley, his grandfather James I and father Charles I were all rather neurotic men with bisexual leanings and domineering wives. The figure of this long-repressed sexuality appears under the left elbow of the seven-year-old Prince Charles in the form of a monstrous boar hound in Van Dyck's 1637 portrait of the five children of Charles I. Although the fabulously large dog has its right paw on the prince's left foot, he seems almost unaware of its presence, as if the hound lurks in the depths of the boy's unconscious, waiting to be redeemed.

Indeed, the old English sensuality was well and truly unkennelled at the time of the Restoration. The inhabitants of London had only to look around them to see the maypoles springing up like a forest in time for the May Day celebrations. The biggest one of all, topped by a gilded crown, was in Nell Gwyn's vicinity at the Strand near Drury Lane.

When we left Nell at the end of the last chapter, she was an urchin queen in the grimy little alleys off Drury Lane, fantasizing about a regal life and commanding the allegiance of a troop of spirited waifs and ragamuffins. Even at ten she was no longer wholly childlike, her knowledge of the world sadly precocious. Central to her fantasies had been the figure of the returning King, and now that he was back, anything seemed possible.

~ 3 ~

Rising from the Ashes

RESTORATION LONDON WAS AN EXCITING place to be for a bright girl of ten whose head was bubbling with dreams of glory. The King was a man who took an interest in human endeavour of every kind. Under his benign – some would say casual – rule, culture flourished: the theatres reopened, the arts and sciences burgeoned, trade boomed, investment soared and the people resumed their sports and pastimes. England once more breathed the invigorating air it had breathed during the heady years of the 1560s under the first Elizabeth. And nowhere was life more vibrant than along the north bank of the King's beloved Thames.

Charles and the Cavaliers brought home a new culture from Paris (and, to a lesser extent, Flanders) in the form of music, painting, fashions, furniture, food, gardens, architecture, the modern stage, court etiquette, gambling (of which Charles disapproved), pornography, champagne and a certain Gallic urbanity that was roundly resented by the bulk of Englishmen. Charles, who favoured the chamber music he had heard at the French court, learnt to play the guitar. Indeed, he was influenced in matters of taste more than he'd have cared to admit by his cousin Louis XIV, and the residence of his mother and favourite sister, Minette, at the Sun King's court kept this connection vital. In effect, Charles planted the seeds of classicism in England. According to Bryant, 'The calm, the balance and beauty of the eighteenth century is Charles's legacy to his people'.

With half a million inhabitants, London was by far the biggest city in the kingdom. There were a hundred parish spires scattered across its face, surmounted by the fatherly bulk of old St Paul's. By and large it was still the medieval city inherited by the Tudors, with narrow streets that became easily jammed with traffic and tall timber-framed houses that leant forward, shutting out both light and air. And although people were supposed to take their household waste to a place where the rakers could cart it off to the laystalls on the edge of town, or failing that leave it outside their doors in tubs or other containers for collection by the 'scavengers', most people tipped their slops into the gutter running down the middle of the street in the hope that the rain would wash them away. Thus not only were the streets dim and airless, they also gave off a terrible stench. Few drank from the city conduits, and the old Celtic suspicion of standing water precluded baths. Pepys records a single bath, if it can be classified as such, in the ten years of his *Diary*.[1]

There were broad streets such as the Strand, but the river served as the city's main thoroughfare, both for commerce and pleasure. Foreign dignitaries were astonished at the sheer volume and variety of shipping on the Thames, from the liveried barges of the nobility to the battered skiffs belonging to vendors of fruit and spirits. Yet, despite the fact that it was London's principal sewer, the river was still 'the silver streaming *Themmes*, / Whose rutty Bancke . . . was paynted all with variable flowers' depicted by Spenser in his *Prothalamion*. People took pleasant walks along its banks and the King himself often went swimming in the river after his early-morning game of tennis, much to the alarm of his doctors.

Less pleasant were the smoke-belching factories of the brewers, dyers, soap-boilers, glass-makers, iron-smelters and lime-burners that had risen in the city and its suburbs, many of them on the banks of the river. Together with the smoke from the widespread use of sea-coal, they produced a high level of pollution in London. Evelyn, who wrote a work suggesting various remedies entitled *Fumifugium* (1661), remarked that the 'columns and clouds of smoke which are belched forth from the sooty throats of our factories are so thick and plentiful that . . . they resist the fiercest winds, and fall down upon the City before they can be dissipated, rendering it in a few moments like a picture of Troy sacked by the Greeks'. He also complained about the

awful coughing in churches and other assemblies, 'where the barking
and spitting is incessant and most importunate'. One of his solutions
was to create a green belt around London, which would surround the
city with air and light, giving much needed refreshment to those
within.

But despite its industry and the grandeur of its principal buildings
and squares, London was still very much a rural town, surrounded by
green fields. There were daily farmers' markets, with livestock wandering in the streets, and country festivals such as May Day were
celebrated in traditional style in the heart of the capital. On 1 May
1667 Pepys wrote in his *Diary*, 'To Westminster; in the way meeting
many milk-maids with their garlands upon their pails, dancing with a
fiddler before them; and saw pretty Nelly [i.e., Nell Gwyn] standing
at her lodgings' door in Drury-lane in her smock sleeves and bodice,
looking upon one: she seemed a mighty pretty creature.'

If a visitor to Restoration London were to travel down river from
Westminster, he would soon pass the great rambling palace of Whitehall, the main residence of English monarchs since 1530, which covered
twenty-three acres and comprised some two thousand rooms. A maze
of galleries, apartments, state rooms, servants' quarters, courtyards and
gardens, Whitehall was home not only to the King but to the whole
royal family, the King's principal mistresses, ministers of state, Ladies
of the Bedchamber, various courtiers and officials (including the royal
chaplains), servants of every rank and all the gilded waterflies that
hovered about the throne. It was a complex of buildings from many
different ages that lacked both rhyme and reason if looked at with the
cool eye of logic, but which was, nonetheless, a fitting reflection of
the nation's idiosyncratic polity. Foreign ambassadors frequently commented upon the inconveniences of this architectural leviathan and
wondered how the King could govern efficiently from it.

At the heart of Whitehall, and hence the nation, was the Stone
Gallery, which housed the bulk of the royal picture collection. Despite
its proximity to the King's apartments it was open to the public, and
both petitioners and officials could be seen walking up and down
waiting for Charles to appear. Opportunities for catching the King's
eye were all too fleeting. Nevertheless, there were consolations: this
was the place to pick up the latest court news and trade gossip of who

was in and who was out; in sum, to feel the pulse of the nation. Whitehall didn't just feed rumour-mongers, it bred them. One of the characters in Wycherley's play *The Country Wife* refers scathingly to 'the whisperers of Whitehall'. If you were a spy or simply an intriguer, Whitehall was your home from home.

Beyond the curtained doors that led out of the Stone Gallery were the King's rooms, where the official and unofficial business of state was carried out: Presence Chamber, Privy Chamber and, holy of holies, the Bedchamber. Strict court etiquette determined who could enter and how far they could go. The Bedchamber was dominated by the King's huge four-poster. There were railings round it in the French courtly style with winged cherubs holding the curtains and silver eagles looking down into the room. The eagles symbolized keenness of sight as well as majesty, while the cherubs were associated with vigilance, and as such were often covered with eyes. Here, between the bed and the window overlooking the Thames, the King wove his own web of secret policy, and the phrase 'backstairs intrigue' entered the language. Charles used the Bedchamber as a political stage much more than either his father or grandfather had: it suited his secretive style, and gave him the freedom to act beyond the ken of officialdom. Careers were made and ruined in the Bedchamber.

There was little real privacy for the King – even his bedroom was a state room – but the genial Charles didn't seem to mind. He prided himself on his accessibility to his people and an informal style of govern-ment. Immediately after the Restoration it was noted that the King kept open house at Whitehall for all comers: ambassadors, petitioners, well-wishers from all over the kingdom, as well as the merely curious. Still others came in the hope of being touched for the king's evil, as scrofula was known. 'Whitehall is like a fair all day', commented one official; yet everyone was received with the King's customary grace and good humour. Nor could he eat his dinner in peace, for throughout his reign people thronged the gallery of the Banqueting Hall to watch him at table. If he wanted privacy, the King had to retire to his Closet, to which there was no unbidden access. Here he kept his favourite treasures, including a collection of over one hundred clocks and watches ticking and chiming 'in exquisite disunion'.

There was quite literally a set of backstairs leading up from the river to the King's Bedchamber, which served for amorous, as well as political assignations. They were carefully policed by two of the King's more colourful servants, who in due time would become good friends of Nell Gwyn: William and Barbara Chiffinch. William was Page of the Royal Bedchamber, Keeper of the King's Private Closet and Keeper of His Majesty's Backstairs; his wife was quite simply the King's Madam Ross, his procuress, and kept a strict register (now lost, alas) of all those women, both casual and regular, who at one time or another ascended the notorious backstairs to take the heat off that 'known enemy to virginity and chastity, the monarch of Great Britain'.

The Bedchamber, then, was the royal arena for both political and sexual transactions of a secretive nature, though Whitehall being Whitehall, rumours both of the King's licentiousness and to a lesser extent his backstairs negotiations quickly spread among the people. Despite his innate furtiveness, Charles was often surprisingly open in his indiscretions, where both his wife and his ministers were concerned, as if he kept deeper secrets beneath the more overt ones. (No wonder then that such a consummate actor was keenly attracted to talented actresses.) Without doubt, the Bedchamber was a place of conquest for the King, sexually and politically, though his sexual successes tended to compromise his political standing.

Before long Whitehall had gained the reputation of a seraglio and the King's demonstrations of power were seen by many as unacceptably oriental in nature. The literature of the time reflected this theme more charitably with its interest in the noble savage, and it seems to me that even Aphra Behn's Oroonoko (the royal slave) was a veiled portrait of Charles. The fact that he toyed with his mistresses in public caused a great scandal. Even Pepys, himself a serial groper, pronounced himself ashamed of the King's licentiousness. And when the City apprentices made their usual holiday assault on the brothels of Moorfields and East Smithfield, they were heard to mutter that the biggest stew of all was Whitehall itself.

So while the 'Black Boy' was playing the king in the White Hall, the girl whose name meant 'Shining White' was making do in the slums of Coal Yard Alley, where she may actually have been a cinderwench, i.e., one who collected cinders to resell as cheap fuel. Certainly the author of the 1681 *Panegyrick* thought so, and he was followed by other satirists later in the decade. Still others had her serving strong waters in a bawdy house, most likely in Lewkenor's Lane (now Macklin Street), or hawking herrings or turnips from a barrow stall in the streets. Marvell, for one, refers to her as one of the oyster wenches, a sorority known for their loud-mouthed garrulity. (To 'talk an oyster-woman deaf' was to talk the back legs off a donkey.)

London awoke to the sound of the hawkers wheeling their barrows across the cobbled streets and crying their wares. You needed a strong voice to be heard above the general cacophony, and Nell doubtless had reason to be thankful for this early training when she came to join the theatre – not just the ability to project her voice but the art of seducing the ear with the lilt of her words:

> Here's fine herrings, eight a groat,
> Hot codlins, pies and tarts,
> New mackerel I have to sell.
> Come buy my Wellsfleet oysters, ho!
> Come buy my whitings fine and new.[2]

Rose too was a street vendor, and one can imagine the two sisters vying to outdo each other from opposite sides of the street. When her shift was over, Nell might well have gone tearing down to St James's Park to see if she could steal a glimpse of the King feeding his ducks or walking his spaniels along the canal. Anything to escape the grimy alleys and feed her fantasies of a more ample life.

The author of 'A Satyr' (1677) claims that Nell threw up her fish to become one of Madam Ross's girls:

> Whose first employment was with open throat
> To cry fresh herrings even ten a groat.
> Then was by Madam Ross exposed to town,
> I mean to those who will give half a crown.

Certainly the new spirit of license in the capital enticed a plenteous supply of girls from the provinces to offer themselves to the new generation of gallants, and not a few of them fell into the clutches of Madam Ross and her ilk. Whether they were pipe-smoking, brandy-swilling dames like Mrs Gwyn and Madam Ross or the more shrewdly sophisticated type of bawd, such as Mother Cresswell, who it was said had some pretty upmarket girls for her clients, one cannot escape the fact that these ruthless women often bought, kidnapped or otherwise ensnared young girls to be trained as prostitutes. They all had networks of scouts in the city. It was a grim education, which, with the high risk of pregnancy and disease, could end in destitution and death.

In the early 1660s nearly one in ten women in London was a prostitute, a quite staggering percentage. They were a common sight on the streets and a sore temptation to young professionals such as Pepys. On the way to a business meeting in March 1665 he seems to have come quite close to succumbing: 'In our way the coach drove through a lane by Drury Lane, where abundance of loose women stood at the doors, which, God forgive me, did put evil thoughts in me, but proceeded no further, blessed be God. So home . . .' For many of the girls it was a chance to better their lot in life by becoming the mistress of a gentleman. As such, the prostitution market was the great melting pot of the time and one of the few ladders to social advancement open to women. Men of an inferior station, however, did not have the same opportunities to meet or make love to well-bred women. Thus the vicious feelings harboured towards the brothels by the apprentices may have had something to do with the fact that those establishments were seen as the means by which desirable girls of their own background were removed from their grasp.

Even Charles himself was known to 'put off the King' and visit the London brothels incognito, which must have satisfied a love of danger as well as a passion for acting, for it was an unnecessary risk to take. His height and dark looks showed through the best disguise, besides which Mrs Chiffinch was only too happy to liaise with the likes of Mother Cresswell to have girls sent to Whitehall (and up the backstairs) for the King's pleasure. It's not inconceivable, given his track record, that Charles paid visits to Madam Ross's establishment. After all, we know that his friend the Earl of Rochester was one of her clients. If so, it may even be that Nell first met the King on one of his forays into the London underworld, well before the start of her theatrical career.

This might explain why Nell was deeply upset (or so the story goes)[3] when the King married his Portuguese bride, Catherine of

Braganza, in May 1662. So upset in fact that she took a lover by the name of Duncan or Dungan, a regular customer at Madam Ross's. According to the editor and antiquary William Oldys (1696–1761), 'One Mr. Duncan, a merchant, taking a fancy to her smart wit, fine shape and foot, the least of any woman's in England, kept her about two years.' The account of the affair in 'The Lady of Pleasure', a contemporary satire, is spiced with obscenities. Referring to Duncan as 'a Cully of the City', it tells how Nell gave her youth, wit and virginity to him in return for fine clothes and good living. We are told that Duncan was the first to wilt ('For either with expence of purse or p---k, / At length the weary fool grew Nelly-sick'), though as a parting gesture of goodwill he provided her with an entrée into the theatre, presumably as an orange girl. If the author of 'Mrs. Nelly's Complaint' is to be believed, Nell returned the compliment in later years by helping him to a commission in the army: 'Duncan, by my great sway and power preferred, / For mounting me well first, now mounts the guard.'

It was through Duncan that Nell left the stifling atmosphere of Coal Yard Alley, living instead in rooms provided by him at the Cock and Pie tavern, which was at the top of Maypole Alley, a stone's throw from where Killigrew was building his new theatre between Bridges Street and Drury Lane. Though illiterate, a girl of her temperament and imagination couldn't help but be fascinated, inspired even, by the new theatre appearing on her doorstep. She was also fast learning how to make beguiling use of her feminine charms and ready wit. The world was suddenly opening up.

The theatre, like prostitution, was an obvious means of advancement for women of modest or lowly backgrounds. It could also provide an entrée to the court. Certainly many of the courtiers who attended the theatre were as interested in the opportunity to flirt with the actresses backstage as they were in the entertainment onstage. Unmarried actresses were always vulnerable to the advances of male suitors once the play was over. As the hack writer Tom Brown put it, '''Tis as hard a matter for a pretty woman to keep herself honest in a theatre, as 'tis for an apothecary to keep his treacle from the flies in hot weather; for every libertine in the audience will be buzzing about her honey-pot.'[4]

During the years of Puritan rule actors were considered a public menace and were relegated to the status of vagabonds. An ordinance passed by the Long Parliament at the beginning of 1647 stated, 'That all stage galleries, seats and boxes shall be pulled down by the warrant of two Justices of the Peace, and that all Actors of Plays for the time to come shall be publicly whipped, and all Spectators of Plays for every offence shall pay five shillings.' It's hardly surprising, then, that Charles II should have been so quick to restore the life of the theatre on his return from exile by issuing patents to Thomas Killigrew and William Davenant licensing the formation of two new acting companies. Their remit included permission to build new theatres anywhere in London for their respective companies. Killigrew's company, which became known as the King's Company, came under the patronage of Charles, while Davenant's players became the Duke of York's Company. All other companies were deemed to be operating illegally and were ordered to be 'silenced and suppressed'. Killigrew and Davenant had a monopoly of theatrical production in the capital.

Although the King was keen to establish a new life of cultural freedom, he was too shrewd to create a wholly independent theatre. What he did in effect was to create a new court theatre in the West End. Unlike Shakespeare's Globe, which catered to all levels of society, play-going in Charles II's time was very much a gentleman's recreation. The servants who had accompanied their masters sat in the upper gallery, but gone were the 'penny stinkards' who swore and fought at the foot of Shakespeare's stage and bantered with the actors in mid-dialogue. Both Killigrew and Davenant had been servants of Charles I (Davenant holding the post of Poet Laureate) and were in tune with the ethos of the court and shared its attitudes. Both men had written plays for the court in the 1630s. They were unlikely to produce seditious works, especially with the King in the audience; Charles knew he could trust them.

Killigrew was a particular friend and had followed the King into exile. He came from a distinguished and slightly eccentric Cornish family and was known to enjoy playing the buffoon. He was on board the *Royal Charles* when the King returned in May 1660 and Pepys described him as 'a merry droll, but a gentleman of great esteem with the King', who told funny stories to while away the voyage. It was later reported that he had been made the King's jester. Once again Pepys had the scoop: 'Tom Killigrew hath a fee out of the wardrobe for cap and bells, under the title of the King's foole or Jester, and may with privilege revile or jeere anybody, the greatest person, without offence, by the privilege of his place.' But this was probably a private joke between two men celebrated for their cynical humour.

The plays Charles watched in France during his exile had been similar to the classical court masques he had witnessed as a child at Whitehall, Windsor and Hampton Court. The collaboration of Ben Jonson and Inigo Jones had brought technical and dramatic innovations from Italy (the proscenium arch and curtain, painted moveable scenery, trap doors) as well as many of the conventions of neo-classical theatre. With the Restoration these innovations were now introduced to the public stage in England, though an Elizabethan-style 'apron' or forestage was kept in front of the new proscenium arch, with entrance doors on either side.

This concession to the past did not, however, succeed in reconjuring the imaginative vitality and depth of the Elizabethan theatre. The proscenium arch in effect turned the stage into a giant screen and signalled a fundamental change in the nature of public entertainment. The audience were no longer active participants in a fiction designed to raise their awareness and knit together the discordant elements of society; rather they were the passive recipients of large doses of escapism. Whereas the Elizabethan theatre invited a person to deepen and refine his identity, Restoration drama invited him to lose it. This is one of the reasons why the latter became a theatre of stars and idols. Nevertheless, for all its faults, the new drama, with its sophisticated playhouse, marked the beginning of modern commercial theatre in Britain. Though he had a few reservations, Pepys declared the King's playhouse at Drury Lane to be 'made with extraordinary good contrivance'.

In the final paragraph of the royal patent issued to Killigrew on 25 April 1662 comes the innovation without which the story of Nell Gwyn would surely have remained untold: 'And we do likewise permit and give leave that all the womens parts to be acted in either of the said two Companies for the time to come may be performed by women so long as these recreations [i.e., plays] which by reason of the abuses aforesaid [i.e., scurrility caused by men acting women's parts] were scandalous and offensive may by such reformation be esteemed not only harmless delights but useful and instructive representations of human life to such of our good subjects as shall resort to the same.' Even though the new actresses were paid considerably less than their male counterparts, and were treated as sexual objects rather than artists by the audience, it was a significant step forward.

While the first Theatre Royal, Drury Lane was being built, a real-life drama was unfolding at court which would have important repercussions for Nell Gwyn. When the Portuguese princess Catherine of Braganza arrived in England in May 1662 to marry the King, Charles was still in thrall to his beautiful and domineering mistress, Barbara Castlemaine. Indeed, she was heavily pregnant with their second child, which was delivered while the royal couple were on honeymoon at Hampton Court. Although Catherine had led an extremely cloistered life in Portugal, her mother, the Queen Regent, had warned her about Castlemaine and made her promise never to tolerate the presence of Charles's mistress at her court. Not only did Catherine take her mother's advice to heart, but beneath her simple and devout exterior she possessed the sort of ardent and redoubtable spirit that was capable of acting upon it. For her part, Lady Castlemaine had also extracted a promise – from the King – that she would be appointed one of the Ladies of the Queen's Bedchamber. It didn't take a seer to predict a mighty confrontation looming between Queen and mistress.

Catherine had come to England with a vast and lugubrious train of black-clad monks and female attendants. The latter were old and smelly and wore immense hooped frames under their black skirts, which meant that extra carriages had to be ordered to take them from Portsmouth to London. None of them spoke a word of English, though their looks of disdain amply told their minds. The King alone among the English contingent seemed unperturbed at the monstrous cortège that clung to his future bride. Her dowry was probably sufficient to dispel any qualms he might have had on that score. More to the point, there was something in this frail but spirited princess that awoke his loyalty and protection, his affection even. Despite the corkscrews of hair that jutted from her temples and which caused

Charles to confide to a chum that at first sight he thought 'they had brought me a bat instead of a woman', he wrote to Clarendon from the coast to say that 'her eyes are excellent good . . . and if I have any skill in physiognomy, which I think I have, she must be as good a woman as ever was born.'

Yet loyalty and fidelity are two different things. When Charles had been crowned the previous year in Westminster Abbey, he had carefully chosen St George's day for the occasion, no doubt to signify his final victory over the dragon of rebellion. But it was the dragon of lust that was his real foe. Even during his honeymoon, the vows of marriage fresh upon his lips, he would slip off to nearby Richmond where Barbara had taken a house following the birth of their son Charles, the future Duke of Southampton. Such was the animal urgency of her appeal, and such the fatal submission of the King, that all the vows in heaven could not prevent their coupling. Catherine was doubtless wise enough to see this and turn a blind eye. But to acknowledge the King's mistress in public and allow her the privileges of the Queen's Bedchamber, *her* Bedchamber, that was a different matter. So when the King presented her with his list of appointees, with Barbara's name at the top, she struck it off in a fury.

Having been brought up in a royal court, Catherine would have understood perfectly what she was being asked to do. The title of Lady of the Bedchamber was neither here nor there: what was at stake was the official status of the King's mistress and therefore the ethos of what was now her – the Queen's – court. She was being asked to confer both honour and legitimacy upon someone regarded by many people both inside and outside the court as a common whore – and this to the detriment of her own honour and happiness. It was a tall order by any measure, and Charles's awareness of his own insensitivity no doubt stimulated his rage at her refusal. Moreover, the King was always vulnerable where deep feelings were concerned, and he suddenly felt out of his depth.

In the end, Charles decided to introduce Barbara to the Queen casually, without forewarning, and hope for the best. There was no reason why they shouldn't hit it off together, woman to woman. Or so he reasoned to himself. Other ladies were being introduced that morning, and Charles knew that Catherine would not recognize

Barbara by sight. And so it happened. Catherine received the stranger graciously and had just allowed her to kiss her hand when Charles leant forward and announced, 'My lady Castlemaine'. At the sound of the name the Queen went deathly pale and grabbed for the arms of her chair. Then she burst into tears, blood gushed from her nostrils, and she fell forward in a faint. She had to be carried out, but the usually considerate King felt too affronted to follow her.

Instead he let it be known that anyone who tried to hinder him in his resolve to have Lady Castlemaine of his wife's Bedchamber would be deemed an enemy for life. Moreover, he sent most of the Queen's retinue back to Portugal and made a show of ostracizing her at court. In this he was abetted by the court wits (his 'counsellors of pleasure', as Pepys termed them), who urged upon him the example of his grandfather Henri IV of France who had forced his wives to accept an exalted status at court for his principal mistresses. It was time, they said, for the King to create the role of *maîtresse en titre* at the English court. Chief among this merry gang was George Villiers, Duke of Buckingham, Barbara's cousin, who was keen to secure his own place beside the throne.

After months of such unpleasantness and several arm-twisting embassies from a reluctant Clarendon, the Queen – in her own good time – suddenly yielded. She was seen to engage Barbara in conversation, and the two of them laughed merrily together. Her devotion to the King had won out. Clarendon, whose sympathies had all along been with the humiliated Queen, had openly criticized the King over his handling of the affair and their relationship quickly deteriorated. He bitterly resented Barbara's influence over the King. For better or for worse, Charles had established the sort of court he meant to keep, and the devil could take the hindmost. Thus it could be argued that the Bedchamber crisis, as it became known, paved the way for an altogether more scandalous mistress in the future, and one who would also enjoy the privileges of the Queen's Bedchamber: Nell Gwyn.

~ 4 ~

A King of Love

THE BEDCHAMBER CRISIS HAD CERTAINLY illustrated Charles's complex and duplicitous dealings with women; it also spoke volumes about his determination not to be dominated by them. He preferred instead to treat them like ministers, playing one off against the other, while maintaining the upper hand. Freedom was the other prize he sought through this tactic, but with it he ran the risk of becoming embroiled in stormy emotional scenes, especially where Barbara Castlemaine was concerned.

Charles's fear of domination can be traced directly back to his relationship with his mother, the formidable Henrietta Maria, herself the daughter of a cold, domineering mother, Marie de' Medici, and a father she never knew (he was assassinated when she was one).[1] From the moment she gave birth to the boy who was so dark that she professed herself 'ashamed of him', Henrietta Maria both tyrannized and dreaded her eldest son, as if she knew that he would one day become the King her weak husband could never be and so break her control over the men in her family. For her, life was about sacrifice and duty and, to be true, love itself had to be dutiful and sacrificial. Affection was secondary. Though a woman of extremely deep feeling, she kept her emotions tightly clamped. When they did break out it was involuntarily, in tantrums rather than displays of maternal love.

This brave, passionate little woman (who stood at a mere five feet in her stockings) seemed cold and controlling to her children. They were never individuals in her eyes, but pawns in the all-consuming drama of her life. Any act of wilfulness or defiance on their part, even as adults, called forth terrifying scenes of rage or, worse still, calculated acts of humiliation. Anything to keep control. When Charles's youngest brother, Henry, Duke of Gloucester, resisted his mother's attempts to browbeat him into the Catholic faith, she had his rooms at the Palais Royal in Paris stripped of furniture and his horses removed from the stables. When he made one final attempt to reason with her, she cut him dead in public. This was in 1655. Henry, who died in 1660 of smallpox, never saw his mother again. Her treatment of her second son, James, Duke of York, when he secretly married a commoner, was hardly less vicious.

It seemed she could only be a true mother to a surrogate child with no ties of blood, over whom she could exercise complete dominance. Such a one was the dwarf, Jeffrey Hudson, who had been presented at about the age of eight to the then childless young Queen by the Duke of Buckingham. Jeffrey had leapt out of a cold pie served before the King and Queen at Burleigh on the Hill. Henrietta Maria took him to her heart instantly, dressing him in the finest clothes and seeing to his education. Here was a pliable child she could recreate in her own image by making a Catholic of him, teaching him to speak French and schooling him in the manners and rituals of the court. She even had her portrait painted with him by Van Dyck in 1633, a picture that reveals the Queen as haughty and exceedingly beautiful in a childish sort of way. Her left hand rests on a monkey which sits on Jeffrey's arm, symbolizing the spirit of mischief shared by the two court outsiders. On one famous occasion at The Hague in 1642, the twenty-three-year-old Jeffrey was mistaken for the Prince of Wales by the Dutch ambassador, who stooped down to kiss the dwarf's hand. He was no doubt fooled by the Queen's easy affection towards the lad, a manner she was never able to replicate with Charles. After the Restoration, when Jeffrey was gone, she adopted a Chinese boy, a stowaway on an East Indiaman, whom she converted and reared as her own.

In Catherine of Braganza Charles had selected a wife with quite profound similarities to his mother. Stubborn, headstrong, volatile, Catherine was capable of digging in her heels when she felt undermined. Physically, both women were fine-boned, doll-like almost, their beauty residing overwhelmingly in their large, dark eyes. The differences, however, were crucial. Whereas Henrietta was a dogmatic Catholic, motivated by political and family allegiances, Catherine was truly devout, mystical even, and for periods throughout her life felt an intense desire to withdraw from the world. She represented the one element of his nature that Charles was unable to express: devotion.

Indeed, Henrietta, who first met Catherine when she returned to London in August 1662, described her in a letter to her sister Christine as a saint. Unsurprisingly, Catherine remained aloof from court intrigue and as the years went by grew steadily in the affections of the people. As early as December 1662, Pepys had heard from Dr Pierce, the Duke of York's surgeon, that Catherine was 'a most good lady, and takes all [i.e., Barbara's intrigues] with the greatest meekness that may be.'

Perhaps the most important difference between the two Queens, however, was the fact that Catherine was never a mother. Having the body of a child, she was reported to be incapable of bearing children. This was a source of deep sadness for both her and Charles. When she fell dangerously ill in the autumn of 1663, Catherine imagined in her delirium that she had given birth to twins, a boy and a girl, and that the boy looked exactly like the King. These phantom twins probably symbolized the true nature of Catherine's relationship with Charles, that of brother and sister. And after the premature death in 1670 of his beloved sister Minette, much of the King's idealistic love was transferred to Catherine. Emotionally he came to rely on her more deeply than most observers realized. He particularly valued her unselfish love, her lack of jealousy towards his mistresses and the kindness she showed to his bastard children.

Barbara Castlemaine, however, followed Charles's mother in using tears and tantrums to bend the King to her will. Their relationship was a degrading power struggle, fuelled by a mutual lust that came near to depravity. Some, including the Queen Mother, attributed Barbara's hold over the King to witchcraft, but lechery and the five children she gave him provide a more obvious explanation. There was something both dangerous and pathetic about Barbara, a winning combination for Charles. She was an orphan of the Civil War (her father, Viscount Grandison, had died in the King's service) and, like Nell Gwyn, had been inducted prematurely into the adult world. Barbara was a nymphomaniac, who had sex with both men and women, and where the satisfaction of her lust was concerned this imperious woman abandoned all pretensions of class. Her lovers were to include an actor, a rope dancer, a highwayman and a violent bigamist. Countless others went unrecorded. And in what was surely her most lurid exploit, she bit the penis off a dead bishop.[2]

Pepys, who adored her from afar, marvelled that her beauty made him construe her actions favourably, 'though I know well enough she is a whore'. He for one was in no doubt about her appeal: 'My Lady Castlemayne rules, who hath all the tricks of Aretin that are to be practised to give pleasure. In which he too [the King] is able, having a large [prick]; but what is the unhappiness is that, as the Italian proverb says, *cazzo dritto non vuolt consiglio* [A man with an erection is in no mood for advice].' The King comes in for much censure in Pepys's *Diary* for doting on Barbara to the neglect of both Queen and government. He deplored the fact that Charles dined at Barbara's house every day of the week and could be seen returning furtively to Whitehall in the wee hours, until even the palace sentries began to gossip.

Whether the King was stimulated by the knowledge of Barbara's other conquests we don't know, though he did draw the line when she made a move on his thirteen-year-old son, the Duke of Monmouth. But *conquests* they certainly were. There was a great deal of anger in her sexual relations with men and very little intimacy, much the same cocktail that was at work in Charles's affairs with the opposite sex. She was greedy and ambitious too, cajoling and hectoring fabulous gifts of property, jewels and monopolies out of the hag-ridden King, much to the disgust of the Parliament and people. In his *Diary* for 23 February 1662 Pepys noted with disapproval that Barbara had been more opulently bejewelled at the recent court ball than both the Queen and Duchess of York put together. She was a political animal, using her feral instincts to increase her power and influence. But she was not interested in politics, any more than her ostentatious conversion to Catholicism bespoke a fondness for religion.

It is doubtful whether all five of the children Charles finally acknowledged as his by Barbara were in fact his, but she bullied him into submission. He did, however, put his foot down with the sixth bastard (her son by Henry Jermyn, Earl of St Albans), even though she screamed at him that she would bring the baby to Whitehall and dash its brains out before his face. 'God damn me, but you shall own it!' she yelled. The King never did acknowledge this child, but a little over two weeks later he was back under Barbara's spell. According to Pepys, the King went to her and she made him beg for forgiveness on his knees and promise never to offend her in the same manner again. Moreover, 'she did threaten to bring all his bastards to his closet-door, and hath nearly hectored him out of his wits.'

She also acted as the King's bawd, so that even if the King wasn't sleeping with her, she could be sure that he would be sleeping with one of her creatures. It was a vicarious way of maintaining her hold over him. But in the case of his young cousin Frances Stuart (and later, Nell Gwyn) the ploy backfired. Frances had been a maid of honour to Charles's sister Minette in Paris, who sent her over to the English court in January 1663 to join the household of the new Queen. Frances was only fifteen and, according to Minette, 'the prettiest girl in the world'. As soon as Barbara saw that the King was smitten, she took Frances under her wing, and even into her bed. Later on, as reported by Pepys, Barbara organized a mock marriage between herself and Frances, which was observed with all due ritual. After the service they retired to bed, watched by the court, and the stocking was flung;[3] 'but in the close', continues Pepys, 'it is said that my Lady Castlemaine, who was the bridegroom, rose, and the King came and took her place with pretty Mrs. Stuart.' ('Mrs' did not necessarily refer to a married woman, but was used of single women too to avoid the term 'Miss', which usually connoted mistress or prostitute.)

This episode took place less than a month after Frances's arrival at court and at a time when Barbara was acknowledged to be the 'Miss of State', which was equivalent to the French *maîtresse en titre*. The incident speaks eloquently both of Barbara's keen understanding of Charles's sexual psychopathology and also of her own desperate ingenuity in maintaining her position as chief mistress. She knew that the King, who hated feeling confined by emotional commitments, required variety, adventure and a touch of the exotic in his love life.

No one woman, not even a sexual buccaneer like Barbara, could hope to satisfy all his amorous desires, hence the necessity in her case of doubling up as bawd and punk.

Frances Stuart was, in many ways, the ideal protégée for Barbara in that she refused to yield fully to the King's advances. She wanted a husband and would not give up her virginity without a ring. Her contemporaries were all agreed that Frances, who loved nothing better than to build castles of playing cards, possessed the mentality of a child. Her innocence maddened the King and drove him to the composition of mawkish poetry about the hell of loving too well. Pepys, who got nearly all his court gossip from the aforementioned Dr Pierce, wrote, 'He [Pierce] told me how the King is now become besotted upon Mrs. Stewart, that he gets into corners, and will be with her half an houre together kissing her to the observation of all the world . . . yet it is thought that this new wench is so subtle, that she lets him not do any thing than is safe to her . . .' In his frustration the King quipped that he hoped he would live to see Frances 'ugly and willing'.

As 1663 progressed, the King began to neglect Barbara for Frances, and when the Queen fell dangerously ill it was rumoured that the King intended to marry her in the event of Catherine's death. The Duke of Buckingham, himself a Villiers and the chief of the court wits, gathered together a committee of his cronies to promote Frances as a future Queen. Even if Catherine survived, they planned to have her kidnapped and placed in a convent. Behind this ludicrous plot lurked an important political concern. It was increasingly clear that Catherine was barren and that the heir presumptive, Charles's brother James, was a secret Catholic (his conversion was not made public until 1669). Buckingham and many like him were keen to secure a Protestant succession. For several nervous weeks, Barbara had to entertain the awful prospect of ending her court career as one of Frances Stuart's maids of honour.

But the intriguers had badly misjudged the King. Charles may not have been faithful to the women he loved, but he was always loyal. Far from seeing an opportunity in his wife's illness, Charles surprised everyone – himself included, perhaps – by the depth of his grief. Catherine's life did indeed hang by a thread. Her head was shaved, dead pigeons tied to her feet and the last rites administered. The doctors and priests squabbled horribly. The King, who spent hours sitting at her bedside, bathing her hands in his tears, begged her to live for his sake. When she eventually recovered and was restored to her wits, the Queen acknowledged that it was her husband's tranquil and loving presence that had saved her life. And it proved more than a simple recovery. In her illness all Catherine's anxieties about her infertility had come to a head and she had given birth to a stream of phantom children. Now that she had come through, she was a new woman. Resigning herself to her condition, she grew merry and affectionate at court, and treated the King with humour and indulgence.

Charles's own son, the fourteen-year-old James Crofts, had been introduced at Court the previous year (having been under the Queen Mother's care in France). He was a year older than Nell Gwyn and would one day find a loyal friend in his father's youngest mistress. Charles doted on the handsome youth, and when he created him Duke of Monmouth in February 1663 it was amid rumours that he was to make the boy his heir. Monmouth himself encouraged the rumour that Charles had married his mother, Lucy Walter, and that he was thus heir apparent. He certainly behaved like the Prince of Wales and Charles did nothing to discourage the boy's presumption, showering him with honours. He was immensely charming and energetic, but lacked brains. Pepys called him 'the most skittish leaping gallant that ever I saw, always in action, vaulting or leaping, or clambering.'

The King's character, especially his attitude to women, defined the tenor of court life. First, there was the royal family, unconventional, rambling, but surprisingly functional, presided over, like some eastern potentate, by Charles himself, who appeared unconcerned by the emotional complexities of his life. One has to admire the man who could get his wife, his principal mistress and his bastard son by a former mistress to travel publicly with him, all in the same coach. Despite the dark undertow of depravity and exploitation, of incest and sedition, Charles was able to maintain the impression of family unity and cultivate for himself the image of the genial patriarch. When a petition was addressed to him as 'the father of his people', the Duke of Buckingham was heard to whisper, 'Of a good many of them'.

Then there were Charles's special cronies, known as the court wits, a group of highborn rakes who modelled their attitudes on the King's.

Two things were of interest to them: love and wit; combine the two and you have their raison d'être: the witty pursuit of love. Their wit, like the King's, was cynical and relied on an apparent disdain for feelings and the ability to prevail by means of a callous brilliance. As for the pursuit of love, their object was to prove that beneath the formal professions of chastity and fidelity all women secretly longed to be seduced. And it was the rake's skilful employment of his wit that secured his conquest and the ultimate prize: sensual enjoyment. Their wit was used to flatter and idealize women; but it was also an aggressive tool, used to humiliate. These were the men who created the Restoration theatre to hold up a mirror to themselves for vanity's sake, and to create a forum where they could celebrate, and indeed enlarge upon, their conquests.

Charles himself was the ultimate rake hero, and he applied the same cynical wit to both love and politics. His quip that he never interfered with the souls of women was typical of the gallant's horror of emotional involvement. Like the heroes of the Restoration drama, he acted on the premise that man is a fundamentally hypocritical creature and that the only sensible way to deal with him is to *outwit* him. Charles's fellow wit Lord Rochester penned the following epigram as a compliment to his sovereign:

> We have a pretty witty King
> Whose word no man relies on,
> Who never said a foolish thing
> Nor ever did a wise one.

Compliment or not, Charles was ready with a witty thrust of his own, namely that his words were his own while his deeds were his ministers'. As the 1660s wore on, Charles's wits increasingly became his ministers, and the public perception grew that the government was in the hands of irresponsible libertines. Sexual intrigue manifested itself in politics through the proliferation of cabals – secret committees on which the principal mistresses often sat – and ministers had to spend more time than was desirable placating Charles's women and trying to keep the lid on court gossip. Skill in public relations, which was another dimension of the rake's much prized wit, was de rigueur.

Again and again, throughout the decade, Pepys complains of the

King's neglect of business and says that the country is going to ruin. He mutters darkly about 'the pride and luxury of the Court' and 'every man looking after himself, and his own lust and luxury'. Then, as today, when to be seen to be doing something seems more important than actually doing it, public perception was crucial to politics. Charles's public dalliances led to the perception that he was idle and neglected business, which couldn't be further from the truth. Charles, as we've seen, was hyperactive. Even if he'd been up half the night at a ball, he would rise before dawn and attend to business after a thorough constitutional. Yet stories of the King's scandalous life made their daily rounds of the capital. Charles declined to take them seriously, even when evidence suggested that they were undermining public confidence in his government.

It is Charles's Byzantine cunning, the King's wit, that still challenges us today. And it may well be that he has outwitted posterity with that same deftness he used to baffle and defy his contemporaries, for the question remains: to what extent did Charles encourage the image of himself as feckless libertine in order to steal a march on his opponents? We shall probably never know, although it is certain that the majority of his political opponents underestimated him, and did so to their cost.

Charles the man determined the temper of the age to an extraordinary degree, through his wit and curiosity, his love of luxury, his passion for women, theatre, science and seafaring. Women generally came to the fore in Charles II's England, and Nell Gwyn was one of those who demonstrated the new independence that was available to talented females. It was in the arts that they made their principal advance, through careers in literature and the theatre. One of the shining examples is the playwright and novelist Aphra Behn, who was hailed by Virginia Woolf as the first woman in England to earn her living by writing.[4] Behn was an admirer of Nell Gwyn (the feeling was mutual) and dedicated her play *The Feign'd Courtesans* to her. In her dedication Behn deliberately draws attention to Nell's lively speech to make a point about female wit: ' 'Tis this that ought to make your sex vain enough to despise the malicious world that will allow a woman no wit . . .' Behn lived a bohemian life that would have been unthinkable in a previous age. And although she herself never had the means to become an out-and-out libertine, she did create a true female rake in the figure of Hellena in *The Rover*, who pursues and wins the hero with her wit.

Hellena or Eleanor, it is hardly a coincidence that Behn's character (who confesses that she 'loves mischief strangely') should have the same name as the heroine of our story, a witty player destined to win the greatest rover of them all.

~ 5 ~

Stepping Up

Fate now for her did its whole force engage,
And from the Pit she's mounted to the Stage.

A Panegyrick, 1681

THE NEW THEATRE BUILT BY Killigrew between Bridges Street and Drury Lane, which opened on 7 May 1663, was for many women the gateway to another, more promising world. Certainly it allowed Nell to escape from the clutches of both Duncan and Madam Ross, for she was one of the first to join the elite sisterhood of orange girls. A few months before the theatre had opened, Killigrew's Company (strictly speaking the King's Company) had granted a licence to one Mary Meggs, widow, 'with full, free and sole liberty, license, power and authority to vend, utter and sell oranges, lemons, fruit, sweetmeats and all manner of fruiterers and confectioners wares'. Meggs, a former bawd commonly known as 'Orange Moll', was an old friend of Madam Gwyn's, and two out of the three places she had for assistants were given to the Gwyn sisters, Rose and Nell. As the author of *A Panegyrick* wrote of the latter,

> But first the Basket her fair arm did suit,
> Laden with Pippins and Hesperian Fruit.
> This first step rais'd, to the wond'ring Pit she sold
> The lovely Fruit, smiling with streaks of Gold.

It's interesting, in light of its symbolism, that the orange has come to be associated so strongly with Nell Gwyn, in particular her vivacity and generosity. As Chesterton reminds us, 'Long after the last of those who had ever seen her face were dead, it remained the custom when alms were distributed at the Savoy Chapel to place near the door a plate with an orange' as a tribute to Nell's charity.[1] First and foremost the orange was a symbol of the sun, both literally and as the spirit informing all life. The oranges – or golden apples – in the mythical Garden of the Hesperides, on the extreme western shore of the world, were the ultimate prize of man's spiritual quest: the radiance of the soul. In Nell's time they were considered an exotic, almost other-worldly fruit and had strong ties with royalty. Charles's grandmother Marie de' Medici, Queen of France, had a famous orangery, and his cousin Louis XIV, the Sun King, was obsessed with orange trees. Significantly, Cinderella gives her ugly sisters a gift of oranges to mark her transformation from cinder wench to princess; oranges too could be said to have marked Nell's induction into royal life.

The girls worked six days a week and received a sixth of their own takings. They stood in the front row of the pit with their backs to the stage, holding their baskets of fruit covered with vine leaves and crying, 'Oranges! Will you have any oranges?' between the acts. According to Wilson, their dress, which must have been provided by Orange Moll, consisted of a white smock, stays, petticoat and a coarse 'stuff' gown. A handkerchief was worn about the neck. Gentlemen would pay sixpence a piece for the small, sweet 'China' oranges, and there were tips to be had too, for the girls acted as go-betweens for the gallants in their amorous intrigues, delivering messages to masked ladies in the audience or to actresses backstage. Thus they gained an education in the idiom and manners of high society. There were unexpected tasks too, as when Orange Moll herself, during a perform-ance of *Henry IV*, saved a man who was choking on his fruit, by thrusting her finger down his throat and so 'brought him to life again'. Pepys was in the audience and confided the incident to his *Diary*. There was social contact too with the actors and actresses, for the orange wenches frequently tagged along when they retired to one of the local taverns after the show.

Meggs picked her girls not just on the strength of their looks but on their ability to banter with the patrons. Soon they came to be prized for their knowledge of the intrigues and assignations made under the theatre roof and could pass on valuable gossip to enquiring gallants. Meggs herself has been described as 'a kind of private broadcasting station for scandal'. In Rawlins's play *Tunbridge Wells, or A Day's Court-ship* a character says, 'She outdoes a playhouse orange-woman for the politick management of a bawdy intrigue.' Certainly it was an excellent apprenticeship for the stage itself, where the management of a bawdy intrigue was an art form; and the managers of the company must have been quick to spot potential in the quality of a girl's voice, the liveliness of her repartee or her ability to raise a laugh. Some of the banter must have been pretty coarse, because the orange girls themselves were fair game for the young blades about town. In later years Nell's great rival the Duchess of Portsmouth told a lady who had commended the former's wit that anyone could tell she had been an orange girl by her swearing.

Coarse or not, it was all heady stuff for a girl from the slums. Nell had never seen so many grand ladies and gentlemen in all their finery. There was also the altogether superior excitement of the King's arrival for a performance. A thrill of anticipation passed through the pit as the royal coach came to a halt outside the main entrance of the theatre. The King could be seen getting out and cheers were heard from the street as well-wishers surged forward to pay their respects. The whole theatre rose to its feet when he entered and remained standing until he had taken his seat. Charles was the first monarch to patronize the public theatre, and his presence guaranteed a full house. Indeed, it often attracted more comment and attention than the play itself. To Nell, her face lit both by the flaming cressets fixed to the stage walls and the candlelit chandeliers that hung from the proscenium arch, it appeared that the entire court had been magicked to her doorstep. Even the actresses must have seemed an otherworldly breed to Nell, for their status as 'stars' led to love affairs with the smart gentlemen and courtiers who eyed them from the pit.

The experience was doubtless made less overwhelming by the presence of her sister, Rose, who had shared the toils and triumphs of her childhood. Rose, by now a young woman, had become sexually involved with Tom Killigrew's madcap son Harry, whose influence she came to appreciate later that year when she was convicted of theft at the Old Bailey. She managed to get a message to Harry, who visited her in jail and sued the King for a pardon on her behalf. Killigrew was one of Charles's grooms of the household and the future Court Jester of William III. Maybe Killigrew junior had got to know Rose as a visitor to Madam Ross's establishment or, more likely, at his father's theatre, where she stood beside Nell. Very little is recorded of her after her release from prison. No portrait has come down to us in paint or words, though it seems that a wild decade in the 1660s was followed by married respectability.

The playhouse itself was a small three-tiered building, largely wooden, measuring 112 feet long by 59 feet wide. It had taken two years to complete, at a cost of £2,400. Inside it was richly appointed, its brilliance – the effect of the chandeliers – nicely offset by an air of cosy intimacy. The floor of the house was taken up entirely by the pit, which ascended in rows of benches covered with green baize and gilt leather. These places were favoured by the young gallants about town (including aspiring gallants such as Pepys) and came at a cost of 2s 6d. Ascending from the back of the pit were three galleries. The first, divided into richly embroidered side boxes, was the preserve of royalty, nobility and visiting dignitaries. These boxes were so little raised above the pit that *œillades* ('most speaking looks') were constantly exchanged between the two levels. The middle gallery, which tended to attract the City merchants and nouveaux riches, was also divided into boxes and at a cost of 1s 6d per seat. Finally, there was the upper, unboxed gallery, which housed the rowdier elements for a shilling apiece, and where footmen, coachmen and other menial attendants could take a pew for free after the curtain had risen on the final act. Prices tended to be doubled on the first night of a play. In all, the theatre accommodated some seven hundred souls.

There was a passageway between the pit seats and the stage, where the orange girls stood and where the spectators could wander up and down between the acts. This separated the world of make-believe from reality. There was an orchestra too in a recess beneath the stage, music being played before the curtain rose and in the intervals. As always with the seventeenth century, claims of comfort must be treated with circumspection. Apart from the obvious fire hazard, the candles made it very hot in summer and Pepys paints us a picture of himself sweating in the pit. In winter they had the opposite problem, because the glazed dome that had been constructed to cover the pit was not impervious to the rain. On one occasion Pepys complains that a hail storm forced him and his wife to rise from their seats and take refuge in a nearby alehouse! There were no toilet facilities, and drinks were strictly forbidden. Performances usually began at 3 p.m.

Pepys, who was there the day after the theatre opened, made the following observations: 'The house is made with extraordinary good contrivance, and yet hath some faults, as the narrowness of the passages in and out of the pitt, and the distance from the stage to the boxes, which I am confident cannot hear; but for all the other things, it is well . . .' Having said which, he goes on to complain about the clarity of the music beneath the stage. Pepys loved to go backstage to ogle the actresses as they were changing, both before and after the performances, as did a great many of his fellow spectators. Many of them went in the hope of making assignations; all made a nuisance of themselves. Privacy didn't exist, even for the 'stars'. Nell's fellow actress Beck Marshall complained directly to the King about Sir Hugh Middleton's unwanted attentions, whereupon Charles issued a decree banning gentlemen from the Drury Lane dressing rooms. There were two tiring rooms, as they were known, one for the men and one for the women, both situated next to the green room where the actors waited for their cues.

With Nell's new employment came a change of lodgings. She moved to the Cat and Fiddle in Lewkenor Lane (now Macklin Street), which, like Coal Yard Alley, was one of the little thief-infested streets off the Holborn end of Drury Lane. It was, apparently, an annexe of Madam Ross's infamous establishment, which suggests that Ross supplied Orange Moll with girls and seems to confirm the close relationship between the bawds and theatre managers. Both were on the lookout for talented girls. Drury Lane and the little cobbled courts and alleys off it were where most of the theatre folk lived. Nell's previous lodgings (paid for by Duncan) had been in Maypole Alley, or Little Drury Lane,[2] from which she could look down into the Strand and see the mighty maypole with its gilded crown. This was the smart end of Drury Lane, the south pole, where the Earl of Craven had his five-storey mansion. The Earls of Salisbury and Peterborough also had houses there, as did Lord Howard, and Weld House was frequently used to lodge foreign ambassadors. Local Catholics were attracted to its chapel in such conspicuous numbers that Drury Lane became known as 'Little Rome'. Further along the street from the nobility were the bohemians and theatre folk, while the north pole towards Holborn housed the slums and brothels familiar to Nell since childhood. With its starkly contrasted poles of experience, balanced and reconciled by the theatre, Drury Lane was indeed an apt metaphor for Nell Gwyn's path through life.

If the King hadn't already met Nell at Madam Ross's house, then there's little doubt that she would have caught his eye crying oranges below the stage. Flushed with the attentions of the gallants, she must have presented an enticing spectacle. According to the anonymous *Memoirs of the Life of Eleanor Gwinn* (1752), 'no sooner had she appeared in the Pit and behind the Scenes with her Oranges, than the Eyes of the Players, and those sparkish Gentlemen who frequent the Theatres were fixed upon her, all anxious to know the Story and Birth of the handsome Orange Wench.' And she in turn must have gazed across the green baize benches of masked ladies and their witty suitors to where the King sat with his auburn-haired mistress, confident that there was everything to play for.

But what would those sparkish gentlemen who frequented the theatres have actually seen when they fixed their eyes upon the delightful orange wench with her back to the stage? She was undoubtedly small and fine-boned (with the smallest and prettiest foot in the country), but with a full figure and the confidence to make it show. According to Dryden's description of her as Florimel, she had an oval face, clear skin, hazel eyes and thick brown eyebrows that contrasted beautifully with her warm, bronze-red hair, which was streaked with gold. Biographer Arthur Dasent, who considers this contrast as 'perhaps the greatest beauty of her face', claims that it is a feature 'seldom or never found in those of plebeian birth'. Her cheeks were dimpled when she laughed and her face alive with mischief. Her portraits too reveal something more profound in those large, melting eyes: the melancholy of the jester.

An engraving of a portrait of Nell by Peter Cross showing her naked but for a pair of Cupid wings was printed with this epigraph:

> Had Paris seen her, he had chang'd his suit
> And for this Hellen giv'n the golden fruit.
> The Subjects' wishes and the Sovereign's Joy,
> Who burns with better Flames our second Troy.
> Wit, beauty, goodness, and good humour too
> Are more than any Venus else can show.[3]

'Hellen giv'n' is, of course, a punning reference to her name, Ellen Gwyn, and as the final two lines make clear, it was her wit and cheerful good nature that made her so attractive to her public. Samuel Pepys, an active admirer of female beauty, was pleased to keep a copy of the engraving above his desk at the Admiralty.

Equally, we might try to imagine the scene that confronted Nell as she stood with her back to the stage, holding her great basket of oranges. If she was expecting good manners and orderly conduct, she would have been sorely disappointed. The pit was little more than a high-class cattle market. The gallants, for one, took every opportunity to exercise their rowdy wit and chat up the masked ladies, or vizards as they were known, even if it meant turning their backs on the action of the play. Frequently drunk, they would stand up on the benches and manage their wigs with great ostentation. They chewed fruit and sweetmeats, scuffled with their rivals and even fought the occasional duel right there in the sawdust. They thought nothing of arriving in the middle of a performance and distracting the house by their disorderly entrance. And when they felt that the author's wit came short of the mark, they wouldn't hesitate to shout out their own 'asides', eager to draw belly laughs from the pit. Or if the play displeased them and the vizards refused their bait, they made great display of leave-taking, and at the most inopportune moment. The playwright John Crowne in his play *The English Friar* gives this description of a gallant's shenanigans on the floor of the house:

> Oh! Sir, you are Governor o' the whole house, no person shall
> hear any more than your noise pleases; you'll take up six
> benches in the pit by sprawling, and pay for none of 'em,

quarrel with the men, talk scurrilous stuff with the Masques in the hearing of all the Boxes; wrestle with the Orange-maids, throw 'em down, kiss 'em, then offer Ladies o' Quality their leavings . . .

And Aphra Behn in the prologue to *The Debauchée* describes the gallants as 'Roaring out Oaths aloud, from Bench to Bench, / And bellowing Bawdy to the Orange-wench'. Indeed, the gallants and their mistresses were actors as well as spectators, diverting the theatre with scenes of unrehearsed scandal. In February 1664 Pepys recorded, 'how the King, coming the other day to his Theatre to see "The Indian Queene" (which he commends for a very fine thing), my Lady Castlemaine was in the next box before he came; and leaning over other ladies awhile to whisper to the King, she rose out of the box and went into the King's, and set herself on the King's right hand, between the King and the Duke of York; which . . . put the King himself, as well as every body else, out of countenance . . .' Barbara, who had been taxing the King's patience of late, had done it, we are told, 'to show the world that she is not out of favour yet, as was believed'.

There was, in fact, no meaningful boundary between stage and pit: they formed a single arena of overweening gallantry. If there was a division, then it's best to think of the stage as a giant looking glass in which the beau monde adjusted its feathers. Sir Carr Scrope, one of Nell's future suitors, uses this image of the mirror to pour scorn on the vanity of the pit in his prologue to Etherege's comedy *The Man of Mode*:

> For Heav'n be thankt 'tis not so wise an Age,
> But your own Follies may supply the Stage . . .
> 'Tis by your Follies that we Players thrive,
> As the Physicians by Diseases live.
> And as each year some new distemper Reigns,
> Whose friendly poison helps to increase their gains:
> So among you, there starts up every day,
> Some new unheard of Fool for us to Play.
> Then for your own sakes be not too severe,
> Nor what you all admire at home, Damn here.
> Since each is fond of his own ugly Face,
> Why shou'd you, when we hold it, break the Glass?

As far as vanity and richness of attire were concerned, the men in their latest French fashions far outclassed the ladies, though, as Richard Ames pointed out, the ladies of the pit were as indifferent to the play itself as the gallants:

> Entrenched in vizor mask they giggling sit
> And throw designing looks about the pit,
> Neglecting wholly what the actors say.[4]

The theatre was a great leveller. Certainly the vizard reduced all the women of the pit, ladies and prostitutes alike, to a single commodity. Whether they fanned themselves modestly or flirted outrageously, it was all one to the predatory gallant. The following exchange at the beginning of Act IV of *The Man of Mode* captures the new ethos of male vanity:

LADY WOODVILL: Well, this is not the women's age, let 'em think what they will. Lewdness is the business now, love was the business in my time.

DORIMANT: The women indeed are little beholding to the young men of this age; they're generally only dull admirers of themselves, and make their court to nothing but their periwigs and their cravats, and would be more concerned for the disordering of 'em, tho' on a good occasion, than a young maid would be for the tumbling of her head or handkercher.

All shenanigans aside, the theatrical world that Nell Gwyn was entering, however obliquely, at the age of fourteen was supported by a wealthy London clientele, drawn from both the court and the growing class of merchants and City financiers (known pejoratively as 'cits'). Trade was flourishing and new industries were springing up, using the endless supply of cheap raw materials from the colonies. Instead of relying on feudal tenures and purveyances, a course that had got his father into so much trouble with Parliament, the King turned capitalist and expanded the nation's overseas trade severalfold. Under Charles's inspiration, the old Elizabethan spirit of commercial adventure returned. Luxury goods flooded into the London markets (principally the Royal Exchange in Cornhill, the New Exchange in the Strand and Westminster Hall), with the result that the theatre-goers to whom Nell called her wares were better dressed and better perfumed than their predecessors. The China oranges that Nell hawked from the pit were themselves exotic goods, though Evelyn and others grew their own and orange trees could be seen at the Physic Garden in St James's Park.

In the previous year, 1663, Charles's brother James and his cousin Prince Rupert had founded the Royal African Company to trade English goods for gold and ivory from the Guinea Coast, which stretched from Gambia to the Congo and where English ships competed fiercely with the Dutch. The guinea, a gold coin worth twenty shillings, was originally minted in 1663. Coffee and chocolate soon became popular drinks in London, and by the beginning of the year there were no fewer than eighty-two coffee houses in the capital. Here men came to discuss the issues of the day free from the hubbub of the tavern: drinking, swearing and gambling were all prohibited. And with Catherine of Braganza's Indian dowry came the new pastime of tea-drinking, as yet affordable only to the wealthy. London was an increasingly cosmopolitan city.

England's colonial expansion inevitably led to conflict with her keenest rivals, the Dutch. In fact, there had long been a state of undeclared war (or state-sponsored piracy) on the Guinea Coast, where the Dutch had tried to enforce a trading monopoly. In his diary entry for 2 February 1664, Nell Gwyn's fourteenth birthday, Pepys wrote,

> to the Coffee-house with Captain Cocke, who discoursed well of the good effects in some kind of a Dutch warr and conquest (which I did not consider before, but the contrary), that is, that the trade of the world is too little for us two, therefore one must down: 2ndly, that though our merchants will not be the better husbands by all this, yet our wool will bear a better price by vaunting of our cloths, and by that our tenants will be better able to pay rents, and our lands will be more worth, and all our owne manufactures, which now the Dutch outvie us in . . .

Later that year, in America, the English took New Amsterdam and renamed it New York in honour of the King's brother. It was a trading post of great strategic importance and by its capture the Dutch were deprived of their only real foothold in North America. England, on the other hand, had secured control over a vast tract of the east coast, from Maine to Virginia. Six of the original thirteen States of America were to be established during Charles's reign, including New York, New Jersey and the Carolinas.

Then, at the very end of 1664, a comet was seen in the night skies above Europe, and the King and Queen sat up all night to view it. The English interpreted it as an omen of war. But it was to be more than this, for the plague had already claimed its first victims in the Dutch ports, and it wouldn't be long before the old medieval curse made its way to the English capital.

After little more than a year with her back to the stage, Nell caught the eye of Thomas Killigrew, the manager of the King's Theatre, who often sat in the pit to watch his company's productions and who heard Nell parrying the advances of the rakehells with commendable wit. As the King's jester, Killigrew had a keen appreciation of the young orange girl's outlandish humour. A great talker himself, especially when 'a little elevated with the juice of the grape', Killigrew was always on the lookout for actors with a talent for improvisation. Thus although a licence had been granted to William Legg in March 1664 'to erect a nursery for breeding players in London or Westminster under the oversight and approbation of Sir Wm. Davenant and Thos. Killigrew to be disposed of for the supply of the theatres', it seems that Nell was provided with a more direct route to the stage. Killigrew introduced her to two of his best and most experienced actors, John Lacy and Charles Hart.

Nor would she have been completely green in the ways of the theatre, for as an orange wench Nell heard up to four different plays each week. With a good ear for dialogue she could gain a fair understanding of the range of voices and actions required for female parts in both tragedy and comedy. More than this, as one of the amorous intermediaries between gallant and mistress, Nell the orange wench was already playing one of the key roles of Restoration drama, the go-between.

Nell was only fourteen when Hart took her under his wing and together with John Lacy began to train her up for the stage. This was not exceptionally young for a theatrical novice, as many girls appear to have joined the two companies when they were fourteen or fifteen. Nell was the first and the most renowned to make the transition from orange wench to actress, but she was by no means the last, the most notorious being Betty Mackarel or 'Orange Betty', who joined the King's Company in 1674. At whatever age they joined the theatre, but particularly if they were in their early to mid teens, the actors and actresses were entering a new family, presided over by the company manager. In the case of the Duke's Company, Davenant provided a special boarding house on the theatre premises for his actresses, in part at least to shelter them from unwelcome attentions at night. A heavily pregnant actress was of little use, which is probably why Killigrew kept a salaried whore at the King's House – to keep the actors from poaching his valuable female stock, whom he boarded nearby rather than at the theatre itself. Nell, for instance, was given lodgings near her old haunt, the Cock and Pie in Drury Lane. Tom himself lived beside the piazza, also in Covent Garden.

Many actresses joined this large bohemian family through marriage, or were the daughters of theatrical parents. Two of the greatest, Elizabeth Barry and Anne Bracegirdle, were adopted by theatrical families. Some married musicians or artists involved in the theatre, or were singers or musicians themselves who adapted their talents to the stage. Affairs within the theatrical family itself were not uncommon, Nell Gwyn's affair with Charles Hart being perhaps the most celebrated and keenly followed.

It's difficult to ascertain who the first actresses were and where they came from. It's possible that those of better birth used false names or deliberately kept their origins secret to avoid the stigma of their profession. According to Wilson, the bulk of actresses during the Restoration came from a 'middle stratum' of decayed gentility. 'The Restoration world had little but domestic service to offer the dowerless daughters of the genteel poor. At least an actress was better paid than a waiting woman.'[5] To my mind Nell Gwyn sprang from ruined gentility, at least on her father's side. Acting certainly required poise as well as a knowledge, however residual, of sophisticated society. Pepys noted in his *Diary* that Moll Davis of the Duke's House was said to be the illegitimate daughter of Thomas Howard, the Earl of Berkshire.

Art was really the only path for a woman wishing to pursue a career and avoid menial labour, for there was no employment market for women. Many gentlewomen whose lives had been ravaged by war, plague or fire had no option but to enter domestic service or become governesses. Pepys's sister Paulina, whom he describes as very plain, was saved from a maid's life by her brother's skill and determination in finding her a husband. (He also provided a dowry.) As Liza Picard puts it, for women 'The normal path to employment led through the front door of a man's house, as a wife, or the back door, as a servant.'

One of the occupational hazards – or perks – of the acting profession for women was being poached by a rich or noble keeper. Many promising careers were either interrupted or terminated by the appearance of a marauding gallant. Given their circumstances, however, it's difficult not to conclude that a great many women became actresses in the hope of finding such a keeper and not out of a passion for stagecraft. Hester Davenport of the Duke's House became the mistress of the 20th Earl of Oxford after only two years on the stage. She was tricked into leaving by a mock marriage but later insisted that their bastard son Aubrey de Vere was the 21st Earl of Oxford. Margaret Hughes, an actress with the Theatre Royal, put in even fewer performances before being carried off by the ageing Prince Rupert, by whom she had a daughter, Ruperta. Mrs Johnson fell prey to the Earl of Peterborough, Elizabeth Hall to Sir Philip Howard, and Susanna Uphill to his cousin Sir Robert Howard. By far the most famous victims of sexual abduction, however, were Moll Davis and Nell Gwyn, both of whom were poached by the King.

The acting companies frequently complained through their author's prologues and epilogues about the depletion of their female stock through excessive gallantry. Addressing the offending gallants in the epilogue to *The Rival Queens*, (1677), Nathaniel Lee wrote,

> . . . Our women who adorn each play,
> Bred at our cost, become at length your prey.

Colley Cibber ruefully refers to the 'many frail fair ones . . . who, before they could arrive to their theatrical maturity, were feloniously stolen from the tree.'[6] Sir Courtly Nice in Shadwell's play *The Disappointment* is less elegiac, complaining that the King's House has become 'a strumpet fair'. Nor were such liaisons always to the advantage of the actress. Tom Wilding in Aphra Behn's comedy *The City Heiress* refers to 'our stage-smitten youth, who fall in love with a woman for acting finely, and by taking her off the stage, deprive her of the only charm she had, then leave her to ill luck.' But the companies were of course powerless to prevent actresses from strutting their wares, when that's exactly what their parts called for. Nor could they prevent gentlemen from pursuing them backstage. Twenty years of Puritanism had made the eye lascivious.

Intriguingly, one Mary Lee, an actress with the Duke's Company from 1670 to 1685, continued to act after she had married Sir Charles Slingsby. As long as she was faithful to her husband – and there is no evidence of infidelity – her previously established career in the theatre was not seen as a stain on her new status, for, as in most matters where human emotion is the guiding spirit, there was a great deal of ambivalence, not to say hypocrisy, in the way that the monied and landed classes treated the theatre. Many gallants, for instance, were intensely jealous of those actors who had married or were seeing beautiful actresses. The latter were as glamorous as the film stars of today and were adept at playing the social equals or superiors of their admirers. It is hard to overestimate the maddening appeal of these socially liberated creatures to the male imagination. William Mountfort, a rising star at the Theatre Royal, whose wife, Susanna Mountfort, was to become one of the most celebrated actresses of the age, was stabbed to death in the street by Captain Richard Hill. Hill had tried to abduct another actress Anne Bracegirdle, and was insanely jealous of Mountfort because he frequently played her lover on stage. Another typically Restoration confusion of art and life.

Nell Gwyn was exceptionally fortunate to have fallen into the hands of Hart and Lacy, though an old family connection may have played a greater part than Lady Fortune, for there is some evidence that Nell's father served with Lacy in Sir Thomas Dallison's cavalry troop during the Civil War. If so, it would be a fitting coincidence if, as some claim, Nell's first role was that of Doll Troop in Lacy's own comedy *The Old Troop*, which was licensed in 1664. It's likely too that Doll Troop, the company whore, was modelled on Nell's mother in her garrison days.

Lacy, then, was of Nell's father's generation. After the Civil War he became a dancing master until the Restoration allowed him to resume his old profession of acting. A large, plain-speaking Yorkshire-man, he excelled in comic roles and humorous dances and was the greatest Falstaff of his day. His bluntness could get him into trouble, though, as when he called the playwright the Hon. Edward Howard 'more a fool than a poet'. When Howard slapped the actor in the face, Lacy beat him with his stick and was confined to the porter's lodge at Whitehall. Had he not been one of the King's servants, Lacy may well have been treated more severely. As it was, he was one of the King's favourite actors, and a portrait of him commissioned by Charles hung at Windsor Castle.

To Nell the humorous old trooper proved a kind and fatherly coach, who taught her to dance on the stage and to speak an epilogue. The satirists have assumed a sexual relationship between master and pupil. The author of 'The Lady of Pleasure' is typical when he writes,

> But there [i.e., in the theatre], what Lacy's fumbling age abus'd
> Hart's sprightly vigour more robustly us'd . . .

There is no evidence of an affair with Lacy and, besides, this particular satirist has exposed his ignorance in another way, for Hart and Lacy were contemporaries. The contrast between 'fumbling age' and 'sprightly vigour' is phoney since Lacy was older by five years at the most.

When Nell Gwyn entered his life, Charles Hart was a mature, charismatic man in his late thirties. Born c. 1627, he was the eldest son of William Hart, whose mother Joan was William Shakspere of Stratford's sister. Thus he was the reputed dramatist's great-nephew. Hart had been a boy actor with the King's Men under the tutelage of the veteran player Richard Robinson until the theatres closed in 1642. As such he played female roles, his first real success coming as the Duchess in James Shirley's tragedy *The Cardinal*, which was registered in 1641.

During the Civil War he served in Prince Rupert's cavalry regiment as a lieutenant, and may well have found himself in Oxford during the conflict. If so, he might have come across Captain Thomas Gwyn or indeed the young Helena Smith. We know he continued to act in makeshift theatres in private houses, because in 1647 he was arrested when soldiers broke up an unlicensed performance of Beaumont and Fletcher's *The Bloody Brother*. The players on this occasion got off lightly: their costumes were torn from their backs and they were bundled out into the street naked, fortunate to escape a branding.

Hart continued to play on and off during the Interregnum, his career only fully flourishing with the return of the King. He was known for his convincing portrayal of men of honour, including Shakespearean heroes Brutus, Hotspur and Othello. He could play kings, it was said, as well as kings themselves and his portrayal of Alexander the Great in Nathaniel Lee's play of that name caused one courtier to exclaim that no prince in Europe should be ashamed to copy him. He was famous too for his intense concentration on the stage, nothing being able to distract him from the emotion of the moment. Once inside a character he possessed it with all the force of his soul. An article in one of the first editions of the *Tatler* (founded in 1709), mistakenly said to be by Sir Richard Steele himself, declared, 'My old friends, Hart and Mohun, the one by his natural and proper force, the other by his great skill and art, never failed to send me home full of such ideas as affected my behaviour, and made me insensibly more courteous and humane to my friends and acquaintance.' He excelled too in comedy and with Nell Gwyn created the type of the mad couple, playing the witty and cynical gallant opposite her wild, independent mistress.

Hart was good-looking, honourable and dedicated to his art, worthy in fact to be Nell's Charles I, as she would later call him. And this being the Restoration, it was inevitable that they would act out their love affair on the stage. Certainly there was no one better in the theatre of the time to direct her talent and coach her in the ways of gentility than Charles Hart. He could also provide her with financial security. As one of the greatest actors of his age and a shareholder in the King's Theatre, Hart made at least £150 a year and was able to buy a house in the country.

But whether or not their love was true love is open to debate. In Dryden's play *An Evening's Love, or The Mock Astrologer*, when Wildblood (played by Hart) asks Jacintha (played by Nell) what a gentleman is to hope from her, she replies:

'To be admitted to pass my time with, while a better comes; to be the lowest step in my staircase, for a knight to mount upon him, and a lord upon him, and a duke upon him till I get as high as I can climb.'

Her ascent had begun.

~ 6 ~

Stars in her Eyes

Next in the playhouse she took her degree
As men commence at University.
No doctors, till they've masters been before;
So she no player was till first a whore.

'A Satyr' (1677)

NELL CAN'T HAVE BEEN AN orange girl for more than a year, for by
November 1664 she had already been marked down for a part in a
play, Tom Killigrew's rambling two-parter *Thomaso, or The Wanderer*,
which would one day be transformed into a brisk comedy by Nell's
friend Aphra Behn. In the list of actors and their roles Killigrew wrote
'Nelly' beside the part of 'Paulina, a courtesan of the first rank'. In the
end, it seems the play was not performed, and what might have been
the fourteen-year-old Nell Gwyn's stage debut was deferred.

But by the following April, Nell was already a household name, at
least among the theatre-going public. Pepys had gone to the Duke's
House to see Lord Orrery's play *Mustapha*, which failed to impress him.
Fortunately, there were compensatory attractions. 'All the pleasure of
the play', he records, 'was, the King and my Lady Castlemaine were
there; and pretty witty Nell, at the King's House, and the younger
Marshall [i.e., Beck] sat next us; which pleased me mightily.'

To have made such quick progress Nell must indeed have been an
apt student; certainly Charles Hart would not have bothered with her

had he found her otherwise, for he was a dedicated professional, known for his high standards. Her quick wit and the talent for repartee she had developed in her previous incarnations gave her a natural advantage, since ad-libbing was an important skill in an age when rehearsal time was so brief. Apart from the gift of the gab, Nell's other marketable quality was her looks. Almost without exception the famous actresses of the time are praised for their black hair and glowing – or melting – black eyes, which are likened to ripe sloes or burning coals. Nell was exceptional in having red hair and hazel-green eyes. In an age when so much emphasis was placed on the appearance and personality of the actresses, her looks marked her out as different.

Nell's relationship with Charles Hart was doubly beneficial. Not only did she receive the sort of personal instruction other up-and-coming actors would have died for, but she was cushioned from the debt and discomfort that was the lot of the majority of her colleagues. (According to *Memoirs of the Life of Eleanor Gwinn* (1752), Hart offered to share his salary with Nell, as if they were husband and wife.) She was probably saved from a life of debauchery too; for acting was a hard-working, poorly paid profession, and actors all too often spent their earnings on drink. As Nell was illiterate, Hart would have had to dictate her parts to her or else teach her to read.

The season lasted from September to June, and over fifty different plays might be acted in this nine-month period. Actors worked six days a week, Monday to Saturday, and Sunday might well be taken up with learning new parts. Rehearsals usually began at ten with a break for lunch, and could last almost until the start of the performance at three in the afternoon. After final curtain, the star actors and actresses would be whisked off for dinner and further entertainments by their admirers, while the lesser artists would gather in one of the nearby taverns for an evening's debauch. (The Rose in Russell Street was a favourite haunt of writers and actors.) Authors, managers and senior actors often complained that members of the company turned up to morning rehearsals with a hangover. If they didn't turn up at all, they could be fined a week's wages. Sometimes there were evening rehearsals after a performance, though these tended to be for the practice of songs and dances; they also gave the manager an oppor-tunity to iron out any technical problems involving scenery and stage machines. On a frantic day, a court performance at Whitehall might follow the afternoon play.

Just as important as group rehearsals, if not more so, was private study, when the actor worked on his own or with an instructor to master his part. There was little true group rehearsal, as practised today, apart from the initial reading of the play by the author and the final or dress rehearsal. The emphasis was on the individual's part rather than the play as a whole, which is why actors and actresses quickly became identified with certain roles and were encouraged by the audience to play them up for all they were worth, regardless of whether such showmanship was in keeping with the spirit of the play. This ethos quickly made idols of the principal actors, who were expected to act like stars and live up to their offstage reputations. Mrs Pepys, who named her dog 'Betterton' after the famous actor, did not go to the theatre to hear a particular play, but to see her favourite actor.

When one considers that three different plays could be performed in a single week, the intensity of an actor's personal study can be fathomed, as well as the strain on his memory. No wonder actors and actresses could be seen walking the streets of Covent Garden muttering and gesticulating to themselves. An anecdote is told of the actor Jack Verbruggen, who went out into the fields beyond London one morning to rehearse his part in a tragedy. Three passing highwaymen found him gesturing violently to himself, rolling his eyes toward heaven and shouting, 'I charge thee not!' to some imaginary foe. Taking him for a madman, they grew compassionate and urged him not to harm himself. When the furious actor told them that he was a player learning his part, they changed their minds and robbed him of his money.[1]

At the time Verbruggen was a famous actor and had money to steal. Most actors, however, lived from hand to mouth, though as servants of the King or Duke of York they could not be arrested for debt. They lived on the edge of the London underworld. Novices were subject to a three-month trial period in which they were not paid at all. If accepted, an actress then started at ten to fifteen shillings a week, a good deal less than an actor. Fifteen shillings would buy you a pair of silk stockings in Restoration London. An experienced actress would earn thirty shillings a week – the price of a pair of boots –

while the top stars such as Elizabeth Barry and Susanna Verbruggen took home fifty shillings a week, roughly £200 in today's money. There were, however, perks for the attractive actress: admirers donated beautiful clothes for them to wear on stage and off, presented them with gifts of jewellery and lace and took them out to dinner.

The production team at Drury Lane during Nell's time consisted of Tom Killigrew, John Dryden and his brother-in-law Sir Robert Howard. Howard and Killigrew were the principal shareholders in the Theatre Royal, holding fifty per cent between them, while Howard and Dryden were the principal dramatists. Both were to write excellent parts for Nell, in particular Dryden, who had a special appreciation of her comic genius. All three became friends and admirers, and in later life Sir Robert acted as one of her trustees and helped manage her financial affairs.

Howard was a skilful, humorous playwright, and a man of extra-ordinarily wide interests, who has been unfairly maligned by posterity, largely as a result of Shadwell's caricature of him as Sir Positive At-All in his play *The Sullen Lovers* (1668). It is a hilarious portrait of a polymathic buffoon, and turned Howard overnight into the satiric butt of the literary world. As late as 1685, seventeen years after the play's appearance, Evelyn was writing in his *Diary*: 'I din'd at Sir Robert Howard's, Auditor of the Exchequer, a gentleman pretending to all manner of arts and sciences, for which he had been the subject of Comedy, under the name of Sir Positive; not ill-natur'd but insufferably boasting.' Elsewhere he refers to him as the 'universal pretender'.

Howard had an affair with the actress Susanna Uphill, who it was said spent all his money and then refused to marry him. She is referred to in a contemporary satire as 'Sir Pos's common jade', while Shadwell lampooned her as Lady Vaine, 'a whore, that takes upon her the name of a lady'. In the end, Howard married her kinswoman Mary Uphill instead. Two of his brothers were also playwrights, the Hon. James Howard, author of *All Mistaken, or The Mad Couple*, in which Nell scored one of her greatest triumphs, and the Hon. Edward Howard. A fourth brother, Col. Thomas Howard, later Earl of Berkshire, was said to be the father of the actress Moll Davis, who became the King's mistress. Like the Killigrews, the Howards were a large, eccentric family of amateur writers.

John Dryden, by contrast, was a professional writer, who was contracted to write three plays a year for the King's Company in return for shares. Though his genius was for satiric verse (he became Poet Laureate in 1668), Dryden was keenly attracted to the theatre, where he created a new English drama, known as 'heroic'. The theatre also helped satisfy his craving for literary adulation and social advancement, but at a steep price: he became the target of unrelenting satire, most famously as Mr Bayes in the Duke of Buckingham's comedy *The Rehearsal*. Yet Dryden did enjoy real celebrity. He was the literary lion of Will's Coffee House and had his own chair by the fire, from which he dispensed epigrammatic advice to aspiring authors.

Dryden's Achilles heel was his envy of the court wits and gentlemen writers. He aspired to be a wit himself, and was desperate for an entrée to the court; but though he befriended a number of the wits at one time or another and married Lady Elizabeth Howard, he always found himself outside the charmed circle. In many ways he was caught between the two worlds of professional and gentlemen writers. Certainly he tried to prove himself by constantly defining and redefining his role and status in literature. Vain, petulant and dogmatic, he was perhaps too concerned about his reputation to be truly great.

He and Sir Robert Howard collaborated on a play called *The Indian Queen*, which first appeared in January 1664 and heralded the arrival of the new heroic drama. Strongly influenced by the French classical tragedies of Corneille (1606–84), the new plays dramatized the conflict between honour and passion, both exaggerated to an incredible degree. The settings of the drama were exotic, the heroes – American Indian princes and princesses – strutting the stage in gaudy costumes and feathered headdresses, like cocks proclaiming a new dawn. A new age was indeed dawning, with the individual now taking centre stage, and this shift in consciousness was marked in the drama by countless images of the sun, principally via the sun kings and sun gods of the Americas. The Ynca of Peru in *The Indian Queen* is the Sun's great son on earth, while Montezuma in *The Indian Emperor* refers to 'the Sun my Father', who gives him life and draws him back up on his beams at death.

It's hardly surprising that extravagant heroism should grace the stage of a conspicuously unheroic age, an age of cynical wit and realpolitik. Samuel Butler wrote in his notebook that although no age 'ever abounded more with those images (as they call them) of moral and heroicall virtues, there was never any so opposite to them all in the mode and custome of life.' In fact, the Indian Queen herself, Zempoalla, gives the game away in her pat definition of honour, one well understood by the gallants of Charles II's court:

> Honour is but an itch in youthful blood
> Of doing acts extravagantly good.

If the human soul forever seeks balance and neutrality, then the taste for sugary-exalted heroism at the Restoration complemented the cynical and mercantile bias of society; but the heroism was all mental. John Crowne in the preface to his play *Juliana* (1671) praises the heroic dramatist Roger Boyle, Earl of Orrery, in these terms: 'In fine it is your Lordship that hath charmed up the ghost of many noble heroes, who otherwise would have lain unlamented in their tombs: and they have walked on the stage in brighter shapes than ever they lived . . .' The gallants may have delighted in honour on the stage, but in real life they derided it. Prince Rupert and his fellow heroes of the Civil War were figures of fun to the new generation of bright, cynical young men.

The new obsession with the heroic on stage meant very few roles for the lower orders, who were excluded from the concept of honour. This was a cosy nostalgia show for the upper classes, the ultimate Cavalier fantasy. Defeated chivalry rose again in a blaze of garish feathers. The exoticism was nine-tenths displaced passion, for this was a cynical, lecherous clique possessed of little true feeling. It was doubtless for this reason that Nell Gwyn could not stomach heroic drama, though she was compelled to make a show of it to advance her career. Pepys is driven mad by her butchery of tragic roles, while Nell herself in the epilogue to Robert Howard's *Duke of Lerma* says,

> We have been all ill-us'd, by this day's poet.
> 'Tis our joint cause; I know you in your hearts
> Hate serious plays, as I do serious parts.

Tragic acting came with a conventional set of rules, dictating tone of voice, gesture and facial expression for different emotions, all heavily stylized, which made it altogether more prestigious – and contrived – than comedy, which for the most part followed the speech patterns and gestures of everyday life. In tragedy, it was not the emotion itself that was important, but its expression according to a professionally accepted formula. There was much booming, face-wringing and sawing of hands. As John Crowne put it in the dedication to his play *Henry the Sixth* (1681), 'when an actor talks sense, the audience begins to sleep, but when an unnatural passion sets him a-grimacing and howling as if he were in a fit of the stone, they immediately waken, listen, and stare.' Hamlet would have been offended to the soul ('to hear a periwig-pated fellow tear a passion to tatters'), while Nell must have been hard pressed to fight back the giggles.

Comedy allowed Nell a much freer rein to express herself, not only because the style was more naturalistic, but also because it involved a strong element of ad-libbing and banter with the audience. Like many famous actors and actresses of her day Nell did more than play her role on stage – *she played herself*. The prologues and epilogues in particular were opportunities to take the audience into her confidence and reveal snippets of her own character. For instance, in the epilogue to Dryden's *Tyrannick Love*, a play in which she has stabbed herself, Nell reminded her admirers that far from being a virtuous Roman princess she is in fact the very spirit of mischief. In other words, she reassures them that the person they've come to see is still alive and kicking. The epilogue is worth quoting in full:

> I come, kind Gentlemen, strange news to tell ye,
> I am the Ghost of poor departed Nelly.
> I'm what I was, a little harmless Devil.
> For after death, we Sprights have just such Natures
> We had, for all the World, when humane Creatures;
> And therefore I that was an Actress here,
> Play all my Tricks in Hell, a Goblin there.
> Gallants, look to't, you say there are no Sprights;
> But I'le come dance about your Beds at nights.
> And faith you'l be in a sweet kind of taking,

When I surprise you between sleep and waking.
To tell you true, I walk because I dye
Out of my Calling in a Tragedy.
O Poet, damn'd dull Poet, who could prove
So senseless! to make Nelly dye for Love;
Nay, what's yet worse, to kill me in the prime
Of Easter-Term, in Tart and Cheese-cake time!
I'le fit the Fopp; for I'le not one word say
T'excuse his godly out-of-fashion Play:
A Play which if you dare but twice sit out,
You'll all be slander'd, and be thought devout.
But farewel, Gentlemen, make haste to me,
I'm sure e're long to have your company.
As for my epitaph when I am gone,
I'le trust no Poet, but will write my own.
Here Nelly lies, who, though she liv'd a Slater'n,
Yet dy'd a Princess, acting in S. Cathar'n.

Because of who she was and where she had come from, her spontaneity and depth of feeling, and her natural agility in stepping outside her role, Nell's presence on the stage must have done much to crack the mirror of vanity that was the gallants' playhouse of the 1660s. Her remarkable unselfconsciousness on stage, so unsuited to tragedy, allowed her to portray the image of a new kind of woman: independent, self-assured, expressive; one who revelled in the power of her individuality. Ironically for an actor, she proved that being someone was less important than being yourself.

Dryden wrote *The Indian Emperor* (also known as *The Conquest of Mexico*) as a sort of sequel to *The Indian Queen*, only this time the Old World intrudes, for the Spanish colonialists under Cortez are the conquerors. As he writes in the prologue, 'The scenes are old, the habits are the same / We wore last year, before the Spaniards came.' It was in this play in March 1665 that Nell had her first recorded part, as Cydaria the Emperor's daughter. Dasent suggests that the part may even have been specially named for her, with its glancing reference to Herefordshire, the land of cyder, but I suspect she was too untested for such an accolade, as well as out of her element. When Pepys comments on a revival of the play two and a half years later in August 1667, he is still unhappy with Nell's performance: 'After dinner with my Lord Bruncker and his mistress to the King's playhouse, and there saw "The Indian Emperor"; where I find Nell come again, which I am glad of; but was most infinitely displeased with her being put to act the Emperor's daughter; which is a great and serious part, which she do most basely.' In other words, she lacked the artifice to feign heroic feelings.

Interestingly, in view of Nell's coming engagement with the world of the court, *The Indian Emperor* dramatizes the clash between the cultures of the New and Old Worlds, represented by the Mexican Indians on the one hand and the invading Spaniards on the other. But the Spanish general Cortez, played by Charles Hart, suffers his own invasion when he is struck by an overpowering love for Cydaria, daughter of the Emperor Montezuma, played by Nell. And just as he is conquered by the charms of this Indian princess, so Restoration London succumbed to the gaiety and artlessness of Nell Gwyn. The following dialogue between Cortez and Cydaria highlights the principal contrast between the two cultures:

> CORT: Our greatest honour is in loving well.
> CYD: Strange ways you practice there to win a heart,
>   Here love is Nature, but with you 'tis Art.
> CORT: Love is with us, as Natural as here,
>   But fetter'd up with customs more severe;
>   In tedious courtship we declare our pain,
>   And ere we kindness find, first meet disdain.

This quality of nature is the very quality Nell would bring to the court. Independence is another trait displayed by Cydaria, for she defies her father to choose the object of her love. Nell too would be led by love to defy the strictures of her birth. And the love interest of the play for the audience was spiced by their knowledge of the real-life relationship between the play's lovers, Charles Hart and Nell Gwyn. No look or gesture between the two would be missed for what it might deliver in terms of the gossip of the day.

By its admirers *The Indian Emperor* was thought to be one of the jewels in the crown of heroic drama, and it managed to hold the stage for twenty-five years. But it had its detractors, especially among the wits. Leading the attack was John Wilmot, Earl of Rochester, aided and abetted by the King's childhood friend, George Villiers, Duke of Buckingham. The heroic drama provided an easy target for these sure-fire cynics, and in their satires they tore couplets apart like dogs mauling a hare. There was an element of envy here too, as Rochester, though fascinated by the theatre, was never able to turn his hand to play-writing with success. He also had a weakness for actresses and was notoriously unfussy about their social background. Wycherley may well have been thinking of Rochester when Mrs Squeamish in his play *The Country Wife* condemns men of quality for spending themselves and their fortunes on 'keeping little playhouse creatures'.

Nell Gwyn may even have been his first thespian conquest. There is a long, scurrilous poem in the Victoria and Albert Museum entitled 'A Poetical Epistle from the Earl of Rochester to Nell Gwin' (in a pamphlet called *A Genuine letter from the Earl of Rochester to Nell Gwyn. Copied from an original manuscript in the French King's Library*). It opens with the line 'Nelly, my life, tho' now thou'rt full fifteen . . .' and is a lecherous hymn to its subject's girlish sexuality. Nell, the author claims, is prepubescent – even at fifteen – and he offers her the gift of a special recipe to maintain this pristine state. ''Tis a receipt,' he tells her, 'found in the Paphian Isles, / Which Venus gave her Graces.' Yet Rochester makes it clear that her purity is something other than sexual innocence:

> Nine times one night I plumb'd the dark abyss,
> And, like Leander, cross'd new seas of bliss.
> So close thou clung'st, so eager in the joy,
> Rapture fresh rapture met, nor knew no cloy.

Though some have doubted the poem's authenticity, it bears the hallmarks of Rochester's style. It was obviously written many years after 1665, once Nell had begun her relationship with the King, for she is compared to Cleopatra. But if the claims made in the poem are true, then Rochester was one of Nell's very first lovers; if so, he may well have been influential in preparing her for the stage, just as he was ten years later with his long-time mistress, Elizabeth Barry. In the

1752 *Memoirs of the Life of Eleanor Gwinn*, Nell is whisked away by a gallant named Deveil, long thought to be a veiled reference to her earliest lover Duncan. But Rochester is a more likely model than the obscure merchant. Dorimant, Etherege's portrait of Rochester in *The Man of Mode* (1676), is famously described by Mrs Loveit as 'a devil' with 'something of the angel yet undefaced in him'. The method of seduction is certainly all Rochester's: 'One day, when she [Nell] was seeing her lover [Hart] perform the part on the stage, in which he most succeeded, *Creon* in Dryden's *Oedipus*, a gentleman stept into the same box, in all the splendor of a consummate beau, and gently whispered a compliment in her ear; she was not long in recollecting her old acquaintance *Deveil* . . .'

When Nell hears his proposals with disdain, he has her abducted in his coach as she steps out of the playhouse, again a device typical of Rochester, whose abduction of his future wife, Elizabeth Mallet, caused a sensation in the spring of 1665. Through Rochester, Nell would have been inducted into the world of the court wits, and her affair with him can be seen as a prelude to her much talked about liaison with Rochester's crony, Lord Buckhurst, in 1667. He may well have coached her too in the ways and manners of the wild mistress or female wit, the role that made a comedic star of her. He is certainly a more likely Professor Higgins to Nell's Eliza Doolittle than Charles Hart, for in the case of Elizabeth Barry, Rochester actually made a wager with the managers of the Duke's Theatre that he could make a great actress of her in six months. And he won.

It was around this time too that Barbara Castlemaine, expecting her fifth child by the King, befriended the young actress. Barbara liked to pick out young girls both for her own pleasure and the King's, and, anyway, patronizing artists was an essential pastime for a *maîtresse en titre*: it enhanced her prestige. In Barbara's case, it enhanced her love life too, for she drew a string of lovers from the ranks of both players and playwrights, including Nell's partner Charles Hart. She even gave Dryden a helping hand after the poor reception of his first play. For Nell, such powerful patrons as Rochester and Castlemaine more than made up for the lengthy interruptions to her career that were waiting in the wings.

It so happened that Nell's theatrical debut had coincided with the outbreak of the First Dutch War, a naval conflict in which Rochester proved an unlikely hero. The sound of the ships' guns could be heard in London. Killigrew complains of low attendance in the pit with so many gallants away at sea, but when bubonic plague followed close on the heels of war, the theatres had to close altogether, on 5 June 1665, for by order of the Lord Mayor and Aldermen of the City of London all plays, indeed all entertainments to which the public gathered, were strictly prohibited. The victorious commanders and sailors returned from sea 'all fat and lusty, and ruddy by being in the sun', but the London to which they made their return was oppressively quiet, with many houses shut up and carts being loaded for the country. In his *Diary* for 7 June Pepys writes,

> This day, much against my will, I did in Drury Lane see two or three houses marked with a red cross upon the doors, and 'Lord have mercy upon us' writ there; which was a sad sight to me, being the first of the kind that, to my remembrance, I ever saw. It put me into an ill conception of myself and my smell, so that I was forced to buy some roll-tobacco to smell to and chaw, which took away the apprehension.

It was the last of the old, medieval epidemics to visit England, carried by the flea-infested rats that entered the city from ships. As the weekly tolls began to mount, there was an exodus from the capital both to the outlying villages of London and further afield. Tent cities appeared on the outskirts, but even these were not free from infection; men and women died like animals on the side of the road, in fields and ditches, in woods and streams, writhing from the awful swellings that erupted from beneath their skin. This dreadful scourge was accompanied by a brief revival of millenarian fervour as people in their terror pointed a finger at the promiscuous court. A brilliant comet was seen in the night sky; the streets swarmed with mock astrologers and 'a wicked generation of pretenders to magic'. The hoarse voice of apocalyptic preacher Solomon Eagle echoed through the deserted streets with the warning, 'Yet forty days, and London shall be destroyed.' According to Defoe in his *Journal of the Plague Year* (1722), 'Another [prophet] ran about naked, except a pair of drawers about his waist, crying day and night, like a man that Josephus mentions, who cried "Woe to Jerusalem!" a little before the destruction of that city.'

London quickly became a ghost town. Weeds grew in the streets, and the houses, sealed to prevent the spread of the disease, became living tombs with infected and uninfected alike holed up together. Makeshift hospitals were patrolled by surgeons in macabre beaked masks. Pepys had to stay put to keep the Navy Office running (after all, England was at war with the Dutch), which was a blessing for posterity, as his *Diary* paints a vivid picture of the deserted capital. The Bill of Mortality for the week beginning 11 September 1665 gave notice of 8,297 deaths, 7,165 of whom died of the plague. On Wednesday the 20th, Pepys wrote, 'But, Lord! what a sad time it is to see no boats upon the river; and grass grows all up and down Whitehall Court, and nobody but poor wretches in the streets!' Bills rose to 10,000 a week at the very height of the pestilence, and when winter's healing frosts brought relief it was discovered that over 100,000 had died in London alone. That's one in five of the population. Most were buried in mass graves beyond the city limits. The stench both there and in the streets was such that it robbed people of their senses.

Helped by John Pritchard, son of the proprietor at her local inn, the Cock and Pie, Nell fled to Oxford with her mother, not to live with her grandfather Canon Edward Gwyn as some have claimed (for he died in 1624), but to follow the King and court. Oxford had been Charles I's headquarters during the Civil War, and his son always thought of it as a second capital. There was no question but that theatrical entertainments would be required during a lengthy asylum, and who better to furnish them than the King's own company? Pepys saw the courtyard at Whitehall full of wagons on 29 June as the royal family and courtiers prepared to leave. On the following day a royal warrant ordered that four yards of bastard scarlet cloth and one quarter of a yard of velvet be delivered to all eleven 'women comedians in His Majesty's Theatre', including one 'Ellen Gwyn'. Nell could now proclaim herself one of the King's servants and wear his livery.

The court spent some time at Hampton Court, then at Salisbury and Wilton before moving on up to Oxford; after Oxford, they repaired to Tunbridge Wells to drink from the chalybeate springs. Whether Nell followed them hither and yond on their progress or kept to Oxford we simply don't know. Nor are there any records of her activities there. If she was Rochester's mistress at the time, then she may well have visited him at nearby Adderbury or his childhood home of Ditchley Park. Having distinguished himself at Bergen,[2] Rochester was in high favour with the King, not that one could do much with the King's favour while London was boarded up and the government removed from the centre of power. Indeed, the whole country came to something of a standstill, and news from the Continent, when it came, did so in a trickle. The death of Philip IV of Spain went unremarked, which suited Louis XIV just fine: he took the opportunity to claim the Spanish Netherlands in the name of his wife, the Infanta Marie-Thérèse.[3]

The King returned to London on 1 February 1666; three days later his wife, who had remained in Oxford, miscarried of a boy at Merton College, the very college in which Barbara had successfully given birth to her fifth child by the King only months before. It was by now clear to everyone that the Queen was incapable of bearing children, but she herself seemed undismayed, so finely tuned was her heart to the consolations of religion. Pepys had found his head growing dizzy when he was shown the King's Closet at Whitehall, crammed with dozens of clocks and pictures and all manner of fine baubles; the Queen's Closet, on the other hand, had been a model of simplicity, for there he found that she 'had nothing but some pretty pious pictures, and books of devotion; and her holy water at her head as she sleeps . . .'

The Queen's faith and that of the whole country was to be sorely tried once more, when on the night of 2 September 1666 London went up in flames. The almanacks and plague-prophets had predicted it, both as scourge and deliverance. Had not a second comet been seen in the skies above London, not cold and phlegmatic like the first but bright with a fierce, rushing sound, and in the shape of a flaming sword? Surely the final judgement was at hand. The sheer scale and ferocity of the fire confirmed it. 'All the skie was of a fiery aspect', wrote Evelyn, 'like the top of a burning oven, and the light seene above 40 miles round about for many nights. God grant mine eyes may never behold the like, who now saw above 10,000 houses all in one flame; the noise and cracking and thunder of the impetuous flames, the shrieking of women and children, the hurry of people, the fall of towers, houses and churches, was like an hideous storme . . .' Birds were roasted on the wing, molten lead poured from the roof of old St Paul's, the houses wept glass; the heavens themselves seemed on fire. Even as far away as Oxford, Anthony à Wood noted that 'the moon was darkened by clouds of smoke and looked reddish', as if the sixth seal of the Book of Revelation had been opened. The French were blamed, so were the Dutch; both had landed forces in the country and were ready to take London – or so the rumours went. Not many people were buying into the story of the baker's oven in Pudding Lane.

The King and the Duke of York both displayed great courage and stamina in directing the fire-fighting efforts, but when on 6 September the King addressed the homeless Londoners assembled on the common at Moorfields, fully one-third of the city had been destroyed, including 13,000 houses, 81 churches and the very hub of the capital, old St Paul's. The medieval city that had been a breeding ground for the plague was well and truly gone. The speed with which both Evelyn and Wren and their fellows in the Royal Society submitted their plans for a new metropolis of brick and stone, with broad avenues and spacious squares, has led some to talk of the fire as intentional.

Whatever the truth of the matter the new London, with the Monument to the fire at its centre, was built by men steeped in freemasonry, who understood the architectural principles that had informed Solomon's Temple in Jersualem and who wished to convey a special message about England's destiny by means of the resurrected capital. If the Stuart royal line was indeed descended from Christ via the Merovingian Kings, as James I had believed, then the English throne was the throne of David, and London the New Jerusalem.

So great was the psychological and symbolic force of the fire that one can almost date the true start of the Restoration to 1666. It was as if the blazing heat from all the sun kings and sun gods in the heroic drama suddenly conflagrated to baptize and purify the nation in fire. The fire of the individual spirit, so long repressed by the demands of the collective, blazed forth. And it was the long-pent-up spirit of women that blazed the brightest, heralded by a remarkable work from one of the most remarkable figures of her day, Margaret Cavendish's *The Description of a New World, Called the Blazing World* (1666).

Born Margaret Lucas near Colchester in 1623, her family had

moved to Oxford at the beginning of the Civil War to be with the King. She became a maid of honour to Henrietta Maria and accompanied the Queen when she fled to Paris in 1644. Margaret, who felt awkward and unable to imitate the manners of the court, described herself as the 'natural fool' of the royal entourage. This immediately allies her with Nell Gwyn, another 'natural fool' at court. Both women possessed the gift of being themselves, and being yourself in the artificial environment of the court meant being that symbol of nature, the fool. Considered eccentric in dress and manners, Margaret's 'folly' was also defined by her keen interest in science, education and philosophy and her courage in writing on such topics under her own name and often from a distinctly feminist point of view.

But her belief in women and their ability to think, to teach, to create and to wield power effectively and beneficently was essentially a belief in the sovereignty of the individual, of whatever sex. In the preface to *Blazing World* she writes,

> I am not covetous, but as ambitious as ever any of my sex was, is, or can be; which makes, that though I cannot be *Henry* the Fifth or *Charles* the Second, yet I endeavour to be *Margaret* the *First*; and although I have neither power, time nor occasion to conquer the world as *Alexander* and *Caesar* did; yet rather than not to be mistress of one, since Fortune and the Fates would give me none, I have made a world of my own: for which no body, I hope, will blame me, since it is in every one's power to do the like.

Blazing World is about a lady who, having been abducted by a lustful merchant and taken out to sea, is rescued by a providential storm that drives the ship up between ice floes and glaciers to the North Pole. Here her captors freeze to death, while the lady, protected by the light of her beauty, continues her journey beyond the Pole to a new, parallel realm ('another Pole of another world'), where she is greeted by all manner of strange creatures, all walking like men. There are Bear-men, Worm-men, Fish-men, Bird-men, Fox-men, Spider-men, Parrot-men, Satyrs and Giants, to name but a few, and they are a cause of great fear and wonder in the lady. Taken for a goddess, she is conveyed to their Emperor, who makes her his wife, and Empress of the whole world. Like Pallas Athene, she is given a spear and shield as symbols of her authority. The remainder of the novel describes the new Empress's understanding, organization and government of the world she now rules, and involves many lengthy philosophical and scientific debates with her various counsellors on the nature of that world.

It is not hard to divine the basic meaning of the allegory. The merchant and his men represent the authority of male lust, which the lady rejects in order to travel to the North Pole, which symbolizes the world of her intellect and imagination. The men cannot follow her there, for it is her own private world, of which she has the absolute government. The fantastic creatures she encounters represent her unused potential – of knowledge, imagination, spirit and worldly power. It is only natural then that they should inspire fear in her at first, for they have been unfamiliar for so long, hidden in a dark corner of the female psyche. In total, the story is about a woman coming into her own and reflects Cavendish's core belief that the way for women to emancipate themselves was by thinking for themselves and so creating their own private mental worlds (or 'life-illusions', in John Cowper Powys's arresting phrase).

Another female trail-blazer in the year of the Great Fire was the playwright and novelist Aphra Behn, who wrote in the preface to her comedy *The Lucky Chance*, 'I am not content to write for a third day only. I value fame as much as if I had been born a hero.' That summer of 1666 she set off for Antwerp to work as a government spy. Acting independently and at great personal risk, she collected valuable intelligence for her King, a task inconceivable to women in a previous age. Thus Nell Gwyn on the stage, Margaret Cavendish with her pen and Aphra Behn through her political initiative all became conscious of their individual power both as valuable members of society and as women.

So when the theatres finally reopened in October 1666, the stage was set for a new drama of the sexes. The genie was out of the bottle. As Margaret Cavendish declared, 'I had rather die in the adventure of noble achievements, than to live in obscure and sluggish security.'[4]

~ 7 ~

The Wild Mistress

LITTLE IS KNOWN FOR CERTAIN of Nell's life during the eighteen-month closure of the theatres, except that she spent some time at Oxford and received the King's livery as a member of his theatre company. We do know, however, that the company's manager, Tom Killigrew, took advantage of the long interlude to make some improvements to the theatre at Drury Lane. On 19 March 1666 Pepys walked over to the playhouse after dinner with his colleague Sir John Minnes and found it 'all in dirt, they being altering of the stage to make it wider'. He went backstage to have a good nose around and saw

> the inside of the stage and all the tiring-rooms and machines; and, indeed, it was a sight worthy seeing. But to see their clothes, and the various sorts, and what a mixture of things there was; here a wooden-leg, there a ruff, here a hobby-horse, there a crown, would make a man split himself . . . with laughing; and particularly Lacy's wardrobe . . . But then again, to think how fine they show on the stage by candlelight, and how poor things they are to look now too near hand, is not pleasant at all. The machines are fine, and the paintings very pretty.

The curious thing here is that Pepys should seem shocked that the theatre is a world of make-believe, as if he'd been expecting to walk through the wardrobe into a fairy-tale world of princes and dwarves. Another demonstration, if one were needed, of the strong escapist element in Restoration drama. Also in the passage is a certain melancholy realization of the transient drama of all life, to which actors are more keenly attuned than most, and which had of course been emphasized in everyone's lives at the time through war, bubonic plague and the Great Fire of London. Few people could have been immune to the idea that for better or worse – or both – a new society was in its birth pangs. The changes did not come overnight, but they were as sweeping as the flames that devoured the capital.

This new society was based on the individual rather than the collective, and was driven by science and commerce instead of religion. Women began to come into their own, albeit slowly, individuality transcending gender. People started to believe that they could recreate the world without God's blessing, and the cast-iron principles of science, together with the material blessings of international commerce, gave them the confidence to proceed.

The two most powerful literary images of the time are unconscious descriptions of this vast new force then breaking free of its moorings. The first is Thomas Hobbes's Leviathan from his work of the same name, which was originally published in 1651 while he was in exile in France. The leviathan, as described in Job, is a primitively fearsome crocodile whose 'teeth are terrible round about', an apt metaphor for the devouring nature of the unbridled ego. The second is Milton's Satan from *Paradise Lost*, which he completed in the year of the Great Fire. Satan in Milton's work represents fallen man, or the intellect cut loose from the nourishing springs of the soul. He it is who persuades Eve that she and Adam will 'be as gods' if they taste of the fruit of the tree, and enjoy sovereign sway over the world. Both Hobbes's Leviathan and Milton's Satan represent the insatiable appetite for power of the prideful ego.

The theatres reopened towards the end of November 1666, despite opposition from the Church authorities, who at least wrung a concession from the two companies that they would give a share of their profits to help those made destitute by the recent disasters. Nell herself had been in the capital for some months rehearsing for the new season. The experience of touring the provinces had sharpened her stage skills, and there had been greater scope for improvisation in the more relaxed atmosphere of the country house. At any rate her very first recorded role of the new season was a starring one, no mean achievement for a sixteen-year-old!

She played Lady Wealthy in the Hon. James Howard's comedy *The English Monsieur*, a character described as 'a rich widow, in love with Welbred'. The latter, 'a wild Gentleman, Servant to the Lady Wealthy', was played by her lover Charles Hart, while Mr Frenchlove, the English Monsieur of the title, was played by Lacy. The humour of the play is extravagant and farcical, as one would expect in a play that targets that well-worn butt of Restoration raillery, the Gallomaniac. Like Sir Fopling Flutter in Etherege's *Man of Mode*, Frenchlove affects all things French to such a degree that he is happy to be rejected by his mistress so long as she does it 'with a French tone of voice'.

To Pepys, it was 'a mighty pretty play, very witty and pleasant. And the women do very well; but above all, little Nelly, that I am mightily pleased with the play, and much with the house, more than ever I expected, the women doing better than ever I expected, and very fine women.' Not for the first time Pepys's judgement may have been clouded somewhat by the alluring female presence on stage or indeed by what was happening beside him in the pit. A keen emulator of court manners, Samuel had become a player in the gallant-and-mistress market, acting out his role in the drama of the pit with ill-disguised relish. Evelyn, on the other hand, hated the idea of women on stage, and refers in his diary entry for 18 October 1666 to 'fowle and undecent women now (and never till now) permitted to appear and act, who inflaming severall young noblemen and gallants, became their misses . . .' He also deplored the court's unthinking adoption of all things French, fearing that England was abandoning its cultural identity. Here is his description of one of the painted waterflies flitting about the court:

> it was a fine silken thing which I espied t'other day [in] Westminster Hall that had so much ribbon on him as would have plundered six shops and set up twenty country Pedlars. All the body was drest like a May Pole or Tom a Bedlam's cap. A fregate newly rigged kept not half such a clatter in a storme as this Puppett's streamers did . . . what have we to do with such forreign Butterflies?

The successful conclusion to the amorous intrigue between Welbred and Lady Wealthy depends on a well-balanced war of wits. Both the gallant and his mistress assert their independence through their wit, but beneath the cool bravura each is anxious to secure a favourable union with the other. The one thing they avoid at all costs is a frank expression of their feelings. Of especial interest to the audience was the way the dialogue between the two characters reflected – or deflected – the true relationship between Hart and Nelly. The following extract gives a good flavour:

> LADY W.: When will I marry you! When will I love ye, you
> should ask first.
> WELBRED: Why! don't ye?
> LADY W.: Why, do I? Did you ever hear me say I did?
> WELBRED: I have never heard you say you did not.
> LADY W.: I'll say so now, then, if you long.
> WELBRED: By no means. Say not a thing in haste you may repent
> at leisure.
> LADY W.: Come, leave your fooling, or I'll swear it.
> WELBRED: Don't, widow, for then you'll lie too.
> LADY W.: Indeed it seems 'tis for my money you would have
> me.
> WELBRED: For that, and something else you have.
> LADY W.: Well, I'll lay a wager thou hast lost all thy money at
> play, for then you're always in a marrying humour.

Here the humour lies in the apparent incongruity of Nell in the role of wealthy widow, though under the surface Lady Wealthy is a comical image of the young actress's growing stature and independence, for now at least she had the wealthy widow's ability to choose her mate. Her stock was high, a bevy of suitors hovered in the wings, and she was no longer dependent on Charles Hart for her welfare. He was a veteran actor of great distinction, old enough to be her father, and her love for him had been in the nature of a schoolgirl crush. Now that her theatrical training was drawing to a close, the early infatuation was replaced by an enduring sense of gratitude and affection.

In one of Lady Wealthy's more reflective moments there is a clear reference to Nell's former calling and a strong reminder of the constant sense of anxiety over matters of status and security in the life of a female artist in the seventeenth century: 'This life of mine can last no longer than my beauty; and though 'tis pleasant now – I want nothing whilst I am Mr. Welbred's Mistress – yet, if his mind should change, I might e'en sell oranges for my living; and he not buy one of me to relieve me.'

Romantic attachments could be so strained and formal in the upper echelons of society that the dream of bucolic love, with its greater emotional freedom, was a persistent theme. Courtiers, City magnates and gallants often had cause to reflect wistfully upon the simple country life, where folk were freer to choose their mates. Welbred's companion, Mr Comely, falls in love with the country wench Elsbeth Pritty, seeing redemption in her sweet looks and innocent ways. Although not a country lass herself, Nell may have conjured up such an image in the minds of her more sophisticated admirers. Pepys, for one, seems to have been drawn into a pastoral fantasy when he saw Nell standing at her lodgings' door on May morning, watching the milk maids dance past with garlands on their pails.

Over the next four months Nell played at least seven different roles, though the true figure is probably nearer ten. New plays, if they survived the first night, ran for three to six days, while the stock repertory could manage up to ten. No wonder improvisation was a necessary skill! In October 1667 Pepys found it pretty 'to see how Nell cursed, for having so few people in the pit.' But there was a practical edge to her cursing, for she knew that a poor audience meant that she would be learning new lines the following morning. Among revivals the plays of Beaumont and Fletcher were extremely popular, not least because of their intimate depiction of court life. Their witty exchanges between courtiers became the foundation of the Restoration comedy of manners. According to Dryden, 'they understood and imitated the conversation of gentlemen much better [than Shakespeare], whose wild debaucheries and quickness of wit in repartees no poet can ever paint as they have done.' A questionable judgement, yet undoubtedly the perception of the time. Their plays were often revised to great effect, the most famous being the Duke of Buckingham's celebrated recension of Fletcher's *The Chances*, a comedy set in Italy.

The story is told of a merry conversation at Rochester's wedding on 29 January 1667 between the groom, his best man Buckingham and Nell Gwyn, in which the two wits playfully persuaded her to learn the role of the heroine Constantia in Buckingham's newly completed *Chances*.[1] They ribbed her about her fabled constancy towards Charles Hart, which they said made her ideal for the role. As it turned out, there were two Constantias in the play, one virtuous and constant, the other a whore. Nell was cast as the latter opposite the gallant, Don John, played by Hart. (But she had the last laugh when she became the King's mistress and proved that she was the two Constantias in one: a faithful whore. Indeed, Buckingham gained first-hand knowledge of this paradox when he attempted to seduce her in the King's antechamber and had his ears soundly boxed.)

It is remarkable how prophetic of her future life some of the roles Nell played at this time were. As Celia in Beaumont and Fletcher's *The Humorous Lieutenant* she played a captive at the court of King Antigonus ('an old man with young desires'), who is courted by both the King himself and his son Prince Demetrius. Her constancy, frankness and sharp tongue affront the court toadies and in the end serve to bring everyone to their senses, including the doting King. Once again, we have the familiar Restoration motif of the spirited girl imprisoned by the authority of an old and lustful king, whose power is broken by the maiden's fidelity to love and truth. It was this spirit of female integrity that was breaking free in Restoration England and that Dryden saw rising from the ashes of medieval London. In the scene in which Antigonus, disguised as one of his own servants, presents Celia with some magnificent jewels, she quickly pierces his disguise and rejects both him and his precious stones. Antigonus is forced to come clean:

> ANT.: Why then I am a King, and mine own speaker.
> CEL.: And I as free as you, mine own Disposer:
> There, take your Jewels; let them give them lustres
> That have dark Lives and Souls . . .

Only two years into her career Nell Gwyn was already a celebrity, popular with audiences and public alike. Pepys had gone to see *The Humorous Lieutenant* and though he didn't think much of the play, the evening was redeemed when his mistress of sorts, the actress Mrs Knepp (or Knipp), took Samuel and his wife backstage to meet Nell. 'Knipp took us all in', he relates, 'and brought to us Nelly, a most pretty woman, who acted the great part of Celia today very fine, and did it pretty well: I kissed her, and so did my wife; and a mighty pretty soul she is.' Knipp arranged for the Pepyses to stay to watch the dancing rehearsal for the next day's play. As they left, Samuel was still thinking of his encounter with the new star: 'And so away thence, pleased with this sight also [i.e., the rehearsal], and specially kissing of Nell.'

The court too had begun to notice her, from her performances both at Drury Lane and at the Whitehall Theatre. And although she was still formally Charles Hart's lover, one senses that she had outgrown the relationship and was casting around for further adventures. Her reputation was now almost as great as his, and she was not one to be hemmed in by the protective embrace of a fellow actor. The players enjoyed a bohemian life in their spare time, mixing with playwrights, musicians and court Wits. They went boating on the Thames, visited the Mulberry Gardens or Vauxhall, or took a picnic out to Finsbury Fields where the old windmills still turned. Such high-spirited expeditions would be followed by supper parties, either at a tavern or a private house. Hot on the heels of dinner came music, dancing and cards. With fidelity a taboo, it was anyone's guess what happened afterwards.

Dryden had been busy during the closure of the theatres. He returned from the country with a play that was to change the course of Restoration drama and which reflected the growing bargaining power of women in their relationships with men. It was also the first of his plays in which he created a comic role specially for Nell Gwyn, that of Florimell, the wild mistress, which became one of the archetypes of Restoration drama. This figure didn't simply reflect a change in female assertiveness, it helped stimulate one. Thus Nell Gwyn came to embody a new breed of woman: witty, independent, unafraid to express her desires, determined to be herself.

Dryden's new play was a tragicomedy called *Secret Love, or The Maiden Queen*, and was performed at the King's Theatre on 2 March 1667. The King was so taken with it that Dryden in his preface to the first edition of 1668 announced that His Majesty had 'graced it with the Title of His Play', and therefore no dedication was necessary. Pepys too was in ecstasies, and his account is worth quoting in full:

> After dinner with my wife to the King's House to see 'The Maiden Queen', a new play of Dryden's, mightily commended for the regularity of it, and the strain and wit; and the truth is, there is a comical part done by Nell, which is Florimell, that I never can hope ever to see the like done again, by man or woman. The King and Duke of York were at the play. But so great performance of a comical part was never, I believe, in the world before as Nell do this, both as a mad girl, then most and best of all when she comes in like a young gallant; and hath the motions and carriage of a spark the most that ever I saw any man have. It makes me, I confess, admire her.

Pepys is always keenly aware of the drama offstage, in the pit and boxes, and here he duly notes the presence of Charles and his brother. In claiming the play as his own, the King was also laying claim to its leading lady. For the seventeen-year-old Nell to have acted with such panache and assurance before the royal brothers says a great deal about her self-possession. Moreover, to have pleased the King in such a public arena meant instant stardom. There was now an unspoken bond between the King and his pretty comedienne, and Nell would have felt a thrill of pleasure whenever she glanced over at the royal box and caught the eye of the dark, melancholy-looking man who was coming to occupy first place in her thoughts.

Court performances soon followed, with special costumes paid for by the King. Nell was kitted out in a man's suit of embroidered purple cloth, a flannel waistcoat, Rhinegraves and 'other furniture'. Rhinegraves (or petticoat breeches) were chiefly worn by men of the court. They were like full-cut knee-length shorts, but effeminate in appearance and worn loose at the hips. They would have flown up as Nell danced. They originated in the Rhineland (*Rheingrafhose*), but had found popularity at the court of Louis XIV, which was the fashion centre of Europe. It was not only French fashions that influenced English Restoration culture; French theatre did too. Dryden himself pillaged French literature for the plots of his plays, despite being an unrelenting critic of French comedies and indeed comedy in general. It could be argued that without the comic genius of Nell Gwyn and others to inspire him, Dryden may well have neglected the genre altogether.

There are two interweaving plots in *Secret Love*, one tragic the other comic, but both deal with the theme of power in relationships. The tragic plot is a tale of thwarted desire and depicts the love of the Maiden Queen of Sicily for a courtier by the name of Philocles. We see how the private passions of a monarch can tear the web of courteous relationships at court and threaten the health and security of the state. We see too how power corrupts love, and how absolute power – the position enjoyed by the monarch – prevents it completely. It is only by sacrificing her love to the duty she owes her people that the Maiden Queen redeems the tottering state:

> The cares, observances, and all the duties
> Which I should pay an Husband, I will place
> Upon my people; and our mutual love
> Shall make a blessing more than Conjugal,
> And this the States shall ratifie.

The comic plot, starring Nell as Florimell and Charles Hart as her gallant, Celadon, is a tale of love's labours won. Celadon, though witty, is something of a bungler, baffled by his own duplicity and infidelity. Florimell on the other hand, though she makes a show of indifference to her suitor, is loyal throughout and both wittier and more purposeful in her pursuit of him. Neither of course will admit to pursuing the other, and marriage at the end is presented as a cruel necessity, though it is eased by the 'proviso' that they make, a set of rules to guarantee freedom within the married relationship. It is Florimell who suggests it:

FLOR.: But this Marriage is such a Bugbear to me; much might be if we could invent but any way to make it easie.

CEL.: Some foolish people have made it uneasie, by drawing the knot faster then they need; but we that are wiser will loosen it a little.

FLOR.: 'Tis true indeed, there's some difference betwixt a Girdle and a Halter.

As for the provisions themselves, though uttered in jest, the key concept is honesty. They speak volumes about the spirit of Nell's future relationship with the King:

FLOR.: But . . . when we begin to live like Husband and Wife, and never come near one another – what then Sir?

CEL.: Why then our onely happiness must be to have one mind, and one will, *Florimell*.

FLOR.: One mind if thou wilt, but prithee let us have two wills; for I find one will be little enough for me alone: But how if those wills should meet and clash, *Celadon*?

CEL.: I warrant thee for that: Husbands and Wives keep their wills far enough asunder for ever meeting: one thing let us be sure to agree on, that is, never to be jealous.

FLOR.: No; but e'en love one another as long as we can; and confess the truth when we can love no longer.

CEL.: When I have been at play, you shall never ask me what money I have lost.

FLOR.: When I have been abroad you shall never enquire who treated me.

CEL.: *Item*, I will have the liberty to sleep all night, without your interrupting my repose for any evil design whatsoever.

FLOR.: *Item*, Then you shall bid me good night before you sleep.

CEL.: Provided always, that whatever liberties we take with other people, we continue very honest to one another.

FLOR.: As far as will consist with a pleasant life.

CEL.: Lastly, Whereas the names of Husband and Wife hold forth nothing but clashing and cloying, and dulness and faintness in their signification; they shall be abolish'd for ever betwixt us.

FLOR.: And instead of those, we will be married by the more agreeable names of Mistress and Gallant.

The proviso makes a nonsense of men's legal power over women in marriage. Nell, both in the guise of Florimell and as herself, tipped the balance towards a more equitable bond between the sexes. If one combines the comic and tragic plots, the message of the play as a whole seems to be that men must relinquish some of their power over women in order to enjoy a more fulfilling relationship with them, for just as the monarch, in this case the Maiden Queen, can be thwarted in love by possessing too much power, so can the ordinary husband. Ironically, the King was unhappy with the proviso scene because it was performed with the Maiden Queen standing silently by, as if in approval. Since it was one of the most popular scenes in the play, Dryden's apology in his preface is less than wholehearted: 'But though the Artifice [i.e., the proviso scene] succeeded, I am willing to acknowledge it as a fault, since it pleas'd His Majesty, the best Judge, to think it so.'

Florimell's journey in the play in many ways symbolizes the growing visibility of women in Restoration England. When she first appears in the action she is wearing a mask, but this is soon set aside, and her wit and purposefulness assert themselves. At the beginning of Act V she disguises herself as a gallant in order to embarrass Celadon in his pursuit of the sisters Olinda and Sabina, for she is determined to win him ('I find I do love the Rogue in spight of all his infidelities'). In fact, she plays the gallant better than the gallant himself, which rather undermines his superiority. It certainly astonished Pepys, wringing from him a frank confession of his admiration for the young actress, as we have seen. And the fact that Nell had no acting models to restrict her doubtless made her wild sallies the more innovating.

The word 'mad' is used again and again to describe both Florimell and Celadon; indeed, they themselves squabble over who is the madder. 'Slife,' exclaims the exasperated Celadon, 'what wouldst thou be at? I am madder then thou art.' 'Mad' in this Restoration sense meant 'wilful' and 'unconventional', which is clearly what Bishop Burnet had in mind when he described Nell as wild and indiscreet. Whatever the exact definition, here was a woman who bested her man in duels of wit, wore breeches to great effect, chose the object of her desire and having won him sought to live on her own terms or at least as an equal partner. And it was Nell Gwyn's performance of Florimell that was the prime mover of this new force in English life, the wild mistress. Nor was it, as some have claimed, a recipe for licence, which was hardly needed. It was more in the nature of social experiment, and as such in the best tradition of radical theatre.

In the same month that *Secret Love* appeared, the first hint of a rivalry came to light between Nell Gwyn and an actress of the Duke's Theatre by the name of Moll Davis, who had joined the company as a child, boarding with Sir William Davenant. It comes in Pepys's *Diary*. Having registered mild disappointment at the play he had attended, a tragedy by John Caryl entitled *The English Princess*, he goes on to praise 'little Mis. Davis' who danced a jig in boy's clothes at the end and gives his opinion that 'there is no comparison between Nell's dancing the other day at the King's house in boy's clothes [i.e., as Florimell] and this, this being infinitely beyond the other.' Matters spilled out into the open when Nell gave a spiked performance of the wild mistress Mirida in the Hon. James Howard's *All Mistaken, or The Mad Couple*, which was performed at the King's House in April 1667.

Moll Davis had won her way into the King's favour by her performance of the song beginning 'My lodging is on the cold ground' in Davenant's play *The Rivals*, an adaptation of Shakespeare and Fletcher's *The Two Noble Kinsmen*. As John Downes, the prompter at the Duke's Theatre, put it, Moll performed her piece 'so charmingly that not long after it raised her from her bed on the cold ground to a bed royal.' Sang she,

> My lodging is on the cold ground,
> And very hard is my fare,
> But that which troubles me most is
> The unkindness of my dear.
> Yet still I cry, O turn, love,
> And I prythee, love, turn to me,
> For thou art the man that I long for,
> And alack what remedy!

Meanwhile Nell was hamming it up as Mirida in *The Mad Couple*, making sport of her hugely obese suitor Pinguister, played by John Lacy. Knowing full well that he is stuck on the ground and can only roll towards her, Mirida mischievously invites Pinguister to come and sit in her lap so that she can try to 'enclose thy world of fat and love within these arms'. Pinguister is in agonies of bitter self-reproach and pity, fearing that the only solution is to weep his fat away, when Mirida suddenly breaks into song with,

> My lodging is on the cold boards,
> And wonderful hard is my fare,
> But that which troubles me most is
> The fatness of my dear.
> Yet still I cry, Oh melt, love,
> And I prythee now melt apace,
> For thou art the man I should long for
> If 'twere not for thy grease.

The audience understood the allusion immediately and howled its delight, not least because Nell performed the piece in mocking imitation of her rival's 'rather coy and petulant tone'. The young blades who frequented the Duke's House swore revenge, but Nell was never more than waylaid at night and, besides, there were gallants aplenty from the King's House to defend her honour. Moll was no great beauty, though she had bright eyes and a trim figure, nor did she distinguish herself as an actress. Her genius was for dancing sugges-tively, which seems to have nettled the Queen, who would not stay to see one of Moll's jigs at court.

The Mad Couple, like *Secret Love* a tragicomedy, is a farcical play full of black humour, in which the bravura comic scenes far outshine the impertinence and stiff banality of the tragedy. Philidor and Mirida, gallant and mistress, are wilder and more mischievous than their counterparts in *Secret Love*, but less witty. They are inveterate prank-sters, and unlike Celadon and Florimell's, their pranks are collaborative efforts, as when they manage to lock all six of Philidor's suitors in a vault with Pinguister. (The latter has just been administered a heavy dose of laxative by his doctor as a way of losing weight, and no sooner is he immured with the hapless ladies than the floodgates open.) As her career at court would prove, Nell herself was a natural born jester, always ready for a caper; the description of Mirida as a 'pretty fairy devil' fits her to a T.

Pepys saw the play later in the year and wrote, '. . . with my wife and girle to the King's house, and there saw "The Mad Couple", which is but an ordinary play; but only Nell's and Hart's mad parts are most excellently done, but especially her's: which makes it a miracle to me to think how ill she do any serious part, as, the other day, just like a fool or changeling; and in a mad part, do beyond all imitation almost.'

But all is not lightness and gaiety. Howard reveals the seamier side of the gallant's life: serial adultery, cruelty, irresponsibility and chronic debt. Philidor, a dead-beat dad with a string of bastards, pays his children's nurses with sexual favours and cynical promises. His pranks are often crude and callous and his witticisms vituperative. Compared to other wild couples in the literature, Philidor and Mirida are a particularly uncompromising pair, and refuse to marry at all at the end. When Mirida finds herself bound back to back with Philidor she orders a fiddler to play her special jig which, we are not surprised to learn, is entitled 'I care not a pin for any man'.

In the scene in which Nell so artfully mimicked Moll Davis, Lacy the fat suitor ended up rolling desperately across the stage to meet her, while she, unknown to him, rolled away to stay beyond his grasp. As Nell rolled, her tumbled petticoats revealed a tantalizing portion of leg and thigh. This so inflamed Charles, Lord Buckhurst that he hastened backstage after the performance and immediately proposed an affair. We don't know what Nell's reaction was, though it's unlikely that she felt anything other than extremely flattered. Here was one of the premier gallants of the age asking her to step out as his wild mistress. No one was better rehearsed to play the part than she. It was time to put her experience on the boards into practice.

Charles Sackville, Lord Buckhurst, who succeeded his maternal uncle as Earl of Middlesex in 1674 and his father as Earl of Dorset in 1677, was one of the original court wits (or 'merry gang', as Andrew Marvell termed them). Cultured, witty, satirical, dissolute, and utterly charming, he exemplified the nonchalant brilliance so coveted by his fellow rakes. A Gentleman of the Bedchamber to the King, Buckhurst was also a talented poet and critic, and the most generous literary patron of his time. He patronized Dryden, Butler, Wycherley and a host of others, and was the first to hail Milton's *Paradise Lost* as a work of genius. Sadly for posterity, he released the bulk of his own wit in conversation rather than composition, and for this he was chided by his fellow authors. Dryden wrote, 'It is a general complaint against your lordship, and I must have leave to upbraid you with it, that, because you need not write, you will not'; while Congreve ruefully observed that Buckhurst 'slabbered' more wit when he was dying than other people had in the prime of life. Looking back from the eighteenth century Pope called him a 'holiday' writer.

Much of the praise of his writing is hyperbolic – Dryden for instance compares him to Shakespeare and Homer! – but this is easily explained as the flattery of a munificent patron. If he did possess genius, it was in the field of satire. According to fellow wit the Earl of Rochester,

> For pointed satyrs, I would Buckhurst choose,
> The best good man, with the worst natur'd muse . . .

In many ways he led a charmed life, and despite some of the obscene and rather nasty pranks he instigated during his youth he always seemed to come away with his reputation as a congenial fellow intact. Rochester even complained to the King about the public's indulgence towards his licentious companion. 'I know not how it is,' he fretted, 'but Lord Buckhurst may do what he will, yet is never in the wrong.' On one notorious occasion at the Cock Inn in Covent Garden after a particularly merry luncheon Buckhurst appeared naked on the balcony with his friend and fellow wit Sir Charles Sedley (known as 'Little Sid') and an obscure Lincolnshire knight, Sir Thomas Ogle. Sedley began by preaching an obscene sermon at the top of his voice, which drew a large crowd in the street below. When he had finished Buckhurst and Ogle went through the motions of buggering each other, while Sedley pissed down onto the upturned faces of the mob. By way of a finale, they pelted the spectators with empty bottles. Stones were thrown in retaliation, and for a moment it looked as though the inn would be stormed. The principals ended up before the Lord Chief Justice, and heavy fines were administered.

Buckhurst, then, could be as crude and obscene as Philidor in *The Mad Couple*, yet as wittily seductive as Dorimant in Etherege's *Man of Mode*. Like all gallants he was inconstant, if not by nature then by principle. He was one of those 'fellows of infinite tongue' decried by

Shakespeare's Henry V, 'that can rhyme themselves into ladies' favours' and 'always reason themselves out again'. He was compellingly attractive to women and, like Rochester, unsqueamish about their social status. One of his lovers had been the notorious bawd Betty Morris, whose reply to a great lady who called her Buckhurst's whore could easily have come from the lips of Nell Gwyn:

> I please one man of wit, am proud on't too,
> Let all the coxcombs dance to bed to you.

What is certain is that he possessed all the qualities, both vicious and commendable, of the true gallant, and what he proposed to Nell Gwyn in the weeks after that first hurried conversation backstage was a quintessential gallant's caper. He suggested they take a house for the summer in the fashionable spa town of Epsom, and to demonstrate that he wasn't interested in a particularly intense or permanent union he announced that they would be accompanied by his co-prankster and fellow profligate Sir Charles Sedley (like Buckhurst a brilliant and irreverent talker, but a mediocre playwright). Both men were in their late twenties, Nell only seventeen, but she knew how to hold her own.

The only qualms she might have had concerned the theatre, for it was a big step to throw up one's parts in mid-season, even if you were the most popular comic actress of the day. Nor could she have been insensitive to the hurt and resentment she would be causing Charles Hart, both personally and professionally. They were the company's star comic turn, and he had been her mentor and protector from the start of her career. His formidable influence in the company had to be considered too, his power to do her harm being commensurately great. Yet, as a contemporary satire, 'The Lady of Pleasure', makes clear, Buckhurst's rank made it imperative that Hart should at least make a show of giving up his girl with a good grace:

> Yet Hart more manners had, than not to tender
> When noble Buckhurst beg'd him to surrender.
> He saw her roll the stage from side to side
> And, through her drawers the powerful charm descry'd.
> Take her my Lord, quoth Hart, since y'are so mean

To take a player's leavings for your Queen.
For tho I love her well, yet as she's poor
I'm well contented to prefer the whore.

Nell's heart's desire at this juncture was for an exciting social life, and that meant witty and vital companions who could broaden her horizons. Her zest for adventure brimming, this was a golden opportunity to spread her wings and test the power of her growing reputation.

The exact date of the merry trio's departure for Epsom is unclear. We know that Nell played one further role that season, that of Samira in Sir Robert Howard's comedy *The Surprisal*. That was at the end of April 1667. Allowing the play, which was not new, a run of ten days, it's probably safe to assume that she made off with Buckhurst some time after the second week in May. The first two or three weeks were spent in London, with Buckhurst inducting Nell into the ways of the merry gang and doing the rounds of smart parties. Unlike Rochester, who was rather brisk and brutal, Buckhurst had the reputation of a sophisticated lover who enjoyed working his charm upon a woman's soul. The trip to Epsom was undertaken once he had the young actress well and truly under his spell, sometime in June.

By the time Pepys got hold of the story it was 13 July: 'I home to dinner, where Mr. Pierce dined with us, who tells us what troubles me, that my Lord Buckhurst hath got Nell away from the King's house, lies with her, and gives her £100 a year, so as she hath sent her parts to the house, and will act no more.' Curiously, Pepys mentions nothing about the merry pair being at Epsom. Yet less than a page later, and in the same entry, he writes, 'So home, and resolved upon going to Epsom to-morrow, only for ayre, and got Mrs. Turner to go with us, and so home . . .' The repetition of 'so home' should warn us that Pepys is not being wholly honest with himself, rather like a stuttering man caught in a lie. Pepys had always been something of a voyeur, certainly a scandalmonger, and it is impossible that his resolution to visit Epsom was unconnected with the news he had just heard of Nell's decampment thither with the rakish Buckhurst. Mrs Turner was presumably commissioned to amuse his wife while he went sniffing about town.

Pepys arrived in Epsom with his wife and Mrs Turner at eight in the morning, having set out just after five. After taking the waters (four pints, no less!), he repaired with them to the King's Head, 'where our coachman carried us, and there had an ill room for us to go into, but the best in the house that was not taken up. Here we called for drink, and bespoke dinner; and hear that my Lord Buckhurst and Nelly are lodged at the next house, and Sir Charles Sidly [Sedley] with them: and keep a merry house. Poor girl! I pity her; but more the loss of her at the King's house.' Whether Pepys went next door to try to present his compliments we shall never know, but it's difficult to imagine him passing up the opportunity. That afternoon he led his companions into the woods, where they got lost in the thickets. When they finally emerged Pepys leapt down a bank and sprained his foot. Nevertheless, they climbed up onto the Downs, where to his delight they found a boy reading the Bible to his father, a shepherd, who looked like 'one of the old patriarchs'. Then they gathered nosegays in the meadows about town and stopped a milkmaid with her pail of milk. Pepys dipped his gilt tumbler into the creamy cauldron and they drank bellyfuls of the stuff. At seven in the evening they headed home, and when it grew dark saw a number of glow-worms illuminated by the side of the road. All in all a most satisfactory day.

It's likely that Nell would have found the same delight as Pepys in the sights and sounds of the countryside in the height of summer. She and her companions went riding on the Downs and spent long lazy afternoons picnicking up on the grassy plains, with Nell quizzing her companions about the King and his court, eager to learn as much as she could. And when they had taken their fill of wine and laughter, they lay down under the sun and drifted off to the music of the skylarks. Sometimes they had in their care Sedley's ten-year-old daughter, Catherine, who would in time become the mistress of the Duke of York[2] and win the same sort of reputation for outspokenness as Nell. Indeed, she became the wild mistress par excellence and refused to be dismissed by her royal lover when he became King. Buckhurst, stung by her rejection of him, would satirize her as Dorinda, whose 'sparkling witt and eyes / United cast too fierce a light'. Her mother, Lady Catherine Savage, was mad, believing herself to be the Queen. Her sudden appearances at the merry house reduced the proceedings to farce.

There were lunch and dinner parties too, given by the local gentry or those with holiday houses beside the spa, though the moon-faced gallant and his puckish whore may have been considered beyond the pale by provincial society. Mary Rich, Countess of Warwick, was present on one such occasion, but as she records in her diary was a little put out by one of the other guests:

> *August 5, 1667.* – Went with Lady Robartes and her Lord to Durdans to see my Lord who was there. At dinner that day dined Sedley [Nelly and Buckhurst's companion], which was much trouble to see him for fear he should be profane. But it pleased God to restrain him: yet the knowledge I had how profane a person he was troubled me to be in his company.

Instead of troubling the local dignitaries, except by way of late-night pranks, they contented themselves with inviting friends down from London. Buckhurst was not a jealous man, nor was he intimidated by the presence of his fellow masters of seduction, Rochester and Buckingham. The satirists of the day were divided over the question of Nell's promiscuity. Some accounts claimed that she had affairs with Buckhurst, Rochester *and* Buckingham, while others averred that she remained a virgin until she gave herself to the King. The latter can hardly be true, and must either be accounted facetious or are based on their authors' subsequent knowledge of her celebrated fidelity to the King. The following lines are from *A Panegyrick*, published in 1681:

> For should we fame believe we then might say
> That thousands lay with her as well as they [Hart and Buckhurst].
> But fame thou ly'st, for her prophetick mind
> Foresaw her greatness fate had well design'd
> And her ambition chose to be before
> A vertuous countess an imperiall whore.

How the wild honeymoon came to an end no one knows, but end it did – and much to Pepys's relief. He had been to the King's Theatre on 1 August, but the play was an ill one and the house 'mighty empty'. Nell's absence doubtless weighed on his mind. Then on 22 August he records his pleasure at seeing Nell back on stage in Dryden's *Indian Emperor*, but hated her performance of the Emperor's daughter, 'which is a great and serious part, which she do most basely.' There was another poor house at *The Surprisal* on the 26 August, but a good chinwag with Orange Moll brought him up to speed with the latest gossip. 'But there Sir W. Pen and I had a great deal of discourse with Moll,' writes Pepys, 'who tells us that Nell is already left by my Lord Buckhurst, and that he makes sport of her, and swears she hath had all she could get of him; and Hart, her great admirer, now hates her; and that she is very poor, and hath lost my Lady Castlemayne, who was her great friend also: but she is come to the House, but is neglected by them all.'

Buckhurst may simply have tired of Nell's unerring wit, or her saucy language may have begun to grate. Money, it seems, had also become an issue. Nell expected to be paid hard cash for playing the role of mistress to his gallant. But whatever the cause of their quarrel, the rancour proved neither deep nor lasting. They both remained members of the merry gang, sharing a determined affection towards the often intolerable Buckingham.

At the very least the liaison had been a valuable apprenticeship for life at court. Buckhurst, as she would later joke, had been her Charles the Second, in succession to Charles Hart. From hart to buck to royal deer: it was an elegant progression. All her lovers had been men of wit and refinement. But in August 1667, ostracized by her fellow actors and lampooned by the wits, her royal redeemer must have seemed a very long way off indeed.

~ 8 ~

Her Charles the Third

Publick matters in a most sad condition; seamen discouraged for want of pay, and are become not to be governed: nor, as matters are now, can any fleete go out next year. Our enemies, French and Dutch, great, and grow more by our poverty. The Parliament backward in raising, because jealous of the spending of the money; the City less and less likely to be built again, every body settling elsewhere, and nobody encouraged to trade. A sad, vicious, negligent Court, and all sober men there fearful of the ruin of the whole kingdom this next year; from which, good God deliver us!

THUS PEPYS SUMMED UP THE state of the nation on the eve of 1667. Many both in government and in the country at large, shared his view. National morale was further damaged the following summer when the Dutch fleet stormed Sheerness, and with London in a panic glided impudently past the English guard-ships on the Medway, broke the defensive chain, set fire to the proudest vessels in the Royal Navy and towed away her flagship, the *Royal Charles*. The Dutch were guided in their daring by English seamen chafed to rebellion by a diet of lousy conditions and no pay. In the City there was a run on the banks, and whole families left for the country with cartloads of chattels in tow. There was talk of treason. How else could such an appalling humiliation be explained? Pepys, fearing that the whole kingdom was 'undone', made his will. Nell, wiser than the worriers, was capering on Epsom Downs.

The whole country burned with shame. Evelyn spoke for everyone when he went to Chatham on 28 June and viewed 'not only what mischief the Dutch had done, but how triumphantly their whole fleet lay within the very mouth of the Thames, all from the North foreland, Margate, even to the buoy of the Nore – a dreadful spectacle as ever Englishmen saw, and a dishonour never to be wiped off!'

The national mood demanded a scapegoat, and the sacrificial dagger fell upon the increasingly obsolete Lord Chancellor, the Earl of Clarendon. The King was the most obvious target, for he ran the court, and the court had not abated its extravagant pleasures to see the sailors paid. (The night the Dutch sailed up the Medway Charles had supped at the Duchess of Monmouth's with Lady Castlemaine, and the whole party had been 'mad in the hunting of a poor moth'.) Yet the King did care about the navy and had urged the fleet to be in readiness for another Dutch war. And he could always point the finger at Parliament for not voting him the funds needed for the proper upkeep of the fleet – a Parliament, moreover, which Clarendon had alienated with his supercilious manner.

Clarendon was an ironic choice of scapegoat for, pompous, domineering and insufferably priggish though he was, he had opposed war with the Dutch from the start. Moreover, he was the severest critic of the culture of court gallantry and had found himself more and more isolated in the rapid-fire world of the wits, whose capacity for government he openly despised.[1] The gallants mimicked him almost to his face and undermined his position with the King. There was no place for Polonius in the merry court of Charles II. Yet it wasn't just the court that turned against Clarendon; the House of Commons and the populace did too. The resentment had been building up for many years, for Clarendon was believed to have engineered his daughter's marriage to the Duke of York as a way of bolstering his own prestige. And he was accused of choosing a barren queen so that his own descendants might one day mount the throne, as both granddaughters eventually did.[2] The humiliating sale of Dunkirk to the French, for which it was said he had taken bribes, was also laid at his door. But the scandal of the Medway was the straw that broke the camel's back; nothing could now alter the public view that Clarendon had become that bugbear of medieval life, the overmighty subject. The court wits were itching to take hold of the reins of government.

The chief architects of Clarendon's fall were both of the Villiers clan: the King's mistress Barbara Castlemaine and the quixotic Duke of Buckingham. These cousins sought to control the King, both directly and by promoting their friends to high office. But it was just as important to provide the King with mistresses as with ministers, and neither hesitated to play the pimp. Both seized upon Nell Gwyn as a potential royal mistress who would be malleable to their desires, just as they had earlier enlisted Frances Stuart. Barbara spotted her first, but seems to have cooled on the idea when Nell ran off with Buckhurst; it was left to Buckingham to pursue the hare, but he found it difficult to concentrate on a single project for long. As Dryden wrote of him in *Absalom and Achitophel*,

> A man so various, that he seem'd to be
> Not one, but all mankind's epitome.
> Stiff in opinions, always in the wrong;
> Was everything by starts, and nothing long:
> But, in the course of one revolving moon,
> Was chymist, fiddler, statesman, and buffoon . . .

According to Bishop Burnet, 'he could keep no secret, nor execute any design without spoiling it'. If there was a fixed notion in Buckingham's life, it was the idea that the titles of royal favourite and chief minister that his father had held under the previous two monarchs were hereditary sinecures of the Villiers clan. But unlike his haughty father, Buckingham yearned to be a popular hero. His father, the last royal favourite to amass the sort of wealth, power and unpopularity that had been Wolsey's undoing, had been assassinated in 1628, the year of his son's birth. Buckingham and his sister Mary, later Duchess of Richmond, were adopted by Charles I and brought up in the royal nursery. Thus Buckingham's earliest playmate and virtual sibling was the infant Prince of Wales, which helps explain why Charles tolerated such impudence from the Duke.

Buckingham had served in the Royalist army under Prince Rupert and proved himself a brave and capable soldier. But, as always, his expectations were too high and he had his first major falling-out with

Charles when he demanded that the King in exile create him General-in-Chief of the armed forces. He won instead the reputation of bon viveur and wit, but chafed at the inactivity of a prolonged exile. Feeling wasted, the restless cavalier turned his thoughts homewards and in a characteristically rash move returned to Cromwellian England. Instead of throwing himself on the mercy of the Lord Protector, he took coach for his old heartland of Yorkshire, bent on retrieving his lands. To this end, he set about wooing Mary Fairfax, the daughter of renowned Parliamentary General Lord Fairfax, who had been granted a substantial swathe of his sequestered estates. And although the banns had already been published for Mary's marriage to the Earl of Chesterfield, Buckingham's preposterous charm won the day and he and the 'spiritless but amiable lady' were betrothed. Cromwell was not convinced of Buckingham's good intentions, but there was little he could do now that the young cavalier was the son-in-law of a national hero.

For her part, Barbara resented Clarendon because he had refused to sanction the transfer of Crown lands and monopolies to 'the Lady', as he snidely referred to her. As a result, she had to rely on the King's privy purse and make do with an Irish title, which was less prestigious. And it was she and her cronies – men such as Arlington, Ashley Cooper (later Earl of Shaftesbury), Buckingham, Coventry and Lauderdale – who planned Clarendon's downfall. As Pepys commented, 'This business of my Lord Chancellor's was certainly designed in my Lady Castlemaine's chamber.' Or so Buckingham was happy to have it thought, for he himself was chief engineer. Greedy and vicious though she undoubtedly was, Barbara did not possess the nonchalant cunning of her more gifted cousin; nor did she understand until it was too late that Buckingham had been using her for his own ends.

Of all Barbara's so-called allies, Buckingham was the only one who could appeal directly to the people. He alone had the power to mobilize the mob. He had taken the part of the disaffected seamen and, even worse from the government's point of view, mixed with religious non-conformists (he had many friends among the Levellers, including the radical Major Wildman).[3] His actions bordered on treason. Thus it was that in the late spring and early summer of 1667 he spent three months in London in disguise, evading a warrant for his arrest. He was also indicted for his dealings with the astrologer

Dr John Heydon. Having cast Buckingham's horoscope, in which he saw greatness writ large, Heydon had begun addressing the Duke in his letters as if he were a prince of the blood. Then it was said that Buckingham had instructed him to cast the King's horoscope, which was a treasonable offence. Presumably Buckingham wanted to know if his own rise would be accompanied by a necessary decline in the King's fortunes.

When Buckingham did finally surrender himself to the authorities on 26 June 1667, he made sure that his journey to the Tower was in the nature of a royal progress. He was cheered by the trades and the City merchants, whose Republican sympathies he shared, as well as the man in the street, who saw him, however mistakenly, as the champion of the people at court. He even stopped off on the way to dine at the Sun Tavern in Bishopsgate, where his companions were fellow wits Lords Buckhurst and Carbery, Charles Sedley's father-in-law Earl Rivers, and the playwright and duellist Tom Porter. Pepys, who tells us that the Duke was 'mighty merry' at dinner, alludes to his apparent popularity for holding the government to account in Parliament, but adds 'they must be very silly that do think he can do any thing out of good intention'. A large crowd gathered outside the tavern, and after lunch Buckingham appeared on the balcony to acknowledge the cheers.

Barbara meanwhile was frantic to get her wayward cousin out of the Tower and back into the House of Lords, where he could cause trouble for Clarendon. She badgered the King, who hated being badgered, and the two fell out. He called her a whore and told her to mind her own business; she called him a fool for allowing his business to be conducted by those who didn't understand it, while imprisoning his most able servants (meaning Buckingham). The King was stung to the quick, yet two days later Buckingham was released and Charles was laughing at his jokes again. As so often, it was Clarendon who saw to the heart of the matter, as attested by this passage from his autobiography, entitled *The Life by Himself*:

The King had constant intelligence of all his [Buckingham's] behaviour, and the liberty he took in his discourses of him for which he had indignation enough: but of this new stratagem to make himself great in parliament, and to have a faction there to disturb his business, his majesty had no apprehension, believing it impossible for the duke to keep his mind long bent upon any particular design, or to keep and observe those hours and orders of sleeping and eating, as men who pretend to business are obliged to; and that it was more impossible for him to make and preserve a friendship with any serious persons, whom he could never restrain himself from abusing and making ridiculous, as soon as he was out of their company. Yet, with all these infirmities and vices, he found a respect and concurrence from all men of different tempers and talents, and had an incredible opinion with the people.

It is true that Buckingham could not help impersonating those he courted as political allies, and it was said that he would rather lose a friend than a jest. His mimicry of opponents had the court in stitches, in particular his skit on Lord Chancellor Clarendon. Hanging a pair of bellows from his belt (representing the great seal in its case of woven silk), he puffed out his belly and limped forward with pursed lip and withering eye, venting high-pitched lamentations on the declining standards of government and the age in general. Before him strode a fellow courtier with a fire-shovel over his shoulder to impersonate the beadle with his mace. Such liberties would never have been tolerated by Clarendon's old master, Charles I. But it was open season now. It suited Charles to be rid of his former mentor, so he let the vultures have their day. When Clarendon emerged from his final interview with the King and was hobbling across the Privy Garden, he heard peals of laughter from one of the windows overhead and looking up saw Barbara in her nightshirt looking triumphantly down from her aviary, surrounded by a gaggle of chortling cronies.

Four days later, on 30 August, Clarendon was forced to resign the Great Seal. Yet, even then, he refused to read the writing on the wall, cherishing the notion that he could somehow reinstate himself through a robust defence of his actions in the House of Lords. But neither the court nor Parliament had any intention of allowing the most eloquent and legally incisive man in the kingdom to defend himself in public. For three months he lingered, until finally, with the Commons clamouring for impeachment, he fled into exile once more, living out his days in Montpelier in southern France: a tragic end for the chief architect of Charles's restoration, and the sturdiest companion of that King's long exile. Evelyn had been to visit him on 9 December, and gives this poignant account: 'I found him in his garden at his new-built palace, sitting in his gowt wheele-chayre, and seeing the gates [i.e., his new garden gates] setting up towards the North and the fields. He look'd and spake very disconsolately. After some while deploring his condition to me, I took my leave. Next morning I heard he was gone . . .'

The fall of Clarendon ushered in a new era, albeit a very different one from that anticipated by his gleeful assassins. Though Buckingham was restored to his former offices, he was not made first minister and the post of Lord Chancellor was dispensed with altogether.[4] Instead Charles himself, whose strength was far subtler and more enduring than that of his counsellors, became his own first minister. This had always been his preferred path in foreign affairs, and now that the Peace of Breda had been signed with the Dutch, he began the treacherous manoeuvres with Louis XIV that would ease his dependence upon Parliament. At the same time he entangled his most senior ministers in a game of cabal, which gave them the illusion of power while indulging their predilection for intrigue. Charles himself sat spider-like in the corner of the web, watching them with dark, imperturbable eyes. As for Barbara, her moment of hysterical triumph at the aviary window turned out to be the apex of her court career, for Charles now began the long-drawn-out process of pensioning her off, which wasn't completed until he created her Duchess of Cleveland in the summer of 1670.

The King's addiction to Barbara was fitful now. Her meddling in politics needled him, and the toll she took on his self-respect was demoralizing. Her arrogance and self-aggrandizement challenged comparison with Clarendon himself, and both in their different ways had become suffocating to Charles. Both too were political liabilities, and hugely unpopular in the country at large. The following Lent (1668) when the apprentices of the City sacked a number of London brothels, as was their wont at Shrovetide, including the house of Damaris Page, chief bawd to the seamen, they put it about that they were not to be satisfied with pulling down the little brothels and should in all conscience turn their attention to the principal bawdy house of London, namely Whitehall. One of the court wits seized the opportunity to write a petition on behalf of the beleaguered prostitutes of the capital, in which they sought protection from the nation's premier whore, Barbara Castlemaine. Entitled 'The Poor Whores' Petition', it was addressed to 'the most splendid, illustrious, serene and eminent Lady of Pleasure, the Countess of Castlemaine' and signed by Madam Cresswell and Damaris Page on behalf of their sisterhood of suffering punks.

Such an attack would have been impossible in the early 1660s when Charles was still in the first flush of his infatuation with Barbara; now the satirists could afford to exploit the widely reported rift between the two and give voice to their pent-up resentments against the royal whore. But it wasn't just the lady herself they were attacking, but a system of government. After all, Charles's affair with Barbara was an affair of state, inasmuch as the lady's bedchamber had become a political arena, where both office and reputation were wilfully dispensed. Charles had been wont to poke his head out of Barbara's closet to intercept ministers on their way to the council chamber, which meant of course that she was privy to most of the political manoeuvring that mattered and could use privileged information to her advantage. Charles explained her away to himself as a necessary ornament to a cultured and sophisticated court; certainly there is no evidence that he ever considered her a useful gatherer of political intelligence.

Having returned from Epsom in August 1667, Nell spent a gloomy first month back at the King's House. Spurned by Buckhurst, there was no one to protect her from the jibes and mocking glances of her fellow actresses. Even Barbara, who had taken a friendly interest in the comedienne's career, marking her down as a potential source of diversion for the King, was not so sure now. Nell's bust-up with Buckhurst was the talk of the town; he had dropped certain ungentlemanly hints about her demand for some sort of pay-off (the sort of jibe to which her low social status made her specially vulnerable),

while the Grub Street rumour mill ground out its lewd satires,
suggesting that Buckhurst had shared Nell out among his gallant mates.
As 'The Lady of Pleasure' subsequently elaborated matters,

> To Buckhurst thus resign'd in Friendly Wise
> He takes her Swinge, and sometimes lends her Thighs
> To Bestial Buckingham's transcendent Prick
> And sometimes, witty Wilmot [i.e., Rochester] had a Lick.
> And thus she Traded on in noble Ware
> Serving the rest with what her Lord cou'd spare.
> For Buckhurst was the Lord o' th' Hairy Manor
> The rest were only Tenants to his Honour.

No doubt the above-mentioned trio had some merry capers with Nell
in and around Epsom, but the picture of depravity the satirist paints is
untrue both of Nell and Buckhurst. There is no evidence of promiscuity or a penchant for orgies in contemporary accounts of her
activities or reputation. Nor is it conceivable that such a scoop, had
it existed, would not have fallen into the hands of Samuel Pepys.
Moreover, all fifteen of Nell's previous biographers have drawn
attention to her remarkable constancy in matters of love.

Nell, it seems, was further depressed by the fact that the comic
roles that might have lifted her spirits were denied her, she being put
to play serious parts. To cap it all, audiences were thin. But as she got
back into the routine of theatre life and the new season brought new
challenges, so her spirits brightened and she began to win back friends
with her accustomed humour.

Nevertheless, at the end of October her affair with Buckhurst was
the subject of an argument with fellow actress Beck Marshall, who
was said (erroneously, it turns out) to be the daughter of the Presbyterian minister Stephen Marshall. Beck was teasing Nell about the
more lurid rumours of her fling when the latter turned and answered
her with the words, 'I was but one man's mistress, though I was
brought up in a brothel to fill strong waters to the gentlemen; and you
are a mistress to three or four, though a Presbyter's praying daughter',
which Pepys declared 'very pretty'. There was clearly a good deal of
jealousy in the tiring room that the seventeen-year-old Nell had

hooked such a weighty fop on her very first cast. Her commitment to her theatrical career was also called in question, though most girls joined the theatre as a means to an end, knowing that there was no better showcase for their charms.

Despite these bleak and testing months the age of Nell Gwyn was dawning, ushered in by Clarendon's fall and Barbara's slow eclipse. Even during the blackest months streaks of light played on the horizon. The brightest of these appeared in the shape of budding dramatist Aphra Behn, the first Englishwoman to use her pen professionally. Behn, whose indomitable spirit had been forged by her early sufferings, was determined to create her own living in a man's world. When her husband, a merchant of Dutch origin, died of the plague in 1665, she took up journalism before being employed as a spy in His Majesty's secret service on the recommendation of her friend Tom Killigrew. This last employment took her to Antwerp where she worked under the codename 'Astraea',[5] gathering intelligence on the Dutch preparations for war. She was treated with callous neglect both by her spymaster Sir Henry Bennet, who ignored all her requests for funds, and by Killigrew himself, who for whatever reason failed to intervene on her behalf. As a result, she fell heavily into debt and was forced to return to London to petition the King in person. But her case never reached him, and she found herself in jail.

The experience would have broken a weaker woman, but it seemed to have the opposite effect on Aphra Behn. After all, she was Astraea, a byword for feminine self-reliance. When she got out of jail, Aphra returned to journalism for a while and began to keep company with the theatre folk. Not one to bear a grudge, she forgave Killigrew, but made a mental note to wring some favours from him in the new career she was planning. She was a bold, magnanimous woman, determined to enjoy her life and more than able to hold her own among the vicious hacks of Grub Street. Regret played no part in her philosophy. Later she would write,

> Give me but love and wine, I'll ne'er
> Complain my destiny's severe.
> Since life bears so uncertain date,
> With pleasure we'll attend our fate,

And cheerfully go meet it at the gate.
The brave and witty know no fear or sorrow,
Let us enjoy today, we'll die tomorrow.[6]

She and Nell were kindred spirits despite the ten-year difference in age, and each had the quality most needed by the other at the time they met. Nell drank deeply of the fortitude and indifference to fortune of the older woman, while Aphra refreshed her jaded soul in the healing fountain of Nell's laughter and ungovernable high spirits. Both revelled in the freedom and challenge of playing the wild mistress; both were cynical about marriage, hedged in as it was by the demands of rank and property. When she came to write, Aphra would fill her plays with characters of both sexes who deplored marriage in the most flagrant terms, as for instance Cornelia in *The Feign'd Courtesans* (a play she dedicated to Nell Gwyn), who exclaims to her lover, 'I rather fear you wou'd debauch me into that dull slave call'd a Wife'; or Willmore, the 'rover' in the play of the same name, who declares marriage to be 'as certain a bane to love as lending is to friendship', adding 'I'll neither ask nor give a vow'.

It was autumn 1667, and there was plenty of entertainment in London for two adventurous young women. Having spent many years of her childhood in Surinam, on the north-east coast of South America, with its rich jungle life, Aphra may well have suggested that they visit the royal menagerie at the Tower of London, where there were lions, leopards, an elephant and a polar bear, which was let out on a lead into the Thames to swim. Or there was India House, with its collection of snakes, 'dragons' and birds of paradise. Failing that, they could indulge their love of theatre by going to one of the puppet shows at Charing Cross, though the finest – if he happened to be in town – was Signor Bologna's, just round the corner at Covent Garden piazza. Then there were the early autumn fairs, such as Southwark and Bartholomew, which boasted entertainers from the Continent as well as from all over England: jugglers, acrobats, tight-rope walkers, clowns and mountebanks vied with dancing bears and helpless freaks. (Some courtiers would dress down and brave the pickpockets in order to scout out talent to bring before the King.) The lunatics at Bedlam were another popular sight.

By October Nell was back in comedic vein at the King's House, playing the title role of Flora in Richard Rhodes's play *Flora's Vagaries*, a comic intrigue set in aristocratic Verona, which worked yet one more variation on the hectic courting life of mistress and gallant. Nell was in her element as the witty and sprightly Flora, named for the Roman goddess of flowers and spring. (Like Flora, Nell was often represented in her portraits holding a garland of flowers.) Pepys went backstage before the performance to help Mrs Knepp rehearse her part. She led him into the tiring rooms 'and to the women's shift, where Nell was dressing herself, and was all unready, and is very pretty, prettier than I thought.' But a few lines later Samuel had taken a closer look and is at his old trick of railing against cosmetics: 'But Lord! to see how they were both painted would make a man mad, and did make me loath them; and what base company of men [himself excepted, of course] comes among them, and how lewdly they talk!' Then in November she played to perfection in *The Mad Couple*, its wild humour helping her to release much of the bitterness of the past months.

Buckingham, who had admired Nell's performance in his adaptation of Fletcher's *The Chances* and got to know her socially during the summer, now felt that the time was right to dangle her before the King. Luckily for his plan, he and Nell were two of a kind, with the same prankish sense of humour and gift for mimicry. Buckingham saw her as his chance to usurp Barbara's place in the King's counsels. He decided on a two-pronged attack, enlisting Moll Davis of the Duke's House as a back-up. For this he had to gain the permission of her unofficial manager, Colonel Howard, the future Earl of Berkshire. Buckingham himself took on the job of 'managing' the seventeen-year-old Nell, for he had warmed to his charge and would not be averse to taking her as a mistress should the King fail to bite. But, from the start, his advice proved suspect. According to Bishop Burnet in his *History of My Own Time*, Nell Gwyn asked the King for £500 a year for becoming his lover. This turned out to be a strategic error, for although £500 a year was a fraction of Barbara's extorted income, it was still a great deal too much for a strolling player who was unlikely to last the course. Moll Davis had much better advice from Colonel Howard's corner, contenting herself with unsolicited royal gifts. Still, the dual bait prepared for the King was swallowed without much hesitation, even if Moll left Nelly in the dust and without her £500 a year. Pepys, who heard the story from his actress friend Mrs Knepp, was not too thrilled to hear 'how Mis Davis is for certain going away from the Duke's house, the King being in love with her; and a house is taken for her, and furnishing; and she hath a ring given her already worth £600: that the King did send several times for Nelly, and she was with him, but what he did she [i.e., Knepp] knows not; this was a good while ago . . .' So much for £500 a year! Moll was wearing on her finger more than Nell was asking as an annuity. But Pepys was writing on 11 January 1668; Nell's turn would come later.

To begin with, the King sent for Nell as an entertainer, and if 'The Lady of Pleasure' is to be believed, Maria Knight, a singer already familiar with the King's embraces, was the go-between. Charles must have been fascinated and delighted with her madcap wit, at once so innocent and penetrating, and loved the way she mimicked the affectations of her superiors. For her part, Nell no doubt relished his urbane humour and saw the loneliness it veiled. She understood him as a man, rather than a king, and would have been thrilled by the sympathy he expressed for her early sufferings. His was a fatherly presence too, and for the first time in her life Nell felt sufficiently protected to let down her guard. Interestingly, one of her roles at this time was Alizia (or Alice Piers), mistress to King Edward III, in Orrery's tragedy *The Black Prince*. Alizia's pride in the King's love might well have mirrored Nell's feelings at the time:

> You know, dear friend, when to this court I came,
> My eyes did all our bravest youths inflame;
> And in that happy state I lived awhile,
> When fortune did betray me with a smile;
> Or rather Love against my peace did fight;
> And to revenge his power, which I did slight,
> Made Edward our victorious monarch be
> One of those many who did sigh for me.
> *All other flame but his I did deride;*
> *They rather made my trouble than my pride:*

But this, when told me, made me quickly know,
Love is a god to which all hearts must bow. [my italics]

Three days later Pepys had Mrs Knepp's story corroborated by Mrs Pierce, the wife of his friend and court gossip Dr James Pierce, surgeon to the Duke of York. She had been to a production of *The Indian Emperor* at Whitehall, acted by members of the court, and had sat near some players from the Duke's House, among them Moll Davis,

> who is the most impertinent slut, she says, in the world; and the more, now the King do show her countenance; and is reckoned his mistress, even to the scorne of the whole world; the King gazing on her, and my Lady Castlemayne being melancholy and out of humour, all the play, not smiling once. The King, it seems, hath given her a ring of £700 [note the increase in value!], which she shews to every body, and owns that the King did give it her; and he hath furnished a house for her in Suffolke Street most richly, which is a most infinite shame.

What irks Samuel is that the King of England is demeaning not only himself but the crown he wears by taking an impertinent slut (read 'actress') as his mistress, and using public funds to adorn and accommodate her. Much worse than her material rewards was the public recognition bestowed upon her by the King. There's no doubt that a number of actresses, such as Elizabeth Farley and Beck Marshall, called in by the faithful Chiffinch, had been led up the privy stairs to the King's chamber over the years, but these were in the nature of one-night stands, fleeting attractions that left no stain upon the Crown.

Curiously, Moll lived for nearly ten years in the house provided for her in Suffolk Street, having abandoned her career in the theatre. She bore a single child to the King, Lady Mary Tudor, and that a full six years after she became his mistress. She clearly kept her head well down and avoided Whitehall, with its snobbishly hostile courtiers. She was not welcome there, spurned even as a performer in court productions. Her subsequent life is distinguished only by its anonymity. Pepys's scathing reaction to the royal favour shown her in 1668 reveals just how astonishing Nell's success would prove. Stigmatized though she was by her life in the theatre, Moll could at least claim to be the bastard of a nobleman. Yet she was persona non grata at court. Nell, on the other hand, armed with nothing but her impudent good nature, took the court by storm and entrenched herself in the esteem and affection of the English people.

Buckingham's medicine evidently worked, for Barbara was well and truly out of sorts. Not only did she have to contend with the King's waning affections, but her very status as royal mistress had been tarnished by Charles's new and disconcerting habit of raising mistresses up from the gutter. Barbara could certainly outshine these upstarts with the riches she had amassed (at one court production she was reported by Evelyn to have worn jewellery worth a staggering £40,000, 'far outshining the Queene'), but she could not prevent the loss of status that her association with them engendered in the public mind. Nor could she avoid the greedy glances that passed between these impertinent sluts and the King, let alone remove the brave little flags they had planted in his amorous heart.

Barbara was aware that she was the leading lady in the biggest show in town: 'Whitehall'. Moreover, the rules and boundaries were well defined, and noises off kept to a minimum. But now low-born actresses, dressed in the glamour and status that their stage roles conferred, were invading her space. Here were stage queens of great virtue and beauty stepping from the land of make-believe into the ill-defined realm, part fiction part reality, of her overblown existence. The public made little or no distinction between an actress and the roles she played, and an actress whisked away to supper at the end of a performance might step into the waiting carriage in full costume. The stage at Drury Lane was as real as Whitehall was fictional. The point is perhaps most vividly conveyed by the fact that when Orrery's *Henry V* was played at the Duke's House on 11 August 1664 the King, the Duke of York and the Earl of Oxford all lent their coronation robes for the performance! When one reflects that Henry VIII considered the impersonation of a king on stage to be treasonable, and had plays at court curtailed for that reason, it is possible to appreciate how diluted 'the divinity that hedges a king' had become by Charles's reign. The public theatre was proving a powerful agent of social change.

Barbara the aristocrat could no longer rely on the privilege of nobility. And anyway, Barbara the aristocrat was also a nymphomaniac with a penchant for slumming it. Her response to the King's affair with Moll Davis and his growing interest in Nell Gwyn was to avenge herself in kind. She took Nell's former lover, the actor Charles Hart, into her bed. Informed by Mrs Knepp, Pepys conveys the news to posterity with breathless excitement: 'She [Knepp] tells me mighty news, that my Lady Castlemayne is mightily in love with Hart of their house [i.e., the King's Theatre]: and he is much with her in private, and she goes to him, and do give him many presents; and that the thing is most certain, and Becke Marshall only privy to it, and the means of bringing them together, which is a very odd thing; and by this means she is even with the King's love to Mrs. Davis.'

Thus, in a delicious twist of irony, Barabara had become Charles Hart's Lady Wealthy, the role in which Nell Gwyn had come to prominence in James Howard's *The English Monsieur*. It had been an incongruous role for Nell; but now it had been taken up by one only too willing to spend money to gain the affections of a well-mannered gentleman – and no one had practised the part of the well-mannered gentleman more scrupulously or effectively than Charles Hart. Once more fiction had encroached on the lives of the celebrated.

If one looks at the corresponding but opposite paths that Nell and Barbara took in their love lives, the crossroads in each case was Charles Hart. For Nell, Hart was her step up into the cultured world of the wits, which in turn led to the King. She had begun with Duncan, the City merchant, then climbed the ladder of her three Charles's. It was up all the way. Barbara, on the other hand, after a brief liaison with the Earl of Chesterfield, had quickly found the King. Affairs with various courtiers followed. The intrigue with Charles Hart marked the beginning of her descent into the underworld. She had always liked to hold men in subjection, thrilled by their grateful self-abasement, and this sense of power she was delighted to find magnified, not diminished, with her less well-born conquests. Hart was followed by Jacob Hall, a rope dancer who could sustain any number of uncomfortable positions in bed, a running footman who has remained anonymous to posterity and with whom she shared a bath, and finally an actor turned highwayman nicknamed 'Scum' or 'Scummy'.

Thus for both Nell and Barbara the theatre proved the turning point in their amorous journey, the one for good the other for ill. But it would be wrong to characterize Barbara as a crude high-class whore, who slipped without reprieve into a life of depravity. She was a cultured patron of the arts, who enjoyed the company of intelligent men and women and was never completely abandoned by either the King or high society. Indeed, even after she had fallen for Jacob Hall and company, she continued to have affairs with men of quality, such as the playwright William Wycherley and John Churchill, later 1st Duke of Marlborough, by whom she had a daughter. The money she paid Churchill he invested to create the foundation of a considerable fortune. When the King caught him slipping out of the window of Barbara's bedchamber one morning he called after him with the words, 'I forgive you, for you do it for your bread.'

Nell, it seems, did not leap into the King's bed, preferring to make friends first, which was the sort of plucky presumption that Charles admired. Nor was she in a hurry to pick up gifts. She was wary after her experience with Buckhurst and was not one to resign control over her destiny lightly. She had, no doubt, heard first-hand stories from her fellow actresses about their short-lived amours with the fickle King, and was determined that any commitment on her part would be reciprocated. Though summoned to the King with pleasing regularity, Nell was happy to pursue her career in the theatre and maintain her modest lodgings in Drury Lane.

Nor was her appetite for pranks any whit diminished. One day early in 1668, having learnt that her great rival Moll Davis was to dine with the King that night, Nell lost no time in inviting her to tea the same afternoon. Being between productions, she spent a lazy day decorating her modest rooms with flowers. Then she sauntered off to take lunch with Aphra Behn, who lived near Lincoln's Inn Fields. After lunch, as arranged, her friend handed her a small packet containing the pulverized root of a medicinal herb that had been introduced to her by the natives of Surinam. The two friends stood giggling together in the doorway for a good while before they were able to compose themselves to say their farewells. On her way back to her lodgings Nell stopped off at her favourite bakery and bought a few sweetmeats. Back at home she removed the powdered root and, mixing it in syrup, added it to the cakes. The substance in question had been extracted from the tuber of the jalap weed, which according to the medical men is 'a cathartic that operates energetically, occasioning profuse liquid stools'. It has even been used by the zoological fraternity to purge elephants, often with dramatic results, and was more than capable of giving her fellow actress a severe case of the trots. One can't help but feel sorry for poor Moll Davis, though perhaps our greatest sympathy should be reserved for the King, who was left to cope with the consequences of Nell's mischief.[7]

Towards the end of February 1668 Nell played the role of Maria in Robert Howard's controversial new play *The Great Favourite, or The Duke of Lerma*, which was interpreted by many as a swipe at the King for his susceptibility to what Clarendon had termed 'petticoat influence'. The play concerns an attempt by the Duke of Lerma, a disgraced favourite who had ruled the country 'in a whirlwind of squandering waste', to prostitute his daughter to the new King of Spain, Philip IV. Although Lerma succeeds in sexual terms, he fails politically, his plans frustrated by the daughter whose integrity he had set at such low rate. If Charles was being chided in the play, then Buckingham – the great favourite of the time, who was prostituting the real-life Maria to the real-life King – must have been sweating in his powdered wig. The play's reflection upon Nell's life is sharpened by the similarity of her character Maria to the Spanish actress Maria Calderon, with whom Philip IV fell madly in love in 1627.

Pepys, who was at the opening performance, mentions that the King and court were present and that Knepp and Nell spoke the prologue together 'most excellently'. But he was less comfortable with the play itself, which was 'designed to reproach our King with his mistresses, that I was troubled for it, and expected it should be interrupted; but it ended all well, which salved all'. Pepys, who kept his own stable of mistresses, was obviously not in a position to feel comfortable about the censure of such a practice, and he mentions his dislike of the play's 'design' again in the very next line. He omits to mention Moll Davis, who was probably being kept at arm's length by the King after *l'affaire du jalap*.

It's certainly appropriate that Nell's last recorded role before her first real 'date' with the King should have been prophetic of the love that would blossom between the two, for in April that year (1668) it is related that during a performance of George Etherege's comedy *She Wou'd if She Cou'd* at the Duke's House Nell found herself sitting in the box next to the King and the Duke of York. Incredibly, she was on a date with a Mr Villiers, a cousin of the Duke of Buckingham, who in his capacity as Nell's manager no doubt devised the caper. The play, a rather lame comedy about the misadventures of a middle-aged nymphomaniac by the name of Lady Cockwood – a skit on Barbara, perhaps – did not hold the attention of the King, who kept leaning over the edge of his box to flirt with Nell. Villiers was greatly discomfited, but there was little he could do. After the play, the King invited them both out to supper. The 1752 memorialist refers to this Villiers as Barbara's brother – a clear mistake – and makes out that he and Nell were lovers. Here is his account of the story:

> Upon this occasion he [the King] came to the play *incog.* and sat in the next box to Nell and her lover. As soon as the play was finished, his Majesty, with the Duke of York, the young nobleman [i.e., Mr Villiers], and Nell, retired to a tavern together, where they regaled themselves over a bottle, and the King shewed such civilities to Nell that she began to understand the meaning of his gallantry.
>
> The tavern-keeper was entirely ignorant of the quality of the company; and it was remarkable, that when the reckoning came to be paid, his Majesty, upon searching his pockets, found that he had not money enough about him to discharge it, and asked the sum of his brother, who was in the same situation: upon which Nell observed, that she had got into the poorest company that ever she was in at a tavern. The reckoning was paid by the young nobleman, who, that night, parted both with his money and mistress.

Other accounts of the supper relate that it was Nell herself who had to foot the bill, and that her exclamation against the company was prefaced by the King's favourite expletive and said in perfect imitation of Charles's deliberate, slightly continental manner of speaking English: ''Od's fish! but this is the poorest company I ever was in!' If true, she must have known that the money was well spent. Buoyed by the respect and sustained attention that the King now paid her, Nell finally gave herself to the man who would be her lover and protector for the rest of her life. As for the other guests at that crucial supper, Villiers (if indeed he was a Villiers rather than Buckingham's idea of a joke) disappeared without trace; dupe or no dupe, it must have been a trying experience, though doubtless the King's brother James kept his attention from Nell by droning on about the poor state of the navy. Lacking his brother's mercurial wit, James would soon be known at court by Nell's epithet of 'dismal Jimmy'.

The fact that Nell remained a member of the King's Company for the following three years says a good deal about her commitment to her art, as well as the pleasure she derived from it. The King clearly recognized its worth in her life and left her to it. He was probably encouraged in this stance by Tom Killigrew, who knew better than anyone the remarkable drawing power of his impudent little comedienne. Nell's departure would have provoked an outcry from another admirer, John Dryden, who had just been created Poet Laureate on the death of Sir William Davenant, Killigrew's rival manager at the Duke's House. The post came with an annuity of £200, but his principal income was still his plays, and their success depended above all on the skill and appeal of the actors. If he wrote a part for Nell Gwyn, such as Florimell in *Secret Love*, and she connected with the audience, then the play was assured a good run and Dryden's revenues went up. The sight of the author sitting in the pit on the opening night of his play, furiously rewriting the script according to the reaction of the audience, was a familiar one.

In May 1668 Nell had three roles to learn in one new play and two revivals. The first was a revival of *The Virgin Martyr* (1622) by Massinger and Dekker, in which she played the role of Angelo, the good spirit or angel who masquerades as pageboy to the martyred maiden Dorothea – hence a breeches role. (Dorothea was played by Beck Marshall.) Pepys, who missed the play but arrived backstage just in time to see the actresses coming off, comments on how fine and noble Beck looks, doubtless in her martyr's robes, while Nell the pageboy angel is 'mighty pretty'. Pepys had seen the play back in February and had been ravished by the wind music that accompanied the descent of the angel.

The second play was Sir Charles Sedley's *The Mulberry Garden*, originally entitled *The Wandering Ladys*. The pit was bristling with wigs that afternoon, but they were to witness an insipid comedy, poorly acted. Sir Charles blamed the actors for not having learnt their parts properly, but the real reason is more likely to have been the play's insincerity, for Sedley, in common with other mediocre playwrights of the time, had played the magpie a little too enthusiastically, creating a patchwork of scenes borrowed from French and Spanish comedies and the works of his more skilful English contemporaries. He was a familiar type in the Restoration theatre: the playwright-gallant who used the theatre to become a celebrity.

This celebrity culture was a new development made possible by the diminishing influence of the court, which was no longer the sole source of patronage and prestige. History does not record what part Nell played, but it's unlikely that she was sorry to see the play fail, for Sedley had joined in Buckhurst's post-Epsom taunts. Pepys was very disappointed by the play, which had been keenly talked up, and seems to have spent most of it stealing glances at the King in order to gauge His Majesty's pleasure ('the King I did not see laugh, nor pleased, the whole play from the beginning to the end'). If the King laughed, a play couldn't fail to meet with success.

The third play was a revival of Beaumont and Fletcher's *Philaster, or Love Lies a-Bleeding*, one of the old romantic tragicomedies that had been assigned to the King's Company when Davenant and Killigrew made their original division of the Elizabethan and Jacobean repertory. Nell played the breeches role of Bellario, loyal page to Philaster, the rightful heir of Sicily, played by Charles Hart. The play, which was a great hit for both Nell Gwyn and Charles Hart, marked the end of their relationship in the public mind. When the play was revived once more in 1695, Hildebrand Horden, who spoke the prologue, gave this tribute:

> The good old play, Philaster, ne'er can fail,
> But we young actors, how shall we prevail?
> Philaster and Bellario, let me tell ye,
> For these bold parts we have no Hart, no Nelly,
> Those darlings of the stage that charmed you there.

When *The Virgin Martyr* had appeared, most of the play-going public read in the title a reference to Charles's saintly Queen, Catherine, who had suffered another miscarriage that month. After six years of marriage she still hadn't produced a child, and she was now a few months shy of thirty. Conception wasn't a problem; carrying a baby to term, with the body of a child, was. Her many visits to Tunbridge Wells to take the waters had proved ineffective. Buckingham, inveterate busybody that he was, initiated a whispering campaign. Pimping for mistresses was all very well, but it would suit his ambitions better if he could pimp for a new queen. Failing that, there was always the succession to worry about, especially now that the King's brother had become a Catholic. Much more glamorous than a King, more charged with his country's hope, is a Prince of Wales, and England towards the end of Charles's first decade as sovereign felt keenly the lack of a royal heir of the King's body. Buckingham's eye fell upon the nineteen-year-old James, Duke of Monmouth, Charles's swashbuckling bastard, who was already cutting a swathe through the court beauties. Might it not be possible that Charles had been secretly married to his mother, Lucy Walter? Flattered and adored by courtiers and commoners alike, the Protestant Monmouth was the ideal vehicle for Buckingham's fantasies of political glory. Thus the battle lines for the exclusion crisis of 1679–81 were already being drawn up. Dashing Jimmy was pitted against Dismal Jimmy.

The previous autumn Pepys wrote in his *Diary*, 'Sir H. Cholmly do not seem to think there is any such thing can be in the King's intention as that of raising the Duke of Monmouth to the Crowne, though he thinks there may possibly be some persons that would, and others that would be glad to have the Queen removed to some monastery, or somewhere or other, to make room for a new wife; for they will all be unsafe under the Duke of York.' But Buckingham was to find Charles maddeningly honourable in the matter of his wife. The King, despite his infidelity, had always been loyal to his Queen, and he would not now divorce her because she was unable to bear children.

By the summer of 1668 everyone at the King's House was aware of Nell's new standing. Her drawing power was even greater than before, and people flocked to the theatre to scrutinize the plays for clues to her developing relationship with the King. Although they kept their snide thoughts to themselves, her fellow thespians must have thought the royal romance would prove another flash in the pan. After all, if she hadn't been able to secure the lasting attentions of witty Buckhurst, a mere gallant, how could she be expected to keep a king, and not only a king, but the gallant of gallants and chief of wits? If such thoughts passed through Nell's mind, she was not one to show it. Indeed, her self-confidence must have been one of the surest arrows in her quiver. She was determined to enjoy the adulation and prestige while it lasted, and delighted in putting on airs to provoke the Marshall sisters. She certainly didn't mind being promoted from the women's shift to her own dressing room with a girl to help with her costume, and 'Mrs. Ellen Gwyn' sounded very nicely in her ears. It was good too to have an escort of gallants whenever the King called for her. Beyond the theatre the people immediately took her to their hearts. She was, in the words of *A Panegyrick*, 'the darling strumpet of the crowd'.

Dryden meanwhile had been scribbling away in the country, desperate to produce a piece worthy of the first female superstar of the stage. The result was an engaging, fast-paced comedy, *An Evening's Love, or The Mock Astrologer*, which opened on 12 June 1668. Though Pepys found it 'very smutty' and vastly inferior to *The Maiden Queen*, and Evelyn — who once again just happened to find himself at the theatre — condemned it as foolish and 'very prophane' ('it afflicted me to see how the stage was degenerated and polluted by the licentious times'), the play was very well received and ran for nine consecutive days, something of a marathon for Restoration productions. Set in Madrid at Carnival time, it tells of the amorous adventures of two English gallants, Wildblood and Bellamy, as they pursue a brace of Spanish belles, Donna Jacinta and Theodosia. Bellamy masquerades as an astrologer to try to win the love of Theodosia, while Jacinta, played by Nell, delights in 'laying baits' for Wildblood, disguising herself first as an African and then as a mulatto. Each time she proves him a perfect scoundrel, a man of 'pernicious wit', as Mrs Loveit would describe him. In other words, we're back in the giddy realms of mistress and gallant.

Bellamy and Wildblood combined (a fair friend ruled by his lusts) seem to represent the King, while Donna Jacinta is perfect Nell. Bellamy at one point echoes Charles's famous saying that he didn't meddle with the souls of women with the words, 'For my part I can suffer any impertinence from a woman, provided she be handsome: my business is with her Beauty, not with her Morals: let her Confessor look to them'; while Jacinta aims the following topical jibe at Charles: 'Heyday, You dispatch your Mistresses as fast, as if you meant to o're-run all Woman-kind: sure you aime at the Universal-Monarchy.' Jacinta's chosen disguises point to her as a creature of nature. Presenting herself to Wildblood as a 'Musullman' [i.e., Muslim] she draws this exclamation from the gallant: 'A *Musullwoman* say you? I protest by your voice I should have taken you for a *Christian* Lady of my acquaintance.' Nell had of course been an oyster wench or 'mussel woman' on the streets of London. In the following exchange there is no mistaking Jacinta's social ambitions, nor for that matter Wildblood's appetite for inferior prey:

WILD.: It has been alwayes my humour to love downward. I love to stoop to my prey, and to have it in my power to Sowse at [strike at] when I please. When a man comes to a great Lady, he is fain to approach her with fear and reverence; methinks there's something of Godliness in't.

JAC.: Yet I cannot believe, but the meanness of my habit must needs scandalize you.

WILD.: I'll tell thee my friend and so forth, that I exceedingly honour course Linnen; 'tis as proper sometimes in an under Garment, as a course Towel is to rub and scrub me.

JAC.: Now I am altogether of the other side, I can love no where but above me: methinks the ratling of a Coach and six sounds more eloquently than the best Harangue a Wit could make me.

WILD.: Do you make no more esteem of a Wit then?

JAC.: His commendations serve onely to make others have a mind to me; He does but say Grace to me like a *Chaplain*; and like him is the last that shall fall on. He ought to get no more by it, than a poor Silk-weaver does by the Ribband which he workes, to make a Gallant fine.

WILD.: Then what is a Gentleman to hope from you?

JAC.: To be admitted to pass my time with, while a better comes: to be the lowest step in my Stair-case, for a Knight to mount upon him, and a Lord upon him, and a Marquess upon him, and a Duke upon him, till I get as high as I can climb.

Buckhurst, who would certainly have been in fops' corner for the opening night, can't have enjoyed being described as grace before the feast. It's nice to think that Nell fixed him with a withering look from the stage as she spoke the words. The King was mightily pleased with the play, though there were many passages to take offence at. He even defended Dryden against his critics. His wild blood was up, and he found Nell's impudence as attractive on stage as off. And he surely muttered amen to himself when Wildblood, having finally secured his prize, declares, '*Jacinta Wildblood*, welcome to me: since our Starres have doom'd it so, we cannot help it: but 'twas a meer trick of Fate to catch us thus at unawares . . .' At any rate, the audience got what they wanted in the way of daring references to the latest 'affair of state'.

If there was one shadow on Nell's newly lit horizon in the summer of 1668, it was at least the oldest problem in the world: her mother. Old Madam Gwyn, a dinosaur at forty-four, had let her fondness for brandy get the better of her. Having hung up her bawdy clogs, she was now a rather dubious operative for Orange Moll, who in addition to her orange-selling business acted as a scout for many of the big bawdy houses in London. The two were old friends and lodgers, and appear to have been satirized together in the figure of Foggy Nan the orange woman in Etherege's *The Man of Mode*. Nan is variously described as an 'insignificant brandy bottle', a 'cartload of scandal' and 'that overgrown jade with the flasket of guts before her'. Now immensely proud of Nell and with time heavy on her hands, one can imagine Madam Gwyn standing outside the Drury Lane theatre, accosting passers-by with the story of her daughter's miraculous rise interspersed with lamentations on her own blasted potential. She was certainly a figure of fun in the taverns, where she was toasted affectionately as the Queen Mother, her tall stories towering like never before.[8]

Not one to disguise her origins, Nell appeared unembarrassed by her mother. Nor would she have worried about the King's reaction, for he had seen too much of life to be put off by the drunken antics of a bawd. But old Mrs Gwyn was a burden upon her daughter's soul. For Nell, like so many younger daughters, had been bred up as the companion of her mother's old age. On her fell the onus of the older woman's loneliness and the stress of her forebodings. Goaded by jealousy and sexual frustration, Helena Gwyn doubtless pried into every nook and cranny of her daughter's heart. And though Nell honoured her as her mother, her stifling presence must have rankled horribly and the old anger cried in her veins.

It must have been with some trepidation, then, that she learnt in July that she was to play the part of Dol Troop in John Lacy's farce *The Old Troop*. The play was about the corrupt doings of a company of Royalist soldiers during the Civil War and was drawn from Lacy's own experience as quartermaster to Lord Gerard in 1642/3. It was said that Captain Gwyn served in the same company, and, as mentioned before, Dol Troop, the company whore, is likely to have been based on Nell's mother. At the beginning of the action Dol is pregnant and uses her condition to extort money from the soldiers, who all seem to have dallied with her at one time or another: 'I cannot say I am with child, but with children; for here has been all nations, and all languages to boot . . . But, for all this, I hope I do not go with above a squadron of children. But to my business. I mean to lay this great belly to every man that has but touch'd my apron strings.' In 'The Lady of Pleasure', Nell was said to have been begotten by 'a battalion of arm'd men'.

In Act II Scene i, Dol meets her match in the company chef, a Frenchman by the name of Monsieur Raggou, who stoutly refuses to be bribed. 'Begar, Madam Dol,' he exclaims, 'you be de great whore de Babylon! Begar, me vill make appear noting can get you wid shild but de maypole in de Strana . . .' From the southern end of Drury Lane, where they lived, both Nell and her mother could see the famous maypole in the Strand, topped by its gilded crown. Given that Dol was played by Nell, the crowned maypole in the Strand clearly stood for the King. There is a second camp follower in the play called Biddy, who maintains her virtue by pretending to be a boy and with whom Dol falls in love. Child-like nymph and brazen whore, Biddy and Dol seem to represent two persistent and vital elements of Nell's nature. Playing Dol Troop must have been a cathartic experience for the young actress, forcing her to delve into her darker nature. The play was a great success, with King and court applauding wildly.

The year 1668 was probably Nell's busiest yet in the theatre, as more playwrights were inspired to write for her. The results, however, were not always worthy of her talent. In the autumn she played Lysette in Richard Flecknoe's *Damoiselles à la Mode*. The play was an abject failure and, according to Pepys, 'when they came to say it would be acted again to-morrow, both he that said it, Beeson, and the pit fell a-laughing, there being this day not a quarter of the pit full'. Flecknoe himself was nevertheless charmed by Nell's performance and sent her a poem entitled 'On a Pretty Little Person' as a mark of his appreciation:

> She is pretty, and she knows it;
> She is witty, and she shows it;
> And besides that she's so witty,
> And so little and so pretty,
> Sh'has a hundred other parts
> For to take and conquer hearts.
> 'Mongst the rest her air's so sprightful,
> And so pleasant and delightful,
> With such charms and such attractions
> In her words and in her actions,
> As whoe'er do hear and see,
> Say there's none do charm but she.
> But who have her in their arms,
> Say sh'has hundred other charms,
> And as many more attractions
> In her words and in her actions.
> But for that, suffice to tell ye,
> 'Tis the little pretty Nelly.

Nell finished the year dressed as an Amazon with a bow and quiver full of arrows when she spoke the prologue to a revival of Ben Jonson's *Catiline's Conspiracy*, though she must have appeared to the audience more as an incarnation of Cupid, the mischievous god of love, than a female warrior. Either way, one of her arrows had lodged firmly in the King's heart, and the following year would reveal the extent of his favour. For now she was the toast of the London taverns, though few would put money on her chances of keeping her footing.

~ 9 ~

A Bastard Grace

WHEN NELL, HALF AMAZON HALF Cupid, had finished speaking the prologue to *Catiline's Conspiracy*, she returned to the wings, from where she witnessed an extraordinary scene. It was one of those classic Restoration moments when art and life wrestled for supremacy. The audience had already been shocked and delighted by the performance of Katherine Corey, the actress playing Sempronia, as soon as it became clear that she was mimicking society hostess Lady Elizabeth Harvey. But there was uproar when Cicero, played by Nicholas Burt, was asked 'What will you do with Sempronia?', for in a flash Barbara Castlemaine had leapt to her feet and was yelling from her box, '*Send her to Constantinople!*'

The joke lay in the fact that Lady Harvey's husband, Sir Daniel, had recently been sent to Constantinople as His Majesty's ambassador to Turkey on one of those cuckold's errands that appealed to the King's sense of mischief. Lady Harvey – who would later befriend Nell Gwyn – was a cultured, slightly bohemian figure who, like Sempronia, meddled in politics. She had once been very close to Barbara Castlemaine and was reputed to be a lesbian. The two women may well have been lovers. Elizabeth's brother Ralph Montagu would later have a scandalous affair with both Barbara and her eldest daughter, Lady Sussex. It was in Lady Harvey's Covent Garden home that Barbara had sheltered after fleeing Whitehall following her furious row with Charles in July 1667 over the paternity of her sixth child, and it was to that same house that the King had gone cap in hand less than a week later to beg forgiveness at the feet of his untamed shrew.

Neither woman would brook obstacles to absolute social and sexual freedom, and both had dropped hints to Charles that their objections would be muted if he was to send their husbands as far away as politically possible, which meant Turkey, not only for Daniel Harvey but for Roger Castlemaine too. 'I hope, Lady Harvey,' said the King, 'that I have pleased you by sending your husband far enough from you.' 'I acknowledge your goodness,' replied the impudent bluestocking, 'and only wish it were in my power to return it by sending the Queen as far from your Majesty.' Nevertheless, some sort of rift – maybe a lovers' tiff – must have occurred between Barbara and Lady Elizabeth in the intervening year, since it was Barbara who had bribed Katherine Corey to impersonate her old friend on stage.

Lady Harvey was hell-bent on revenge. She had a word with her cousin Edward Montagu, Earl of Manchester, who as Lord Chamberlain was responsible for policing the theatres. He had the offending actress thrown in jail.[1] But Barbara got the King to overrule the decision; more than that, she bullied him into commanding a repeat performance of the play, a stellar occasion which found her perched imperiously beside him in the royal box. And Katherine Corey, further coached by Barbara in the minutiae of Lady Harvey's mannerisms and clearly enjoying the scandal her previous performance had excited, took her caricature of the unfortunate aristocrat even further. But Harvey herself did not go unprepared. She hired a bunch of ruffians to hiss the actress and, when that didn't work, pelt her with oranges.

The King, who had spent £500 on costumes for the production, sat in astonishment as an orange whistled past his nose on its way to the stage. It seems he was the only one in the theatre that day who had not known what to expect. Nor was it the first time that Barbara had used him as a foil for her personal vendettas. The episode led to a full-scale feud at court between the supporters of the two women, and as ever the King was dragged through the mud. In a further exchange of insults Barbara called Lady Harvey a 'hermaphrodite' and claimed to have rejected her advances.

Pepys's colleagues at the Navy Office were talking of nothing else: 'They speak mighty freely of the folly of the King in this foolish woman's business, of my Lady Harvey. Povy tells me that Sir W. Coventry was with the King alone, an hour this day; and that my Lady Castlemayne is now in a higher command over the King than ever – not as a mistress, for she scorns him, but as a tyrant, to command him ... and so we are in the old mad condition...' Barbara may not have wielded the power of a mistress any more, but she knew how to blackmail Charles emotionally, just as Henrietta Maria had done. Charles grew up in the belief that the world would fall apart if he crossed his mother's will. Barbara seems to have tuned into this vague but deep-seated fear in order to keep the upper hand in her dealings with the King. Her tantrums almost never failed to bring him into line.

The Harvey–Castlemaine furore illustrates the extent to which the theatre, having received the wholehearted and active patronage of the King, had become a subsidiary court, where men and women of influence made amorous conquests, traded gossip, vied for position and upstaged their rivals. It had always been a foraging ground for Barbara, who loved the buzz of the big arena. It was also a forum where contentious political issues could be debated and enacted, both on and off the stage – the crucible, in fact, of the nation's passions. Beneath the veil of fiction cast by the drama people felt freer to voice their true thoughts. Violence was frequently the result. Nor should we forget how vulnerable the King himself was sitting in his box, both to the assassin's sword and to the stinging jibes of the playwrights. It says much of his magnanimity that he subjected himself to this trial by fire with such regularity and evident pleasure.

But Charles was a master at covering discretion with a coat of folly, and the theatre, with the possible exception of the park, was his favourite turf for gathering political intelligence and the gossip of the town. Much to the delight of his people, Charles was the first king to attend the public theatres, a habit his father and grandfather would have found unthinkable. Indeed, it could be said that it was through Charles's familiar habits and ready condescension that the monarchy during his reign lost much of its former mystique. But his patronage was more than his presence: Charles actively encouraged writers and promoted their plays. He was well read in the dramatic literature of France, Italy and Spain, and would often suggest a theme or plot to a dramatist by referring them to a continental source which he had read in the original. Thus he drew John Crowne's attention to the Spanish play *No Puede Ser* ('It Cannot Be'), and from this seed grew the comedy *Sir Courtly Nice*, whose finicky hero sends his clothes all the way to Holland to be laundered. It's said that Charles supervised the writing of the opening scenes himself. All in all, the King played a vital role in influencing the drama of the time and in particular in developing what has come to be known as the comedy of manners, which flowered in the plays of Sheridan and Wilde as well as in the drawing-room comedies of Somerset Maugham and Noel Coward. Charles, we must remember, was a master of the one-liner and judged a play by one criterion alone: entertainment value.

The King's taste in dramatic literature was matched by his appreciation of beautiful actresses, and his example quickly spread through the ranks of the nobility. In May 1669, for instance, crotchety old Prince Rupert made public his relationship with the actress Margaret ('Peg') Hughes by inviting her to leave the stage and go live with him. (Their daughter Ruperta was born in 1673.) This was the same Peg Hughes whose brother William was killed in an argument with one of the King's servants over who was the prettier woman, his sister or Nell Gwyn. Another measure of Charles's deep involvement in the theatre and his fascination with literary types was the number of court intrigues that sprang from literary or theatrical feuds. If a Buckingham was unable to oust a rival by political means, you can be sure that he would attempt it on the stage.

Attending and promoting the theatre was an important way for Charles to show that he shared the tastes and humour of his people. The King's House reflected the King's nature with as much if not more fidelity than Whitehall. Here amidst the music, acting and gossip the King was in his element. And though he was at an unfair advantage when it came to picking mistresses from the theatre, Charles was not without his own gallant code of honour. He did not actively poach other men's mistresses, and in return expected those ladies who enjoyed his favour at any given time to be his alone. But it rarely worked out in practice.

It seems to me that Charles's fascination with the theatre was strongly connected with his fascination and compassion for women.

Having known what it was to be stripped of status and despised by those in authority, Charles tended to sympathize with the inferior lot of women in society. He was keenly aware of the need imposed upon them to hide their talents and feelings and so make an art of dissimulation. And as a man who was himself condemned to wear a mask, Charles was naturally attuned to the mental life of both women and actors. When the two combined so gracefully and impudently in the person of Nell Gwyn, it is little wonder that the King should have been smitten. Yet there was a further dimension to this new love. The experiences of Charles's exile had given him a soft spot for the underdog, and it was this soft spot that became the cradle of his love for Nell Gwyn. It was a love founded on compassion. Childlike and uninhibited, Nell must have appealed strongly to the bohemian and unconventional in Charles, and her presence seems to have stimulated him to give rein to the private man. Because a monarch must cultivate tact and caution to an unnatural degree, Nell's indiscretion no doubt acted as a tonic to the King's wary soul and reawakened in him the greater freedom of spirit that had been his in exile.

That said, we should not underestimate the extent to which Charles was running the gauntlet of court and public obloquy by plucking a mistress from the gutter. Pepys's critical fury each time Nell acted a tragic part (such as a grave and virtuous princess) probably had more to do with his social snobbery than her acting ability. That such a punk should presume to imitate royalty drove the upwardly mobile Samuel to his wits' end. On 7 January 1669 Pepys found himself at the King's playhouse with his wife 'and there saw "The Island Princesse" [a tragicomedy by Beaumont and Fletcher], the first time I ever saw it; and it is a pretty good play, many good things being in it, and a good scene of a town on fire. We sat in an upper box, and the jade Nell come and sat in the next box; a bold merry slut, who lay laughing there upon people; and with a comrade of hers of the Duke's house, that come in to see the play.' Pepys's tone of shocked disapproval rings out from the passage not only in the flagrant epithets he applies to the actress but also in his use of the vivid present 'come', which exposes his feeling that Nell had some-how trespassed upon his social turf by entering the box next to his own. In Pepys's book, as in society's, it was one thing to have a fling with your wife's maid, but quite another to confer status upon her by making the relationship public.

An incident in the House of Commons the following year under-scores how jittery both Charles himself and the nobility were about their association with actresses. A motion had been brought forward to levy taxes on the theatres. It was opposed by the court, with Sir John Birkenhead stating that 'the players were the King's servants and a part of his pleasure'. By way of response the member for Weymouth, one Sir John Coventry, asked 'whether the King's pleasure lay among the men or the women that acted', a clear jibe at Charles's affairs with Moll Davis and Nell Gwyn. Though motivated more by the humour of the moment than any studied malice, Sir John would live to regret his reckless words. King and court were furious when they heard. Charles's bastard son Monmouth, being the offspring of a whore, was stung to the quick and mobilized a band of the King's Guards to ambush Coventry on his way home from Parliament. As his assailants leapt from the shadows in Suffolk Street on 21 December 1670, Coventry grabbed a torch from his servant and, setting his back to the wall, drew his sword in self-defence. He fought valiantly, disabling a couple of the guardsmen, but he was no match for twenty. Having been disarmed, he was pinned to the ground and his nose slit to the bone.

At the time of Sir John's taunt in the House, the King was already the father of a son by Nell Gwyn. She was no longer a casual mistress, and he may have felt she had been sufficiently elevated and blessed by his attentions to merit more respect from the likes of Coventry. After all, the King could dignify others by his association, but he himself could not be debased by theirs. Such was the absolute theory of kingship. One additional point suggests itself: because Charles felt so emotionally at home at the theatre, he was peculiarly vulnerable to unkindness on that score. The image that Coventry's words conjured of a royal predator in the pit was probably uncomfortably close to the truth. Andrew Marvell in his poem 'Upon the Cutting of Sir John Coventry's Nose' directed much of his venom at Nell herself, who was of course not actually named by Sir John in his speech:

But if the sister of Rose
Be an whore so anointed
That thus the Parliament's nose
Must for her be disjointed;
When you [Parliamenteers] come to name the prerogative whore,
How the bullets will whistle, and cannons will roar!

As for the general public, represented by the average Londoner, there was undisguised delight that the King had taken up with one of their own. According to Churchill in his *History of the English-Speaking Peoples*, 'It was with relief that the public learned that the King had taken a mistress from the people, the transcendently beautiful and good-natured Nell Gwynn, who was lustily cheered in the streets . . .' Nor would the King's reputation as a womanizer have bothered the man in the street, though it may have raised a chuckle and a line or two of bawdy banter. There were disaffected groups, such as the City apprentices, which denounced Charles's philandering, but on the whole the King's sexual prowess was seen in a positive light.

The literature of the time portrayed him as the noble savage, nowhere more graphically than in Aphra Behn's short novel *Oroonoko, or The History of the Royal Slave*, which, though written in the 1670s, wasn't published until after the King's death. Oroonoko is an African prince sold into slavery by the treachery of English colonialists. His struggle for freedom, in which he is sustained by his mistress Imoinda, the daughter of a general and now a slave herself, ends in excruciating death. Behind Oroonoko lurks the unmistakable figure of that 'tall black man', King Charles II, both in Behn's physical descriptions of the negro prince, as well as in her portrayal of his character and philosophy.[2] Here was a king who ruled by nature or instinct rather than dogma, and whose restoration had brought the promise of a golden age, unriven by the doctrinaire feuds of preceding decades. But it was not to be, for Charles had his hands bound from the start, a slave to the demands of Parliament and that Puritan stronghold, the City.

Charles was also portrayed in the literature of the time as the fertility god Pan ('the Royal Pan' as Otway called him), who was half man and half goat, and whose realm of Arcadia neatly metamorphoses into England. Pan was the god of shepherds and herdsmen as well as wild places, and as part of the conscious myth-making of Restoration England the impression was created of a country returned to its pastoral and idyllic roots after the stresses and terrors of the Civil War. Charles, for instance, improved and opened St James's Park to the public. It had been a royal hunting domain much used by Henry VIII, though it was so marshy that Charles's grandfather James I had kept crocodiles there as part of his private zoo, as well as an elephant that drank a gallon of wine a day. Charles had it landscaped and opened to the public; it became a favourite haunt, where he could saunter at leisure and mingle with his people. Indeed, many an unsuspecting walker must have felt a surge of panic (the special feeling Pan inspired) when he turned a corner in his morning stroll to come face to face with the King of England.

Edmund Waller in his poem 'St. James's Park Newly Restored by His Majesty' (1664) describes Charles as 'the people's pastor' and draws attention to the political virtue of the King's strength and beauty (his noble savagery):

> His shape so lovely, and his limbs so strong,
> Confirm our hopes we shall obey him long.

And if the pubescent Nell developed a juvenile crush on the King, as some have surmised, it is quite likely to have taken root in St James's Park. One can certainly imagine her stealing off from her street-hawking duties to catch a glimpse of Charles feeding his ducks and pelicans on the canal. (St James's would become special for her again when Charles gave their son and his descendants, the Dukes of St Albans, the privilege, shared with the monarch alone, of driving down Birdcage Walk along the southern boundary of the Park.)

The pastoral theme was strong too in Nell's life, albeit in a slightly metaphorical sense. In as far as London prostitutes – more often than not fresh-faced girls from the country – administered relief from the stresses and strains of urban life, they were purveyors of pastoral care, at least in the minds of certain eighteenth-century sentimentalists. John Cleland in his *Memoirs of a Woman of Pleasure* wrote of whores as 'the restorers of the golden age and its simplicity of pleasures, before their innocence became so unjustly branded with the names of guilt and shame'. One of the most famous portraits of Nell from the studio of Lely depicts her in simple rustic dress caressing the head of a sheep. Her blouse is open and in her right hand she holds a garland of flowers.

Nell, in contrast to the other principal royal 'misses' of the reign, quickly established herself as Charles's country mistress, and was even credited with teaching him to fish. Already in the spring of 1669 they were off to Newmarket together for the racing, and were regular attenders together at the spring and autumn meetings for the following fourteen years. Their friendship blossomed in the informal atmosphere of the old Suffolk racing town. Both King and mistress sauntered about in old clothes, much endearing themselves to the townsfolk, whom they encouraged to attend the races. Here the King felt free of the constraints of his office, a freedom that the new girl in his life must have embodied with special vivacity. But Charles found it hard to be idle for long, especially where such an overriding passion was concerned, and he was soon busying himself restoring and expanding his stables, improving the race course and setting up new breeding facilities for the next generation of pampered racehorses.[3] He bred twelve horses a year and kept four jockeys-in-ordinary. He also donated trophies and purses for both breeding and racing, introduced the use of racing silks and even raced himself.

Royal patron, jockey, trainer, adjudicator of races, Charles could be seen out on the flat in the early morning watching the training sessions, and during the races themselves the crowd was treated to the spectacle of the King galloping along the side of the course to see the runners over the line. Indeed, such was his enthusiasm for the racetrack that he would sometimes leave London at 3 a.m. to reach Newmarket in good time for the day's events. Cromwell had banned racing because he disapproved of betting and suspected that race meets were a convenient cover for subversive political gatherings. Now racing had found a true champion in Charles, and the effects of his enthusiasm are with us today.

It was natural that he should be popular with the townsfolk of Newmarket, as his visits there, accompanied by a large retinue and much of the court, brought an influx of business into the town. The races were attended by several thousand people. In addition to buying the estate of Audley End about seventeen miles away, Charles commissioned Wren to build a 'palace' (really a large house) for him in Newmarket itself as well as a more modest establishment for Nell opposite the Maiden's Inn. Evelyn visited the palace before it was completed and was thoroughly unimpressed. He complained that it had been 'place'd in a dirty streete, without any court or avenue, like a common one, whereas it might, and ought to have ben built at either end of the towne, upon the very carpet where the sports are celebrated'. Even Charles complained about the height of the ceilings, which were too low for a man of six foot two inches. Wren, who was a foot shorter than his sovereign, insisted that they were quite high enough. 'Aye, Sir Christopher,' replied the King, stooping down towards his diminutive architect, 'I think they are . . .'

When he rode in the races Charles did so under the name of his most prolific stallion, 'Old Rowley'. This nickname quickly caught on, and 'The Song of Old Rowley' or 'Old Rowley the King' became an endless ballad of his amorous conquests. As in a game of consequences, each new exponent of the song added a flourish or anecdote of his own. One day at Whitehall, from behind a chamber door, the King overheard a snatch of the song being sung by a female voice (it was Dorothy Howard, niece of the Earl of Berkshire). He listened in amusement for a while, then knocked. And when the lady asked who it was, he flung open the door with a flourish and announced, 'Old Rowley at your service, ma'am!' According to the *Richardsoniana*,[4] however, the King took his nickname from another creature completely: 'There was an old goat that used to roam about the privy-garden to which they had given this name [i.e., Old Rowley]; a rank lecherous devil, that everybody knew and used to stroke, because he was good-humoured and familiar; and so they applied this name to Charles.'

Two other country retreats in the early days of Charles and Nell's romance were Bagnigge House and Windsor Castle. We don't know how Nell acquired the house at Bagnigge Wells, which was near King's Cross, but the place became a fashionable spa in the 1760s. She and the King used to swim together on summer mornings in the nearby Fleet, a tributary of the Thames. According to G. W. Thornbury in his *London Old and New*, it was here amid fields that 'she entertained Charles and his saturnine brother with concerts and merry breakfasts in the careless Bohemian way in which the noble specimen of divine right delighted.' The wells at Bagnigge had once belonged to the nuns of St Mary, Clerkenwell and had been called collectively the Well of the Blessed Virgin, which sorts well with the symbolism of Nell's name and birthday discussed earlier.

Nell's stage career was inevitably winding down. Having played the part of Pulcheria in a revival of James Shirley's *The Sisters* in January 1669, she is not recorded as having played another role until June that year when she took the part of Valeria, daughter of the Roman Emperor Maximin, in Dryden's tragedy *Tyrannick Love, or The Royal Martyr*. The play, presented before the King and Queen, was a great success, running for fourteen consecutive days. It was another of Dryden's heroic dramas and treats of the martyrdom of St Catherine of Alexandria.

St Catherine herself – the virgin martyr – was a favourite female icon of the times, and many of the leading ladies of Charles II's court, including Barbara Villiers, were painted in the garb of the fourth-century Alexandrian saint. Such an identification might seem grotesque until we accept that Catherine's martyrdom was a metaphor for women's struggle for independence: their determination to decide their own fate, in particular their sexual fate.

Nell herself, though no martyr, certainly imitated Valeria in giving the King constancy without expecting or receiving it in return. On the other hand, she enjoyed the sort of freedom in their relationship that was denied to the great generality of women, including the choice to remain constant. It is interesting in this regard to consider Valeria's penultimate speech before killing herself:

> My Father's Crimes hang heavy on my head,
> And like a gloomy Cloud about me spread;
> I would in vain be pious, that's a grace
> Which Heav'n permits not to a Tyrant's race.

The crimes of the father are those of patriarchy in general, from whose iron grip Valeria, representing the female spirit, struggles to free herself.

The figure of the virgin martyr rising from the ashes of the old patriarchal dispensation is a common one in Restoration tragedy. Indeed, Valeria quite literally rises from the dead when she gets up from her stretcher to speak the epilogue (quoted in full in Chapter 6), though by now she has been metamorphosed into a mischievous spirit called Nell Gwyn, much relieved no doubt to be restored to the world of comedy.

Curll in his *History of the English Stage* (1741) tells us that Nell as Valeria 'so captivated the King, who was present the first Night of the Play, by the humorous Turns she gave it, that his Majesty, when she had done, went behind the Scenes and carried her off to an Entertainment that Night'. It would certainly have been ironic if true, because the play was widely thought to have been written as a tribute to Charles's Queen Catherine, who was in what turned out to be her final pregnancy while Dryden was writing the play. Sadly, she miscarried not long before the opening night, when Charles's pet fox sneaked into her room and leapt up onto the bed. Catherine had herself been painted as St Catherine by Jacob Huysmans in 1664 and was certainly a martyr to Charles's serial infidelity. It was now clear that she would never produce children. The effect of her sterility was to turn the Queen into another mistress; indeed, with Barbara's eclipse, she was now *maîtresse en titre* in all but name! Onlookers like Marvell probably thought that the King had finally lost interest in her:

> Our great King, Charles the Second,
> So flippant of treasure and moisture,
> Stooped from his Queen infecund
> To a wench of orange and oyster;
> And for sweet variety, thought it expedient
> To ingender Don Johns on Nell the comedian.[5]

Yet far from abandoning his Queen, Charles enjoyed the new sense of excitement that her de facto conversion to mistress kindled. She was able to entice him to bed more often and call him to her to indulge her passion for dancing. She took to wearing risqué and avant-garde dresses. On one occasion she was reported to have 'exposed her breast and shoulders without even . . . the slightest gauze; and the tucker instead of standing up on her bosom, is with licentious boldness turned down and lies upon her stays'. She also liked dressing down and would wander through the streets of London incognito, 'not[ing] the qualities of people'.

Despite its obvious connections with Catherine of Braganza, *Tyrannick Love* was dedicated not to the Queen but to her stepson the Duke of Monmouth, who was to become something of a royal martyr himself the year his father died. Charles adored him, in public at least, and showered him with honours both civil and military, but in private he found it hard to tolerate his son's ebullience and headstrong nature. For his part, Monmouth resented the indelible mark of bastardy conferred upon him by his father and he minded terribly that his mother, Lucy Walter (or Barlow), had been a whore. There may have been good sport at his making, but he, Monmouth, had to live with the consequences for his entire life. The one thing that Charles could not give him was the one thing he wanted above all: legitimacy. And yet this was just the thing that Charles had seemed to promise.

As for Monmouth's relationship with women, this 'universal terror of husbands and lovers' was superbly attractive to the opposite sex and always gorgeously attired, yet the apparent emptiness at the core of the man made it impossible for him to hold the interest or affections of those he had seduced. For all his brilliance and bluster, failure of wit generated angry feelings in him, and his dealings with women, which were extensive, began to lack finesse. De Grammont had hailed him as 'the new Adonis', and like Adonis Monmouth quickly preferred hunting to women.

From the moment she made her first appearance at court, Monmouth was drawn to Nell Gwyn, emotionally and sexually. Although they were exact contemporaries, she became something of a mother figure to him, a shoulder to cry on, while he played the role of errant son. There were many parallels in their early lives. Monmouth too had been a child of the streets, in Rotterdam rather than London. Deprived of his father, his childhood had been dominated by the figure of his dissolute mother. Nell understood his feelings of alienation, knowing well what it was like to be the outsider; yet she was ruthlessly honest with him and tried to discourage his fantasies of kingship. On one occasion after he had failed yet again to persuade

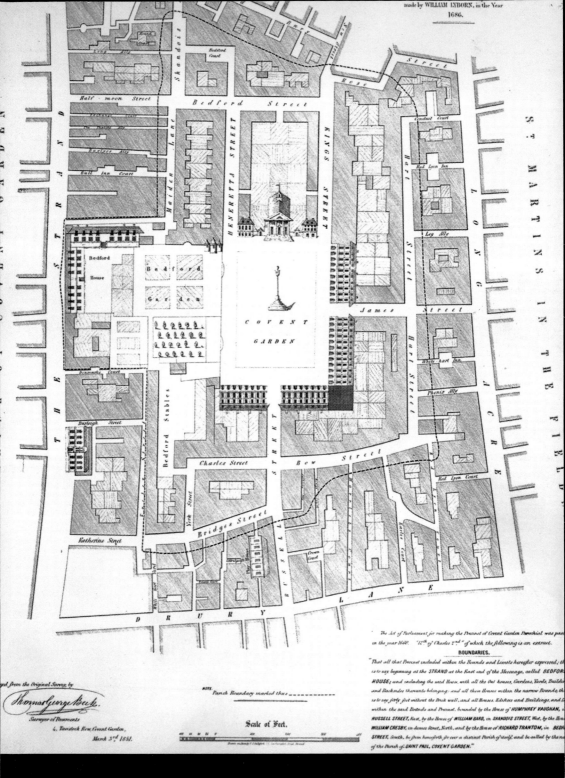

Map of Covent Garden as Nell Gwyn would have known it. (Guildhall Library.)

Above. Nell Gwyn with her first son, Charles, later Duke of St Albans, 1671.
Portrait by Sir Peter Lely. The King used to enjoy attending the sittings
at Lely's London studio. (Bridgeman Art Library.)

Opposite. Aphra Behn (1640–89), Nell's admirer and the first female
playwright to make her living by writing. (Bridgeman Art Library.)

Nell Gwyn with pearls
in her hair, c.1675.
Engraved by Valentine
Green from a painting
by Sir Peter Lely.
(From the Crofton Croker
album, by kind permission
of the Duke of St Albans.)

Nell Gwyn as Cupid, c.1672.
Pepys hung a copy of this
painting over his desk at the
Admiralty. Engraved by
Richard Tompson from
a painting by Peter Cross.
(From the Crofton Croker album,
by kind permission of the Duke
of St Albans.)

Opposite.
King Charles II (1630–85)
by unknown artists.
(National Portrait Gallery.)

Above.
The two sons of Nell Gwyn,
Charles and James, c.1676.
Portrait by Gaspar Netscher.
(National Portrait Gallery.)

Left.
Catherine of Braganza
(1638–1705), wife of Charles
II, in the year of their
wedding. Portrait by
Dirck Stoop, 1662.
(National Portrait Gallery.)

Barbara Palmer (née Villiers) (1641–1709), later Countess
of Castlemaine and Duchess of Cleveland. Charles's first mistress
after the Restoration. She bore the King as many as five children.
Portrait by John Michael Wright, 1670. (National Portrait Gallery.)

Frances Theresa Stuart, Duchess of Richmond (1647–1702), known for her exceptional beauty as *la belle Stuart*. She confounded the King with her chastity and ended up as the model for Britannia on the nation's coinage. Portrait by William Wissing and Jan Van der Vaart, 1687.
(National Portrait Galley.)

her to champion his cause, he threw up his arms and called her a guttersnipe. 'Was Mrs Barlow better bred than I?' she shot back.

Nell was one of the very few to whom Monmouth could speak his heart, and it's not hard to see why he would be attracted to a bold and beautiful woman of Welsh ancestry who had captured the heart of a king, for his mother had been such a one. I suspect that Nell loved him as a son, nothing more. She certainly never yielded to his advances. At the same time, it would be wrong to underestimate the importance of the friendship to her. Not only was Monmouth a powerful ally to have at court, but his obvious dependence on her would have done much to boost her confidence as she stepped out onto this newer and bigger stage. Though not political allies in the strict sense, the Protestant Duke and the Protestant Whore, as they became known, remained fast friends.

Even more useful to Nell in the early days of her affair with the King were the Chiffinches, William and Barbara. As mentioned, William was Keeper of the King's Closet and Pictures, as well as of His Majesty's Backstairs, and Page of the King's Bedchamber, while Barbara was Laundress to Queen Catherine. But they were much more than these titles imply, for they held positions of unique trust. Charles relied on them to grease the wheels of his private life, and in William's case to protect his privacy. Apart from the King, Chiffinch was the only person with a key to His Majesty's Closet (his study where he kept his favourite pictures and other knick-knacks and dealt with his private correspondence). No one but he could enter unbidden, not even the Queen. The Whitehall apartments belonging to Chiffinch and his wife, together with the King's Closet, constituted 'the Backstairs', and were used by those who met privately with the monarch. If you went by water to the Privy Stairs, a landing stage on the Thames at the back of Whitehall, proceeded up to the lobby and knocked at the first door on your left, you would find yourself face to face with William Chiffinch, Esq. There was no access to the backstairs without his cooperation.

Politically, Chiffinch was vital to the King, for he facilitated the secret diplomacy that was intrinsic to Charles's modus operandi. During the Popish Plot of 1678–81, for instance, he was an effective go-between for the King, arranging private meetings for him with spies and informers acting on behalf of the Whigs, as well as with Catholic leaders who could not be seen coming up the front stairs.[6] It was in Chiffinch's apartments, too, that Charles's secret payments from Louis XIV were negotiated with the French ambassador, and it was Chiffinch who received the subsidies themselves as well as other secret service funds paid by order of the King. Of obscure origins, he remained a shadowy figure despite his vast network of contacts. Harbouring no political ambitions for himself, he died a wealthy man and took his master's secrets to the grave. It's certainly difficult to disagree with David Ogg that this most private of royal servants 'performed a great and honourable service to the Stuarts by not writing his memoirs'.

Whereas William alone dealt with political assignations, both he and Barbara managed the King's social life, and in particular his amorous appointments, for which it was said they were paid the fantastic sum of £1,200 a year. Many a green girl, heart pounding, was led up the backstairs to satisfy the King's sexual curiosity, and their names duly entered in a book, later destroyed, with a mark indicating whether a return visit was considered appropriate. (If the King ended up with 'the pox', meaning venereal disease, they were doubtless struck from the roll, while the King hastened to his laboratory to prepare an antidote.) Husband and wife were, in effect, the King's pimps. The Chiffinches' apartments were also the scene of private dinner parties, at which Barbara Chiffinch sometimes acted as unofficial hostess. William too was inevitably one of the company, acting as Charles's eyes and ears. And sometimes they entertained without the King, in which case it was William's job to extract valuable intelligence from guests by plying them with drink, while he himself remained sober by taking the King's drops, a powerful restorative based on a recipe devised by Cromwell's old physician Dr Jonathan Goddard and perfected in the King's own laboratory. All in all, if you wanted private access to the King, it wasn't a bad idea to cultivate the friendship of Mr William Chiffinch.[7]

Nell quickly became a favourite with both William and Barbara and was a frequent guest at their Whitehall lodgings, both with and without the King. The table always rang with laughter when she was there, and the Chiffinches would have seen that her affection for the

King was heartfelt and without calculation. But it was their job to be cunning, and it may be that they exploited her naivety and indiscretion as well as her knowledge of the London underworld to add to their stable of royal paramours. At the very least she was a useful channel to the theatre. But even if Nell involuntarily pimped against herself, the rewards of her friendship with the Chiffinches far outweighed any drawbacks. They not only secured her access to the King in the early days, but it was through William that she received what tokens of the royal bounty came her way. She saw them too at Newmarket, where they had a house next to the King's, and as their guest at Philberds in the parish of Bray, near Windsor, where the King liked to hunt.

It was largely through the influence of the Chiffinches that Nell received her first invitations to state dinners. In June 1669, during the run of *Tyrannick Love*, she was invited to a banquet in honour of Prince Cosimo, heir to the Grand Duke of Tuscany. Count Magalotti, one of the Prince's entourage, who left an account of the visit, was bemused to see Nell at the table 'quaff[ing] a great goblet of canary', a strong sweet wine. Indeed, he was altogether astonished by the amount of alcohol consumed at court. The Prince, having visited the Royal Society, went to the King's playhouse to see Dryden's latest success and thought the theatre 'superior to anything in Florence'. Given her presence at the banquet, a curiosity that would have been eagerly reported in the news-sheets, and her newly acquired celebrity, it is little wonder that Nell should have found herself the principal attraction of *Tyrannick Love*. It was certainly one of the many ironies of her life that just at the point when her appearance on stage could ensure a play's success her career came to a sudden end.

Over the summer Nell began to see more and more of the King, and once again it was the Chiffinches who ensured her safe arrival at Whitehall by sending a coach to Drury Lane or making sure that there was a boat waiting for her if she decided to make the short walk from her lodgings down to the Thames. And if an anecdote from Sir Francis Fane's *Commonplace Book* is to be believed, she had further reason to be grateful to them. One night that summer Charles had sent word to his Queen that he would be keeping to his own bed as he was suffering from a cold. Catherine, who rose early to say her prayers, decided to make a dawn visit to her ailing husband. Fortunately,

Barbara Chiffinch got wind of her intention and ran to warn the King, who had spent an amorous night in the arms of Nell Gwyn. Barbara hid her young charge behind the bed hangings, but in the rush Nell lost a slipper.

The King, who was an early riser, managed to sit up in bed and greet his wife with careless affection. The Queen expressed herself delighted that he was completely recovered and turned to go. But the King, no doubt feeling guilty, patted the bed and invited her to sit down beside him. Catherine, secretly elated by this gesture of intimacy, walked forward to take up his invitation when she spotted the slipper. She stopped short and shook her head indulgently. 'I will not stay for fear the pretty fool that owns that little slipper might take cold,' she sighed. And turning once again, she left the room.[8]

Charles was also in the habit of visiting Nell, who just that summer had moved into new, more spacious lodgings at Newman's Row on the northern side of Lincoln's Inn Fields, a short walk, up Great Queen Street, from her old stamping ground. As was the case with most of Restoration London, it was an area of stark contrasts. It had first been developed as a site for smart townhouses in the 1630s by William Newton. It was then that the London season had begun in earnest and many aristocrats and rich landowners took to spending the months from November to June in the capital, where they could enjoy the the busy social life as well as cultivate their political and business interests. Houses were built along three sides of the Fields, the eastern side being left open to the gardens of Lincoln's Inn proper. The Fields, being unlit, had long attracted prostitutes of the ordinary tavern-door kind, who conducted their clients there. Whetstone Park, just to the north of Nell's new house in Newman's Row, was crawling with punks. It wasn't a park at all, but a dark alley. Also, by Charles II's time, Lincoln's Inn Fields had attracted a number of City merchants who were looking for larger properties, as well as members of the artistic community who were drawn to the Duke's Theatre situated on the south side of the square, in Portugal Row. Visiting the theatre remained a chief pleasure throughout Nell's life.

There were less salubrious approaches to Newman's Row than Great Queen Street, as the French ambassador, Colbert de Croissy, found out, for there were many occasions on which his audiences with the King, especially in the middle of the day, took place at Nell's modest house. Londoners would gawp at the sight of the powdered and bewigged diplomat, with page and secretary in tow, picking his way through the debris-strewn alleys of what is now Kingsway to deliver a message from Charles's cousin, His Most Christian Majesty, King Louis XIV of France. Once at Newman's Row he would be greeted by a scene of cosy domesticity.[9] Charles and Nell would be playing at cards and chatting, with a few close friends in attendance, while a homely meal of pigeon pie was prepared in the modest kitchen. Washed down with goblets of canary, the meal would be followed by the gentle sounds of royal snoring. The King didn't mind one whit that he should be seen by de Croissy with such a conspicuous absence of ceremony. One of Charles's chief private pleasures was to be *underestimated* by others.

For a man who in exile had grown to appreciate the virtues of the simple life, these informal lunch parties with Nell, when he could 'put off the King', were no doubt important periods of relaxation, essential to his overall health. For Nell, it was a double victory to have the King on her own turf; it gave her more power in the relationship and was evidence that the King enjoyed her for her company rather than as an ornament of his court. It also fuelled her fantasies of keeping house for Charles, as if they were husband and wife. Nell was compelling on her home ground, and even the courtly de Croissy laughed with Charles at her 'buffooneries'.[10]

Windsor, like Newmarket, was another country retreat that Charles and Nell enjoyed together. After its neglect during the Interregnum, when for a time it had been occupied by squatters, Windsor Castle was ready for a facelift, and Charles with his great appetite for projects, especially those involving building and landscaping, rose to the challenge. Having installed Prince Rupert in the Round Tower as Constable of the Castle, where he invented mezzotint engraving, the King relieved the gloom of the old medieval fortress by introducing large windows, levelled the skyline by dropping the turrets, and brought verve and colour to the interior with painted ceilings in the Baroque manner and panelling decorated by the masterly hand of Grinling Gibbons. Outside, the King extended the north terrace round to the south and east and had it 'curiously turfed', planted avenues of elms and limes and created an enchanting canal for water-fowl. He also commissioned a fountain from Sir Samuel Morland that shot water dyed with red wine sixty feet up into the air. Finally, the park was restocked with deer from Germany and a new tennis court constructed.

Here by day Nell joined the King in a favourite pursuit, hawking, while the evenings saw great tables laid beneath the oaks for candlelit 'picnics', the diners serenaded by the King's Italian musicians. In the water meadows surrounding Windsor, which must have reminded Nell of the Oxford meadows of her early childhood with their ancient willows, the couple loved to walk together or sit on the river bank watching the dragonflies. Charles built a summer house at nearby Datchet, which he had decorated by Verrio, and it was here that he developed his passion for fishing. His tutor, appropriately, was his low-born comedienne, for angling, unlike hunting, was not considered an aristocratic pastime, nor indeed much of a sport. It was a good metaphor, however, for Charles's political technique, with its twin hallmarks of patience and camouflage, though the satirists construed his passion less charitably. An anonymous libel, attributed to Roches-ter, entitled 'Flat-foot the Gudgeon Taker' contains the following lines:

> Methinks I see our mighty Monarch stand,
> His pliant Angle trembling in his hand.
> Pleas'd with the Sport, good man; nor does he know
> His easy Scepter bends and trembles so.
> Fine Representative indeed of God;
> Whose Scepter's dwindled to a fishing rod! . . .
> Too well, alas, the fatal Bayt is known
> Which Rowley does so greedily take down
> And how ere weak and slender be the String,
> Bayt it with Whore and it will hold a King . . .

Flat-foot, like Rowley, was the name of one of Charles's stallions at Newmarket. If Nell coached Charles in the mysteries of hook, line and sinker, he made sure that she mastered the principles of horseman-ship. It proved something of a struggle, as Nell was not a natural horsewoman. She loved watching the races at Newmarket and gambling on the horses, and the animals themselves excited her admiration, but she was never particularly comfortable in the saddle and declined to join the hunt. Therein no doubt lies the reason for her partiality to pursuits such as fishing and hawking, which required both feet on the ground. Besides, her equestrian incompetence would have provided a good excuse for sharing the same horse as the King. One can imagine the thrill of a dawn gallop through the park at Windsor with the King holding her hands upon the reins!

It was at Windsor in August 1669 that Nell conceived her first child by the King. With Barbara eclipsed, Louise yet to appear on the scene and Parliament prorogued, Nell had Charles all to herself during those perfect summer months. When she returned to London for the autumn season, she seems to have cut back her stage appearances for the duration of the pregnancy, though the absence of recorded roles is not conclusive evidence. In September, probably around the time that Nell realized she was pregnant, Charles's mother Henrietta Maria died at Colombes, a village a few miles from Paris where she had a summer house on the banks of the Seine. She was in her sixtieth year and had been in poor health for some time. Charles's sister Minette, who had just given birth to her second daughter, was beside herself with grief. There was anger too at Vallot, the French King's doctor, who had administered a grain of laudanum to help the old Queen sleep, even though she had earlier refused it not only on the grounds that she had reacted badly to narcotics in the past but also because an astrologer had once told her that 'a grain' would be the cause of her death. As the Duchesse de Montpensier commented tartly, 'She could not sleep, so the doctors gave her a pill to send her to sleep, which it did so effectually that she never woke again'.

Charles, who was informed while out hunting in the New Forest, took the news in his stride. He had never been able to shake off that feeling of weariness that he had conceived towards his temperamental mother during his exile. And though he hadn't seen her for over four years at the time of her death, she had remained an emotional and financial drain to the bitter end. As it happened, her death proved a double release, for it seemed finally to break the power of Barbara's spell over him. She would always be a strong presence in his life, but never again a controlling one. It heralded the start of a new decade, marked also by Nell's pregnancy, in which Charles found his full independence and authority as a monarch. One wonders whether Henrietta Maria had heard of her son's relationship with the former orange girl or, God forbid, that she was expecting his child. The shock would surely have hastened her departure.

Much more to Henrietta Maria's taste would have been the political design that Charles was concocting with his sister Minette, which involved his public conversion to Catholicism in return for hefty subsidies from Louis XIV. After long years of enduring Parliament's bullying parsimony, Charles's patience had worn thin and he longed to be free of his humiliating dependence upon its handouts. Indeed, his personal situation had become so dire that the Crown would find itself bankrupt if action wasn't taken to remedy the deficit. Hence Charles's attraction to the creative, but desperately dangerous solution offered by Louis and Minette, which came to be known as the Secret Treaty of Dover.

On the surface, the treaty was essentially commercial and military; for instance, England would support France's annexation of Holland, hoping thereby for mastery of the seas. But there was a secret crux, kept hidden from Protestant ministers such as Buckingham and Shaftesbury, in which Charles agreed to convert publicly to the Catholic faith in return for French gold. And Charles's conversion, backed by French arms, meant England's conversion.

The dangers were obvious. Here was a King who at the outset of his reign had stated his determination never to go on his travels again, and yet if he could have devised a foolproof means of losing his throne, this was surely it. Quite apart from the risk of exposure through the indiscretion of his own ministers, he was handing Louis XIV the perfect means of blackmailing him. His anxiety is expressed to Minette in a letter of 20 January 1669: 'I shall be very just to the King, my brother, in never mentioning what has past betweene us, in case this negociation does not succeede as I desire so I expect the same justice and generosity from him, that no advances which I make out of the desire I have to obtain a true frindship between us, may ever turne to my prejudice.' So why did Charles embark on such a perfidious scheme with nothing to protect him against the treachery of the world but his wits?

Firstly and most obviously, there was the despair of his indebtedness. People do silly things for money. Secondly, it seems he never intended to risk a revolution at home by going through with his conversion. And thirdly, whether consciously or not, he was still smarting over Parliament's treatment of his father and family. We should never forget, as Charles certainly didn't, that at the Restoration he was returning to a country whose Parliament had murdered his father, despoiled his palaces, disparked his parks, defaced his statues and eliminated the very concept of royalty on which the lives of father and son had been founded. Moreover, it had put a price on his head and forced him to eat the bitter bread of banishment. Little wonder, then, that despite his political policy of forgiveness and thoroughgoing tolerance, or perhaps because of it, there should have seeped up from the depths of his being a barely recognizable feeling of vindictiveness which expressed itself in a desire to deceive Parliament and even, in this case, to usurp its power. Despite his professions of good faith, Charles possessed a strong unconscious urge to punish Parliament for the murder of his father. And what could not be accomplished openly, because hostile to the calculations of the political mind, was done through duplicity.

We don't know whether Charles took Nell into his confidence over the Secret Treaty, but I suspect it was too early in their relationship for him to trust her with sensitive political material. We do know, however, that the treaty was discussed in broad terms when Colbert de Croissy visited the King at Nell's house in Lincoln's Inn Fields, and that the French ambassador informed Foreign Minister Hugues de Lionne that Nell could be of little use to the French King in his plans for bringing England back to the Catholic fold because of her well-known friendship for the anti-Catholic Duke of Buckingham, who at that moment was planning how best to effect a legal divorce between Charles and Catherine.

It's doubtful anyway whether Nell's thoughts at this time could be fixed upon politics for long, for she was in a state of elation. Her dreams had come true: the King's child – a royal child – was quickening in her womb. Whatever became of her now, she knew she would always have a hold both on the King's affections and on his purse strings, for Charles, an affectionate if distant father, always provided for the mothers of his children.

Childbirth, however, was a perilous enterprise, especially, it seems, if a midwife was present. Many in the medical profession of the time blamed the unnecessary interference of midwives for up to two-thirds of stillbirths, miscarriages and maternal deaths in childbed. And if the child itself survived, a plethora of diseases vied for the hapless infant's first embrace. The 'lying in' took place at home, in a room carefully sealed against draughts and usually filled with female friends and relatives. In Nell's case her mother and sister Rose and a couple of girlfriends from the theatre are likely to have attended. An observer from the court, possibly Barbara Chiffinch, would also have been there to verify the birth, as this was to be a royal child.

The baby turned out to be a healthy boy and was born on 8 May 1670. The Oxford antiquarian Anthony à Wood wrote in his *Life and Times*, a sort of rambling diary, 'About the 14 or 15 [of May], Elianor Quin, one that belongs to the King's play hous, was brought to bed of a boy in her house in Lyncoln's Inns feilds, next to Whetstones Park – the King's bastard.' It took the news a week to reach Oxford, though it is fitting that the birth should be registered for posterity in the town where Nell herself was most probably born. In mentioning both Whetstone Park and Lincoln's Inn Fields, Wood draws attention to the social limbo into which the royal bastard was born, midway between a den of prostitutes and a row of aristocratic townhouses.

The days following a birth were known as the 'upsitting', during which the new mother's bedchamber became a salon for well-wishers. Nell had a stream of visitors, including John Dryden, who was eager to have her back at the theatre as soon as possible. Charles was busy preparing to travel to Dover to meet Minette, who was coming to England to seal the Secret Treaty, when news of the birth reached him. There is no record of his reaction, but he surely rejoiced in his heart when he saw the baby's mother beaming with pride. Nell had already decided to call the boy Charles, and the father gave his wholehearted approval. The matter of the surname would have to wait until Charles returned from Dover. Nell's little boy Charles was the King's seventh son (by five different mothers) so it was fortunate that he was spared the name Septimus Fitzroy. There had already been a James, three Charleses, a Henry and a George, so not only was this child Nell's Charles the Fourth, but he was also the King's fourth

Charles. There is no record of a christening; certainly Charles would not have wanted a public service, with all the ribald commentary such an event would draw. Maybe Nell opted for a private ceremony at her house; we don't know. Strangely, the child was given no surname until six and a half years later, when he was granted his first titles. In the meantime he was not even described by the generic surname used for royal bastards of the time, 'Fitzroy'. He was plain Charles.

But for now this was of no concern to Nell, as she unwrapped the gifts sent by the King's sister from Dover. Though she could never be *maîtresse en titre*, she was, for a few glorious months at least, the King's chief mistress.

~ 10 ~

Final Curtain

THE DAYS THAT CHARLES AND Minette spent together at Dover in May 1670 could not have been sweeter. Brother and sister had not seen each other since the first year of Charles's reign, a decade earlier, when Minette had visited London as a girl of sixteen. The sun shone down upon a halcyon sea, and once the formal business of the treaty had been dispatched, no effort was spared to entertain the French party. The importance that Louis XIV attached to the Secret Treaty was reflected in the size of Minette's escort, which numbered some two hundred souls. Not to be outdone, Charles had surrounded himself with his entire court. Accommodation was a problem. The English royal family together with Minette and her immediate train were housed in the castle, while the town itself was forced to find lodgings for the generality of courtiers, not to mention servants, priests, secretaries and hangers-on.

Banquets were held both on land and at sea, the revelling and dancing being almost continuous. The festivities reached their climax on 29 May, Charles's fortieth birthday and the tenth anniversary of the Restoration, the royal banquet at sea challenging comparison with the feast that Pompey hosted on his galley off Misenum to celebrate his treaty with Caesar and Antony. There was yachting too, and hawking, and day trips to Canterbury, where they were entertained by the Duke of York's Company and feasted in the great hall at St Augustine's Abbey. And of course there were the private interviews, at which Minette poured out to her brother all the dammed up woes of her marriage to the sadistic Duc d'Orléans. They talked too of the happy times spent at Colombes during Charles's exile, when they had discovered each other for the first time. Rich gifts were exchanged, in both gold and the heart-warming courtesies of friendship.

When the time came for Minette to return to France, the distraught Charles followed her part of the way across the Channel. When he boarded her ship for the last time, there were tears on both sides. Colbert de Croissy wrote that he

> had never seen so sorrowful a leavetaking, or known before how much royal personages could love one another. It had appeared during her stay at Dover that she had much more power over the King her brother than any other person in the world, not only by the eagerness the other ministers have shown to implore her favour and support with the King and by the favours he has accorded simply at her request . . . but also by the King's own confession and the tears he shed on bidding her farewell . . .

And well may he have shed tears, for it was to be the last time that they would see each other. By the end of the month the twenty-five-year-old princess was dead. Poison was suspected, and rumours at the French court circled about her husband's homosexual lover, the Chevalier de Lorraine.

Despite the real dangers to King and country in the Secret Treaty, the effect of Minette's zealous diplomacy and her sincere desire to see her brother enhance the strength and prestige of his kingdom was to rouse Charles in his throne and make him alive to the greatness of the crown he wore. The last fifteen years of his reign would see a more ruthless and determined King.

One of the plays performed before the French and English bigwigs at Dover excited great controversy and caused both hilarity and resentment, depending on the nationality of the spectator. It was John Caryll's comedy *Sir Salomon, or The Cautious Coxcomb*, specially selected by the King. The part of Sir Arthur Addell, 'a noisy bawling fop', was taken by the up-and-coming comedian James Nokes. But in this case it wasn't what he said that caused offence, but what he wore. In clear mimicry of the clothes then fashionable among the French gallants, Nokes had on an absurdly abbreviated lace coat, secured by a fancy girdle, and a broad-brimmed hat of ludicrous dimensions. According to Downes, 'his appearance was so ridiculous, that at his first entrance he put the King and Court into an excessive laughter; and the French were much chagrined to see themselves aped by such a buffoon as Sir Arthur'.

The hat joke at the expense of the French was a telling one. The vast hat itself, quite apart from the literal, sartorial joke, symbolized the grandiose thoughts of France, which were concentrated on her ambition to swallow up the rest of Europe. This ambition, which was really Louis's grandiose thought, was the object of both hatred and mirth in England. To the English, who had fought with their lives against a king's tyranny, French concepts of a universal monarchy – with Louis at the helm – appeared dangerous, despite the bombast. As Forneron wrote, 'The Protestant passions of the people, and the Liberal ideas of the aristocracy, inevitably placed England in conflict with an absolute, and a Catholic king'. Hatred is not too strong a term for the feelings harboured by the average Englishman towards the French. Later in the decade the French ambassador de Courtin told how a London crowd, mistaking a Venetian for a Frenchman, was on the point of throwing the unfortunate Italian into the Thames.

Though Charles's political enemies tried to compare him with Louis, he had no taste for absolute monarchy. Indeed, the notion ran counter to his nature. Louis was vain and humourless, exalting glory above personal happiness, always desperate to project an image of infallibility. Indeed, he took to wearing a wig because loss of hair, he feared, would give the French people a glimpse of his mortality. Charles, on the other hand, was humorously self-deprecating and a keen solicitor of the happiness of the moment. When the painter John Riley presented him with his portrait, Charles asked him if it was really a good likeness. When told that it was, the King laughed and said, 'Then, 'Od's fish, I am an ugly fellow!' Charles found humanity a truer weapon than infallibility in his dealings with his subjects.

As for mistresses, it would have been unthinkable for Louis to take a mistress from the lower orders, let alone allow her the run of the court. It would be wrong, however, to suppose that Nell's relationship with the King and the birth of their child were welcomed by Englishmen everywhere. There was a group of Republican MPs, among them the poet Andrew Marvell, that denounced Nell's presence at court as a national disgrace. These coarse lines from the satire 'The Lady of Pleasure' give vent to their bitterness:

> And now behold a Common Drab become
> The glorious Mate for th'English Monarch's Bum.
> Nor was it long before the Artful Slut
> Had got the length of her Great Stallion's Foot.
> She knew so well to wield the Royal Tool
> *That none had such a Knack to please the Fool.*
> *When he was Dumpish, she would still be Jocond*
> *And Chuck the Royal Chin of Charles ye Second.*
> Come Dear, quoth She, I hate this Melancholy –
> Then out She lug'd the Handle of his Belly –
> And with her Heels lock'd in the Amorous Cully.
> Such Dalliance as this, and Royal Puke,
> At length produc'd the great St. Alban's Duke.
> Thrice happy Nell that had'st a King so gracious
> *To poke for Princes in thy Dust and Ashes.*
> And well done Charles, when thou can'st get no Heirs
> To stock thy Peerage with St. Martin's Peers
> And stain the Lines of all thy old Nobility
> With Scoundrel Whores, and *Cinder-drabs Fertility.* [my italics]

Once again, even in the vortex of such vitriole, the image of Cinderella rises to the surface. As for 'great St. Alban's Duke', that was the title that Charles eventually conferred upon the son that Nell bore him. Marvell in his 'Royal Resolutions' has Charles say,

> I'll wholly abandon all public affairs,
> And pass all my time with buffoons and players,
> And saunter to Nelly when I should be at prayers.

Nell was not a naturally maternal mother, being a child herself, and an artist to boot. And not just a child, but a love-starved child, who had been left to fend for herself at a premature age. It was probably just as well, then, that she had a wet nurse on hand to suckle the child, as well as a nanny to cope with the daily chores. As the visits of her fellow actors increased, so Nell began to feel a restless desire to return to the stage. John Dryden brought her the part of Almahide, the Moorish Queen from his new play in two parts, *The Conquest of Granada*, which she enjoyed rehearsing in her bedroom, not because she relished the tragedy itself, but because she liked dressing in mock-oriental garb and making Charles take the part of her jealous husband, Boabdelin. What really delighted her, however, was the prologue, to be 'spoken by Mrs. Ellen Gwyn, in a Broad-brimmed Hat, and Waist-belt', for news of Nokes's sensational success in the part of Sir Arthur Addell had already reached her. She knew immediately the sort of uproar *she* could cause. Not only would she be in her element, but there would be the added fascination she could now command as the mother of a royal bastard.

The birth of their child was a complex turning point in the relationship between Nell and the King. She immediately trusted to a deeper, more affectionate alliance, and in her most private thoughts allowed herself to dream of that which all royal mistresses at some stage dream: marriage. It was a wild and improbable fantasy, but irresistible to an imaginative and ambitious girl of twenty, whose life had already followed impossible flights of fancy. Charles, on the other hand, seems to have fought feelings of growing intimacy with the deft use of his trusty shield, wit. On the whole he was attracted to younger, immature women who didn't burden him with emotional demands and whom he could keep at arm's length with the authority and invulnerability of a father. Nell, however, was the exception. More than honours or wealth, she demanded love, intimacy and friendship.

Both Charles and Nell had been exiled from the carefree pleasures of childhood and initiated before their time into the weary responsibilities of adult life. Perhaps as a consequence, both were prey to bouts of depression throughout their adult lives. Nell, at least, had had her band of street urchins; the theatre too had helped to put her in touch with that fund of good-humoured mischief that impressed her contemporaries. Yet, she appears never to have lost that aura of the child left out in the cold (like the wounded child beneath the winter tree in Oscar Wilde's *Selfish Giant*) and it was perhaps this image of her above all that struck a deep, sympathetic chord in Charles. He too was that neglected child, and each was able thaw the frozen patch in the other's garden. It was a painful process, particularly for the King with his formal upbringing. How he treated Nell henceforth became a test of his compassion not only for himself, but for his people. Truly, as the historian Brenda James has pointed out, Nell's little hand in the King's was the hand of his people.[1]

His love for both Lucy Walter and Barbara Castlemaine had been erotic and compulsive, while the ties of affection that bound him to his Queen drew what strength they had from notions of duty and chivalry. His love for Minette, whom he hardly ever saw, had been almost spiritual. Nell was something quite different: she challenged the King to a deep and intimate friendship. Charles and Nell were drawn together in the first place by their love of theatre and an irreverent sense of humour. They laughed at the same things and soon found that they enjoyed discussing ideas, for her understanding was as quick as his. More than this, they shared a philosophical bias: life was a divine comedy and the key to happiness was discovering your part and playing it to the hilt, without taking yourself too seriously. Both were strong individuals who rejected pretension, and it was this quality of truth that cut to the heart of their friendship. True friendship is between equals; more than that, *it creates equals*. As such, it's a kind of rebellion, creating a separate world of special interests and sympathies.

In the case of Charles and Nell, the nature of the rebellion is clear: it was social. Never before had an English King – except in literature – made a social outcast, possessing neither wealth nor status, his equal. And, whatever his intentions, the hand he reached out to her set in motion a revolution in relations not only between the sexes but also between the different estates of men. What the King effectively said was, 'Whoever is worthy of my friendship is my equal'. Revealingly, Sir Francis Fane makes the following entry in his *Commonplace Book*: 'The old Duchess of Richmond said she could not abide to converse with Nell and the rest of the gang, which Nell told the King of, who replied that those he lay with were fit company for the greatest woman in the land.'

This social change, accompanied as it was by a great deal of new money in the country, is charmingly illustrated – almost in the form of a parable – by the following story from *Richardsoniana*, related by Cunningham in *The Story of Nell Gwyn* (1903):

A cutpurse, or pickpocket, with as much effrontery of face as dexterity of finger, had got into the Drawing-room on the King's birthday, dressed like a gentleman, and was detected by the King himself taking a gold snuff-box out of a certain Earl's pocket. The rogue, who saw his sovereign's eye upon him, put his finger to his nose, and made a sign to the King with a wink to say nothing. Charles took the hint, and, watching the Earl, enjoyed his feeling first in one pocket and then in another for his missing box. The King now called the nobleman to him. 'You need not give yourself,' he said, 'any more trouble about it, my Lord, your box is gone; I am myself an accomplice: – I could not help it, I was made a confidant.'

What better image for a City trader than a cutpurse dressed as a gentleman! Yet Charles, in his eagerness to encourage free enterprise, stimulated the growth of this class at the expense of the nobility. He was indeed an accomplice to the theft.

Charles introduced Nell to status, wealth, gracious living, beautiful surroundings and a dazzling social life. With these came insight into the world of the upper classes, a knowledge which she could take back to the streets. He was also a father figure, who provided her with a sense of security, though it is unlikely that she ever felt totally secure, for she was too keenly aware of the place she had come from and to which she might at any moment be forced to return. In one sense, she was a free woman, neither bound to the King by ties of marriage or family, nor, as an actress, beholden to him for her daily bread; yet emotionally she must have begun to feel a certain dependency, and this, I think, made her anxious. Remaining detached from emotional alliances had been part of her stock in trade; loving the King probably made her feel vulnerable and out of control. This could explain why she returned to her career, even after the birth of their child.

For her part, Nell kept the King in touch with his popular and humanitarian instincts. She gave him a knowledge of London street life and a vivid sense of how its poorer citizens lived. As his all-licensed fool she delivered disinterested and forthright advice on the state of the nation. She brought spontaneity and laughter, and provided him with a place of peaceful retreat from the cares of office, where he could relax sufficiently to enjoy sex. Finally, and most challengingly, she put him in touch with vulnerable and neglected elements of his nature that had remained mummified since childhood. The instinctive fun-loving Charles, as opposed to the wittily cynical King, prospered under her influence.

As the 1670s progressed, however, the covert resentment of Charles's cohorts towards a relationship they didn't understand and found socially unacceptable brought intense pressures which, though weathered, almost certainly led to private fights between the couple. But the friendship was too strong to be defeated by conventional malice. In a letter to the new king after Charles's death, Nell gave this poignant testimony to their years together: 'He was my friend and allowed me to tell him all my griefs and did like a friend advise me and told me who was my friend and who was not.'

For those romantic souls who wish to speculate on a secret marriage between the King and Nell Gwyn, possible clues may be found in the literature of the time. Such a union would require no more than an exchange of rings and the plighting of their troth, though its force would be more emotional than legal. However, if such a contract ever existed, it would be impossible to separate truth from fantasy, for those who appeared to know the truth may simply have been indulging in wishful thinking. If anyone actually knew such a truth, it would surely have been Nell's friend Aphra Behn.

In her short novel *Oroonoko, or The Royal Slave*, the story of Oroonoko (whose slave name is 'Caesar') and his mistress-wife Imoinda, can be read as a parable of the relationship between Charles and Nell. Certainly, there seem to be deep insights into the meaning of a possible union and the forces that may have moved to prevent it, as well as a wealth of more trivial echoes. Intriguingly, Imoinda's slave name is 'Clemene' (i.e., 'Little Orange'), and it is through a secret rendezvous in an orange grove that she spends her first night with Oroonoko. The daughter of a general, it is her truthfulness and nobility of spirit that are stressed throughout. For this reason the other slaves show her extraordinary respect and do her work for her. It is said that 'no man, of any nation, ever beheld her that did not fall in love with her; and that she had all the slaves perpetually at her feet'. In her dedication of her comedy *The Feign'd Courtesans* to Nell in 1679, Behn writes, 'even those distant slaves whom you conquer with your fame pay an equal tribute to those that have the blessing of being wounded by your eyes . . .' Moreover, she emphasizes how naturally Nell moves in the upper circles of society: 'and so well you bear the honours you were born for, with a greatness so unaffected, and affability so easy, an humour so soft, so far from pride or vanity, that the most envious and disaffected can find no cause or reason to wish you less . . .'

Also in the dedication of *The Feign'd Courtesans* is a curious eulogy of Nell's sons. Behn, having stated that heaven in its particular care of Nell can confer no further blessings on her, mentions its greatest gift in 'bestowing on the world and you two noble branches, who have all the greatness and sweetness of their royal and beautiful stock; and who give us too a hopeful prospect of what their future braveries will perform, when they shall shoot up and spread themselves to that degree, that all the lesser world may find repose beneath their shades . . .' Curious because it echoes a passage in Ezekiel 17, much quoted by British Israelites,[2] who see in it a reference to the legitimate royal dynasty of Britain, descended from David, King of Israel: 'Thus saith the Lord God; I will also take of the highest branch of the high cedar, and will set it; I will crop off from the top of his young twigs a tender one, and will plant it upon an high mountain and eminent: In the mountain of the height of Israel will I plant it: and it shall bring forth boughs, and bear fruit, and be a goodly cedar: and under it shall dwell all fowl of every wing; in the shadow of the branches thereof shall they dwell.'

The tender shoot transplanted from the royal tree of David was the daughter of King Zedekiah of Judah, who was taken to Ireland by the prophet Jeremiah during the Babylonian captivity of the Jews. There she married the Heremon, or King of all Ireland, Eochadh II. From them descended a thousand-year dynasty of Irish Kings until the year 506 AD when King Fergus, whose royal standard depicted the lion rampant (of Judah), crossed to Scotland where he was crowned King of the Scots. One of his eventual descendants was James VI of Scotland and I of England, grandfather of Charles II. Thus Nell Gwyn's sons by Charles were offshoots of this Davidic line, and it was to the elder son, Charles, that the King gave his executed father's ring. This descent from King David was one of the most keenly cherished secrets of

Scottish Rite Freemasonry, which was brought to England by the royal house of Stuart.[3] Aphra Behn, with her connections to the world of espionage, was well placed to infiltrate such secret knowledge. She was certainly a robust apologist for the royal house of Stuart.

Charles, however, did not concern himself with abstract or far-reaching speculations when it came to politics; instead he kept his eye firmly on the ball. Whatever the distractions of the moment, he concentrated on one thing: remaining in charge of his destiny. When news of Minette's death reached him, he was inconsolable in his grief. Locking himself in his Closet, he gave himself up to bitter tears. 'My grief for her is so great,' he told a friend, 'that I dare not allow myself to dwell upon it, and try so far as possible to think of other things'. But there was fury too, all the more potent for being unaccustomed, for Charles suspected foul play. In private he cast aspersions on the King of France's brother, Minette's kinky husband. But both grief and anger, compelling though they were, were subordinated to the King's political designs. He saw clearly that if he continued to humour the French, the Treaty of Dover could ensure both his own security and England's.

In the wake of Minette's death, Charles sent Buckingham as his envoy to France to represent him at Minette's funeral and make formal thanks to Louis for his condolences. There was one further errand, of a more sensitive nature. On the eve of Minette's departure from Dover, Charles had given his sister some exquisite jewellery and in return begged her — somewhat slyly — to furnish him with one of her own jewels as a keepsake. Minette immediately ordered her maid of honour, a pretty Breton girl with black hair and fair skin, to fetch her casket and asked Charles to choose anything he liked. Whereupon he took the blushing maiden by the hand and declared that she was the only jewel he desired. But Minette had refused, claiming that she had a duty to the girl's parents. Now two months later Charles was making a formal request to Louis through Buckingham that the girl be permitted to come to England as a maid of honour to Queen Catherine.

Her name was Louise de Kéroualle, and she had been introduced into Minette's household as a possible mistress for Louis XIV. Pipped to the post by another Louise, Louise de la Vallière, she would nevertheless become the last principal mistress of Charles II, and Nell Gwyn's chief rival for his affections. Buckingham, who fancied himself as a procurer and manager of royal mistresses, was only too delighted to take up the commission. Straying from his script, he told Louis that the only way to ensure Charles's good faith over the alliance with France was to present him with a beautiful mistress, the finest that France could offer. Once again, Louis was ahead of the game and had already planned to use Louise as political bait. Not only could she be employed to gather political intelligence, but she could step into the shoes of her dead mistress, Minette, in ensuring that Charles kept his vow to convert publicly to Catholicism. Finally, and most significantly, she could – if all went well – become a symbol of France's control over England, which was vital if Louis was to keep continental Europe subservient to his grand design. Nor need that control be real; the appearance was enough.

But Charles had designs of his own. He knew the political virtue of keeping a French mistress at his side. For although the satirists would have their day, it would mean that he could postpone his public conversion indefinitely. Louise would be his pledge of good faith, the visible symbol of his French sympathies, and would leave him free to act in bad faith. He was in fact playing the same game that Elizabeth I had played with her hideous French suitor, the Duc d'Alençon, whom she nicknamed her Frog. By continually holding out the prospect of marriage, Elizabeth was able to maintain the balance of power in Europe between England, France and Spain. In a sense, both monarchs eventually came to believe their own propaganda and half fell in love with their political victims.

Privately Louise de Kéroualle jumped at the chance to exchange a mediocre life on the periphery of Versailles for the prospect of royal courtesanship. But she had been well coached by her highly placed mentors, so that when Charles's offer was made to her, she shook her head wistfully, saying that her only desire now that her mistress was dead was to live out her days in a convent. Buckingham, ignorant of this new charade, told her that the King of England was in love with her, but she merely pouted. So he pulled out his trump card, and with it reverted to his favourite theme: the King's marriage was, he said, doomed, the clear implication being that young Louise could find herself angling for a crown. Finally, he had her attention. With his

Gallic flair for political choreography, it was left to Louis himself to persuade her to take up this important post for the sake of France, or at least those were the stage directions. Buckingham got her as far as Dieppe, then succumbed to one of his spells of madness, leaving Louise in some seaside dive to rush back to England and into the arms of his pregnant mistress, Lady Shrewsbury. Arlington had to send a yacht to rescue the stranded girl, who was never to forgive the Duke for his neglect. De Grammont, who had accompanied Buckingham to France, stayed with Louise in Dieppe and advised her on how to handle the English King. The example he implored her to follow was that of Frances Stuart, whose evasions and coy refusals had driven the King half mad with love.

Louise had one special advantage with Charles, initially at least: she wore the fragile glamour of his departed sister. Nor did she scruple to take full advantage of this rather macabre fascination with which fate had endowed her, and would talk for hours about Minette and even deploy some of her mannerisms. She had been devoted, she said, to the King's sister. All this dissembling came quite naturally to Louise, who even at twenty was known for her esprit froid. She was dark, sulky, baby-faced, phlegmatic, vain, manipulative, covetous and prudish. In many ways, she was Henrietta Maria without the tantrums. Her voice was soft with the softness of repressed anger. She had what contemporaries described as a languid walk, and a slight cast in one eye drew from Nell Gwyn the nickname 'Squintabella'. Nell also called her 'Weeping Willow', for she had a gift for sobbing on cue. The English generally, who couldn't or wouldn't pronounce Louise's name, referred to her as 'Mrs Carwell', which Nell modified to 'Cartwheel', a reference to the craze for huge, broad-brimmed hats among French ladies. Charles called her 'Fubbs', a name she was to share with one of his luxury yachts. A 'fubb' or 'fubbs' was a small, chubby person, while 'fubsy' meant fat and squat. 'Fubbery', less endearingly, meant deception.

In the famous portrait of her painted by Pierre Mignard, when Louise was thirty-two, she appears almost lifeless, like marble, her pale cheeks daubed with rouge, her eyes cold, her mouth prim and spinsterish. Her right arm rests on the shoulders of a negro boy who offers her gifts of pearl and blood-red coral, but she gazes ahead, apparently unconscious of his presence. The symbolism is fascinatingly apt in a number of ways, especially if one takes the black boy to be Charles and his gifts the twin realms of soul and instinct neglected by Louise. She had not entered into a cordial loving relationship with the King, preferring to weave her web of intrigue. Her concerns were overwhelmingly mundane (she points to the ground with her left hand), and already by early middle age true emotion, which she had so often faked, appears beyond her grasp. An inner petrification has taken place.

Judging from a number of her portraits, as well as the comments of contemporaries, Louise was in fact very pretty, but the childishness of her looks promised a vitality that was absent. She was, if anything, unnaturally demure and had a sort of sedative effect on Charles, which probably contributed to his overall welfare. Her pallor, her round face and the black hair 'puffed in small ringlets' about it, gave her the appearance of a doll. Hers was the rather unnatural beauty in vogue at the court of Louis XIV. As Jesse remarks, 'The countenance of the Duchess of Portsmouth [which she later became], though undoubtedly beautiful, possessed the worst of all faults, a want of expression'.[4]

Louise Renée de Penancoët de Kéroualle, to give her her full name, was probably still a virgin when she arrived in England in September 1670, though her name had been coupled for some time with that of a debauched young Parisian, the Comte de Sault. She had had a strict convent upbringing, and spent her holidays under the eye of devout, slightly severe parents. Her coy glances, then, were not complete affectation. She flirted with the King, but would not allow him to kiss her, holding herself aloof, both to distinguish herself from the English mistresses and to demonstrate her class. She had to be won.

The de Kéroualles were an ancient but impoverished Breton family, who coated the bitter pill of poverty with pride of ancestry. Thus, Louise grew up a snob, who used hauteur to hide both her sense of inferiority and a burning desire to acquire riches worthy of her status. As soon as she arrived at Whitehall, she affected to despise the English Court as provincial. Its ladies and gallants were insufficiently polished, its culture barely more than improvised. Her standard of sophistication was Versailles; Whitehall could never pass muster. Like all inveterate intriguers, she felt marooned outside the city. Country estates were of no interest to her; she preferred gifts of jewels and cash to property. Instead she stayed put at Whitehall. The courtier's life, which Evelyn described as 'anxiously tedious', was Louise's trade. Even as she crossed the Channel, she relished the thought of playing the grande dame and bringing something of the flavour of Versailles to Charles's cloddish court.

Imagine then her sense of shock when she found not just the royal court but also the King's heart inhabited by a low-born, loud-mouthed actress, who thought nothing of sophistication, made it her business to ridicule the great and the good and whose pranks were not merely tolerated by the King, but actively abetted. Not only did this guttersnipe not respect her, she took every opportunity to cock a snook. Several years later the Marquise de Sévigné, watching with amusement from the safety of Versailles, wrote to her daughter,

> Kéroualle saw well her way, and has made everything she wished for come to pass. She wanted to be the mistress of the King of England; and behold, he now shares her couch before the eyes of the whole Court. She wanted to be rich; and she is heaping up treasures, and making herself feared and courted. But she did not foresee that a low actress was to cross her path, and to bewitch the king. She is powerless to detach him from this comedian. He divides his money, his time, and his health between the pair. The low actress is as proud as the Duchess of Portsmouth [Louise], whom she jeers at, mimics, and makes game of. She braves her to her face, and often takes the king away from her, and boasts that she is the best loved of the two. She is young, of madcap gaiety, bold, brazen, debauched, and ready witted. She sings, dances, and frankly makes love her business.

The contrast with Nell Gwyn could not have been more striking. Nell was bold and downright, and her mischievous voice echoed brightly through the corridors of Whitehall. Her swearing was legendary, and in 'Mrs. Nelly's Complaint' she is made to boast of her pre-eminence in the art:

He [the King] ne'er heard swearers till Mall Knight and I.
Loudlier we swore than plundering dragoons;
S'blood followed s'blood, and zoons succeeded zoons;
Till at the last the bawd's weak forces failed,
And I by noise and impudence prevailed.

Louise found it hard to hide her irritation with Nell, and when she did retaliate found that she didn't have the wit to embarrass her rival. Years later, when one of the court ladies happened to comment on Nell's wit and beauty and excellent bearing, pronouncing her to be as much a lady of quality as anyone at court, Louise cut her off with the words, 'Yes, madam, but anybody may know she has been an orange wench by her swearing.' Such snobbery was simply another source of mirth to Nell, who was quick to seize on the insecurity at the heart of Louise's pride. The Marquise de Sévigné records Nell's refreshingly frank analysis of the situation: 'As to [Nell Gwyn], she reasons thus: this duchess, says she, pretends to be a person of quality. If she be a lady of such quality, why does she demean herself to be a whore? She ought to die for shame. As for me, it is my profession; I do not pretend to anything better.' Later in the same letter, the Marquise cannot help recording her admiration for Nell: 'This creature gets the upper hand, and discountenances, and embarrasses the duchess extremely. I like these original characters . . .' So too did Charles II.

Louise was immediately given the finest apartments in Whitehall, where the French ambassador, Colbert de Croissy, spent his afternoons. Leading French exiles, such as de Grammont and Saint-Evremond, whom Charles had created Governor of the Isle of Ducks in St James's Park, also paid court to her and offered advice on handling the King. First among the English ministers seeking influence over her was Secretary of State Arlington, who found Nell Gwyn far too boisterous and her pranks altogether too broad to bear with. Colbert wrote to Paris,

My Lord Arlington told me recently that he was very glad to see the King his master attached to her [Louise], for although His Majesty never communicated state affairs to ladies, nevertheless as they could on occasion injure those whom they hate and in that way ruin much business, it was better for all good servants of the King that his attraction should be to Mademoiselle Kéroualle, whose humour was not mischievous and who was a lady, rather than to lewd and bouncing orange-girls and actresses, of whom no honest man could take the measure . . .

Louise's bedchamber soon became known as the true cabinet council, and an anonymous wag, possibly Rochester, urging the inevitable, pinned a notice to her door which read,

> Within this place a bed's appointed
> For a French bitch and God's anointed.

When Buckingham failed to wheedle his way back into Louise's graces, he once more joined forces with Nell. The merry pair had plenty of matter for mirth during the first few months of Charles and Louise's courtship. Charles, caught between grief and lust, was so overcome with tenderness when he saw Louise that the tears would come to his eyes; while Louise, a perfect Mock Turtle, sobbed the louder, for Minette, for France, for her family, for the loss of that exquisite taste that only Versailles could confer. At the all-night dinner parties that Buckingham threw for his fellow wits, he and Nell performed a hilarious skit of Louise and Charles weeping tenderly as they sat stiffly opposite each other. Buckingham, impersonating the King, would heap jewels in Nell's lap, while she – mimicking Louise's heavy French accent – sobbed out the words, 'Me no bad woman. If me taut me was one bad woman, me would cut mine own trote'.[5] When word of such capers reached Charles, he merely laughed.

Then there was Louise's incessant chatter about Catherine's ill health and her expectation of stepping into the Queen's shoes. Her promoters counselled tact and caution, but the seed that Buckingham had sown in Paris sprouted regardless. Colbert confided to the French King his fear that Louise would make a laughing stock of herself 'because she does not keep her head sober, since she has got the notion into it that it is possible she may yet be Queen of England. She talks from morning to night of the Queen's ailments as if they were mortal.' If she couldn't actually be the Queen, Louise was nevertheless determined to live like one and, before long, her apartments were reported to be a good deal more opulent than Catherine's.

Ultimately, it is difficult to pin down Charles's feelings towards Louise. One thing is certain: they were not simple. He may well have felt a slight thrill that he was finally about to consummate his love for Minette. There's small doubt that his loyalty to Louise had more than a little to do with his enduring feelings of love for his departed sister. The glamour never wholly wore off. He also seemed grateful for Louise's sexual placidity; unlike Barbara, she didn't exhaust the King with compulsive carnal demands or impugn his virility. By the early 1670s Charles seems to have become sated with sex and was looking to stimulate a deeper, more spiritual nerve. Rumours of royal impotence were rife, and the King frequently paid in cash what he couldn't give in seed, which might explain why so many of his mistresses became compulsive gamblers.

In the end, however, love for Charles was a political game and monogamy did not suit the complexity of his designs, quite apart from the fact that he had a number of galleries to play to. What seemed like emotional chaos to others was to Charles a satisfying mood music, completely reconciled in its contradictions. Indeed, one could argue that Louise and Nell, far from being rivals in the King's affections, complemented each other, for they represented two different sides to his nature, each of which craved expression. If Charles had chosen between them he would have impoverished both his emotional and his political life. The one was fair and genial, the other dark and cunning; the one natural, the other political. This theme of the King's dual nature was explored repeatedly, if subliminally, in the drama and literature of the time.

Louise's arrival in London coincided with Nell's return to the stage after four months of doting on little Charles, the nameless one. As the King's mistress, and with a royal child to boot, it was an extraordinary thing to do and a measure of how seriously she took her career. It wasn't so much a convention she was breaking as a taboo. For a woman to tread the boards in those days was to announce her availability, be she never so chaste, and to present a target for the gallants and City men. And brazen though Charles was to criticism in these matters, he was certainly not immune to jealousy and had already sent Buckhurst on a diplomatic mission to keep him out of temptation's way. Nell's act of defiance gave him pause for thought, especially now that she was the mother of his child. Maybe it was Nell's way of trying to jog him out of his infatuation with Louise, or perhaps it was just Nell being Nell. As she was to prove over the next fifteen years, she had no intention of straying sexually, but nor would she be prevented from steering her own course.

There may have been a measure of protest in her act, for the birth of her son, while naturally turning her thoughts to worldly considerations of place and security, had not stimulated the King's largesse. It is true that in August she had moved to accommodation in Pall Mall, but her small rented house was at the dilapidated eastern end of that prestigious avenue, a good quarter-mile from the stately townhouses. According to Wilson, the tax on Nell's house was only sixteen shillings a year, very modest indeed for that neck of the woods. Whether it was her decision to move or Charles's, we don't know; perhaps it was a temporary move agreed between them until something better became available. One contemporary wrote, 'Nell Gwin, beinge asked why shee removed from ye good ayre in Lincolsin fields to worse neare Whit-hall, replyed shee had but on [one] good friend in ye world & shee loved to gett as neare him as shee could.' Although her only friend, Charles Stuart, paid her rent, it was clearly not what Nell had in mind for herself and her son. The King had yet to grant her an income, and until he did she would not be forsaking her professional salary.

The trouble was, her relationship with the King broke new ground; there were no precedents for Charles to follow, and men like Arlington would be quite happy to see Nell tossed back into the streets. As a result she lived in social limbo. She had no real allies at court and was not invited to the masked ball at Whitehall that Christmas, at which Louise was fêted. And her simple appellation of 'Nelly', if affectionate, was also condescending, one to grace a pet or an innocent. Her general absence from the letters and diaries of the time suggests rather eloquently that most people simply didn't know how to react to her. Like Cinderella, she could appear at Whitehall and set tongues wagging with her beauty and confidence, but when midnight struck she must hurry back to her modest lodgings, with nothing to console her but a dream.

Such obstacles might breed surface fears, but, underneath, Nell knew that she and the King were deeply – fatefully even – involved with one another. The birth of her child had instilled a new determination in her, and she could now plead her cause by pleading his. Madame de Sévigné, in the letter to her daughter already quoted, gives these words to Nell Gwyn: 'The King keeps me; ever since he has done so, I have been true to him. He has had a son by me, and I'm going to make him own the brat, for he is as fond of me as of his French miss.'

The same month that Nell moved into her new digs in Pall Mall, the King created Barbara Baroness Nonsuch, Countess of Southampton and Duchess of Cleveland. According to the patent, the honours were bestowed 'in consideration of her noble descent, her father's death in the service of the crown, and by reason of her personal virtues'.[6] ('If everybody minded their own business,' the Duchess said, in a hoarse growl, 'the world would go round a deal faster than it does.') She received a grant of the revenues of the Post Office worth nearly £5,000 a year, £10,000 a year from the farmers of the Customs, a further £10,000 from the farmers of the county excise on beer and ale, together with a host of other leases and places to sell. (A naval officer at that time earned in the region of £60 per annum.) As Andrew Marvell commented, 'All promotions spiritual and temporal pass under her cognizance'. Yet Barbara, who had, in the words of Bishop Burnet, 'abandoned herself to great disorders' since leaving the King's bed, still managed to find herself short of cash, spending thousands on the upkeep of her déclassé lovers. Even the mansions bestowed upon her were either divided into plots and leased or torn down to sell as building materials, having first been plundered of their contents. As for good Queen Catherine, Charles moved her to Somerset House, leaving Whitehall as the arena for the hugely entertaining contest between Louise and Nell.

In December 1670 Nell made her much anticipated return to the stage in the character of Almahide, Queen of the Moors in Dryden's two-part epic *The Conquest of Granada*. (The second part was produced in January 1671.) Nell sauntered onto the stage to speak the prologue in the same garb that James Nokes had worn before the French at Dover in May, only her hat was the circumference of a coach wheel. The house roared itself hoarse, while it's said that the King all but suffocated with laughter. With her opening words she craved the audience's indulgence:

> This jest was first of the other house's making,[7]
> And, five times tried, has never failed of taking;
> For 'twere a shame a poet should be killed
> Under the shelter of so broad a shield.
> This is that hat, whose very sight did win ye
> To laugh and clap as though the devil were in ye.
> As then, for Nokes, so now I hope you'll be
> So dull, to laugh once more for love of me.

Later in the prologue Nell refers to herself and Nokes as 'two the best comedians of the age'.

It should be remembered that the prologues and epilogues performed at the beginning and end of plays were miniature shows in their own right, and in the right hands could be the saving grace of a bad production. The prologue was like a warm-up act to get the audience into a responsive mood, while the epilogue, which Nell was wont to round off by dancing a jig, might well ensure the only enthusiastic applause of the evening. As Buckingham wrote in his epilogue to *The Chances*,

> . . . the author dreads the strut and mien
> Of new-prais'd poets, having often seen
> Some of his fellows, who have writ before,
> When Nell has danc'd her jig, steal to the door,
> Hear the pit clap, and with conceit of that
> Swell, and believe themselves the Lord knows what.

The production of *The Conquest of Granada* had been delayed for a year to allow Nell to have her child, and this is alluded to in the epilogue when the author apologizes rather artfully to the house:

> Think him not duller for this year's delay;
> He was prepared, the women were away;
> And men, without their parts, can hardly play.
> If they, through sickness, seldom did appear,
> Pity the virgins of each theatre:

For, at both houses 'twas a sickly year! [owing to pregnancies]
And pity us, your servants, to whose cost,
In one such sickness, nine whole months are lost.

As we have seen, the plays Nell acted in reflect to an uncanny degree the inner tensions in her life at the time of their production. *The Conquest of Granada* was no exception. The play tells the story of the siege of the Moorish stronghold of Granada by the Spaniards at the end of the fifteenth century, with its classic interweaving tales of love and war, honour and perfidy. The Moors, led by Boabdelin, Moham-med XI of Granada, a weak, unprincipled King, seem doomed until their salvation appears in the form of Almanzor, a stranger from Africa, who performs miracles on the battlefield.

Almahide (played by Nell), the loyal wife of Boabdelin, falls in love with Almanzor (played by Charles Hart); though constant to the King in duty, she is caught between the two men. Boabdelin and Almanzor represent the two sides of Charles's nature, the one faithless, the other true. Boabdelin doesn't allow himself to trust Almahide's love, for he judges others by his own treachery; he is the calculating politician, forever caught in his own lies. Almanzor, on the other hand, is our old friend the noble savage. Passionate and committed in his love for Almahide, he accuses the King of trying to win her with titles instead of 'blood and dangers'; he is an exile, a wanderer, for whom con-science sits above policy. Almahide at one point loses patience with the King's equivocations and shouts at him, 'How dare you claim my faith, and break your own?' She tries to make him understand that it is true love that she is after:

> Yet I declare, and to the world will own,
> That, far from seeking, I would shun the throne,
> And with Almanzor lead a humble life:
> There is a private greatness in his wife.

In the end Almahide is united with Almanzor, the natural man. Thus the final image of Nell's theatrical career gave her the promise of a deeper, more private union with the King.

Although Nell would make further threats to return to the stage, none of her reported appearances after 1671 seems valid. The old

Dictionary of National Biography listed seven parts for her in the late 1670s and early 1680s, including the role of Queen Elizabeth in John Banks's tragedy *The Unhappy Favourite, or The Earl of Essex* (1682), but the publicity that would have attended such a comeback is absent. We know that she attended the theatre regularly and kept up with her thespian friends, but her professional days were over. The theatre had been good to her. It had provided her with a surrogate family, and she must have missed the daily comradeship of her fellow professionals, as well as the applause and adulation of an enthusiastic public.

In assessing Nell's seven-year career (1665–71), it's interesting to speculate about what might have happened had she never met the King. Would she have become one of the great actresses of her age, on a par with Elizabeth Barry or Anne Bracegirdle? Almost certainly not, for her aversion to tragedy would have disqualified her, in the minds of the critics at least. She was a comedienne, whose genius for being herself made her a box-office hit. Of particular note were her loud, clear voice, which had once cried oranges and could cope with the most fractious of hecklers; her comic timing, which was impeccable; and her finely judged aptitude for exaggeration. The idea of training to be what she wasn't could never have appealed to her. If challenged on that score, she might have claimed – and with good warrant – that the repertory of the time did not give sufficient rein to her talents. Even Dryden proved incapable of exploiting her irreverent humour to the full. In this respect, she would have been better served by the modern age, with its television sitcoms and stand-up comedy. By any criteria, however, her career was meteoric. She retired at the tender age of twenty-one, and had stamped her mark with such distinction upon certain popular plays, most notably Dryden's *Secret Love*, that it was to be a full decade or more before they were performed again. There was simply no one to replace her.

Nell's return to the theatre clearly had the desired effect upon the King, for in February 1671 she moved into 79 Pall Mall, a grand townhouse in brick at the smart, western end of the street, shaded by stately elms. Incorporating four bays with long windows on the first two floors, it had a street frontage of almost thirty-five feet and contained seventeen fireplaces. It was almost brand new, part of an extensive property development laid out by Henry Jermyn, Earl of St Albans, who had also been granted a site for a thrice-weekly market in Pall Mall fields. It had been home to the Earl of Scarsdale, but he had been prevailed upon to give it up to the King's agent, George Hewitt, who was instructed to transfer the lease to the King's mistress for a term of forty-nine years. But Nell was not interested in a leasehold and, not being one to bully or badger the King, she employed her surest weapon, wit. The house, she insisted, must be hers 'free under the Crown', because she herself had given her services free to the King! The King, who was always persuaded by a jest, yielded to her quixotic reasoning and a few years later the property was hers to keep. It was to be her principal residence for the rest of her life and was inherited by her son Charles.

In addition to three storeys and extensive cellarage, there was attic accommodation for servants. The house possessed a fair-sized garden, which adjoined the King's garden at St James's Palace and looked out onto the park beyond, with Whitehall visible in the distance. As we learn from Evelyn, this provided for easy communication between the two lovers:

> I had a fair opportunity of talking to his Majesty . . . in the lobby next the Queenes side, where I presented him with some sheetes of my Historie. I thence walk'd with him thro' St. James's Parke to the garden, where I both saw and heard a very familiar discourse between [him] and Mrs. Nellie as they cal'd an impudent comedian, she looking out of her garden on a terrace at the top of the wall, and [he] standing on the greene walke under it. I was heartily sorry at this scene. Thence the King walked to the Dutchess of Cleaveland [at nearby Berkshire House], another lady of pleasure, and the curse of our nation.

Moreover, wherever Nell took up residence, and this is true of Pall Mall, Newmarket and Windsor, legends sprang up of a secret subterranean passage between her house and the King's neighbouring palace or castle. Such tales, whether true or not, are suggestive of the deep emotional connection between Nell and Charles in the popular mind.

Charles didn't expect much these days when he sauntered over to Barbara's house; he went, in the main, to see his children. He was never quite sure in whose arms he would find their mother. Her latest conquest was the playwright William Wycherley, whom she had snared in Pall Mall by means of a literary allusion. As their carriages had passed the Duchess had leaned out of her window and bellowed, 'You! Wycherley! You are the son of a whore!' The stunned writer looked round to see the lady collapsing back onto her seat in fits of laughter. Fortunately Wycherley possessed a quick mind, and he had gone less than fifty yards when he realized that the Duchess's insult had in fact been a pick-up line of considerable bravura, a compliment even. He ordered his driver to turn around, and an assignation was made for the same evening. The venue was the King's Theatre, Drury Lane, where Wycherley's comedy *Love in a Wood, or St. James's Park* was receiving its debut. Barbara had already seen it, and her audacious greeting had referred to its famous 'song against marriage', which was in praise of bastards. It's not hard to see how Barbara might have taken the following verse of Wycherley's song as a compliment to her children, then used it as she did to commend the playwright's good looks and exceptional wit:

> When parents are slaves
> Their brats cannot be any other;
> Great wits and great braves
> Have always a punk for their mother.

True to her word, Barbara sat in the front row of the King's box that night, and Wycherley, standing in the pit below her, entertained his new mistress throughout the performance. But nothing could disguise the fact that Wycherley, like the blasé gallant that he was, had little real interest in the outcome of his flirtation. Barbara was by now an object of contempt.

The play gives us an interesting insight into Nell's new neighbourhood, for the wood referred to was just over her garden wall in St James's Park. Its shady groves were a favourite place for night-time assignations among people of quality, introducing a note of urban pastoral into the lives of the jaded gallants, who could imagine themselves as love-lorn shepherds, albeit in high heels. Their mistresses were the shepherdesses of Lely's court portraits, alluring in their studied simplicity. Lady Flippant, who trawls the park at midnight, loaded for gallant, might well have been played by Nell Gwyn had she still been a member of the King's Company that spring.

Whether at midnight or not, Nell's assignations with Charles proved fruitful, for by the end of March she was pregnant again. She spent the spring furnishing her new house at the King's expense, employing the necessary staff and getting to know her neighbours. Sir Francis Fane wrote, 'Most of the great men's Misses [i.e. mistresses] have houses in the Pall Mall where the Countess of Portland hath likewise a house and is very kind to Nell Gwinn by reason she procured a 1000 li. [i.e., pounds] out of the Exchequer. They call it Portland Park.' Her immediate neighbour was one Edward Griffin, a Groom of the Bedchamber to the Duke of York, whose wife Anne had just died at the age of thirty-three. Also nearby were Barbara, now Duchess of Cleveland, the singer Maria Knight, Charles's former mistress Catherine Pegge, now Lady Greene, and the Countess of Shrewsbury, whose husband had been killed in a duel by her lover, the Duke of Buckingham.

Nell worked quickly on the interior of her house, for she was determined to have it ready for Charles's birthday at the end of May. The party would double up as a house-warming. Her pièce de résistance was a *salle des miroirs*, a reception room lined from floor to ceiling with mirrors, which her mother was unable to enter without yielding to a 'fit of the dizzies'. In the afternoons she took a sedan chair over to Lely's house in Drury Lane, where she sat for her portrait. On a couple of occasions she brought the one-year-old Charles with her, for they were being painted together as Venus and Cupid. The boy's father would drop by nearly every day and chat merrily to Nell as she tried her best to keep still. She was naked but for a strip of white satin draped loosely over her loins. In the finished work, now across the road in the Army and Navy Club, Cupid has grabbed one end of the drape and looks as if he might at any moment expose his mother with a sudden jerk of the arm! As a joke, Nell set the portrait up in her hall of mirrors. Flirting with her guests was now out of the question for Charles, for wherever he turned her eyes would be upon him. A copy was delivered to Whitehall.

Lady Shrewsbury heard of the party through Buckingham and had him inform the King that she expected to be invited. When Charles passed the information on to Nell, she was quick to refuse, saying that 'one whore at a time was enough for his Majesty'. Though in tune with the people on this and many other issues, Nell herself inevitably became a target of satire for the coffee-house men, especially in the City. The coffee houses had been branded 'lay conventicles' by the beer-drinking fraternity, and they were the only places of public resort where the Geneva skullcap was not an object of derision. These neo-Puritans were a new breed, more subtle and cynical than their predecessors, and were content to fight their propaganda war from the wings. Coffee was a revelation to them: a clean drink that stimulated the revolutionary nerve. High on caffeine, they scribbled away late into the night. And inasmuch as she kept the King from his devotions, Nell was 'the dunghill wench', yet one more roadblock on England's highway to salvation. Garroway's Coffee House listed her in an 'Advertisement for a sale of choice goods': 'Twenty-four ells of Nell Gwyn's virginity in three pieces, 1 yellow, 2 black, full yard broad and a little better, at 3 s. per yard, to advance 2 d. each bidding.'

While Louise continued to keep Charles on heat by urging him to honour his marriage vows, Nell decided to let the dust settle in her new home and headed off to Windsor with her son for the summer. There the King put them up in a house in Church Street, though they spent their days up at the castle in lazy country pursuits. Prince Rupert was there with his mistress, Nell's former colleague Peg Hughes. Nell took an instant liking to him and prevailed upon him to tell tales of his exploits during the Civil War. For his part, Rupert enjoyed her forthright manner and lack of pretension; he could no doubt tell that her father had been a military man.[8] Charles, as was his wont, shuttled back and forth between Windsor and London (Louise sat out the summer at Whitehall), and was always ready to find an excuse to sneak off to Datchet for a day's fishing with Nell. Girolamo Alberti, the Venetian ambassador who translated Walton's *The Compleat Angler* into Italian, witnessed Charles's earliest efforts at the sport, ably guided by Nell, and the growing intimacy that their shared hobby fostered. Contrary to the prevailing ethos of the smart set, both Charles and Nell enjoyed the backwoods, their rambles taking them far from the beaten track.

September saw the court setting out once again for Newmarket and the autumn races, but this time there was no question of Louise remaining in the capital. Colbert himself, prompted by an exasperated Louis, took matters into his own hands and arranged with the Arlingtons that Mademoiselle would be brought to stay at their country seat of Euston in Suffolk. The King, who was made privy to the plan, would come up from Newmarket to make a final assault upon her chastity. Despite the efforts of the court gallants to keep the King in Newmarket with a series of stag nights, all went according to plan. Evelyn, who was a house guest at Euston for the duration, wrote this account in his *Diary*:

> During my stay here with Lord Arlington neere a fortnight, his Majesty came almost every second day with the Duke [of York], who commonly return'd to New-market, but the King often lay here . . . It was universally reported that the faire Lady [Louise] was bedded one of these nights, and the stocking flung, after the manner of a married bride; I acknowledge she was for the most part in her undresse all day, and that there was fondnesse and toying with that young wanton . . .'twas with confidence believed she was first made *a Misse*, as they call these unhappy creatures, with all solemnity at this time.

Exactly nine months later Louise gave birth to her only child by the King.

When Charles returned to Newmarket in triumph, the gallants were still revelling and Buckingham had arrived with the Countess of Shrewsbury and his band of fiddlers. The King was given a lusty welcome. Even Nell affected to be amused by Weeping Willow's calculated submission, and to a degree she was. But as a woman seven months pregnant with her second child by the King, she had a little correction in mind for her errant lover. It would have to be a prank, of course, or the message would be ignored. So Nell joined forces with her old comedy double the Duke of Buckingham and between them they hatched a plot. That night Buckingham and his mates took Charles to a notorious Newmarket brothel, only Buckingham, who knew all the doxies in the joint, had been there earlier in the day to prepare the ground. Charles duly enjoyed his whore, who retired as soon as the King had taken his pleasure. When he came to put his clothes on, Charles discovered that he had been robbed of his money; worse still, his fellow stags had deserted, leaving him to face an irate landlord alone. The constable was sent for and the King threatened with all manner of humiliations, when a local customer, recognizing the coronation ring, drew the landlord aside and revealed the identity of the royal miscreant. Back at Nell's house, Charles's pleas for sympathy fell on deaf ears. Instead she reminded him that dabbling with whores could be a costly business.[9]

Nell was relieved to get back to her new home to prepare for the festive season. It was to be a particularly happy one for her: on Christmas Day she gave birth to another healthy boy, whom she named James as a compliment to the King's brother.

A Chargeable Lady

JAMES, NELL'S SECOND SON BY Charles, was the King's eighth and penultimate acknowledged son. His final one, Louise's son Charles Lennox, had already been conceived by the time of James's birth and would be born in July of the following year. Whether Charles's sexual powers were failing was a moot point even at the time, but it is surprising that after Louise's son he fathered only one further child during the remaining thirteen years of his life, his daughter by Moll Davis, Lady Mary Tudor, who was born on 16 October 1673. There would be one other serious mistress during the last decade of his reign, but there were certainly no children by her, even though Charles was only in his mid-forties.

It may be that both venereal disease and the mercury he used to treat it caused impotence in the King. Or perhaps, as legend has it, there really was a Dr Condom at the court of the merry monarch, who supplied the King with prophylactic sheaths made from sheep's intestine.[1] My own feeling is that Charles had been sated to the gills with his compulsive womanizing, and this mental and physical satiety impaired his performance. This certainly explains the appeal of the chubby and epicene Louise; there were no erotic demands from that quarter. As for Nell, she had to work hard to enjoy the King's body, at least if Rochester is to be believed. Here are some lines from towards the end of his poem 'A Satyr on Charles II', written in January 1674:

To Carwell, the most dear of all his dears,
The best relief of his declining years,
Oft he bewails his fortune, and her fate:
To love so well, and be beloved so late.
For though in her he settles well his tarse,
Yet his dull, graceless ballocks hang an arse.
This you'd believe, had I but time to tell ye
The pain it costs to poor, laborious Nelly,
Whilst she employs hands, fingers, mouth, and thighs,
Ere she can raise the member she enjoys.

Given that Barbara's first son by Charles, born in 1662, was the only one he acknowledged as his without appalling duress, it seems likely that Nell was the only mistress of the King's to provide him with more than one son. The name James, however, as so often in the Stuart family, proved unlucky and Nell's second son was not destined to live out his childhood. Born once Nell was comfortably established at 79 Pall Mall, James turned out to be a less feisty and more accommodating lad than his brother Charles, as if his mother's new-found security told favourably upon his disposition. As a result of this, and maybe too because of a premonition that she would not enjoy him for long, little Jimmy certainly usurped first place in Nell's affections. Like young Master Charles, the latest addition to the royal Stuart family had to wait a good many years before he received a surname. For now he was simply 'Master James'.

Nell had two spheres of power, her home at 79 Pall Mall and the court – usually at Whitehall, but wherever it happened to be. In the first Nell was able to create her own, very individual salon, where statesmen and ambassadors rubbed shoulders with artists, writers, actors and fops; and although old Madam Gwyn was usually too drunk to be presentable by late evening, no attempt was made to exclude her from the festivities. Nell did not allow political calculations to determine her choice of guests, indeed she didn't make political calculations; she simply invited those she liked or found interesting in some way. It was this very neutrality that proved useful to Charles, for 79 Pall Mall was a place where political opponents could be observed 'off guard' and wound into the King's confidence. Here, in a sense, Nell Gwyn continued the social experiment she had begun on stage by creating a melting pot in which many of the old taboos and prejudices turned to vapour. Her friends, however meanly bred, were worthy to rub shoulders with the King of England. Without knowing it, she was recreating the sort of social gathering that Charles had so relished in the bohemian days of his exile.

Always the actress, she made sure there were skits on political figures and events of the moment, as well as musicians and singers. On one occasion, after a concert at which the young actor Henry Bowman had sung for the guests, the King was unreserved in his praise of both the music and its interpreters. Nell, who knew the life of the struggling artist and always looked for opportunities to put money in the purses of aspiring performers, was quick to seize the moment. 'Then sir,' quoth she, turning to Charles with a hint of mischief in her eye, 'to show that you do not speak like a courtier, I hope you will make the performers a handsome present.' The King, having fidgeted in his pockets, was forced to admit that he had no money about his person. To cover his embarrassment he turned to his brother James for assistance. But the Duke of York was no better off. Nell, in a rerun of the apocryphal tavern supper of April 1668, took the King by the hand as if presenting him to the assembled guests and, mimicking his rather grave manner of expression, cried, ''Od's fish! what company am I got into?'[2] She seems to have been the only person who got away with teasing the King in public.

It was certainly unusual at that time for a monarch to attend private parties, as is made clear by Cosmo III, Grand Duke of Tuscany, who on his visit to London in the summer of 1669 was reluctant to accept invitations to parties at the houses of English noblemen until prompted to do so by the example of the King. The Grand Duke's secretary, Magalotti, recorded that Charles and James were 'frequently seen in the private houses of gentlemen at dinner and supper, divesting themselves, for the sake of recreation, of that reservedness which is indispensably observed at most other courts, where it is by no means permitted to attend similar entertainments'.[3] (Charles dined in state at Whitehall for the midday meal, where he could be viewed from a gallery by the public. It was only in the evenings that he had a choice of venue.) Louise was certainly a stickler for the stricter, continental etiquette and did her best to ensure that Charles dined at her Whitehall apartments as frequently as possible. But being a man of restless curiosity, who read people as others read books, Charles preferred the sort of private entertainment where he was able to circulate freely among the guests in a relaxed fashion. And at 79 Pall Mall, it being his mistress's house, he could make himself at home and take upon himself the role of host, which meant that there was less likelihood of strained courtesy or conflicts of rank. With the King beneath her battlements, so to speak, Nell could give herself up to the delicious fantasy that they were man and wife.

Nell held both soirées and supper parties (dinner parties were at midday), the only real difference being that there was no sit-down meal at the former, therefore people arrived later having already eaten their evening meal. Food was of course served, but not in such great quantities as on the latter occasions, when there were many fewer guests. Whereas sixteen might be invited to a supper party, twice that number would appear for one of her soirées. With the King present, a degree of formality was unavoidable, since he would come with his taster and footmen, who would be required to serve His Majesty on one knee. Whether he dispensed with this ritual at Nelly's more intimate supper parties is not known; but this King, having helped himself to the rudest fare from hedgerows and in sodden woods, was not one to stand on ceremony if he could help it.

Nell would have served nine or ten courses – more accurately, dishes – all placed on the table at once and from which people helped themselves. (Pepys proudly lists all the dishes on the table at one of his dinner parties: 'We had a fricasée of rabbit and chickens, a leg of mutton boiled, three carps on a dish, a great dish of a side of lamb, a dish of roasted pigeons, a dish of four lobsters, three tarts, a lamprey pie, a dish of anchovies . . .' Nine in all.) Naturally, this could make for a very crowded table. Nell had a dinner service of solid silver embossed with the initials 'E.G.', which shone splendidly in the candlelight, and a large silver bowl filled with rose water, in which guests could dip their napkins when minded to clean hands, face or teeth. The room was decorated with baskets of fruit and flowers. High above the table, like a huge diamond, hung a magnificent rock-crystal chandelier with lighted tapers.

A typical soirée at 79 Pall Mall would begin with people sitting at tables or standing in groups around the room, talking and listening to the musicians playing light music in a corner of the salon. Some played fashionable card games such as hazard, quadrille, ombre and basset, usually for considerable sums, while others stood around watching, as much to ensure fair play as for enjoyment of the game itself. (Cheating was considered an art and was by no means discouraged in the manuals of the time.) Wine, decanted from barrels into special jugs, would be served in beautifully wrought glasses. A number of dishes would be laid out in the dining room, rather like a buffet, so that people could wander in when they felt hungry and either sit down at the main table or make use of one of the small, movable ones that had recently come into fashion. Once everyone had arrived and the party was in full swing, the guests might be called to order for a special musical performance or a skit or two, or there might be a game of crambo or forfeits, both popular among gallant society for the opportunities they gave for displays of wit.

On a summer's evening the doors to the garden would be open and the garden itself lit with torches and candles. There would be music and dancing in the open air and maybe an acrobat or two. Some hostesses did their best to secure the latest daredevil act in town. Lady Sunderland, for instance, was keen on conjurors, showmen and fire-eaters. In March 1676 at one of her soirées, Evelyn saw 'a fellow swallow a knife, and divers great pebble stones, which would make a plaine rattling one against another'. As evening turned into night, the games tended to become rowdier and more physical. 'Hoodman Blind' (i.e., 'Blind man's buff'), 'Hot cockles' and 'Hunt the slipper' were all favourites of the time. 'Hot cockles' was a game of French origin in which one player knelt down with his face in the lap of another while stretching one of his hands full length behind him. This hand would be struck by each of the other players in turn, either softly or with force, and the recipient would have to guess the name of his assailant. Another, more riotous pastime was the Restoration equivalent of pillow fighting. Pepys witnessed it while a guest at Lord Sandwich's Berkshire estate of Cranbourne: 'anon to supper, and then my Lord going away to write, the young gentlemen to flinging of cushions, and other mad sports . . .'

Nell's parties often ended up in St James's Park in the wee hours, for she and her guests had but to slip through a slim-gated arch in her garden and they were soon among the moonlit groves and meadows of that rural retreat in the heart of London. And what a picture it must have been to see barefooted Nell, with the daintiest feet in England, skipping like Syrinx across the silver sward, with the King in hot pursuit. Or if they were feeling less adventurous, they could hop over into the Palace gardens, for as Rochester reminds us in his poem 'A Ramble in St. James's Park', the park at night often became the haunt of insalubrious characters:

> Each imitative branch does twine
> In some loved fold of Aretine,
> And nightly now beneath their shade
> Are buggeries, rapes, and incests made.
> Unto this all-sin-sheltering grove
> Whores of the bulk and the alcove,
> Great ladies, chambermaids, and drudges,
> The ragpicker, and heiress trudges.
> Carmen, divines, great lords, and tailors,
> Prentices, poets, pimps, and jailers,
> Footmen, fine fops do here arrive,
> And here promiscuously they swive.

Back at the house Nell would give her guests another light meal and a warm alcoholic drink, such as a sack posset (eggs, wine and spices scalded with sugared cream) to see them on their way. If Charles could be persuaded to stay the night, she doubtless led him upstairs to the nursery to see their sleeping sons before taking him off to her great silver bed, which was the talk of London. There, in the comfort of their shared privacy, they could mull over the satisfaction of a successful evening at which they had acted as host and hostess, and laugh over the follies of their guests. Charles, too, was wont to seek out Nell's opinion of this fellow or that, for he valued her judgement of people.

As can be seen from her surviving household accounts,[4] Nell provided her guests with a more than adequate table, no doubt supplied in part from the market in Pall Mall Fields. Her accounts show an impressive variety of foods. Apart from the usual run of domestic fowl, which in Nell's case included plentiful supplies of pullets (with their eggs) and capons, she kept her three poulterers – Will Scott, John Jones and Mary Hack – busy with orders for pigeon, partridge, plover, woodcock, duck, duckling, swan, goose, snipe, lapwing and lark. Larks seem to have been a particular favourite of Nell's and could be had for one and a half shillings the dozen. There is even an order for 'cockes combes' at sixpence. They also provided her with rabbit and hare. Swan was an especial and rare delicacy, being a royal bird, and equally dear: the swan pie that appears on her bill for 28 February 1676 cost £1 5s 4d, the equivalent of £100 in today's money. Having cried herrings as a girl, Nell continued to support the fishmongers when she became a lady of means: there are frequent bills for herring, red herring, salt fish, anchovies, smelts, whiting, salmon, pike, flounder, gudgeon, shrimp and oysters (two and a half shillings for 'a barrill'). Nell didn't have a particular fish-monger, relying on her general supplier of goods, one Mary Smith, to pick and choose on her behalf.

Inevitably at a time when meat was the staple diet, the bills of Nell's butcher, Will Tompson, loom large. Bacon, pork, veal, lamb, mutton and beef all appear and in vast quantities. On one bill there is an item for fifteen stone of beef! (The King, we're told, was especially partial to mutton, but there may have been a confusion of meaning here, for 'mutton' was also the slang for 'prostitute'. Rochester no doubt had the latter meaning in mind when he referred to Charles as 'our mutton-eating king'.) More exotic viands in Nell's accounts included tripe, neat's foot, cow's udder, cow's heels, hog's foot, tongue, sweetbreads, tripe, lamb's testicles, black pudding, hogs' pudding and marrow pudding. For one party on 17 February 1677 she ordered in '3 stone of beef, a legg of beef, a shoulder of veal, [and] a dish of lamb, stones & sweet breads'.

Comparing the range and delicacy of French cuisine with the coarseness of the English (a favourite theme), Count Magalotti wrote, 'Nevertheless, in [Paris], though the inhabitants are more numerous, the consumption of butchers' meat is much greater in London, either because there are no abstinence-days, or in consequence of their voracity, the English eating more meat than any thing else; and on this account, there are slaughtered there, every day, besides other animals three thousand oxen, with large joints of which their tables are covered.' Having dined at the Portuguese Embassy in London, Evelyn dismissed the dishes as 'trifling, hash'd and condited after their way, not at all fit for an English stomach, which is for solid meate'. What English tables lacked in quality, they made up for in quantity; nor were matters likely to improve in Magalotti's view so long as English noblemen failed to employ French chefs. When the King told de Grammont that he was served upon the knee at dinner, an ancient custom of the English court, the Frenchman replied mischievously, 'Is that so, sire? I thought it was by way of apology for giving you such a bad dinner!'

Of course, no dinner could be prepared or rooms heated without large quantities of fuel. A bill from Francis Smith dated 10 September to 5 November 1675 lists '1 Tun of Scotch Coale' at £1 12s 0d, '2000 of Billetts [thick pieces of firewood]' at fifteen shillings the thousand, and '1/2 1000 of Oake Billetts' at nine shillings. A further bill dated 24 January to 17 February provides for two tons of 'Grete Coales' at £3 4s 0d and '5000 of Beech Bill[ets]' at £3 15s 0d. We know from the six-monthly hearth duty of seventeen shillings that she paid in April 1675 that there were seventeen hearths at 79 Pall Mall. The chimney sweep charged a shilling a chimney. Fires were also a source of light. In addition, candles had to be bought in bulk. In the third quarter of 1675 William Miller provided Nell with 42 dozen candles at £10 12s 6d, roughly £800 in today's money. These were supplemented by 'a doz wax lights' of superior quality from Henry Preedy at £1 3s 0d, and in the first quarter of the following year Thomas King, wax chandler, supplied her with fifty-seven 'wax flambres' [flambeaux] at £5 4s 6d, over seven pounds each in today's money. Flambeaux were flaming torches comprising several thick waxed wicks.

If the English ate a deal of meat, they washed it down with great quantities of alcohol. Magalotti was impressed by the different kinds of beer (among which he includes ale and cider), describing the bottled ones as 'exquisite'. One kind of beer, he tells us, was 'made with the body of a capon, which is left to grow putrid along with the malt'. For those preferring wine, the Italian is full of praise for the imported wines available in London, and singles out 'the clarets of Provence and

Languedoc, those of the Rhine, of Candia, of Naples, and of Florence, of which there is an abundant supply at the tables of the English nobility'. Malmsey, a strong sweet wine from the Greek islands, was also popular among the upper crust, but expensive, as was Sillery wine, the still champagne produced on the estate of the Marquis de Sillery. Dearest and most prestigious of all was real champagne, which was first brought into England by the French exile Saint-Evremond in 1661. There were English wines too, from fruit trees and flowers as well as vines. Nell's accounts show orders for claret, sack (i.e., *sec*, dry white wine), canary (sweet white wine), ale and of course brandy, which was her mother's favourite tipple. No doubt the cellars at 79 Pall Mall were kept well stocked, as several barrels could be drained in the course of a boisterous evening. Nell's order for a single party on 5 November 1675 was as follows:

To The Right Honn: Madam Gwinn
ffor 1 doz bott Canarey 1–4–0
ffor 2 doz bott wtt [white] wine 1–4–0
ffor 9 gall Clarrett for ye pint bott 1–16–0
ffor 3 gall Clar: 0–12–0
paid ye porter 0–1–6

The bill comes to £4 17s 6d, roughly £390 in today's money, and provides for the equivalent of a hundred bottles of wine. Not bad for an evening's drinking for thirty-odd people! Glass bottles had now replaced their older stone brethren, and wads of oiled hemp were supplanted by corks as we know them today. Nell had cut–glass goblets in which to serve her wine, which may well have come from her friend the Duke of Buckingham's glassworks in Lambeth, whose products Evelyn declared superior to the Venetian.

There are no orders for cider, which is a comfort to those who reject Hereford as her birthplace. Her wine merchant was one James Prouis, probably one of a growing number of naturalized Frenchmen in the English capital. Ale, made from malted grain and water, and beer (with hops added) were drunk throughout the day, for the water was unsafe. Even children drank weak beer, known as 'small beer', with no obvious ill effects. At dinner parties frequent toasts were called, as the surest means of getting the stuff down quickly, copiously and convivially. Nell's accounts also show orders for tea – a rare commodity at twenty-eight shillings (£110) a pound – and coffee, but these were drunk during the day rather than after supper.

Vegetables were certainly eaten, though still rather despised as poor man's food. Only an enlightened few recognized their exceptional nutritional value and health-giving properties. John Evelyn, who was among the few, wrote *A Discourse of Sallets*, in which he cautions against using garlic in salads, 'for sure 'tis not for a ladies palate, nor for those who court them'. Nell clearly valued vegetables, and makes regular orders for onions, carrots, turnips, squash, potatoes, mushrooms, capers, sallet, and 'herbs and roots'. She also uses barley, rice and oatmeal, while named herbs and spices include sage, chamomile flowers, cinnamon, saffron, mace, cloves and mustard. Although she ordered in breads, cheesecakes, tarts, 'biskits' and custards, many of the desserts she served would have been prepared by her own cook. Fruit was served to clear the palate after the main courses and came with a large selection of sweetmeats and nuts. These were often enjoyed in a separate room, where they could be arranged with considerable skill and splendour, for the confectioner's art (imported from France) was elaborate and full of conceits. Citron and lemon pills were also available to sweeten the breath. Of all the fruits she orders – apples, oranges, lemons, prunes, blue figs, cherries, pears, currants, raisins, gooseberries and grapes – oranges appear most frequently on the lists. One imagines that they had become something of a lucky charm for Nell.

The colour orange has long been recognized as a symbol of ambition, and the fruit itself an emblem of immortality. It can also symbolize pride and luxury, and there's little doubt that Nell took great pride and delight in her luxurious surroundings. Given her background, it would be strange if she hadn't. Although her instinct was to make light of such matters, she was ambitious to own beautiful things and to be seen as beautiful and accomplished. Contemporary comment acknowledges her stylish and original taste both in the way she dressed and in the furnishing and decoration of her house, and she herself delighted in having her things flourished with the initials 'E.G.', be it her silver tableware, her napkins or even her window panes. Her accounts throughout the 1670s reveal frequent orders placed with painters and decorators, silversmiths, drapers, portrait and still-life artists, as well as dressmakers, tailors, haberdashers and hair-dressers. Considerable expenditure was also laid out on a coach and four and a sedan chair, not to mention the bills from harness-makers, farriers and those that supplied fodder for the horses (whose hay in those days was all but buttered). Although she had 'inherited' a good deal of furniture from the previous occupant, Lord Scarsdale, in the form of chairs, chests of drawers, cabinets, couches and bookcases, Nell was quick to stamp her own mark on the house. She commissioned portraits and still lifes, had curtains and drapes made and kept the silversmiths busy with fine objects and decorative work.

Her most magnificent possession, and one which became the talk of the town, was an ornate four-poster silver bedstead fashioned by John Coques, a master silversmith who lived on the north side of Pall Mall and numbered the royal family among his clients. Nell herself designed the bed. She seems to have used the King's bed at Whitehall as a model, with its silver eagles, crowns, and cherubs, but added many humorous touches of her own. It was made as a sort of shrine to celebrate her love for the King, but there was nothing solemn about it. Reading between the lines, the bed told the story of her bold triumph in the King's affections. The two main figures were Charles and Nell, who it seems were presented as mythical figures or characters from literature, possibly Oroonoko and Imoinda, as they were accompanied by 'ye slaves'. Their children no doubt appeared in the faces of the cherubs. Then there were cleverly wrought jibes at the other principal mistresses. Firstly there was the figure of 'iacob halle [Jacob Hall] dansing upon ye robbe [rope] of Weyer Work', in other words Barbara's acrobatic lover dancing on a silver wire. Given that her relationship with Hall marked the end of her physical relationship with the King, the message is clear: as Barbara descended the social scale, putting herself beyond the King's embraces, so Nell rose up to take her place.

There was also a silver Louise depicted 'lying in a grave with an unnamed eastern potentate',[5] which sounds like the ending to one of Dryden's heroic dramas. It was actually more likely to have been a snide reference to Louise's habit of going into mourning each time some obscure monarch died, for which Nell teased her mercilessly.

Louise was also known to have a penchant for African princes, a weakness that Nell no doubt hoped would bury her prospects of a lasting relationship with Charles. And looking down serenely from the crown of the bedstead upon this farcical tale of love was the King's head, weighing 197.5 ounces (as much as a fully grown cat). The total cost of the bed, together with one or two other small objects on the same bill, was £1,135, almost £100,000 in today's money. Her bill was delivered at the end of 1674, and was headed, 'Worck done for ye right Hon'ble Madame Guinne: John Cooqus Silversmyth his bill'. It was indicative of her newfound status that Coques felt he must give her some sort of honorific.

A typically Baroque mixture of the exalted and the grotesque, Nell's silver bed was both tribute and monument to her love for the King and speaks volumes both about her desire to mythologize that love and her extraordinary sense of humour. Silver, Nell's favourite metal, was allied to the moon and symbolized both enchantment and madness. The bed was certainly a bower of charms, designed to restore the King's waning virility and maybe even conjure those spirits that might seal Nell's dreams of becoming his wife. But they were dangerous dreams that could lead to the bitterness of illusion. Some might say that the bed itself was an act of egregious folly, for its extravagance must have stretched Nell's income to breaking point. She also had a silver warming pan made for winter nights, on which were engraved the words 'Fear God, serve the King'.

There is another record of an attempt by Nell to immortalize her relationship with the King. A receipt dated 11 November 1675 reads, 'Received then of Tho: Growndes by Order of Madam Gwin the sum of one hundred & thirty pounds in part for a silver fframe for a Glass weighing 600. ounces. I say recd in part − − − − − by me X X' [the signature is illegible]. This is the frame for her famous looking glass, which was elaborately embroidered using coloured glass beads and wax as well as gold and silver thread to create figures in high relief. It may well have been worked by Nell herself. Charles stands at the top of the mirror in his robes of state, Nell at the bottom in her court dress. Then again Charles is on the right-hand panel in his hunting dress opposite Nell on the left, who looks very pretty in her negligee. Beneath the King sits a lion, while Nell has a leopard for her dæmon.

Other panels include a sphinx, a winged serpent, roses and what look like phoenixes, one on each side, signifying immortality.[6]

Other silver items for which we have records include a sugar box, a pepper box, a mustard pot, a pair of cruets in a silver stand, two silver bottles, candlesticks, cups, fruit knives, hampers (i.e., cases for goblets), andirons and a teapot. All appear to have been made, repaired and cleaned by John Coques and his staff. The teapot is listed in the catalogue of chattels sold in Brussels in 1786 by the 3rd Duke of St Albans, Nell's profligate great-grandson. Also on one of his bills Coques lists 'ye making of a greatte ciffer for ye charette painter', a reference to the silver badges bearing her initials that were fitted to her chariot or carriage. Only one gold item is recorded: Coques charges 2s 6d for 'ye mending of ye goold hower glass'. Nell's time on earth may have been short, but it was golden.

Nell was determined to make a masterpiece of her bedchamber. In addition to the silver bed, she had sky-blue satin curtains made for the windows, which were reglazed with the best Normandy glass; and two wainscot seats were installed 'with compass ends' carved with her initials and the King's. It was all about creating a luxurious, yet homely love nest to tempt the King to spend his nights with her. Her dressing table was covered with damask silk and flanked by two life-sized black boys carved in ebony that served as candelabra, while her fireplace was embellished with stately silver andirons. Her upholsterers (the interior decorators of the day) were Edward and Anne Traherne, and the total refurbishment, including the bed, cost our taffeta punk in the region of £1,700, a cool £130,000 in today's money.

Nell also spent money on adorning herself and clearly took great delight in making a splash. Now that her credit had the name of a king to back it, shopping for fine fabrics at the New Exchange was a carefree pleasure. Situated in the Strand, it contained 'two long and double galleries, one above the other, in which are distributed, in several rows, great numbers of very rich shops of drapers and mercers, filled with goods of every kind, and with manufactures of the most beautiful description'. The shops were run for the most part by stylishly dressed women, who attracted custom as much by their arch looks as by the wares they displayed. The Exchange was also a favourite place for assignations among the gallants. Nell's bills show that she bought a dazzling array of fabrics from a number of different drapers, mercers and haberdashers: yards of scotch cloth, sheeting, towelling, holland, white thread damask, white silk damask, green satin, filemot ducape, white paragon (a type of fine cloth of Angora goat hair), gold and silver silk, pink ribbon and gold, green, silver and black lace. George Bird, William Wayte, Samuel Howard, Charles Rise and Sara Meare supplied her materials, while Humphrey Dutton and George Hookett made up her dresses and hose, as well as her gowns. A typical bill from Dutton, dated January 1674, reads,

A bill for the wright honored Lady gwine
ffor silke & making 2 night gounds 0—5—0
ffor making 2 coates Last [laced] 1—4—0
ffor silke & ribon for 2 pettecoates 0—2—6
ffor making 2 pettecoats 0—1—0
ffor making a sattin coate Last 0—12—0
ffor making 2 nightgounds 0—5—0
ffor making a pinke & white Lutestring coate 0—12—0
ffor making a Last frock 0—8—0
ffor making a pinke & white sasenit [sarsenet] coate 0—12—0
ffor making a Last frocke 0—8—0
ffor making making [sic] 2 sattin coates Last 1—4—0

This totals £5 6s 0d, approximately £410 in today's money.

Ladies' skirts were open in front or looped to reveal the underskirts or petticoats, and we know from de Courtin's reports to the French Foreign Minister that Nell was particularly proud of her sumptuous petticoats. She was also keen on red satin nightgowns, pearl-coloured hose, vivid silk stoles and scarves, sarsenet hoods and scented gloves. And like many ladies of the time, she favoured Indian gowns for casual morning wear; there was nothing like a full-length silk negligee for pottering around the house in. Items on an October 1675 bill from George Hookett include 'making up a pare of hoses & 12 silke poynts', '12 ounses & half & half quartr of Crimson fring', and '12 silk poynts ingrayne [i.e., dyed in grain]'. We know that Nell liked to dress in men's clothes, as did the Queen, who had the same brisk figure. Forneron writes that Nell 'had such success on the stage in *Florimel*, and other masculine characters, that men's clothes, which in the seventeenth century were bright in colour and very dressy, became the rage among the ladies at Whitehall.' Ladies in hose could show off their legs and be more active generally.

How stylish she was we don't know. Gilbert Burnet, who was catty towards all Charles's mistresses, wrote that after her elevation to royal mistress she continued to 'hang on' her clothes with the same slovenly negligence as before. But it is more likely that the good bishop was confusing negligence and panache. As someone who delighted in being herself, Nell had the confidence to wear anything, however unconventional. Hers was not a laborious, heavily pasted beauty, but nimble, unaffected, elfin. Whatever she wore she made her own, and people noticed her. 'Some of your news I heard,' wrote Ursula Wolryche to her daughter Lady Wrottesley, 'as concerning Nell Gwine. They say there is the greatest gallantry maybe in towne; silver and gould lace all over peticotes and the bodies of their gounes; but sleeves and skirts blake [black]; abundance of curles very small on their heads, and very fine their heads dressed.' Nell certainly went in for the mass of small curls, but other portraits show her with her hair straight down over her shoulders or in a topknot on the crown of the head. It helped, of course, when the hair was thick and plentiful. Hairdressing was clearly expensive, as attested by this curious bill dated 14 March 1676:

for My Lady Goin [i.e., Gwyn] Bill
for two Lesse quaisfe 03:10:00
for tw: Coronettes 02:10:00
for a quaisfe 01:15:00
for two Coronettes 01:10:00
Some 09:05:00
ffor two great primers
and a Coife 03:10:00
In all 12:15:00

The total of £12 15s 0d is the best part of £1,000 in today's money, but Nell's steward clearly demanded a discount of one pound, because the final amount paid is given as £11 15s 0d. What these strange head-dressings are is anyone's guess; the writing on the receipt is certainly very clear.

In a number of her portraits Nell can be seen wearing pearls round her neck and, most attractively, in her hair. On 7 December 1682 she paid the fantastic sum of £4,520 to the executors of Prince Rupert's estate for the pearl necklace that he had given his mistress Margaret Hughes.[7] This could be the necklace Nell is wearing in the portrait by Verelst, completed in the early 1680s. Other pieces of jewellery, gifts from Charles to Nell, were in the ownership of the Dukes of St Albans until very recently. They included a cushion-shaped diamond cluster ring with a fluted gold sunburst back, a pavé-set diamond hairpin and a blue enamel and pearl watch set with rose diamonds. The watch was on a gold chain with two cameo seals, a polished carnelian heart and a small locket with a miniature of Charles I. The heart, a simple love token, is particularly affecting. At the time of her death she wore a gold mourning ring containing a miniature of Charles under crystal and bearing the inscription 'C:II:R Feb:6 1684' [old-style date]. Nell also hired jewellery for special occasions, as the following receipt attests: 'March 19th 1675 rec'd then of Madam Gwin at ye hands of Thomas Growndes ye sum of five poundes for ye use of a parcell of jewells wch I formerly lent to her, and do hereby acknowledge yt I have rec'd them all back againe, I say rec'd. By me John Marlowe.'

As for cosmetics, these were obtained from the apothecary. Blessed with a clear, rosy complexion, Nell did not require the many vicious compounds in use to camouflage blemishes or heighten the colour of the skin. Freckles, which were considered a defect, could apparently be removed by an ointment made from cowslips. She did, however, use a variety of washes, lotions and scents to freshen and perfume her skin, as well as 'pomatum' (pomade) for the hair. Orders have survived for Queen of Hungary's water (spirit of rosemary), rose water, orange flower water, mint water, oils of lilies, roses and nutmeg and other 'waters for the face'. These waters were sometimes a substitute for washing and could be applied to a linen cloth for rubbing down the whole body. Nell did not splash out for the more exotic waters mentioned by Evelyn's wife in her *Mundus Muliebris*, such as puppydog water, concocted from wine and roast puppy! More seriously, the consequences of over-painting could sometimes be fatal. Nell's friend Henry Savile, writing to his brother Lord Halifax in April 1686, gave him the news that 'My Lady Henrietta Wentworth [Monmouth's mistress] is dead, having sacrificed her life to her beauty, by painting so beyond measure that the mercury got into her nerves and killed her'.

Nell was famous for the prettiest feet and ankles in the kingdom and, judging from the list of fabulous shoes and slippers that she ordered in May 1674, she liked to show them off. The bill, which proves that Nell's fairy godmother was no slouch, is worth presenting in full:

Mad: Guin her Bill

Your Laste Bill I delivered you came to ye sume 07:00:00
1 paire of pinck colloured Satin Slipers with Silver and Gold Lace
    very rich 01:00:00
1 paire of Sky Colloured Satin ribin shooes with gold 01:00:00
1 paire of Sky Colloured Satin ribin with gold & sil. 00:18:00
1 paire of Green Lace Shooes Mr: Charls 00:04:00
1 paire of Shooes and Slips your Sister 00:06:00
1 paire of pinck Satin ribin with Silver Lace 00:18:00
1 paire of Sky Colloured Satin Slipers 00:18:00
1 paire of Sky Coll: Satin ribin shooes wth Gold Lace
and a paire of velvet [?] very rich 01:09:00
2 paire of pinck Coll: Laced Shooes for ye Children 00:09:00
1 paire green Satin ribin Shooes wth Gold Lace 00:18:00
1 paire of Scarlet Satin ribin Shooes very richly Laced 01:10:00
1 paire of Green Satin Shooes w:th Gold and Silver Chaine and
    Laced very rich 02:00:00

The bill, including the seven pounds from her previous order, came to £18 4s 0d, roughly equivalent to £1,400 today.

Walking abroad in such dainty footwear was not advisable, nor would Nell have dreamt of it. She now had a splendid carriage to carry her about the capital, which like most fashion accessories in Restoration London was of French design. Luxuriously upholstered inside, painted and japanned on the outside with her 'cipher' blazoned in silver and her initials cut into the windows with a diamond, it was drawn by four horses. She also displayed a coat of arms, designed for her by some obliging herald at the College of Arms. It was based on the shield of the Gwyns of Llansanor and shows a blue lion on a field of silver and gold (per pale argent and or a lion azure rampant and guardant). She also had a 'chariot'; these were lighter and more elegant than coaches and sometimes known as 'flying chariots', excellent for skimming along the Mall of a spring morning. A receipt dated 26 April 1675 acknowledges payment of ten pounds to Nathaniel Baker towards 'the painting & gilding of a Chariot' for Madam Ellen Gwin.

Like all the gallants and ladies of quality, she would drive round 'the Ring' at Hyde Park to show off her coach in person. This was one of the inevitable social rituals of the season lasting from spring to autumn. The King and Queen, as well as the Duke and Duchess of York, all indulged. It was the custom for ladies and gentlemen to greet members of the royal family once only as they circled the Ring; to do it more frequently was considered poor form. Also an edict of 1661 forbade the excessive gilding of coaches and chariots, ostensibly to save gold, but it was universally ignored. This was, after all, an age of gaudy display. To avoid crowding and confusion, footmen and other servants were not allowed in, but had to wait at the gates of the park for their masters. Pepys went there one day with Mr Povy, who was treasurer to the Duke of York's household. It was 19 March and the first day of 'the tour', as driving round the Ring was known. Pepys notes that there were 'many brave ladies; among others, Castlemayne [i.e., Barbara] lay impudently upon her back in her coach asleep, with her mouth open'.

Poor roads could subject the carriage to a good deal of wear and tear, especially if Evelyn was right in his claim that the English drove so fast that 'all coaches in London seem to be driving for midwives'. Certainly Nell's coachmaker, Edmund Aubrey, was frequently called upon to make repairs and carry out servicing work. One such service in July 1675 cost Nell £3 4s 0d, getting on for £250 in today's money. Service work was also carried out by the harness maker Richard Lloyd. In his quarterly bill for July–September 1675, there is an entry 'for oyleing and cleansing ye coach & 6 harness and bridles', which cost nine shillings. He also mended the harness, reins and collar, cleaned the gilt harness, fastened straps to the coach box seat and fitted brass buckles, a brass ring and leather thongs to the harness. The gilding and paintwork was seen to by Nathaniel Baker, the same man who had decorated her bedroom. Keeping and feeding the horses was also an expensive business, requiring grooms and stabling and tons of hay, straw, oats and beans. We have a bill submitted by Nell's farrier, John Willes, who probably doubled up as a vet, in September 1675 'for a quarters worke Done to 7 horses', which includes an item for horse-shoes, 'drinkes' (medicines?) and dressing for the animals' heels. His bill comes to £5 2s 10d, almost £400 today.

Nell had a couple of coachmen, too. Thomas Johnson and John Cooke, who seem to have alternated between the posts of coachman and footman. One of them was involved in a notorious altercation, recounted in many versions over the centuries. This version is from Henry Fielding's novel *Tom Jones* (1749):

> The famous Nell Gwyn, stepping one day, from a house where she had made a short visit, into her coach, saw a great mob assembled, and her footman all bloody and dirty. The fellow, being asked by his mistress the reason of his being in that condition, answered, 'I have been fighting, madam, with an impudent rascal who called your ladyship a whore.' 'You blockhead,' replied Mrs. Gwyn, 'at this rate you must fight every day of your life. Why, you fool, all the world knows it.' 'Do they?' cried the fellow in a muttering voice, after he had shut the coach-door; 'they shan't call me a whore's footman for all that.'

The anecdote speaks colourfully of Nell's artless approach to her newfound wealth and status. Though skilful at playing the part, she refused to put on airs. She may have been dressed in the finest silks, but she still swore like a trooper.

She also had an elegant sedan chair made with all the trimmings, as attested by a bill presented to her on 5 March 1674. Items include 'iron worke' on the body of the chair, 'the best neats leather ffor the outside', 'workemanshipe trimming the chair inside & outside', '1300 of nailes ffor shankes [i.e. shafts] guilt with water gold', '1000 ingraven nailes white ffor inside edges', '5 glasses the best sorte 24 inches longe dark glasse' [this item for smoked glass is the most expensive of the lot at thirteen pounds – £1,000 in today's money], 'pinns for the windowes', 'curtaine rodes', 'guilt staples for the inside & tassells', 'guilt nailes ffor to sett one the silver ropes', 'leathers and case ffor the seate', 'canvisse to put under the leather' and more gilding work for the irons and both sides of the windows. The total came to £38 7s 6d, approximately £3,000. The sedan chair, which required two footmen to carry it, was named after the French town of Sedan on the Meuse, where it was first seen in use by an English traveller and was ideal for short trips about town. The first person to use them in England was the 1st Duke of Buckingham, King James's favourite, in 1623. The spectacle caused an uproar, with Buckingham being accused of 'degrading Englishmen into slaves and beasts of burden'. It was a leisurely form of transport (walking pace), but excellent for creating an impression. One can imagine the people stopping to cheer and wave as Nell was borne past them at eye level in her best gown.

Nell was generous with the use of her sedan, often lending it to friends; she also hired other chairs both for herself and for others, as the chairmen's bills in her surviving accounts testify, most of them submitted by chairman William Callow. In his entries Callow several times refers to Nell as 'yor Ladyship'. Such conspicuous wealth clearly excited a certain amount of deference in the lower orders.

Nell's least favourite means of transport was probably the river, and I have found only one entry in her accounts that marks her use of the Thames: 'for a waterman from Chell: [Chelsea]'. The trip, made in March 1677, cost one shilling. It was a dirty, noisy and often dangerous way to travel, especially for women. The stairs, bridges and landing stages were muddy, slippery and crowded, and you were at the mercy of the tides. Low tide could mean wading into or being carried over yards of Thames ooze. The watermen themselves were a rough and boisterous bunch and often took advantage of the riverside hubbub to ease their customers of money and jewels.

Nell hired coaches as well as sedans, not only when hers was out of commission, but when she wished to travel anonymously, for she was a huge star now, her relationship with the King and her former popularity in the theatre having cast a mantle of considerable glamour about her. Ordinary Londoners left flowers outside her door as a mark of their affection, and her appearances in the streets drew crowds of curious admirers. There must have been times when she craved a little privacy. She also sent coaches for her friends, and seems to have been most generous towards Lady Sandys and Maria Knight, the singer. She was always treating them to coaches to Whitehall and to the theatre. Indeed, Nell's travel accounts provide us with an interesting cross-section of her friends. Among the ladies are Maria Knight, Rose Cassels, Nell's sister, the King's seamstress Madame Younge, Barbara's nemesis Lady Harvey, Lady Lucy Sandys (one of the St James's set), Lady Greene (née Catherine Pegge), Lady Shannon (née Elizabeth Killigrew), Lady Southesk, Frances Jennings, whose sister Sarah became the wife of the 1st Duke of Marlborough, and Arabella Churchill.

Only one among them was an aristocrat by birth, and that was 'the innately dissipated and unrestrainable' Anne Southesk, who was the daughter of the Duke of Hamilton. No fewer than five, however, were or had been royal mistresses. Maria Knight had been a minor, rather fleeting mistress of the King, while both Lady Greene and Lady Shannon had borne him children before the Restoration: Shannon a son, Charles Fitzroy, in 1650 and Greene a son and daughter, Charles Fitzcharles in 1657 and Catherine Fitzcharles in 1658; Lady Southesk had been the Duke of York's mistress at the Restoration until her indignant husband returned from Scotland (according to Pepys she gave the Duke 'a clap [i.e. the pox] upon his first coming over'), while Arabella Churchill became the Duke's most enduring mistress, following him into exile in France and bearing him three children, all of whom became naturalized French subjects. She was the sister of Barbara's lover John Churchill, who later became Duke of Marlborough.

Clearly the spirit of the harem prevailed over any feelings of jealousy. The mistresses could discuss their experiences with the King and his brother, and in several cases lament their nebulous status as mothers of royal bastards. There is even an entry in Nell's accounts which reads 'for a chaire carring my lo: [i.e., Nell's son] from ye dutches of Portsmouth', which could suggest that there were periods of truce between Louise and Nell or that their rivalry was exaggerated for political reasons. The bill in question is dated 14 February 1677, only a couple of months after the boy was ennobled. Perhaps his title made the six-year-old Charles eligible for the honour. It may suggest that Nell was not one to bear a grudge and, if anything, was probably a little too ready to respond warmly to gestures of goodwill. Many of Nell's girlfriends were a good deal older than her and may have acted as mentors, helping her to navigate the treacherous waters of court preferment. Lady Shannon, for instance, had been born in 1622 and knew how to steer clear of trouble.

As for Nell's sister, Rose, she remained close to her sister and they enjoyed visiting friends together. Both she and Nell were as capable as anyone of courteous and proper behaviour in the salons of the wealthy and yet could provide welcome relief from the monotony of unrelenting formality with their salty repartee. Rose also did some sewing work for her younger sister and shopped for the materials herself, which included yards of Nell's favourite pink ribbon. On the bottom of one receipt, she wrote or had someone write, 'I have sent you the rest of the ribbon and lace that was left. I was in twenty shops looking for cheaper but could not [find any] for my life'. Nell, who could rely on the King's credit, was not in the habit of bargain hunting, so it was probably as well that she sent her thriftier sister every now and then. Rose also enjoyed shopping at the markets for groceries, and one item reads 'for apals [apples] mis Casels bought'.

Rose had married Captain John Cassels as her first husband, and in 1672 Nell had the King confer a grant of £100 per annum on the couple. Rose, who was childless herself, spent a good deal of time with her two young nephews and would take them out into St James's Park on summer afternoons to feed the ducks, one of their father's daily rituals. Captain Cassels was killed in Holland in the autumn of 1674 fighting Louis's Anglo-French war against the Dutch, and thus was, indirectly, a victim of the Treaty of Dover. Samuel Pepys made a yacht available to Nell so that Mr Philip Pigeare could be sent over to Dieppe to sort out the dead man's affairs and arrange for the return of the body. As a widow, Rose's pension was increased to £200 a year.

Nell liked to keep up with her old friends from the theatre and the bohemian community in general. One of her passions was singing, an art she had tentatively mastered at the playhouse, but which was perfected by her friendship with Maria Knight, who sometimes sang at Nell's supper parties, and made a tour of Italy not long after Nell moved into 79 Pall Mall. Evelyn was certain that her voice had 'the greatest reach of any English woman'. Nell and Maria enjoyed singing ballads together, and there is an order for song sheets among her household bills. Her accounts show that she sent coaches for the actors

Henry Harris and Joseph Haines to visit her. Harris was an actor with the Duke's Company, a witty man much admired by Pepys, who pronounced his performance of Henry V in Orrery's play of the same name 'incomparable'. Samuel even commissioned a portrait of him from John Hale, dressed as the victor of Agincourt. Harris was also a bon viveur, as a letter from Nell to Laurence Hyde in August 1678 attests: 'My lord of Dorscit [i.e., Buckhurst] apiers worse in thre munths, fo he drinkes aile with Shadwell & Mr Haris at the Dukes house all day long.' Haines, on the other hand, was a male version of Nell Gwyn. He sang and danced with gusto and excelled in parts requiring comic exaggeration. He was also a masterly performer of prologues and epilogues and an inveterate practical joker who often proved too wild even for his fellow actors. Charles Hart once cast him for a small and uncongenial part in *Catiline*, a play well known to be a showcase for Hart's own portentous tragic style. Aggrieved at this decision, Haines walked out of the wings in comic dress holding a pipe and pot, and sat himself down on a stool at the back of the stage, from where he made faces behind Hart's back. The audience roared with laughter, but Hart, famed for his deep concentration, ignored his tormentor and continued with his performance. After the final curtain, however, he went calmly backstage and fired the impertinent comedian on the spot. Both Harris and Haines were arrested for debt at different times in their careers.

Whether Nell invited these actors to her home to take part in skits before her guests or for purely social reasons, we don't know. The theatre, however, remained an important part of her social life, and she frequently paid for side-boxes, which she filled with friends, at both the Theatre Royal and the Duke's House. The King's Theatre had burnt down in January 1672, the fire having started below stage in the cubbyhole kept by Orange Moll for her stores of fruit and sweetmeats; when it was reopened to Wren's specifications in March 1674 Nell had use of the royal box. In a sense the fire of 1672 marked the end of Nell's theatrical era, as well as the end of the heroic drama. The death knell of the latter had been sounded the previous December with the production of Buckingham's comedy *The Rehearsal*, an hilarious satire of Dryden and the bombastic form of drama he had created. 'What a Devil is the Plot good for, but to bring in fine things?' cries Dryden's double, Bayes, when his captive audience flees at the noise and absurdity of it all.

There are many items in Nell's accounts that record her visits to the theatre, which were as frequent as two or three times a week. Sometimes she went with her sister, Rose, in which case the cost was eight shillings at the public theatre or ten shillings for two at Whitehall, but more often than not she took a party of four and sent a coach to take them there. There are bills too for 'maskes', which ladies often wore to the theatre, and for 'fruit at ye kings play house' (usually three shillings, which would buy you six oranges). In addition to contemporary comedy, Nell had a particular fondness for Shakespeare, who was by no means top billing in Restoration London, but then her first lover had been his great-nephew. Between September and December 1674 she saw *The Tempest* four times, *Macbeth* once and *Hamlet* once; then in June 1675 she attended a performance of *King Lear*. Indeed, as another of her biographers, Graham Hopkins, discovered, between September 1674 and June 1676 Nell attended the Duke's Theatre at Dorset Gardens no fewer than fifty-five times, taking in at least forty-two different productions, including six performances of Thomas Shadwell's opera *Psyche*.

It is not difficult to plumb the attractions of *The Tempest* for Nell Gwyn. The story of a magician-king marooned on an enchanted island with his teenage daughter must have corresponded nicely with her own fantasies of an exclusive relationship with Charles. In both her age and her dependence upon the King, Nell was very much in loco *filiae*, and in terms of *The Tempest* could be seen as a sort of spirit daughter of the King, a cross between Ariel and Miranda. When Prospero abjures his magic powers at the end of the play, he rejoins the human race. For Nell, watching intently from her box, it would have been easy to imagine Prospero as Charles, renouncing his kingly status to become the private man with whom she longed to unite.

Nell also took an interest in up-and-coming actresses and was called upon by the Earl of Rochester to help train Elizabeth Barry for the stage after the barrister's plain daughter had been rejected by the Duke's Company as hopelessly wooden. She later became the greatest actress of the age. And towards the end of 1674 the playwright Thomas Duffett dedicated his comedy *The Spanish Rogue* to Nell in the most flattering terms: 'You still are Mistriss of so much obliging Affability, so free from sullen Pride, and affected Stateliness, the usual attendants of extraordinary Felicity; not contented to be safe in the barren praise of doing no ill, but so readily and so frequently doing good, as if it were not your Nature, but your Business; that, next to your Beauty, these Virtues are the greatest Miracle of the Age.' It had been acted at the King's House in May 1673, with Nell's old friends in the cast.

Nell was invited to many parties attended by the King, even if her hosts didn't particularly care for her, as it was a way for them to ingratiate themselves with Charles. Lord Arlington was certainly no friend of Nell's, but one entry in her accounts for November 1675 reads, 'for 2 chareman of Sunday night at my Lord arlindons [Arlington's]', the cost being two shillings. Tantalizingly, many of the names entered are either illegible or botched, as William Callow and his partner would simply have heard the name, often imperfectly, and then done their best to spell it. The Duke of Buckingham, on the other hand, was a close friend and fellow buffoon and a frequent guest at 79 Pall Mall. One entry for 20 March 1677 reads 'for ye Duke of buckinghams foot man 10−0'. He must have performed some signal service for the equivalent of forty pounds. Another name that crops up, in 1678, is that of 'Mr. Bridges', who was presumably the George Bridges who married the widowed Countess of Shrewsbury and was known for his extravagant revels. Nell knew the Countess well through her former lover, the Duke of Buckingham, and would have relished the company of her new husband.

Relishing her new life altogether, Nell appears to have been quite undaunted by the responsibilities of running a large household. As the mistress of a house with no master, she was in something of an anomalous position and probably relied more heavily than was usual on her steward. She had a permanent staff of about fourteen and treated them as an extended family. In return, they served her with love and loyalty. At the bottom end of the scale were the pageboys, probably two in number, who ran errands both about the house and in town in return for board and lodging and gifts of clothes. Given Pepys's accounts of the terrible 'bastings' he gave his house boy, caning and birching him to within an inch of his life (once even grabbing a salted eel for the purpose), Nell's boys probably considered themselves lucky to be working for a mistress, and a kind-hearted one at that. Footmen were paid around four pounds a year (approximately £320 in today's money), and Nell would have kept four or five, both to serve at table and to accompany their mistress when she travelled out in her coach, whether she was going shopping, visiting friends, popping in to see the King at Whitehall or on one of her many trips to the theatre. They worked closely with the coachman, who was in charge of travel: both the vehicles themselves and the care of the horses. It was his task too to record travel expenses for Nell's frequent trips to Windsor and Newmarket. One of her coachmen, John Cooke, seems to have lived at 79 Pall Mall, while the other, Thomas Johnson, lived over the stables, where the coach and horses were kept. They were paid up to six pounds a year. The porter's job was that of door-keeper, welcoming visitors, receiving messages to pass to his mistress and making sure that undesirables stayed outside. (There were other porters too, who acted as deliverymen.) His salary was three to four pounds a year, supplemented by tips from Nell's aristocratic friends. The male servants would wear Nell's livery, a uniform with a distinguishing badge, but sadly no description of her household colours exists. There is, however, a bill from April 1674 for their headgear, which reads, 'for 5 french hatts for ye footmen at 10 [shillings] a piece' and 'for 4 English hatts for ye other men at 7 and 6 a piece'.

The cook, who was probably a woman, was paid four pounds a year and had under her a kitchen maid, who was expected to work very hard for her shilling a week. The chambermaid, who received the same as the cook, kept the rooms clean and helped with the laundry; separate payments are listed in the accounts for a 'washer woman', who came in specially on washing days and a 'card match-woman', whatever that was. Another casual servant was one Gamor Hill, who seems to have come in most weeks. Her work must have been skilled as she was paid one and six a day. In charge of the children was a nursemaid, and she too could expect in the region of four pounds a year.

Chief among Nell's female servants was her waiting woman, or lady's maid, an educated girl who acted as both secretary and companion and would entertain her in dull moments by reading, singing or playing an instrument. Great trust was invested in the position, as the waiting woman would write letters for her mistress and handle a good deal of confidential business. She would also dress and undress her, comb out her hair, help choose her clothes and be consulted on matters of style and taste. Equally, Nell would enjoy treating her companion to a fine dress or suit of clothes. A 1675 account for three pairs of silk shoes reads, 'one for yourself, another for ye sister, and another for yor woman'. She ate with the family, and in Nell's case may have taught the children to read and write. A tutor would not have been hired until they were older. And like Emilia, Desdemona's waiting woman in *Othello*, she could end up not only as confidante but as best friend, uniquely privy to the secrets of her mistress's heart. Such deep trust was worth between twenty and twenty-five pounds a year. It is a thousand pities that we do not know the identity of Nell's waiting woman.

In overall charge of the household was Nell's steward, Thomas Groundes, a gentleman who would have earned between sixty and one hundred pounds a year. Good stewards were worth their weight in gold, for they kept the household running smoothly and could save their masters a fortune through prudence and good management. Groundes was in charge of Nell's accounts and supervised the catering. Fuel, lighting, house maintenance, the stocking of larder and cellar, hearth taxes – all came under his supervision. He paid her bills and, where appropriate, managed to get the totals rounded down a pound or two. For instance, on the second sedan chair she had made, in June 1675, the joiner Mr Wright, under pressure from Groundes, accepted thirty pounds in full payment of his bill for £34 11s 0d. On that one deal alone Groundes saved Nell the equivalent of £350 today. Most bills seem to have been paid promptly and in full, though payments 'upon accompt' (or part payment) are fairly common, presumably when funds were low or Nell had been on a spending spree. One bill, for work on her bedroom in 1674, wasn't paid for fifteen months, but such belated payments were rare. Nell tended to buy on impulse, yet Groundes seems to have been pretty effective in imposing some sort of fiscal regimen. All receipts carry the same formula: 'Rec'd then of Madam Ellen Gwin at ye hands of Thomas Growndes ye sume of *x* poundes in full of this Bill and all other accompts and demands to this day, I say rec'd'. He was also responsible for discipline among the other servants, paid their salaries, distributed gifts to them from Nell and was able to hire and fire them in consultation with his mistress. Nell was responsible for providing health care for her servants and also made it her business to help them with any personal or family problems. When her coachman John Cooke fell ill in March 1676, she ordered in a sweating potion, six 'glysters' (enemas, using an ivory pipe and bladder) and buckets of special cordials, all to be administered by the apothecary Mr Brace. Servants in Nell's house were cared for and treated as members of an extended family.

Nell was not only beloved by her own staff, but was popular with servants in general for her willingness to stop and chat and for her generosity in tipping. She was known to be a favourite with the guards at Whitehall and outside St James's Palace, and there is an item in her accounts for March 1677 which reads, 'for ye yeomen of ye gard at ye tower 5–0 [five shillings]', a tip of almost twenty pounds. On some of her bills there are separate sections under the heading 'The poor'. Street beggars, who came to her door or approached her outside the playhouse, were usually given sixpence (about two pounds today), though some items record higher sums, such as the gift of half a crown (about ten pounds) 'ffor a poor woman at ye door' in October 1675. On another occasion she tipped 'my La. Southast [Southesk's] man' fourteen shillings (about fifty-five pounds). Regardless of the religion, politics or background of the individual, Nell always seems to have responded to suffering, whether emotional or financial. She famously gave Oliver Cromwell's old porter a handsome bible when she heard that he had been taken to Bedlam suffering from religious mania. And on another occasion she stopped her coach on Ludgate Hill to rescue a clergyman who was being arrested for debt. Having discharged his obligations, she managed to secure some sort of preferment for him from the King, who was equally moved by tales of individual suffering.

There would have been about twenty souls in all living under Nell's roof, and until March 1676 one of them was her mother, old Mrs Gwyn. There are entries in the accounts for her necessities of life, such as brandy, lemon and brandy, and 'plague water', which was a tonic of herbs steeped in brandy. But we mustn't suppose that brandy was Mrs Gwyn's only drink; she liked to sit up in bed in the mornings with a pot of sack which put her in a good humour to receive her daughter and royal grandsons. She had some health problems in the last quarter of 1675, and Nell's apothecary Mr Brace was called in to administer 'clysters', 'plasters' and 'cordial mixtures'. But there was little for it, as both the cause of the ailment and the patient's favoured cure were one and the same: brandy. Then in February and March of 1676 there is a great toing and froing between Pall Mall and Chelsea, as the account entries reveal: 'ffor a Coach goeing to Chellsey', 'ffor 2 hackney coaches to Chellsey', 'ffor ye gates to Chellsey', 'ffor a porter goeing to Chellsey', 'ffor a waterman from Chell:', and, inevitably, 'for a pore man at Chelsy'. Suddenly, a different kind of evacuation had taken place. Old Madam Gwyn had been carted upriver.

There are no clues as to why she was moved, but it could hardly have been on her own initiative. It seems to be that either the King had told Nell that he considered the old soak unsuitable company for his young sons or else her alcoholism was putting an intolerable strain on the household. Nor do we know exactly where she lived in Chelsea, but it may well have been at the house that Nell rented at Sandy End, Fulham, near the King's Road, and where she is reputed to have spent the summer months when not at Windsor. Mrs. S. C. Hall visited the house in Victorian times and wrote up her account for the 'Pilgrimages to English Shrines' series in the *Art-Union Monthly Journal*. At first, she had no luck with directions, but then she was advised to visit old Hill, the rat-catcher, who had an eccentric little cottage in the Fulham Road. Old Hill was 'a man of powerful frame with a massive head . . . deep, well-set eyes, and a quiet smile', and having ushered Mr and Mrs Hall into his front room, hung with cages full of songbirds of every description and ranged about with hutches of rats and ferrets, he launched into this priceless peroration:

'Oh, oh! Nell's old house. Nell Gwynne's house at Sandy End, where runs the little river they deepened into a canal – the stream I mean that divides Chelsea from Fulham – Sandford Manor House! Ay, that I do, and I'd match it against any house in the county for rats! – terrible place – I lost two ferrets there this time two years, and one of them was found t'other side of the canal; it must have been a pleasant place in those days, when the king was making his private road through the Chelsea fields [the King's Road], and the stream was as clear as a thrush's eye and birds of all sorts were so tamed by Madam Ellen, that they'd come when she'd call them. Ah, a pretty woman might catch a king, but it's only a kind one that could tame the wild birds of the air; I know that; I'll show you the way with pleasure.'

Mrs Hall duly made her tour of the house and garden, not without many sentimental reflections on Nell's virtue and honesty in a sinful age, but had to concede that there was nothing left to recall her presence there, except one of three walnut trees planted by the King. She also admitted that she crossed the garden, 'but could find no trace of the pond in which tradition reports Madam Ellen's mother to have been drowned', though, to be fair, the good dame was supposed to have drowned in the stream dividing Chelsea from Fulham which old Hill mentions. Whatever the truth of the matter, the mother certainly lived out the last three years of her life in Chelsea, far from the public eye, and it appears probable that she lived in a house provided by her daughter, who agreed to spend a couple of months a year with her. She had been a comical and slightly disturbing presence in the lives of her two grandsons, whose other grandmother, the youngest daughter of Henri IV of France, had died before they were born. Which was probably just as well, as Henrietta Maria would hardly have relished sharing such a role with a brandy-swilling bawd.

Nell was determined that her sons should want for nothing. There are numerous items in her accounts for 'play things for my Lords', as well as specific purchases of toys such as 'a gig & a whip', 'a gig pin', 'a topp for my lo:', '2 gunns for my lo:', followed by 'gunn balls', '2 coloring broshes', and 'a Cornett'. There are also orders for cards and dice, but these were probably for Nell's basset table. She purchased a pet donkey for the boys to ride about the garden under supervision, and in the park too. They also drank its milk, which was considered safer than cows' milk. Nell paid various people to look after the animal: five shillings 'for milking ye Asse', one pound 'for keeping ye Asse' and a shilling 'for a porter brought the Ass home'. She also bought two tame pigeons, which seems a little unadventurous when so many households could boast monkeys and all manner of exotic birds. The King himself had a pet starling in his Bedchamber, which, according to Pepys, whistled and talked better than any bird he'd ever heard. Sir William Batten, on the other hand, kept a gorilla. Included also in a section marked 'the chare man's bill' are these entries: 'for carring my lords about the garden 2–0' and 'for carring my lo: about the yard 2–0'. It seems extraordinary that Nell's household servants couldn't have been called upon to give them a piggyback round the garden; though perhaps they enjoyed the more formal entertainment. It may be that Nell regarded her royal offspring with a measure of awe and was determined to attune them to the formalities that awaited them at court.

Naturally enough, the two boys were fitted out with the best clothes by the King's French tailor, leaving little on Nell's books except fancy shoes, coats and gloves. It is telling, however, that a bill for gloves submitted at the end of December 1676 shows that she bought no fewer than ninety pairs in the space of six months, sixty-eight for the children and twenty-four for herself! There are white, cream and coloured kid gloves, the children's costing a shilling a pair and the ladies' sometimes twice that amount. On a separate bill for the previous year 'I doz: of halfe hands' are also listed. Gloves and shoes seem to have been something of an obsession with Nell. She can't have forgotten how she had walked the streets of London in winter with her toes and fingers ready to drop off from the cold, and how Poor Dick the linkboy had presented her with a gift of stockings to keep her warm.

Nell was solicitous for her children's health. They suffered from the usual run of coughs, colds, fevers and colics, for which there were plenty of homely remedies. The accounts show regular orders for 'sugar cande', 'pectoral sirup', 'hartes horn', 'plaisters' and so forth. In October 1675 a special 'cordiall julep with pearls' was prescribed for Master Charles. Master James seems to have been of a weaker constitution and became a source of frantic concern in February 1676. A bill for that month shows two identical entries that read 'a coach for ye surgeons' at four shillings a time, and for three shillings 'a coach for nurse goff'. Weeks later he was still being treated, though we don't know the nature of his complaint (the prescribed remedy rarely gives a clue). He was given an enema, three doses of purging powder, a cordial and two ounces of 'diascordium', a medicine made from the dried leaves of water germander. Whether Charles sent his personal surgeon, George Moretto, to treat his sons we don't know, but Nell moved heaven and earth to see her boys restored to health. Nameless and untitled though they still were, they were her guarantee of royal goodwill in an uncertain and often vicious world.

~ 12 ~

Foreign Honours

THE SPLENDOUR THAT SURROUNDED AND decked Louise was on an altogether grander scale, and she was soon to receive the honours to complement it. Never venturing beyond the opulent template laid down by the French King, she created a set of Whitehall apartments that, for all their lustre, were utterly derivative. She was not without a certain sparkle and sophistication, but both were compromised by a failure of imagination. John Evelyn provides an invaluable description of Louise's establishment:

Following his Majesty this morning thro' the gallerie, I went, with the few who attended him, into the Dutchesse of Portsmouth's *dressing roome* within her bed-chamber, where she was in her morning loose garment, her maids combing her, newly out of her bed, his Majesty and the gallants standing about her; but that which engag'd my curiosity was the rich and splendid furniture of this woman's apartment, now twice or thrice pull'd down and rebuilt to satisfie her prodigal and expensive pleasures, whilst her Majestys dos not exceede some gentlemen's ladies in furniture and accommodation. Here I saw the new fabriq of French tapissry, for designe, tendernesse of worke, and incomparable imitation of the best paintings, beyond any thing I had ever beheld. Some pieces had Versailles, St. Germain's, and other palaces of the French King, with huntings, figures, and landskips, exotiq fowls, and all to the life rarely don. Then for

Japan cabinets, screenes, pendule clocks, greate vases of wrought plate, tables, stands, chimney furniture, sconces, branches, braseras, &c. all of massive silver, and out of number, besides some of her Majesty's best paintings.

In other words, her apartments were stuffed with imitation classics and Louis XIV furniture from the Gobelins factory in Paris. The effect was clearly overpowering, as Evelyn's next lines attest: 'Surfeiting of this, I din'd at Sir Stephen Fox's, and went contented home to my poor, but quiet villa. What contentment can there be in the riches and splendor of this world, if purchas'd with vice and dishonour!' The same approach extended to her hospitality. Her salon was full of the finest people drinking the finest champagne and listening to the finest musicians in the finest surroundings. There were no midnight capers in the park for Cartwheel and her toadies; for one thing she was too hated to show herself in public. Hers was an alternative salon to the Queen's, more sophisticated, but less lively. Through it the 'creature of France', as Shaftesbury described her, strove to impress the King and enlarge her own sphere of influence in the state. According to Airy in his biography of Charles, Louise alone among the mistresses cultivated *la haute politique*: 'she alone in that ignoble Court could command the respect and co-operation of statesmen and ambassadors. She met the vulgar furies of the Duchess of Cleveland and the banter of Nell Gwynn with quiet disdain; she held her own with a certain dignity against the anger of the Commons, the hatred of the people, the attacks of politicians, and the waywardness of Charles, and for many years she was virtually Queen of England.'

The relationship between Louise and Charles was in the nature of a political dance, each using and serving the other in a faultless game of social and diplomatic gambits. Both were vital to the other's ambitions. Charles alone could raise Louise to the pinnacle of gracious living she so coveted, while she was his guarantee of good faith in the eyes of France. So long as she kept her salon at Whitehall, Charles could flatter the French into believing his Catholic and francophile overtures. With it, however, he ran the gauntlet of considerable unpopularity. The butt of anti-French, anti-Catholic paranoia, Louise was detested up and down the country. Yet she provided a comfortable haven for Charles amid the hurly-burly of Whitehall. Her soft voice calmed him, and the whispered French reminded him of intimate moments with his mother as a small boy. And in a court that could be coarse and prurient, he could rely on Louise to restore him to the pale of taste and decorum with all the sophisticated arts of a geisha. She could be seductive, erotic too if a literary or mythical context could be found, and a political motive.

We know of one occasion at least (towards the end of 1673) when Louise played the wanton, following a sumptuous banquet in her apartments at which the whole company – herself excepted – had become uproariously drunk. As dawn came on and the guests began to disperse, Louise insisted that the King stay for a game of Questions and Commands with her and two other titled ladies who had remained behind. As he hesitated, Louise began to undress and her companions followed suit. With gallantry and lechery vying for the honour, the King rushed to assist them. 'Not unlike the three goddesses, Juno, Pallas, and Venus before Paris, did those three naked ladies stand before the King, who was ravished with the sight, and examined every part about them with his own hands and eyes, with all imaginable curiosity.' When it came to the game itself, the other ladies questioned Charles about their beauty and his desire, and squandered their commands by ordering him to drink a goblet of wine to their healths. But wily Louise, the Pallas of the three, was never wanton without good purpose. Her part was rehearsed and, though she stood before the King without a fig leaf, less than innocent. Firstly, she asked him whether he would like to govern without Parliament, to which he replied in the affirmative. Her second question – who he thought the happiest monarch in the world – also received the desired reply: Louis XIV. Whereupon she delivered her command: Charles was to prorogue Parliament the very next day. In the event the King complied, but only because her command anticipated his own intention. He wished to save one of his principal ministers, the Duke of Lauderdale, from impeachment by the Commons.

Their son Charles, Charles's fifth Charles, was born on 29 July 1672. Louise, who treated the child from the start as a sort of heir presumptive to the throne, was shocked and hurt that Charles, as was his wont, did not instantly acknowledge him. To her it was further proof that they did not know how to do things at the Court of St James. After all, the King of France had shown special favour to his bastard children by Louise de la Vallière and the Marquise de Montespan, even going so far as to legitimize them. Her indignation was mollified a year later when on 25 July 1673 Charles created her Baroness Petersfield, Countess of Farnham and Duchess of Portsmouth in the English peerage. She was only the second Duchess in her own right in the country and the title was traditionally a royal one. Louise was over the moon, and threw a ball for the whole court at Barn Elms. Among her 'creatures' the celebrations lasted a full fortnight. But whether Louise had taken the prerequisite step of becoming a naturalized English subject, without which her titles were void, is still a moot point.

Nell was furious. She went straight to the King and demanded that he show the world how much he valued her. She knew the truth of their friendship and her artless, democratic spirit could not, would not, acknowledge the politics of the matter. For her it was a simple question of loyalty. The King was caught in a tight spot and, after much humming and hawing, promised to make her a countess, just as soon as he could discover how it would go down among the people – *not* the court, but the people. Charles, cunning as ever, knew that it was popular opinion, rather than the prejudices of the court, that mattered to Nell. Seeing the look of childish joy on her face, he even went so far as to mention a specific title: Countess of Plymouth. Naively, Nell swung into action, only to learn a harsh lesson about the aristocratic establishment of which the King was head. This entry in Sir Francis Fane's *Commonplace Book* tells the sad story: 'Nell got a pattent drawne to bee Countess of Plymouth but ye L: Keeper refused to seale itt before hee first spoak with ye King who told him, hee was but in iest with her.' (Two years later the King granted the Earldom of Plymouth to his bastard son by Catherine Pegge, now Lady Greene, on the boy's coming of age.) Nell also took the opportunity to press once again for the freehold of 79 Pall Mall. In a letter to Sir Joseph Williamson on 25 August 1673 the civil servant Henry Ball wrote, 'The people say, Madam Guinn complains shee has no house yett . . .'

Gossip was rife in the summer of 1673 that Nell had in fact been created Countess of Plymouth, causing feelings of alarm among nearly everyone who mattered. But when the rumours were scotched, alarm turned to derision. Rochester gently mocked her as 'the countess o'th'Cockpit' in his satirical poem 'Signior Dildo', suggesting that Nell might have to make do with playing countesses on stage (the Cockpit being the name of a theatre at Whitehall). Certainly, titles appealed to the actress in Nell. Life was a pageant, and she would prefer to have a costume that stood out. Besides, whatever her conscience told her, there was always that sneaking suspicion that, in the words of Bishop Burnet, she was being treated 'not . . . with the decencies of a mistress, but rather with the lewdness of a prostitute'. Ultimately, though, the establishment proved too powerful. Cecil Chesterton, brother of G. K., cuts to the heart of the matter: 'The dignity and power which a peerage conferred were highly esteemed and jealously guarded; these honours were not then sold by politicians like so much butter as they are to-day. To have made the orange-girl a peeress would have been an affront to something much stronger than the moral sentiment of the middle classes; it would have been an affront to the idea of aristocracy.'[1]

One possible consolation for Nell lay in the fact that her ability to wound Louise with her retorts would have been undermined by a title, for women of the same class were expected to be catty towards each other. As plain 'Mrs Nelly' the insolence of her sallies struck deeper, especially since Louise was peculiarly sensible to social distinctions. One day when Nell appeared at court dressed to the nines, Louise decided to give her a good ribbing. 'Nelly,' quoth she, 'you are grown rich, I see, by your dress; why, woman, you are fine enough to be a queen.' To which Nell shot back, 'Quite right, madam; and you are whore enough to be a duchess.' She was of course reflecting the mood of the average Englishman. And not so average ones too, for even Louise's own brother-in-law Philip Herbert, Earl of Pembroke, had said as much. A savage man, who chewed table legs and beat his wife, Pembroke had been chosen by Louise for her sister Henriette with little regard for his character. When she grew alarmed and threatened to complain to the King about his behaviour, Pembroke swore that he would drag Louise to the street corner and hang her by her heels with her skirts about her ears, so that the world could see the source of her power. Needless to say, the marriage was an unhappy one. King Charles gallantly paid the girl's dowry and settled an annuity of £600 on her.

The aristocracy in general shared Pembroke's view of Louise and was outraged at her elevation to its highest rank. As far as they were concerned, being a whore to the King did not merit ennoblement; being French was a further disqualification. Moreover, when her sister arrived in England towards the end of 1674, Louise was in a state of horrible embarrassment. She had always hated sharing the King with other women, and now it had been brought home to her that there were definite occupational hazards in courtesanship, however thick the veneer of virtue and sophistication. The King had caught the clap from some backstairs doxy and passed it on in his democratic fashion to the *maîtresse en titre*. Louise was advised to take the waters at Tunbridge Wells, but when she arrived she found the house she had taken already occupied by the Marchioness of Worcester, who, far from gracefully stepping aside, berated her for being no better than a common whore. The King, learning of Louise's distress, sent a guard to escort her to Windsor, where he put his personal physician at her disposal. Epsom, Bath, Tunbridge: Louise was thereafter shunted from spa to spa for the best part of a year, desperately seeking a cure, while Nell appointed herself *maîtresse en titre* in her absence. Louise's only real consolation were the pearls and diamonds sent her by Louis XIV, who felt indirectly responsible for her plight.

Charles preferred not to argue with his mistresses and knew better than to suggest that Louise might have caught her pox elsewhere. But such a suggestion would hardly have been unwarranted, as in time Louise would be widely suspected to have shared her favours with Lord Treasurer Danby and a string of aristocratic French visitors. She was not faithful to Charles for the simple reason that she was not in love with him. Each respected the fact that the other had a political game to play.

The so-called Cabal of top ministers that Charles had formed in the wake of Clarendon's fall had never been united in their aims; now the Treaty of Dover had severed them further. Only Clifford and Arlington of the five had been privy to the secret clauses; the remaining three (Lauderdale, Ashley and Buckingham), though suspicious, had been effectively hoodwinked. The Test Act of February 1673, imposed by Parliament in retaliation for Charles's Declaration of Indulgence, delivered the final blow. It meant, among other things, that only those who took the Anglican communion could hold public office. Lord Treasurer Clifford, a devout Catholic, returned home to Devon, where he committed suicide. Even the Duke of York was forced to resign his command of the fleet, Prince Rupert being made Lord High Admiral in his stead. Grilled by Parliament for their dealings with France, Arlington and Buckingham were forced from office, while Shaftesbury was dismissed by Charles for backing the Test Act. The Cabal was over.

The man who replaced Clifford as Lord Treasurer in the summer of 1673 was Sir Thomas Osborne, later Earl of Danby, who effectively became Charles's chief minister. A brilliant and devious strategist, Danby was the perfect servant for Charles. He was a cold fish, 'of excellent natural parts, but nothing of generous or grateful'. He realized that the key to making the Crown solvent lay in the management of Parliament. To this end he set about creating a party of court loyalists within Parliament through the use of patronage (i.e., bribes); in order to gather the necessary funds for such a project he insisted upon a complete overhaul of the royal finances. He also warned the King that patronage alone would not suffice; Charles himself must be seen to give his unequivocal support to the Anglican Church. With dirty money coming in from both France and Spain, Danby's strategy quickly prospered, and the Court Party was born.

Opposing Danby was the Earl of Shaftesbury who, smarting from his dismissal by the King, set about organizing a group inside the Commons hostile to the court. A political agitator of the first order, Shaftesbury was an opportunist prepared to use any person or principle that might advance his ambitions. Charles, who nicknamed him 'Little Sincerity', was quick to take the measure of the man. On one occasion, during a performance of *Macbeth* at the King's Theatre, Charles contemplated the fierce looks of Banquo's assassins with the words, 'Pray, what is the reason that we never see a rogue in a play, but, 'Od's fish! they always clap him on a black periwig, when it is well known that one of the greatest rogues in England always wears a fair one?' Shaftesbury was blond. 'I but take off my gown to buckle on my sword,' he said, as he prepared to challenge the royal prerogative both in Parliament and on the streets of London. The Country Party quickened in the Earl of Shaftesbury's spleen and won the support of many landed MPs and a handful of influential peers, including the Duke of Buckingham, who in a speech to the Commons in his own defence said in reference to the King and his brother, 'that he was weary of the company he was joined with, for a man might kill with a pack of beagles but could not hunt with a brace of lobsters'.

Two other major factors influenced the rise of the party system. The first was James's open avowal of Catholicism, which caused huge political tensions, for he looked certain now to inherit his brother's throne. As the de facto leader of the Catholics in England, James became in his usual tactless fashion the most feared and hated man in the kingdom. It was easy for the new parties to crystallize in their respective solutions to this problem, which was further precipitated when James, despite Parliament's opposition, took the fifteen-year-old Italian princess Maria d'Este of Modena as his new bride. The princess arrived in England on Guy Fawkes Day 1673. That night, according to Evelyn, 'the youths of the Citty burnt the Pope in effigie, after they had made procession with it in greate triumph, they being displeas'd at the Duke for altering his religion and marrying an Italian lady'. It marked the beginning of a decade of pope-burning processions.

The second major factor was usury. Parliament's policy of bleeding the King dry unless he bent to its will had forced Charles into the hands of the London goldsmiths, who lent the King money against his Parliamentary revenues. The goldsmiths were the bankers of their day and bought up all the major political offices in the City. By charging the King heavy interest they helped generate the national debt, which the Bank of England was subsequently created to manage. They also began issuing what was in effect paper money, which had to be backed up by the bullion brokers of Amsterdam. They worked hand in glove with Parliament (a number of MPs had strong interests in the City) to try to strip the King of his prerogative powers, and even put forward a bill which would have deprived the Crown of the administration of its revenues, granting the privilege instead to the Chamber of the City of London.

The gulf of misunderstanding between City and court was widening by the day, and embittered former ministers such as Buckingham and Shaftesbury looked increasingly to the City for support in opposing the government. Not that they were prepared to forsake the gay and dissolute existence of their court companions; instead they lived a double life, alternating between skullcap and plumes as the occasion demanded.

The beginning of the party system led naturally enough to a culture of bribery in Parliament, or what the French ambassador Ruvigny described as '*le sale traffique*'. No member, it seems, was exempt, while some took advantage of the confusion to take bribes from opposing sources. The bribing powers were France, Spain and Holland, with France dangling by the far the heaviest purse. Louis XIV was in effect playing the same game as the bankers, helping to create the Punch-and-Judy system of politics that has kept governments in line for centuries. The bribery was indiscriminate, and came in kind as well as cash. For instance, one MP might receive six dozen bottles of champagne, while the wife of another would be presented with rich gifts of jewellery or fabrics. Buckingham was paymaster for the French King, but that didn't stop him opposing Charles's policies, while Shaftesbury took bribes from both the French and the Dutch to fill his party coffers. Andrew Marvell, who became Dutch paymaster under the sobriquet 'Mr Thomas' (even though he had described Holland as 'this indigested vomit of the sea'), found it hard to determine who was spying for whom. Before we accuse the King of hypocrisy, we would do well to reflect upon the moral fibre of his Parliament.

As mentioned, Danby's manipulation of Parliament in the King's interest was accompanied by a tightening of the royal finances, and among the first disbursements to be controlled were the allowances granted to the royal mistresses, or 'chargeable ladies', as Shaftesbury acidly christened them. This is why Louise lost no time in cultivating Danby's favour, and was even said to have become his lover. There is no doubt that of all the mistresses she was the most successful in getting her grants approved by the new Lord Treasurer. After the clampdown, Barbara received £6,000 a year for life (roughly £450,000 in today's money) and £3,000 a year for each of her three sons; Louise and her son received £8,600 per annum, but this had risen to £19,000 (an exorbitant £1.5 million) by the 1680s. Nell's income was modest in comparison, at £4,000 a year, plus £1,000 for the upkeep of her children, nor was it stipulated 'for life', but rather 'during the King's pleasure' – one of the drawbacks of being a commoner. On the other hand, she was clearly trusted to spend her child benefit on the children, for she alone of the mistresses received the payments for them directly from the Treasury.

These figures were supplemented by other fees and licenses, as well as by income from grants of Irish land. Nell for instance received the 'farm' of certain Irish properties in Dundalk and Carlingford, which yielded her a further £800 a year, but she had to fight for them. Fortunately, she had influential agents in Rochester, Buckhurst and Thomas Felton, a retainer of the Duke of York, and they were able to exert the necessary pressure upon the Lord Lieutenant of Ireland, the Duke of Ormonde. When the deal was done, Sir Robert Howard, Auditor of the Exchequer, wrote to the Duke to thank him on Nell's behalf. The terms in which the thanks are expressed reflect Nell's frank and genial nature, as well as her easy confidence in addressing people of the highest rank: 'Mrs. Nelly has commanded me to present her among your true servants and does think herself so much obliged to Your Excellency, that unless within a little time you command her something that she may serve you in, she swears she will pick a quarrel with you, for she vows she loves you entirely.'

In 1681 Louise boosted her total unearned earnings to an obscene £136,668, the equivalent of £10.5 million today. Indeed, she had so much of the stuff that she was reported to have thrown handfuls of gold from her windows, in the hope that stories of her fantastic wealth would reach the aristocrats of Paris. It's easy to see why the people grew angry, but the truth is that Charles wasn't actually paying for her. Louis XIV, through his secret subsidies, was the ultimate paymaster. The expense of Charles's bastard children was also resented. In his 'Dialogue between two Horses', Marvell has Wool-Church say,

> While these brats and their mothers do live in such plenty,
> The nation's impoverished, and the 'Chequer quite empty;
> And though war was pretended when the money was lent,
> More on whores, than in ships or in war, hath been spent.

Sometimes when cash was short the King would grant warrants to his mistresses, allowing them a share of goods from captured Dutch vessels, but here again Danby quickly scuppered the arrangement. In September 1673 he made it clear that 'neither Madam Kerwell's nor the Duchess of Cleveland's nor Nell Gwyn's warrants would be accepted'. This came at a bad time for Nell, who was still enduring the heavy start-up costs of becoming a lady of substance, and she went straight to the King to ask for some cash. He replied that he had none, which was doubtless true. 'Then,' said she, 'I will tell you how you shall neiver want, send ye French into France again, sett me on ye stage againe, & lock up your own Codpiece.' If the people of England could have spoken with one voice, those might have been their exact words. Whether Nell would have made more money than before as an actress is debatable, as funds at the theatres were limited, and she surely knew that returning to the public stage would mean the end of her established relationship with Charles.

Naturally enough, there was fierce competition among the mistresses for the substantial, yet limited resources available, especially in the months immediately preceding Danby's reforms. Rumours were rife about the various sums meted out and the lengths to which the royal doxies had gone to secure the biggest prizes. On 14 July 1673 one Henry Ball wrote to secretary of state Sir Joseph Williamson,

> A pleasant rediculous story is this weeke blazed about, that the King had given Nell Gwinn £20,000, which angrying much my Lady Cleaveland and Mademoiselle Carwell, they made a sopper at Berkshire House [Barbara's residence], whither shee being invited was, as they were drinking, suddainly almost choked with a napkin, of which shee was since dead; and this idle thing runs so hott that Mr Philips askt me the truth of it, believing it, but I assured him I saw her yester night in the Parke. The people say there has been £100,000 given away within these last five weekes, so ready are they to blaze pernitious lyes.

The story probably had some truth to it. Nell may have been grilled about her income by the other two ladies or been the object of their spiteful comments; if so, she may well have choked on her champagne. The rumour of Nell's death is interesting and probably betrays the fears of the London citizenry, who had come to value her as a charm against the subversive influence of Charles's two Catholic mistresses. One can certainly imagine the popular outcry that would have accompanied the rumours of her death, as well as Nell's mischievous protestations that she was very much alive.

Nell was not a mother for the working day. When Lely painted her as a mother in early 1671 it was as Venus, the sensual pleasure-loving goddess, and she looks directly out at us, not at her child. Having witnessed the darker side of life from birth, Nell had learnt how to fend for herself in practical terms from an early age, yet emotionally she remained a child looking for a childhood. Consequently, I suspect she was something of a bewildering figure in the lives of her children: doting, wilful, commanding, glamorous, charismatic, mercurial, elusive. And her strong fear that they might reject her in favour of their father's world could perhaps have made her overprotective and controlling at times.

The age of gallantry did not celebrate motherhood; if anything it reviled it. There was a strong reaction against the homely culture of the Puritans, in which motherhood was exalted over all other expressions of the feminine. The age of gallantry was the age of the *puer aeternus*. Its hero was the philanderer, who has a horror of maternal sexuality and does not want to be reminded of the generative potential of intercourse. His mistress was fantasized as the wild and witty girl, who is rarely – if ever – saddled with the burdens of motherhood. Hence too the proliferation of nymphs, virgin martyrs and even female warriors in the literature of the time. All were elevated above the maternal. It was the whore, in fact, who conformed to the Restoration ideal of womanhood, for she satisfied men without encumbering them with children or conjugal responsibilities, and so managed to remain chaste in the male imagination.

The culture of gallantry did much to create an epidemic of bastards

among the upper classes in Restoration society, while bastardy itself
and the legacy of the Civil War made it an age of absent fathers. In
Thomas Shadwell's comedy *The Virtuoso* (1676) Gimcrack's uncle
Snarl, who is always harking back to the good old days, says, 'I am
afraid the next age will have very few that are lawfully begotten in't,
by the mass. Besides, the young fellows are like all to be effeminate
coxcombs, and the young women, strumpets, in sadness, all strumpets,
by the mass'. It is hardly surprising, then, that Restoration comedy is
full of uncles, cousins and guardians, but contains very few parents.
Snarl is remarkably astute psychologically: fatherless daughters became
whores, fatherless sons vain coxcombs. The shame of bastardy, however, was projected not onto the father (the gallant with his horror of
the maternal body), but onto the mother. This was partly because the
bastards, having no father's name or inheritance, fell completely under
her power. One sees this clearly with Monmouth, and it's reasonable
to assume the same dynamic in the case of Nell's bastard sons.

The culture of gallantry was not, however, an exclusively male
affair; women colluded in the denial of motherhood by embracing the
role of the wild mistress. A court masque written by John Crowne
and first produced in February 1675 vividly exposes the dynamic of
love at the court of Charles II. The masque was entitled *Calisto*
[Crowne's spelling], and seems to have been the only one produced at
court during Charles's reign, for Charles, unlike his father and grandfather, did not believe in the superiority of courtly art, nor in the
necessity of using it to promote the divine right of kings. His
preference was for a more casual presentation of kingship, reflected
in his patronage of the public theatres. For all Crowne's efforts to
bowdlerize the Greek myth of Callisto to make it acceptable to the
two young Stuart princesses (the Duke of York's daughters), Mary and
Anne, who were to act the leading parts, it nevertheless reads as an
exposé of that putrid philosophy of love, gallantry.[2]

The original Greek myth, as retold for instance by Ovid in his
Metamorphoses, is about the rape of Diana's favourite nymph, Callisto,
by the king of the gods. The tale is set in Arcadia, a wild and
mountainous land, traditionally the home of Pan, where nymphs and
satyrs, shepherds and shepherdesses live a life of bucolic simplicity,
'exempt from public haunt'. Jupiter is wandering through the country,

repairing the damage done by Phaeton's collision with earth, when he spies Callisto in a glade of the forest, taking a rest from hunting. Disguising himself as her mistress, Diana, he begins by wooing the nymph with fair words, but when talk turns to kisses Callisto rejects the god with scornful indignation. Jupiter, however, proves too strong and having had his way with her flies back to heaven. After rejoining Diana's retinue, Callisto's shame is exposed when the goddess proposes a bathing party at a woodland pool and the ravished nymph is forced to undress. The wrathful Diana dismisses Callisto from her service, leaving her to give birth alone in the forest. When a son, Arcas, is born to the nymph, Juno is consumed with jealousy and descending to earth turns the wretched Callisto into a bear. (In some versions of the tale it is Diana herself who metes out this punishment.) Several years later, Arcas is out hunting one morning when he comes across the bear, who recognizes him instantly as her grown son and reaches out to embrace him. Arcas, in fear of his life, raises his spear and is about to hurl it when Jupiter, taking pity on the creature he has wronged, gathers mother and son up into the heavens and fixes them there for all time as the neighbouring constellations of the Greater and Lesser Bear.

The theme was certainly an unnecessarily thorny one for Crowne to choose, given that the two princesses who were to act the roles of Calisto and her sister, were twelve and ten respectively. But, more than that, why run the gauntlet of presenting a royal rape before a king with Charles's track record? For even if the part of Jupiter proved inoffensive to Charles, surely Juno's ranting jealousy would grate upon his Queen? In the event, Crowne deviated from his story in several vital respects: no rape, no bear and no son. For Arcas he substituted a sister, Nyphe, which gave him a part for the Princess Anne, and he added an evil nymph called Psecas. At the end of the masque it is Calisto and Nyphe who are made into stars.

The effect of Crowne's butchery of the myth was to turn a deep cautionary tale into a frivolous comedy. Nevertheless, those watching the production would have known the original myth of Jupiter and Callisto, most likely in Ovid's racy version, and the deeper message would not have been lost on them. Jove is of course Charles himself, the ultimate gallant, who descends to earth to taste the pleasures of mortal love, and like a typical Restoration gallant flies back up to the stars once his dirty deed is done. (Jupiter repairing the land of Arcady after Phaeton's crash is Charles healing the breaches caused by the Civil War.) Callisto is the wild mistress, or virgin huntress, for whom motherhood is a source of shame. Indeed, the condition has to be forced upon her through rape, and no sooner has she given birth than she is turned into a bear, thus making vivid the connection between motherhood and woman's animal nature. Ultimately, Callisto's shame is the result of an unwitting collaboration between Jupiter, who commits the rape, Diana, who dismisses her pregnant nymph in disgust at her condition, and Juno, the jealous wife who punishes the victim of her husband's lust by turning her into a bear. Men alone cannot bear the blame for the nymph's degraded state; it has taken the collusion of her fellow women. Thus was it with the cult of gallantry in Charles's reign: it relied on a collaboration of the sexes.

The Restoration cult of love, then, took its character from the peculiar love life of the King. Charles was married, but his wife was a child, incapable of bearing children. The royal line could not be extended through her. Charles might be the father of the nation, but there was no mother. Instead there was a jealous wife, who was forced to master her jealousy by aping the wild mistress stereotype. Catherine took to dressing in men's clothes (like Florimel in *Secret Love*) and going in for all the wild frolics that she knew excited the King. Meanwhile, her place was frequently usurped by the King's bona fide mistresses, as she took solace in her devotions. It was as if England didn't have a queen at all, but a king and his harem. There was no mother archetype in the life of the nation, while the example of the wife was of one humiliated and exiled from the conjugal bed (like Juno in Crowne's *Calisto*); or else the wild mistress appeared in her place to cheat the cheating husband. It is difficult to imagine Charles and Catherine not squirming in their seats at this tirade delivered by Juno (who was played by the teenage Lady Sussex, Barbara's elder daughter by the King):

> O! servile state of conjugal embrace!
> Where seeming honour covers true disgrace.
> We with reproaches mistresses defame,

But we poor wives endure the greatest shame.
We to their slaves are humble slaves, whilst they
Command our lords, and rule what we obey.
Their loves each day new kindnesses uphold,
We get but little, and that little cold!
That a poor wife is with her state reproached,
And to be married is to be debauched.

Following a row with her husband at Windsor, the Queen had been heard to complain that 'the mistresses govern all'. Of course, without mothers and wives, the roles of father and husband were themselves degraded. As Lady Gimcrack's lover Hazard says, 'Nay, I think a husband is a very insipid, foolish animal and is growing mightily out of fashion.'

If there were beneficiaries of the cult of gallantry, they were the gallants themselves. Its victims were mothers and children, in particular mothers and sons. To be a wild mistress and a mother at the same time was to be feared and rejected by your children. The bastard himself, meanwhile, grew up into a dashing gallant, who like Monmouth possessed no heart. In his case, he was saved in the end by the King's patronage; for Charles, like Jupiter, could raise him up to the safety of the heavens through honours, titles and wealth.

Calisto proved extremely popular with the court, no doubt because those who wanted to read between the lines could, while the vain and squeamish could satisfy themselves with the surface glitter. It seems to have run for several months, with over thirty performances being given. Many of Nell's friends and acquaintances took part: Frances Jennings, who once disguised herself as an orange wench in order to visit a notorious mountebank, was Mercury; Lady Mary Mordaunt was the evil nymph Psecas; Moll Davis was the River Thames; Maria Knight, Nell's neighbour, played the role of Peace; and her old lover Charles Hart impersonated Europe. Asia, Africa and America were also represented. Moll Davis and Maria Knight doubled up as shepherdesses. There were many dances, songs and interludes to punctuate the story: choruses of carpenters, shepherds, gypsies, cupids, Basques and Bacchae, not to mention nymphs, shepherdesses and African women. The production was directed by the Bettertons and cost in the region of £5,000. The costumes were lavish, America's dress being decorated with '6000 swan's feathers of several colours'.

Nell must have found it excruciatingly difficult to sit quietly in the audience, while her friends and colleagues acted, sang, danced and frolicked on the stage of the Hall Theatre. In the end, it seems, she took advantage of the state visit of Philip William, Prince of Neuberg, in the summer of 1675, to steal a dance-on part as an Arcadian shepherdess. Marie Catherine, Baronne d'Aulnoy, who was one of the Prince's entourage, recorded 'the arrival of Nelly Gwynne' in pastoral attire at an unnamed court masque, saying that she 'danced the *contre danse* (which she did very well, although her manners were as singular in dancing as they were in everything else that she did) . . .' One can see Nell making the most of her moment in the limelight, no doubt stepping outside her role to add a few singular measures of her own, or a comic turn or two. It may well be that she had been asked to dance one of her famous jigs to wind up the performance, for as soon as she had finished, 'she cried out that the heat of the room was unbearable, and that they must have some air, that of a truth the season was unsuitable for such amusements, & it was uncomfortable to stay shut up with so many people, and so many candles'.

The women were perspiring in their heavy costumes and jewelled gowns, the men under their mountainous periwigs. A banquet had been prepared for the royal and noble actors as well as for members of the court audience, Nell included; the array of steaming dishes increased the temperature still further, and endless toasts of Rhenish wine enflamed the laughing faces. Nell, making use of her fool's prerogative, had the windows heaved open, much to the relief of the silently suffocating. The Queen and Louise de Kéroualle, not used to fresh air, sat shivering like chihuahuas. It was only when the women began fainting that Nell was able to take command of the situation by announcing that the party was to be continued in St James's Park; whereupon she proceeded to organize the removal of the food and drink, as well as the musicians and their instruments (violins, flutes, oboes). Finally, she played the shepherdess in good earnest, leading her flock of gaudily attired guests out into the moonlit park. The sky was exceptionally clear and the trees stirred softly in the night breeze. The musicians struck up, and Nell, kicking off her silken shoon, led the first dance across the bowling green, like Titania leading forth her fairy train. According to Baronne d'Aulnoy, 'her spirits were such that it was difficult to remain long in her company without sharing the gaiety'. Though it was past midnight, a crowd gathered to watch the royal party dancing and revelling the night away.[3]

The following evening, buoyed by the success of her whimsy, Nell suggested taking the Prince and his entourage up the Thames to Hampton Court. This time she had prepared one of her ingenious pranks. They travelled in painted barges, with the finest Italian musicians to speed them on their way. Baronne d'Aulnoy once more takes up the story:

> One of her [Nell's] schemes which was previously arranged, proved very amusing. She suggested to the King that they might stop awhile, the better to enjoy the beauty of the evening and music; this done she had some fishing tackle produced; it was all painted and gilded, the Nets were silk, the Hooks gold. Every one commenced to fish, & the king was one of the most eager. He had already thrown his line many times & was surprised at not catching anything. The Ladies rallied him, but calling out that they must not tease, he triumphantly showed his line to the end of which half a dozen fried Sprats were attached by a piece of silk! They burst into laughter in which all the Court joined, but Nelly said it was only right that a great king should have unusual Privileges! A Poor Fisherman could only take Fish alive but his Majesty caught them ready to eat!

Highly amused, the Prince decided to cast his line one more time, joking that they would need more sprats if they were to feed the whole company. When he began reeling in, the heavy pull on the line convinced him that he had hooked a rock. Instead, he was thrilled to find a gold purse woven with precious stones, which concealed an exquisite gold locket containing the picture of a court beauty with whom he'd fallen in love. When he saw the picture, the Prince let out a cry of joy and the whole court laughed at his good fortune. No one laughed louder than the King, who, with a wink at Nell, laid the blame on the famous water nymphs of the river Thames. Nell had in fact taken a leaf out of Cleopatra's book by employing divers to fix the catches to the lines while they were under the water. Cleopatra had had a salted fish attached to Antony's line, an expedient she sometimes employed to make up for his deficiency as an angler. 'General,' she had chided him, 'leave the fishing rod to us . . . your game is cities and kingdoms and countries.' Charles too was an average, if extremely enthusiastic fisherman. As for Neuberg, he was so delighted by Nell's elegant strategem that he sent her a gift of fine lace on his return to Germany.

Louise, meanwhile, had been going through a rough patch since returning from her spa-hopping the previous autumn. Though physically recovered, she still bore the mental scars of her undignified tussle with the clap. She was suddenly plagued by the idea that the satirists and libel-mongers were right: perhaps she was just another whore after all. But just as Louise was beginning to lose heart, Charles made things better by whisking their son up into the heavens and fixing him there for all time as Duke of Richmond, Earl of March and Baron Settrington. It was an astonishing thing to do, especially as the child was only three. Even the darling Monmouth had been made to wait until his thirteenth birthday. And the choice of principal title was itself mischievous in the extreme, for it had belonged to the young husband of Frances Stuart, whom Charles had driven to diplomatic exile – and an early death – in Denmark. His crime had been to marry a girl whom the King had marked out for his own special favour and enjoyment. It was a chilling reminder of Charles's ruthlessness in matters of love, which had surfaced once before when Clarendon attempted to challenge the propriety of his relationship with Barbara.

There is no doubt that politics played a large part in the premature ennoblement of Louise's son. Firstly, Louise had the Earl of Danby under her thumb, and it was his responsibility as Lord Treasurer to approve and sign the patents for new peers, once they had been cleared by the King. Secondly, and most importantly, at a time when he had made peace with the Dutch and was facing unruly parliaments at home, Charles needed to send a clear signal to France that he was still honouring the spirit of the Secret Treaty. In this respect, Louise proved the ideal stalking horse for Charles's pursuit of his own peaceful, trade-based foreign policy.

When Barbara got wind of Louise's plans for her son in the summer of 1675 there was an unseemly scramble for honours between the two titans of the bedchamber. Barbara was determined that the King should honour her sons Charles and Henry Fitzroy, who were thirteen and eleven respectively, before the infant son of a French upstart. It was all a matter of precedence. Both women pestered the King incessantly, clawing his throne like a pair of harpies, until finally he declared that both patents would be signed simultaneously, which was of course impossible. Louise, however, being on intimate terms with the Lord Treasurer, discovered at the last moment that he was slipping off to Bath the very night before the day appointed for the patents to be passed. So she had her attorney rush over to his apartments at midnight, where he found Danby on the point of stepping into his coach. The Lord Treasurer, mindful of his 'obligations' to the great lady, duly signed the patent before leaving the capital post haste. When Barbara arrived early the next morning, patents in hand, she was dumbfounded to learn that she had been outwitted. And to this day the Duke of Richmond takes precedence over the Duke of Grafton, the title granted to Henry Fitzroy on Danby's return from Somerset.

Nell, who had no time for the humbug of political niceties, was exasperated by this latest show of favour towards her hated rival. 'Even Barbara's brats,' she cried, 'were not made Dukes until they were twelve or thirteen, but this French spy's son is ennobled when little more than an infant in arms!'[4] Nell felt snubbed and undervalued, and was only partially consoled by her appointment to the post of Lady of the Queen's Privy Chamber. This may have been at the King's prompting, but from what we know of Catherine it's more likely to have been a spontaneous gesture of goodwill on the part of that kind-hearted Queen. The post was essentially a sinecure, and allowed Nell access to Her Majesty's apartments. Above all, it conferred the status, if not the title, of 'lady' upon the former orange girl, which probably afforded her a great deal of private satisfaction. It wasn't proof against the snobbery of the court ladies, but it was at least a badge of dignity.

13

The Court Jester

DIGNITY AS PRACTISED BY THE majority of court ladies, that is to say self-love, was of no value to Nell. She made it her business to pull faces at dignity, the more grotesque the better. For her, the court was simply another theatre, and the part she chose to play was that of the fool or jester. Like the joker in a pack of cards, which is free to 'go wild' and stand for any other card, Nell could mimic whomever she liked, the King included. As such, she stood outside the formal hierarchy of relationships that constituted society. This gave her the freedom to do and say as she pleased, provided she retained that all-important license – the King's indulgence. With it, her charter was indeed 'as large as the wind', to blow on whom she pleased.

The honourable history of the licensed fool came to an end during the reign of Charles I, when in April 1637 the King's jester, Archie Armstrong, was expelled from court for calling Archbishop Laud 'a Monk, a Rogue, and a Traitor'. He was carried to the Porter's Lodge at Whitehall, where they pulled his coat over his ears and booted him out into the street. Archie had gone too far, but there were collective powers at work as well. The monarchy was besieged by the forces of democracy, and the fool's primary function was undermined by the growing power of Parliament, which acted as a check on the King's absolute authority. His pungent commentary on affairs of state and his chiding of the King's folly were now supplanted by printed broadsheets and satires, available for men to read at their local coffee houses. It was in the time of Charles's grandfather James I that Archie had had his heyday. As John Southworth writes in his *Fools and Jesters at the English Court*,

> It was among the mass of ordinary Londoners, whose prejudices he shared, that he [Archie] became a popular figure. Like them, he was disapproving of bishops, suspicious of foreigners, and resentful of the tyranny of over-mighty ministers. At a time when any expression of what we would now describe as 'public opinion' was ruthlessly suppressed, reports of his taunts against such establishment figures as Northampton, Buckingham and Laud were greeted with delight in the City taverns, and endlessly repeated.

These words could easily be applied to Nell Gwyn, who was in many respects Archie's heir. Curiously enough, having survived his expulsion from Court by thirty-five years, Archie died in March 1672 just as Nell was beginning to shake her bells in earnest. Having 'jested himself into a fair estate', Archie had been living in comfortable retirement with his family up in Cumberland. With singular aptness he was buried on April Fool's Day.

The ethos of the time, quite apart from the new political dispensation, was unfavourable to the profession of fooling. In the theatre the formal, classical stage of the Restoration had no room for the spontaneous outbursts of the fool; stage management was too strict. Moreover, the noblemen and gentlemen who patronized the theatres wanted to see themselves hoisted onto a heroic plane far removed from the impertinence of fools and clowns. There are no fools in Dryden, for to his mind they were anti-heroic and violated 'the decorum of the stage'. He and the other heroic dramatists prided themselves on the sophistication of the new drama. As for the Restoration court, it was consciously modelled on the continental type, especially the French, and it, too, liked to consider itself sophisticated and cosmopolitan. The fool's bladder would have seemed impossibly coarse. Besides, the court wit was himself a sort of fool of the sophisticated sort. The same dynamic was evident in France, where the Sociétés Joyeuses (Societies of Fools) died out in the reign of Louis XIV, whose cult of infallibility precluded ridicule.

The King appointed Tom Killigrew as Court Jester shortly after the Restoration, but it was probably a joke, as Killigrew had many disqualifications for the role, not least his high level of literacy. Moreover, he held other formal appointments both in the theatre and at court which prevented that dedication to folly which is the hallmark of the true fool. It also meant that he couldn't serve as the King's constant companion. (The true fool *belonged to* the king, and was his most faithful servant.) Also, by the time Nell was wielding her marotte at court, Killigrew, who was born in 1611, was already in his sixties. Nevertheless, the recorded anecdotes of his jibes and pranks ably demonstrate his jesting skills. He never lost an opportunity to remind the King of the lamentable state of his affairs, and on one occasion offered the following neat solution: 'There is,' said he, 'a good honest able man that I could name, whom if your majesty would employ, and command to see all things well executed, all things would soon be mended, and this is one Charles Stewart, who now spends his time in employing his lips and lusts about the Court, and hath no other employment; but if you would give him this employment, he were the fittest man in the world to perform it.'[1]

On another occasion he was employed by Nell herself to goad the King into attending the Council, which he had been neglecting of late. Nell met the Duke of Lauderdale returning from the King's Closet and, learning of his failure to persuade Charles, laid a wager of £100 that she would have better luck. Whereupon she sent for old Tom Killigrew and instructed him in his part with all the skill of a practised thespian. Having got himself ready, Killigrew burst into the King's Closet in full travelling gear – cloak, hat, riding boots and crop – with a look of the utmost urgency on his face. 'What, Killigrew!' cried Charles, 'where are you going in such a violent hurry?' 'To hell,' replied the earnest madcap, 'to fetch up Oliver Cromwell to look after the affairs of England, for his successor never will.' According to Nell's earliest biographer, 'This Expedient, concerted by *Nell Gwinn*, and executed by *Killegrew*, had the desired Effect; for he [the King] immediately went to the Council, and, as long as he could bear the Badges of Royalty, continued with them'.

Nell, on the other hand, possessed all the essential qualities of the court fool, being completely uneducated, of small stature and devoted to the King. Her life too had followed the pattern of the great court fools of the past: from humble beginnings, a gift for entertainment had brought her to the attention of the monarch. Traditionally, as long as he pleased the king, the fool was safe and lived a privileged life; but there was always the possibility that he would go too far and find himself out in the cold again.

There were two principal types of court fool, the natural and the artificial, and Nell embodied aspects of both. The natural fool was by nature foolish or simple, retarded even, and possessed a childlike faith in the goodness and abundance of life. In medieval England these fools were considered close to God and in Mediterranean cultures were thought to ward off the evil eye. They might be the one source of innocence in a corrupt court. Nell was not, of course, a simpleton; on the contrary, she was known for her sharp wit. Nevertheless, she possessed an unschooled innocence that won her the goodwill of the people and a certain immunity at court. It was also proof against the corrupting influence of sudden wealth and status. It meant that she could remain in the court, but not of it. This was a vital element of all true court fools: though their privileged position made them insiders, they could never be anything but aliens at heart.

Outwardly Nell wore the fine apparel of the court, but deep down she was an outsider. As an innocent of sorts, she was the butt of much condescending humour from her superiors, who absorbed the shock of her presence at Court by dismissing her in their minds as a mere child, tolerating her as they might a performing monkey. Otherwise, the threat to the social order was obvious. For Charles, however, who had been brought up in an upside-down society, where the king had been executed and his nobles abolished, there was something familiar, even comforting, in the presence of his 'tricksy spirit'.[2]

The artificial fool, on the other hand, was anything but foolish. Because he made it his business to be blunt, he could appear crude and simple, but this was part of an artful disguise. In a corrupt and sophisticated court, that lived from the neck up, the fool represented the wisdom of the instincts. It was his task to keep the king in touch with his heart and remind him of his humanity, so that power was tempered with compassion. In a court where flattery was the monarch's staple diet, the fool was the truth-teller. He alone spoke out with impunity, hence the term 'licensed' or 'allowed' fool. As Olivia remarks in *Twelfth Night*, 'there is no slander in an allowed fool though he do nothing but rail'. To point out the king's folly was to point out his vices, for in the fool's book vice was the only real folly. Kindness and wisdom were one.

But the artificial fool wasn't simply there to counsel the king; he was there to make him laugh, and if he could do both at once, so much the better. If the king was melancholy (considered in those days to be a state of temporary folly or madness), then he would more often than not call for his fool, who like Nell usually had singing and dancing in his repertoire, as well as clowning. According to the satirical poem 'The Lady of Pleasure', no one had such a knack for pleasing the King as Nell: 'When he was dumpish, she would still be jocond / And chuck the royal chin of Charles ye Second.' As Bishop Burnet commented, 'She acted all persons in so lively a manner and was such a constant diversion to the King that even a new mistress could not drive her away.' Nell's wit, in the tradition of the medieval fool, was sharp but earthy, full of homely metaphors that brought pretension crashing to the ground. With it she exploited the hypocrisy and vainglory of those around her, as when on a visit to the Duchess of Cleveland one day she 'thought ye Dutchess lookt a little coyly at her, soe [she] clapt her on ye shoulder, & sade shee perseaved yt persons of trade loved not on[e] another'.[3] In Nell's book the Duchess of Cleveland, for all her bells and whistles, was a whore like any other, and there was an end of the matter. And when Mary Kirke, the wife of the Keeper of Whitehall Palace, called her a whore, Nell retorted that she wouldn't have minded if it had been any one else, but to be called whore by someone who had been 'an old notorious whore even before whoreing was in fashion' afflicted her.[4]

There are many instances of Nell's blunt humour towards the King, used more often than not to goad him into action. Indeed, the 1752 memorialist claims that Nell was 'so far . . . from drawing aside the King from an Attention to his Affairs, that she often excited him to Diligence'. One day the King, being badgered on all sides both by members of Parliament and his own ministers for the threadbare state of the national purse, retired to Nell's apartment in a state of considerable dejection. When he asked her what he could do to satisfy his critics, her response was swift: 'Dismiss your Ladies, and mind your

Business; the People of England will soon be pleased.' Thus, even though Nell was one of those very ladies, her duty to speak the truth came before self-interest. The memorialist ends with the following observation: 'This good-natur'd Prince was never more delighted than to have Truth told him in a pleasing facetious Manner; and as Nell was sensible of this, she fell upon a Number of Expedients to divert him, and at the same time put him in mind of his Affairs.'

On another occasion, Nell told the King that the only way to placate Parliament was to treat it to a meal of her devising, namely 'a French ragou, Scotts collops, and a calf's head'. The French ragou was Louise, the Scotts collops the Duke of Lauderdale – hated in Scotland for his enforcement of episcopal power – and the calf's head was Danby, feared for his high-handed treatment of Parliament. (Calf's Head Day was the Puritan term for Charles I's execution day.) The King laughed, but Nell, sensing that she was not being taken seriously, added a savage coda: 'Hang up the Scotch dog and the French bitch!' That was in March 1675. As usual, Nell was in tune with the national mood, for in the next session of Parliament moves were initiated against Lauderdale and Danby, and derogatory remarks made about the ambitions of the de Kéroualle family.

The fool was also the scourge of vanity, and in this Louise qualified as Nell's primary target. Her constant air of pride and righteous indignation seems to have called forth an impish spirit in her English rival that dogged her every step. And the more the Duchess tried to ignore 'the frisking comedian', as de Courtin described her, the more outrageously mischievous she became. One of Louise's favourite ways of advertising her lofty social connections was by going into mourning at the death of foreign dignitaries. Public mourning had its own strict etiquette in those days, at least in high places, and only close relatives of the deceased could wear funeral weeds and drape their coaches in black. Thus, for Louise, ostentatious mourning was a way of claiming kinship with the high-born of the world.

When news of the death of the Chevalier de Rohan reached England in December 1674, Louise appeared in deepest mourning. Sobbing words of grief into a black handkerchief, pacing fitfully back and forth, wringing her hands in torment, she sought to wrench the whole court into a like frame of mind. On the orders of the King, she was escorted back to her apartments, where her ladies did everything they could to console her; but she kept returning to the Presence Chamber, muttering prayers for the Rohans, to whom she appears to have been completely unrelated. In fact, the object of her mourning on this occasion turned out to be rather ill-chosen, for though he was indeed a prince of the blood, the Chevalier had died a traitor's death.[5]

The very next day Nell herself appeared at court in full mourning garb, and clearly convulsed with grief. She sobbed and moaned and tore at her hair, and grabbed the arm of a bewildered courtier to prevent herself from falling. 'He is gone, he is gone!' she cried, staring wild-eyed into the man's astonished face. If Louise had been overcome with grief, Nell had gone one better – she was in paroxysms of sorrow. Even the King, who was well used to Nell's pranks, was a little bemused, while the Duchess, still in mourning for the Chevalier, looked nervously over at her rival. When Nell had been made to calm down a little, one of the gentlemen about the King enquired what the matter was. 'Why!' she exclaimed, 'have you not heard of my loss in the death of the Cham of Tartary?' 'And what relation, pray,' asked the gentleman, 'was the Cham of Tartary to you?' 'Oh,' replied Nell nonchalantly, as if retailing common knowledge, 'exactly the same relation as Rohan was to Cartwheel.' The King was unable to suppress his laughter, though it meant a tearful exit from the insulted Duchess. As for the courtiers, they roundly applauded the King's jester for dispelling the pall of gloom cast by Louise's mummery. It was a stroke of genius on Nell's part to have lighted upon the Cham of Tartary, whose name was a byword for anything far-fetched. In Congreve's *Love for Love* Sir Sampson Legend interrupts Foresight's bragging by crying out, 'I know the length of the Emperor of China's foot; have kissed the great Mogul's slipper, and rid a hunting upon an elephant with the Cham of Tartary . . .'

After her initial humiliation Louise continued to flaunt her grief for a host of deceased European sovereigns, and each time, by judicious priming of her diplomatic contacts, Nell was able to trump her. The luck of the devil was with Nell. When, for instance, Louise went into mourning for the King of Sweden, the very next day saw Nell gifted with news of the death of the King of Portugal (Queen Catherine's brother). Sometimes, though, she had to fall back on her imagination, as when she put on funeral weeds for the 'Boog of Oronooko', no doubt inspired by Aphra Behn's tale of the tragic African prince. Finally, by way of a fitting end to her mourning jests, Nell suggested that she and Louise should divide up the world between them: she would take the kings of the south, and Louise could have the kings of the north — that way they wouldn't trespass on each other's grief. It was certainly fitting that the phlegmatic Louise was assigned the northern hemisphere, while Nell with her joie de vivre claimed hegemony over the south.

Nell loved to copy Louise in other ways too, and the fact that her victim always rose to the bait made the trouble worth it. In the autumn of 1674 Louise sat for Henri Gascar, the French portrait painter who had just arrived at court. Pictured as Venus holding a dove, with her son Charles Lennox as Cupid, Louise wore a special full-length red and white satin chemise trimmed with lace and lined with pink silk, which was open at the chest. She was seated on a bank of cushions (a sort of couch) backed by heavy purple drapes, with a view of St James's Park over her left shoulder. Nell employed some mischievous body about the court to filch the chemise, and had herself painted in it by the same artist, with herself as Venus and her sons as cupids. Gascar, unfamiliar with the rivalries at the English court and thinking that the portrait was a harmless piece of flattery, willingly complied with Nell's instructions. Where Louise had sat on a couch, half reclining, Nell lay back full-length on a bank of flowers to show off the chemise to best effect. The background is identical, only Nell could not resist a little one-upmanship: across the water on the other side of the canal stands the King, gazing across at his mistress, while the younger cupid, James, holds a burning torch between his parents to signify the ardour of their love. One can picture Louise's exasperation when she saw the portrait over the fireplace at 79 Pall Mall.

Yet Nell seems to have found it in her heart to be genuinely friendly from time to time, and even invited Louise for tea and cards. Both women were incorrigible gamblers, and Louise rarely declined an opportunity to take money off her less wealthy colleague. Nell's basset table was renowned as a place of bonhomie and merriment, where fantastic sums could change hands in the course of an afternoon. Basset, having the highest stakes, was *the* court game, though the King himself did not take part and tried his best to discourage gambling among his ladies, for obvious reasons. But the craze had too strong a hold on gallant society, and skill at cards had become a mark of good breeding. In *The Complete Gamester; or, Full and Easy Instructions for Playing the Games now in Vogue*, published in 1674, Richard Seymour wrote, 'Gaming is become so much the fashion among the *beau monde*, that he who in company should appear ignorant of the games in vogue would be reckoned low-bred and hardly fit for conversation.'

If anything, the ladies were more addicted than the gallants, who began to complain that their mistresses were neglecting them in favour of the gaming tables. It was said too that they were ruining their looks by sitting up all night at cards, and consuming large quantities of alcohol while they were at it. Aphra Behn, herself a bon viveur, gave this warning in her prologue to *The Moor's Revenge*: 'Yet sitting up so late, as I am told, / You'll lose in beauty what you gain in gold.' The playwright Susanna Centlivre even wrote a comedy on the subject, entitled *The Basset Table*, which takes place at the Covent Garden lodgings of Lady Reveller at four o'clock in the morning. Even Sunday was desecrated by the new passion. Pepys, who was scandalized, wrote, 'This evening going to the Queen's side [at Whitehall] to see the ladies, I did find the Queen, the Duchess of York, and another or two, at cards, with the room full of great ladies and men; which I was amazed at to see on a Sunday, having not believed it; but certainly flatly denied the same a little time since to my cousin, Roger Pepys.'

Gambling parties and state dinners aside, Nell would sometimes share a table with Louise at one of the King's intimate suppers at Whitehall. On one occasion they were dining *à trois* in the King's private apartments. Boiled chicken was on the menu, and there were two of them on the table. Louise, who liked to venture the odd jest herself, declared that there were in fact three chickens on the table. When Nell asked her to explain, she pointed to the first one and said, 'Zer is one,' then pointed to the second and said, 'And zer is two. One and two makes tree. Zer are tree shicken on ze table.' 'Why, so there are!' cried Nell. And with that she put the first one on the King's plate, took the second for herself and bid Louise take the third.

Their contrasting reactions to danger are also revealing. When her coach was waylaid on the old Portsmouth Road out of London by the notorious highwayman known as 'old Mobb', Louise attempted to face off the old ruffian with a show of icy dignity. She began by asking him if he knew who she was. 'Indeed I do, madam,' replied old Mobb with insolent composure. 'I know you to be the greatest whore in the kingdom and that you are maintained at the public charge.' Louise blushed to the roots of her hair and told him that he would pay dearly for this affront. But old Mobb had heard that sort of bluster before and proceeded to rob her, telling her that he cared not for her haughty French spirit, so long as her money was English. He concluded with his own delicious brand of pride. 'I would have you know that I am king here,' he said, drawing himself up. 'And I have a whore of my own to keep at the public expense, just the same as King Charles has.'

Nell was held up on a different stretch of the same road while crossing Bagshot Heath, but with very different results. Her assailant was another well-known prince of thieves, Pat O'Bryan, a former sentinel in the Coldstream Guards, who had the brass neck to ask her for a little something for himself once he'd completed the formal task of robbing her – which may suggest that he was part of a cartel that divided their takings. Nell was so delighted by his effrontery (Captain Smith relates that she 'laugh[ed] heartily at his bull') that she rewarded him with a kiss. Overcome by this unexpected boon, O'Bryan promptly returned her rings and, having doffed his hat, turned to go. But Nell hadn't finished with him; she called him back and handed him ten guineas.[6]

Another anecdote reveals the public mood towards the rival mistresses. A leading goldsmith of the early eighteenth century, looking back to his days as an apprentice, recalled the time in Charles's reign that his master was making an expensive service of plate on the King's orders. It was a gift from His Majesty to the Duchess of Portsmouth. But when the people heard about it, they formed a crowd outside the shop, jeering and hooting, and, as he said, 'threw a thousand ill-wishes against the Duchess, and wished the silver was melted and poured down her throat; but 'twas ten thousand pities his Majesty had not bestowed this bounty on Madam Ellen.'

Barbara, too, came in for her fair share of ribbing from Nell, but she seems to have taken it in good part. Having enjoyed many lovers from outside her social circle, she didn't stand on ceremony in the way that Louise did. At around the time that she began her affair with Wycherley, Barbara took to driving about London in a coach and six, traditionally the privilege of royalty. So Nell hired an old cart and six oxen and drove past Berkshire House cracking her whip and shouting 'Whores to market, ho!' But Barbara was not to be a target for much longer. In March 1676 she went to live in Paris, her life in England having become too much of a farce, even for her. In the French capital she was able to start all over again, using her erotic reputation to take a string of high-class Gallic lovers.

One thing of a practical nature that strikes one about Nell's pranks is how painstaking they were. Considerable time and expense must have been involved in researching the deaths of foreign kings and having the necessary funeral weeds made, or in hiring a cart and six oxen, or indeed in filching a favourite chemise from the Duchess of Portsmouth. This was not simply spontaneous high spirits; it was conscientious fooling in the best medieval tradition.

Nell was also a member of what Andrew Marvell termed 'the merry gang', a group of court wits, most of them sympathetic to the Country Party, who made it their business to poke fun at the government and all things officious. They met at Nell's Pall Mall home for afternoons of political discussion and, inevitably where Buckingham was concerned, lively intrigue. They even generated a cabal or two, which Nell joined more out of good humour than conviction. The merry gang was, in a sense, the equivalent of the old Sociétés Joyeuses in France which, as Enid Welsford relates, was an institution 'whose members, in their capacity as fools, were pledged to more or less continuous representation of the whole of society as a "great stage of fools"'. Courtiers, poets, satirists, politicos, pranksters and voluptuaries, the merry gang that met at Nell's house was remarkable for its ever-shifting interests and allegiances.

Among its members were many old friends, such as Rochester, Buckingham, Sedley, Harry Killigrew (Tom's son) and Sir Carr Scrope, known as the 'ugly *beau-garçon*'. Others included Rochester's great friend Henry Savile, a former lover of Barbara's (who wasn't?), Bab May, Keeper of the Privy Purse, Nell's future steward Fleetwood Sheppard, the Earl of Mulgrave, a poet and politician of extraordinary vanity who was given the nickname 'Numps' (i.e., fool) by his fellow wits, Henry Guy, who together with Harry Killigrew had secured Rose Gwyn's release from jail in 1663 and the playwrights Wycherley and Etherege. Dryden's relationship with the group was uneasy, reflecting both envy and contempt, and eventually turned to hostility. He had once been tempted to describe them as Augustans, harking back to the witty circle that gathered round Ovid: 'We have,' he said, 'our genial nights, when our discourse is neither too serious nor too light, but always pleasant, and for the most part instructive; the raillery neither too sharp upon the present, nor too censorious on the absent, and the cups only such as will raise the conversation of the night, without disturbing the business of the morrow.' Witty they certainly were, and most of them, like Ovid, suffered banishment from court at least once in their careers, but Dryden's civilized commentary does not do justice to their wild escapades, nor the vicious in-fighting among them that produced some of the tartest libels of the age.

It was very much a boys' club, and Nell seems to have been the only female to be admitted to its mysteries. Many of the friendships between its members were remarkably pure and affectionate, and she partook of these as well. Rochester, in particular, was always solicitous for her welfare at court and proferred some astute advice. In a letter to his dear friend – and hers – Henry Savile in June 1678, Rochester wrote,

> But to confess the Truth, my Advice to the Lady you wot of [i.e., Nell], has ever been this, Take your measures just contrary to your Rivals, live in Peace with all the World, and easily with the King: Never be so Ill-natur'd to stir up his Anger against others, but let him forget the use of a Passion, which is never to do you good: Cherish his Love where-ever it inclines, and be assur'd you can't commit greater Folly than pretending to be jealous; but, on the contrary, with Hand, Body, Head, Heart and all the Faculties you have, contribute to his Pleasure all you can, and comply with his Desires throughout: And, for new Intrigues, so you be at one end 'tis no matter which: Make Sport when you can, at other times help it.

But Rochester wasn't always so sound. In June 1675 he, Savile and other members of the gang succumbed to a spell of midsummer madness. On leaving Whitehall after 'drinking and roistering all night with the King', they stumbled upon the great sundial in the Privy Garden, a rare construction of glass spheres considered to be one of the finest in Europe, and Charles's pride and joy. The whole structure was cone-shaped, and to the drunken Rochester decidedly phallic. Coming to a sudden halt in front of it – for it blocked their path – he was seized with blind indignation. 'What!' he cried. 'Dost thou stand there to fuck time?' And drawing his sword, he rushed upon the offending object. His companions followed at his heels, and in a trice the masterpiece was no more. Charles was furious and banished the entire pack to the country.

Rochester, as was his wont, spent his time in the country writing libels on his enemies at court, for he had well-placed spies that fed him the latest gossip from Whitehall. But it only brought him further trouble. Indeed, no sooner was he back at court in the autumn of 1675 than he managed to offend the Duchess of Portsmouth with one of his pungent verses ('Portsmouth's Looking Glass'), and was rusticated once more, this time for a whole year. But he was incapable of spending twelve months in the company of his wife and children, surrounded by fields, so he crept back, not to the court itself, but to the City, where he disguised himself as a trader and lived under a false name. There he wheedled his way into the society of rich merchants, winning their approval with his invectives against the dissolute court and by singling out a certain Earl of Rochester for particular obloquy. His purpose all along was to seduce their wives. When he tired of this, he took other lowlier disguises, such as a porter or a beggar, in order to augment his knowledge of the London underworld, which had always fascinated him, and to enjoy the poor man's opinion of the court. Bishop Burnet was impressed by Rochester's dedication as a man of disguise: 'At other times, merely for diversion, he would go about in odd shapes; in which he acted his part so naturally, that even those who were in the secret, and saw him in these shapes, could perceive nothing by which he might be discovered.'

Finally, he embarked on the elaborate hoax that he'd been planning for many a month. Setting himself up at lodgings in a goldsmith's house next door to the sign of the Black Swan in Tower Street, he dispersed bills throughout the City announcing the arrival in London of the famous Italian pathologist Doctor Alexander Bendo, who would be at the service of all comers 'from three of the Clock in the afternoon, till eight at night'. Pathologist meant mountebank, a familiar type both on the streets of London and in Restoration drama, notorious for his home-brewed remedies for all ailments from bad breath to syphilis. And in an age whose science was still fantastical in many respects, fuelling as much as dispelling superstition, there was a rich store of credulity for the mountebank to feed on. As was his hope, word soon spread to the court, and first the ladies' maids then the ladies themselves beat a path to his door. Rochester qua Bendo was a sort of doctor of vanity, who in addition to his remedies for diseases 'Peculiar to Women' practised 'rare Secrets for the help, conservation, and Augmentation of Beauty and Comeliness'. He also practised physiognomy, interpreted dreams and made astrological predictions, all arts guaranteed to fascinate his female clientele. He owed his success at divination to his intimate knowledge of the court ladies, their love interests and the particular scandals that attached to them. Being Bendo added to his vast store of prurient knowledge.

Rochester was not alone in his strange despair. The aristocracy in general was undergoing a crisis of identity. Noblemen experimented with a plethora of different roles, as their ancient sense of public duty was confounded by a newer, more urgent call: self-exploration. They sought a deeper identity, beyond that conferred by their titles and hereditary offices. Cromwell had proved that neither the monarchy nor the nobility were permanent; it was a realization that sent many noblemen scurrying off to become poets, dramatists, scientists, explorers, philosophers or simply gamesters. And sometimes, of course, the inner journey took darker forms; brilliant men such as Rochester could spend whole weeks inebriated, using his wit 'as a torch to light himself to Hell thereby'. In the end it was through illness and an early premonition of death that Rochester came to a poignant realization of his folly: 'It is a miraculous thing,' he wrote, 'when a man half in the grave cannot leave off playing the fool and the buffoon; but so it falls out to my comfort.'

Even Nell sometimes found herself on the wrong end of a prank or two. Harry Killigrew, a madcap like his father, eventually appointed Court Jester by William III in 1694, was famously hot-headed and often in trouble (duelling had been going out of fashion until he turned up). When his wife died at the end of October 1677, Nell qualified her condolences with the reservation that he was now at liberty to 'play the fool again'. She could not have been more right, for hardly had a month elapsed than she became his first victim. Louise had fallen dangerously ill at the beginning of December, and her life hung in the balance for several very long days. Many of the younger court beauties were on their knees, praying for her death. But they were to be disappointed. Louise suddenly rallied, and Killigrew seems to have got the news hot off the press. Arriving at Nell's house at four in the morning and as drunk as a lord, he set up an unholy din, beating upon the door and bellowing for her to come down. When she put her head out of the window and demanded to know his business, he announced that he had come hot-foot from Whitehall specially 'to acquaint her with the good news of the Duchess of Portsmouth's recovery'. Nell told him what she thought of his lousy prank, whereupon he proceeded to 'rall[y] her with his abusive tongue extremely'. Nell was so incensed at this display of ill nature that she reported the incident to the King, who banished Killigrew from court.

Maybe Nell herself had been praying for Louise's death, for her reaction to Killigrew's outburst was uncharacteristically peevish. Indeed her toleration of others' foibles was such that she sometimes found herself imposed upon, and there was never a time when some poor outcast from the storms at court wasn't lodging beneath her roof (Buckingham, Monmouth, Scrope, to name but three). But much as she valued the underdog and the scapegrace, she nevertheless expected high standards of personal hygiene from them. William Fanshawe, one of Rochester's cronies in his hell-raising days, was another of Nell's creatures. A minor court official, who was inordinately proud of his marriage to Monmouth's half-sister Mary, Fanshawe was noted for his cynicism in a notably cynical age. 'Lame and lean, with mouth awry from the pox', he was, according to Rochester's mother, 'a pitiful fellow, upon all accounts but mischief'. When his first child was born in the autumn of 1677, Nell urged a modest christening in order that her friend might 'reserve himself a little to buy him new shoes that he might not dirty her rooms, and a new periwig that she might not smell him stink two stories high' when she opened the front door.[7]

Sir Carr Scrope, Rochester's 'purblind knight, / Who squints more in his judgment than his sight', was another defective character to find shelter beneath Nell's broad wing. A wit himself, he seems to have been a perpetual target for his fellows, who attacked his ridiculous appearance as much as his petulant versifying. Sir Carr seemed to excite Rochester to his wicked best: he was, he said, 'love's scarecrow'. This wretched figure fell in love with Nell and became a frequent visitor to her house, paying court in his own inimitable way. It amused her for a while, for he could write charmingly at a pinch and made her laugh, but when he began to press his attentions upon her she rebelled. In a letter of June 1678 to Lory Hyde, son of the former Lord Chancellor, Nell wrote, 'the pell mel [Pall Mall] is now to me a dismale plase sinse I have uterly lost Sr Car Scrope never to be recovrd agane for he tould me he could not live allwayes at this rate & so begune to be a littel uncivil which I could not sufer from an uglye baux garscon.' In other words, Scrope got bored with literary love-making; he wanted the real thing.

Nor was Nell afraid to chide Rochester himself for his churlish and unchivalrous behaviour. When her friend Elizabeth Barry gave birth to Rochester's child in November 1677, Savile wrote to the Earl, who was ill in the country,

> The greatest news I can send you from hence is what the King told me last night, that your Lordship has a daughter borne by the body of Mrs. Barry of which I give your honour joy. I doubt she does not lie in much state, for a friend and protectress of hers in the Mall [i.e., Nell Gwyn] was much lamenting her poverty very lately, not without some gentle reflections on your Lordship's want either of generosity or bowels towards a lady who had not refused you the full enjoyment of her charms.

Nell's most regular partner in folly was Buckingham. The two were wont to reduce her guests to tears of laughter with their mischievous skits on Danby and his deranged wife. But Buckingham was a dangerous ally to have, for his licence for folly had long expired and the government was keeping a close eye on him. He had been at the peak of his influence in the autumn of 1670, but he lacked political guile and was quickly outwitted by his opponents. There was also his demoralizing affair with the Countess of Shrewsbury, whose husband Buckingham killed in a duel in 1668. From that moment, things began to unravel for him. Nell was one of the very few who remained loyal to him in his declining years, not only because she remembered his role in introducing her to the King, but because constancy in both love and friendship was her watchword. And though Buckingham had made some clumsy attempts at seducing her, Nell was quick to forgive such desperate acts of gallantry. Buckingham still believed that the King could be controlled through women and kept what was jocularly known as 'the convent' in his London home, a group of rooms reserved for promising young girls, to be loosed upon the King when the time was ripe. But it was an obsolete fantasy.

Buckingham wasn't even in the lists when Charles's final serious mistress arrived in England in December 1675. The lady in question, a thirty-year-old Italian adventurer, celebrated as much for the scandal that had dogged her life as for her rare beauty, landed in Torbay, having travelled incognito all the way from Savoy to Amsterdam to escape detection by her husband's agents. She was met ten miles outside London by Ralph Montagu, who with the help of his sister Lady Harvey set himself up as her 'manager'. They were joined in this enterprise by Lord Arlington, who was looking for a way to oust Louise as *maîtresse en titre*. The lady was Hortense Mancini, Duchess Mazarin, the fourth of the five Mancini sisters who had grown up under the care of their powerful uncle, Cardinal Julius Mazarin, virtual ruler of France during the minority of Louis XIV. Hortense had been his favourite niece and the chief beneficiary of his will. She and her husband were left the greater part of his fabulous fortune, amounting to some twenty-eight million livres (approximately £140 million today), and lived in quasi-royal style at the Palais Mazarin. Charles himself had been a suitor to the teenage Hortense in the days of his exile, but Mazarin had not fancied the young man's prospects. The Cardinal changed his tune after the Restoration, offering a dowry of twenty million livres, but Charles's advisers feared the match would prove unpopular with the people and the offer was rejected. Now, finally, fifteen years later, the King had an opportunity to taste what he had missed.

Ironically, it was Hortense's marriage that had been the great misfortune of her life. Her husband, Armand de la Porte, Marquis de Meilleraye, was created Duc Mazarin by the Cardinal so that the Mazarin name would live on through his niece and her children. The new Duc, however, was not one to play second fiddle to his wife, and marriage soon brought out his domineering strain. Worse than that, Hortense seems to have fertilized the seeds of madness in him, and intense jealousy quickly turned to paranoia. He dismissed any servant found conversing with his wife and virtually put her under house arrest. Any suggestion of sex drove him to frenzy. A maniacal prude, he claimed to be acting on the advice of angels. Women on his estates were forbidden to milk cows, lest the action of pulling the animals' teats should excite sexual thoughts in them, and he vandalized the Cardinal's priceless collection of classical nudes by hacking off their private parts. Then when a series of visions convinced him that he was in fact a tulip, he ordered his servants to plant him in the garden and pour water over his head.

Hortense eventually managed to escape and so began an errant life of adventure, wandering across Europe often disguised as a man, seeking refuge among her many highly placed relatives and admirers, though convents often proved the safest hideouts. Nearly always, she managed to stumble upon the good life. After her expulsion from Savoy, her one-time friend Sidonia de Courcelles wrote, 'But what is so strange is that this woman triumphs over all her misfortunes by an excess of folly which has no parallel, and that after receiving this set-back she thinks of nothing but enjoying herself. When she passed through here she was on horse-back, befeathered and bewigged, with a train of twenty men. She talked of nothing but violins and hunting-parties and everything else that can give pleasure.' The good citizens of London must have stopped and stared as they saw this female cavalier ride through the streets of the capital with her moth-eaten but colourful train. In fact she had eight servants with her, including her little Moor, Mustapha, who had been a present from the Duke of Savoy and swam 'like a fish'.

The purpose of the Montagu–Arlington–Harvey cabal was not simply to oust Louise, but to break the Danby–Portsmouth axis, which strongly influenced domestic and foreign policy and the appointment of ministers. Whether Hortense came to England at the invitation of

Montagu is unknown, but the rumours that she was somehow an agent of the French King can be dismissed as incredible. Indeed, it wasn't long before the French ambassador, de Courtin, was so concerned about Hortense's intimacy with King Charles and her likely power to harm French interests, that he wrote to Louis asking that he find a way of ordering her back to France. What is certain, however, is that Hortense found London very much to her taste. Women there led freer lives than their sisters on the Continent, and she was soon the mistress of a bohemian salon, open all hours of the night and mighty gallant. De Courtin was probably correct when he described England as a haven for all women who had quarrelled with their husbands. Having come to London on a whim, the vagabond duchess was to remain until her death nearly a quarter of a century later.

In many ways Hortense was the ultimate wild mistress. She shared Nell's happy-go-lucky attitude to life and had a reputation as a madcap, but she was never a conscientious fool, for she lacked wit and purpose. Her pranks were of the high-spirited, public-schoolgirl variety, and rarely went beyond making apple-pie beds for the nuns in France or fencing in her dressing gown in St James's Park. Unfortunately for her promoters, Hortense resisted any interest in politics and was too volatile to be used effectively. Nor was it her ambition to rule the King of England's heart; she was, however, more than happy to have a fling with him, both for variety's sake and because it brought an annuity of £4,000 a year. But as Charles found to his disgust in the summer of 1677, he could not expect constancy in return for his money. Hortense's well-publicized affair with the Prince de Monaco exposed him to ridicule.

To a high-class gamester like Hortense, £4,000 a year meant the ability to continue living and entertaining while she indulged her passion for gambling. (Nell was said to have lost £5,000 to Hortense in a single evening.) Saint-Evremond, who had done his best to gather about Hortense a cultured salon of philosophers and literati, found his enterprise undermined by her addiction to the card table. Another exile from Paris, the wily croupier Morin, soon engrossed her attention and the quality of her company deteriorated. Hortense no longer had time for the verses Saint-Evremond used to read to her and like Lady Reveller in *The Basset Table* seemed surprised at his indignation: 'He

[Lord Worthy] had scarce begun [i.e., reading his verses] when I, being eager at a piquet, he rose up and said he believed I loved the music of my own voice crying "nine and twenty", "threescore", better than the sweetest poetry in the universe, and abruptly left us.'

Hortense's arrival eclipsed Louise, who seemed to fall into despair. Certainly the threat to her pre-eminence at court appeared real; after all, Hortense was to the manner born and possessed the sort of natural sophistication and easy familiarity with European royalty and nobility that Louise could only dream about. She was, in fact – pranks and frivolity aside – the epitome of all that Louise desired to be. Hortense had no sooner paid her compliments to the King than Nell went into mourning yet again; but this time the object of her grief was not a crowned head, but one that would dearly like to have been – Louise herself. The duchess's hopes were dead and buried, said Nell, and it was only proper that she should pay solemn tribute to her former rival. Indeed, at times it seemed as if the whole court was egging Charles on to have an affair with the Italian, simply to spite the French. De Courtin found Louise sobbing her eyes out at her Whitehall apartments, stung to the quick as much by Charles's callousness as by Hortense's sudden influence, for the King seemed to relish her discomfort and laughed at Nell's mockery. The French ambassador counselled her to hide her sorrow from the King, for sullen moods would alienate his affections still further. Meanwhile he wrote to Paris, 'I have ascertained beyond doubt that [the King] passes nights much less often with her [i.e., Louise] than with Nell Gwynn; and, if I can believe those who are most about with him, his relations with the Duchess of Portsmouth have subsided into a virtuous friendship. As to the Duchess Mazarin, I know he thinks her the finest woman that he ever saw in his life'.

With his waning virility, Charles's delight in women was probably more ocular and conversational than physical. He wasn't sleeping with Louise or Barbara any more and it's doubtful whether he had any real success with Hortense. It was important, however, that the King be seen as virile and capable of commanding the love of the most beautiful women, if only as a political gesture. The imputation of impotence could affect the pride and lustre of his harem, as well as undermining his ability to project an image of power.

Charles's elder daughter by Barbara, the fifteen-year-old Anne Sussex, herself pregnant with her first child, developed a teenage crush on Hortense and the two were inseparable. Cards, fencing, shuttle-cock, reading, chatting, playing pranks, they did everything together, even sleeping in the same bed. Anne now occupied her mother's old apartments directly above the King's Bedchamber. There was a stair-case linking the two, and every morning the King ascended in the hope of catching Hortense in bed with his daughter. De Courtin remarked how familiar Hortense seemed with the King, whispering in his ear and never once addressing him as 'Your Majesty'. There were reports too that he visited her house at night, not returning to Whitehall until five in the morning.

The love contest between Nell, Louise and Hortense became a matter of public interest. They were portrayed as the three classical goddesses vying for the golden apple, with Charles as an ageing and rather indifferent Paris, determined as usual not to be tied to a judgement. In Edmund Waller's poem 'The Triple Combat', Nell, the native beauty, is portrayed as Chloris, Hortense as the Roman eagle and Louise the representative of Little Britain or Brittany. Their respective supporters turn out in force:

> Legions of Beauties to the battle come,
> For Little Britain these, and those for Rome.
> Dressed to advantage, this illustrious pair
> Arrived, for combat in the list appear.
> What may the Fates design! for never yet
> From distant regions two such beauties met.
> Venus had been an equal friend to both,
> And victory to declare herself seems loth;
> Over the camp, with doubtful wings, she flies,
> *Till Chloris shining in the field she spies.*
> *The lovely Chloris well-attended came,*
> *A thousand Graces waited on the dame;*
> *Her matchless form made all the English glad,*
> *And foreign beauties less assurance had;*
> Yet, like the Three on Ida's top, they all
> Pretend alike, contending for the ball;

Which to determine, Love himself declined,
Lest the neglected should become less kind.
Such killing looks! so thick the arrows fly!
That 'tis unsafe to be a stander-by.
Poets, approaching to describe the fight,
Are by their wounds instructed how to write . . . [my italics]

Waller had been a mentor to the court wits and was a close friend of Buckingham, who esteemed him as the grand old cavalier of English letters. The Duke was always whisking the ageing poet off to his mansion on the Thames for supper, but, as this note to his wife makes clear, Waller found it difficult to keep up with the younger set: 'The Duke of Buckingham with the Lady Sh[rewsbury] came hither last night at this tyme and carried me to the usual place to supper, from whence I returned home at four o'clock this morning, having been earnestly entreated to supp with them again to-night, but such howers can not be always kept, therefore I shall eat my two eggs alone and go to bedd.' He lived round the corner from Nell in St James's Street, where Rochester also had a house, and sometimes accompanied Buckingham to 79 Pall Mall for an afternoon of witty conversation and court gossip. His portrayal of Charles as 'Love himself' confounded by his range of choice corresponds with de Courtin's assessment towards the end of 1676. According to Forneron, 'Courtin pitied Charles, who wanted to be well with every one – a hard problem to solve, surrounded, as he was, by jealous women. He had to face the anger of the Duchess of Portsmouth for drinking twice in twenty-four hours to the health of Nell Gwynn, with whom he still often supped, and who still made the Duchess of Portsmouth the butt for her tickling sarcasms. The rakes of the town met the king at her supper table, and said freely before him whatever came uppermost to their heads.'

Even though Hortense made no effort to oust Louise or set herself up as a rival, the latter almost brought ruin on herself by her sense of foreboding. Never had she felt such keen envy of another woman, nor been less able to disguise it. As Iago says of Cassio, so Louise might have said of Hortense, that she had 'a daily beauty in [her] life / That makes me ugly'. In the end Louise shrank from contact with her tall, black-haired opponent, fearing the unfavourable comparisons of the court pundits. Instead, she wended her way down to Bath, with a heavy cortège of staff and baggage, to take the waters. And although Charles and Hortense continued their game of 'Shall we, shan't we?', it was Nell who reaped the benefits of her absence. And Nell it was who greeted her noisily some six weeks later. According to Forneron, 'The Duchess of Portsmouth . . . was assailed on her return by the strong jests of Nell Gwynn. The latter armed herself in every possible way, to shelter herself from the resentment Louise might be expected to harbour because of the visits Nell received from the king in her absence'.

De Courtin, who was teased by his colleagues at the Ministry of Foreign Affairs back in Paris for having fallen in love with Hortense, now made it his business to bring the two duchesses, French and Roman, together. He still believed that Hortense was capable of wrecking Louise's influence, and was determined to exercise his talent for conciliation. The ambassador invited both ladies to dinner at the French Embassy and, taking them upstairs, locked them in a room together. When he tiptoed to the door several hours later and gingerly turned the key, the two women came skipping out hand in hand and danced down the stairs together. As far as Hortense was concerned, there had never been a feud to patch up. The scorpions had all been in Louise's head.

With Barbara in Paris, Louise in a state of eclipse and Hortense too wild and inconstant to pose a threat, Nell considered the time ripe for a fresh assault upon the King. She was determined to see her sons ennobled and went about it in the only effective way she knew: fooling. Two different tales recount how she went to work to remedy the situation, and both may be true. According to the first, one day at court the King asked to see their elder son, who was playing in a corner of the room, whereupon Nell cried out to the boy, 'Come hither, you little bastard!' A shocked silence fell on those present. The King himself was indignant and reproved her for her harsh language. But she was unabashed. Quoth Nell, 'I have no other title to call him by'.[8] Charles had been trapped, and had the good grace to acknowledge his negligence. Though, for a king who knew the art of letting events ripen, there had probably been neither neglect nor delay.

With the boy's education beginning in earnest, it would have been difficult to hold out much longer. With typical disregard for the conventional, Nell appointed one of the merry gang, Fleetwood Sheppard, as Charles's tutor. 'A ribald wit and farceur', he had for some time been living on the bounty of Nell's former lover, Charles Buckhurst, now Earl of Dorset, and had been one of Rochester's co-vandals in the sundial escapade. For all his debauchery, Sheppard was described by the latter as 'a Man of a fluent Stile and coherent Thought', and it's likely that the two wits preferred him for the post. He had an MA from Oxford and had studied at Gray's Inn, and in a more sober reign would become Gentleman Usher of the Black Rod.

According to the second, less plausible story, the King was approaching Nell's house through the garden one morning when he heard shouting and screaming from a top-floor window. Looking up, he saw her holding their son Charles out of the window by his legs and threatening to drop him if the King refused to ennoble him. Always quick off the mark, Charles called up, 'God save the Earl of Burford!' In some accounts of the story, the venue is not Pall Mall but Lauderdale House, where Nell was reputed to have been a tenant for a while.

Either way, a patent was drawn up on 27 December 1676 creating the six-year-old Charles Baron Heddington and Earl of Burford, both in the county of Oxfordshire. And the following month a further warrant was granted assigning arms to him and his younger brother James, who was given (rather strangely) the place and precedence of the eldest son of an earl. In other words, uniquely among the King's bastards, he wasn't made a peer. Charles may have intended to raise him to the peerage later on. Equally, he may have been sensitive to the charge that he was creating a future court party from his own offspring. As the surname granted to the brothers was 'Beauclerk', the younger became Lord James Beauclerk. The brothers' shield depicted the royal arms of King Charles II, representing England, France, Scotland and Ireland, overlaid by the baton sinister to signify illegit-imacy. For young Charles Beauclerk the shield was surmounted by an earl's coronet and supported on the right by a white antelope, marking his collateral descent from Henry IV, and on the left by a white greyhound, a symbol of his great-great-great-great-great-grandfather Henry VII. His crest was a gold lion crowned with an earl's coronet.

The motto selected was *Auspicium Melioris Aevi* (An Omen of a Better Age), meaning perhaps a return to a more chivalric one. One is reminded too of the words of Aphra Behn in her dedication to Nell of *The Feign'd Courtesans*. She refers to the Beauclerk boys as 'two noble branches . . . who give us . . . a hopeful prospect of what their future braveries will perform . . .' In 1818 the same motto was adopted by the Order of St Michael and St George.

The choice of surname is significant and stands out among all the generic Fitzroys and Fitzcharleses. 'Beauclerk' or 'Beauclerc', which among other things connotes fine penmanship, was a French variant of 'steward' and so a pun on the King's surname of 'Stewart'/Stuart. Why Charles chose to honour Nell's children with this most personal of names is not known, but he did. 'Beauclerc' was also the sobriquet given to King Henry I (1100–35), youngest son of William the Conqueror, for his literacy and the importance he placed on learning, and is usually translated as 'fine scholar' in this context. Interestingly, too, Henry raised many talented men of lowly birth to positions of prominence to offset the power of the barons; and his roll of illegitimate children was as impressive as Charles's. In Charles II's time the name Beauclerk was sometimes rendered 'Beauclaire' (fair light), which nicely reflects the meaning of the name Nell Gwyn (shining white).

There is a fine print engraved by R. White which shows the six-year-old Charles Beauclerk in his newly made earl's robes, accompanied by his brother. Looking self-possessed, even a little blasé, he rests his left hand on his hip while almost dangling the coronet from his right, as if it was no more than a bauble. His curly, shoulder-length hair rests on his silken robes. It was a proud time for Nell, who was also finally granted the freehold of 79 Pall Mall as well as the reversion of the Registrarship of the High Court of Chancery, an hereditary title that remains with the family today, though the office itself lapsed during the reign of George III. Her birthday party for James that Christmas turned into an extended celebration of all the bounties showered upon her by the Crown. A constant stream of coaches and sedans arrived at her door for their owners to offer their congratulations in person, not to mention all the written compliments which she answered with visits of her own.

After the Christmas hubbub was over, Nell went one January

afternoon to St James's Palace with her friend Lady Harvey to thank the Duchess Mazarin for her kind compliments on the ennoblement of her sons. When they arrived they found two other visitors present: the French ambassador de Courtin and the Duchess of Portsmouth. The awkwardness did not last long, and soon the four women were chatting gaily under the indulgent eye of the diplomat. Even Louise felt magnanimous enough to congratulate Nell on her sons' honours. Nevertheless her early departure seemed to dispel the last vestiges of formality and was succeeded by an episode of pure Gwynian mischief. Forneron takes up the story:

> . . . when the Duchess of Portsmouth left, Lady Harvey's fair friend [i.e., Nell], who was of the bold, laughing sort, turned round to De Courtin and asked why it was that the King of France did not send presents to her, instead of to the Weeping Willow who had just gone out? She vowed that he would have more profit in doing so, because the King of England was her constant nocturnal companion, and liked her far the best. The other ladies had heard of the luxurious fineness of Miss Nelly's under-clothing, and asked if they could judge of it for themselves. Without more ado she let them raise each petticoat, one by one, and before all in the room examine them on her.[9]

De Courtin, whose correspondence from London betrays a strong voyeuristic streak, was clearly titillated by the sight. On 18 January 1677 he wrote to Simon Arnauld, Marquis de Pomponne, the French Foreign Minister, in Paris to tell of Nell's petticoats and finished with these words: 'I never in my life saw such thorough cleanliness, neatness, and sumptuosity. I should speak of other things that we all were shown if M. de Lionne were still Foreign Secretary. But with you I must be grave and proper; and so, Monsieur, I end my letter.' Knowing the delight she took in exhibiting them, the 'other things' referred to were perhaps her pretty feet, ankles and legs. Even the famously formal Pomponne was charmed by what he read of Nell's artless exhibitionism. 'I am sure you forgot all your troubles,' he purred, 'when you were making Mistriss Nesle raise those neat and magnificent petticoats of hers.' Once again, Nell's folly had been her inspiration.

In his 1678 dedication to Nell of his *Lives and Histories of the Heathen Gods, Goddesses, & Demi-Gods*, Robert Whitcombe complimented her judgement and candour, saying that she was 'more addicted to forgive than censure'. 'Apollo told me,' he continued, 'that in you only he should meet with his Primitive Wisdom.' Apollo, or Phoebus, was 'the shining one', and the primitive wisdom attributed to him by Whitcombe was also shared by the fool. Licensed or not, Nell would need all her primitive wisdom to guide her through the political storms of the next five years.

14

Politics ~ A Deadly Pursuit

JANUARY 1679 SAW THE END of the Cavalier Parliament, which had sat for eighteen years, and with it the end of the Age of Gallantry. Gone were the Sir Fopling Flutters, Sir Frederick Frollicks and Sir Joslin Jollys.[1] The Popish Plot and succession crisis changed all that. Revolution cast its menacing shadow once more, eclipsing for ever the carefree court of the merry monarch. The theatre suffered generally, and if there was a vogue, it was for Tory political drama set in the 1650s to point up the threat of republicanism. As Aphra Behn wrote in the prologue to *The Feign'd Courtesans* (1679),

> The devil take this cursèd plotting age,
> 'T has ruined all our plots upon the stage;
> Suspicions, new elections, jealousies,
> Fresh informations, new discoveries,
> Do so employ the busy fearful town,
> Our honest calling here is useless grown . . .

The Tories controlled the playhouses with Royalist propaganda, while the Whigs took theatre to the streets with their Pope-burning pageants. The latter were masterpieces of their kind written by enlisted playwrights such as Elkanah Settle, whose broadsides entitled *The Solemn Mock-Procession of the Pope* are dramatic records of the parades. The Duke of Buckingham, who had a flair for large-scale productions, orchestrated the action. Their two gala days were 5 November (Guy Fawkes Day) and 17 November (Queen Elizabeth I's Accession Day).

The first Pope-burning of Charles's reign, on 5 November 1673, was described as 'acted with great applause in the Poultrey, London, on Wednesday night', as if it had been a play rather than a political demonstration.

In 1676 the Green Ribbon Club began organizing and sponsoring the pageants, and they became larger, more elaborate and politically more daring. The club, formed by Shaftesbury in the early part of the decade, started life as a political dining club for various peers and members of the Commons who shared the great-man-turned-citizen's plans for a fully constitutional monarchy that would be run by talented ministers. But it soon became the executive committee first of the Country Party and then of the Whigs. Their headquarters at the time of the Popish Plot was, according to Roger North, 'in a sort of Carrefour at Chancery Lane, in a centre of business and company most proper for such anglers of fools. The house was double balconied in front . . . for the clubbers to issue forth *in fresco*, with hats and no perukes, pipes in their mouths, merry faces, and dilated throats for vocal encouragement of the canaglia below . . .' If the Popish Plot was hatched anywhere, it was here.

Effigies of the Pope and his cardinals weren't the only figures used in the pageants; real actors were there to engage with the audience, drawing the crowd into a dark, impromptu theatre of vengeance. Some, dressed as priests, would hand out pardons 'to all those that would murder Protestants'; others solicited donations for the Jesuit missions to England, a move guaranteed to whip up the fury of the mob. The people were encouraged to shout slogans such as 'No popery! No slavery!', and when the pontiff was tried, they became jurors and pronounced the guilty verdict.

The Pope, drawn along on a painted cart, was gorgeously attired in scarlet and ermine, his hair curled and lips rouged to identify him with the Whore of Babylon. His belly was filled with live cats that squealed horribly as he was lowered into the bonfire. At his shoulder stood the devil, 'frequently caressing, hugging, and whispering to him, and oft-times instructing him aloud to destroy his Majesty, to forge a Protestant plot, to fire the City again, to which purpose he held an infernal torch in his hand'.[2]

Equally magnificent, and standing against everything for which the

Pope stood, was Good Queen Bess herself, true champion of the true Church. The analogy did not need to be spelt out. Elizabeth had saved the realm from a Protestant holocaust by executing the Catholic Mary Queen of Scots; it was now up to Charles to ensure that his brother James never came to the throne. They weren't asking for his execution, only his *exclusion*, but the words sounded eerily similar. After 1678 the spectacles became true revenge tragedies, when a ghostly effigy of the murdered magistrate Sir Edmund Bury Godfrey was paraded around the fire to 'milk the maudlin eyes' of the crowd.[3]

The pageants came within a whisker of compassing treasonable designs. Indeed, many of the King's supporters feared that one of the pageants might be used as cover for a coup d'état. The pageant of 17 November 1680, at the zenith of the Exclusion crisis, saw 200,000 people taking to the streets of London, the equivalent of 4,000,000 turning up for a rally in the capital today. Bringing politics to the streets through what were in effect mass demonstrations was characteristic of Shaftesbury's modern, revolutionary approach. Nor did he leave matters to chance, but used trained bands of thugs – his 'brisk boys' – to whip up popular feeling and ensure a large turnout.

On 5 November 1678 Nell had held her own Pope-burning party in the street outside 79 Pall Mall, to which people of all estates had come. Her whole household had had fun making the Pope, who 'sat in a great chair, with a red nose half a yard long, with some hundreds of boys throwing squibs at it'. It reminded her of the street parties of her childhood, and was the sort of feast of fools over which she presided with artless zeal.

Nell never deliberately involved herself in politics: she was drawn to the ministers of pleasure rather than the ministers of state and her only allegiance was to the King. Of course, the Whigs were keen to claim her as one of their own, and she herself played along with the title of 'Protestant whore', but without ever openly espousing their cause. She was careful, too, not to accept the invitations of the Whigs to join in the official processions. Such a move would have offended the King deeply. Danby certainly saw Nell's political use, for she brought the King into regular contact with leading Whigs through the parties she gave, while Charles himself valued her as a symbol of his commitment to the Chuch of England.

When in the spring of 1677 Buckingham had colluded with Shaftesbury and two other peers to try to force a dissolution of Parliament on a technicality, he had been committed to the Tower. Nell, who was described by Savile as Buckingham's 'great friend and faithful counsellor', successfully interceded for him with the King and made frequent visits to her friend as a sort of envoy of the merry gang. On one occasion she carried a letter from Buckhurst, which read, 'The best woman in the world brings you this paper, and at this time, the discreetest. Pray, my lord, resign your understanding and your interest wholly to her conduct. Mankind is to be redeemed by Eve, with as much honour as the thing will admit of. Separate your concern from your fellow prisoners, then an expedient handsome enough and secret enough to disengage yourself [shall be found]: obey, and you are certainly happy.'

Buckingham, who liked to think of himself as above the political fray, a statesman by inheritance, always appealed to the King on personal grounds. Having been assured by Nell that Charles was well inclined towards him, he wrote rather disingenuously to his sovereign that he was 'so surprised with what Mrs. Nelly has told me that I know not in the world what to say', and later on, 'What you have been pleased to say to Mrs. Nelly is ten thousand times more than ever I can deserve'. Buckingham was released for a few days, ostensibly to visit the mansion he was building on the Thames, but a secret meeting had been arranged with the King, who was seen leaving the Duke's house at the dead of night. Back in the Tower, Buckingham penned a jovial note to Buckhurst: 'My lord, I am now very busy drinking your lordship's health, and shall very shortly have the honour to receive your and Mrs. Nelly's commands.' Six weeks later he gained what proved to be his complete liberty on the grounds of ill health, though technically still a prisoner of the King's. Andrew Marvell in a letter to fellow puritan Edward Harley, wrote, 'The D: of Buckingham petition'd only that he had layd so long, had contacted severall indispositions and desired a moneth's aire. This was by Nelly, Middlesex (Buckhurst), Rochester, and the merry gang easily procured with presumption to make it an intire liberty. Hereupon he layd constantly at Whitehall at my L: Rochester's lodgings leeding the usuall life.'

After his release, Buckingham ended up staying at Nell's house, which further angered Danby. Her hospitality towards the Duke had no political purpose, however; what motivated her was loyalty to an old friend. Nor was his stay without its trials, for the Duke, who had never had much concept of personal hygiene, was in a state of some decay. Nell, who was always loath to offend a friend, on this occasion insisted that her august visitor have his wig deloused and his false teeth replaced. For his part Danby, sensitive to Nell's influence with the King, realized that she had to be taken seriously as a player at Whitehall. When he wrote to his wife from Newmarket in the autumn of 1677, he cannily instructed her to visit Nell's son: 'Remember to send to see my Lord Burford without any message to Nelly, and when Mrs. Turner [the governess] is with you, bid her tell Nelly, you wonder she should be your Lord's enemy that has always been so kind to her, but you wonder much more to find her supporting only those who are known to be the King's enemies, for in that you are sure she does very ill.'

But Nelly's friends could oppose the Crown politically without being disloyal to the King, hard though it was for some Tories to grasp this novel concept. Only a tiny minority of extremist Whigs were out-and-out Republicans. Even Shaftesbury professed to favour monarchy. According to Evelyn, the Earl had confided in him that 'he would support [the monarchy] to his last breath, as having seene and felt the miserie of being under mechanic tyranny', though it's difficult to take such statements at face value.

Nell's only real political weapon was her wit, and she was happy to direct it against the man who had blocked her ennoblement. If she was dangerous at all, it was as a jester. As Cardinal Wolsey found to his cost with Henry VIII's fool Will Somers, when the joke is on you it can prove fatal. Sir Robert Southwell could see the writing on the wall for Danby as early as the autumn of 1677: ' 'Tis certain', he wrote, 'that Buckingham passes a great part of his time with Nelly, who because the Lord Treasurer would not strive to make her a countess, she is at perfect defiance with him, so that the treasurer's lady [Danby's wife] is there acted, and the King looks on with great delight, which has a fatal prognostic unto some.' And the following February the Earl of Arran referred to the trouble that had been brewing for Danby 'since those entertainments at Nelly's . . . and the scenes of abuse there passing on Lord Treasurer'.

If the age of gallantry did end in 1678, it certainly went out with a bang in an episode that illustrates the way that sexual scandals could rock the state in Charles's reign. And as befitted the original wild mistress, Nell was swept up in the quickly unravelling events, for she was an easy target for political manipulators. The focal point of the crisis was the sexual and political life of Ralph Montagu, Charles's ambassador in Paris. Montagu embodied the archetype of the ruthless gallant, who used women to advance his career. Grammont described him as 'no very dangerous rival on account of his person, but very much to be feared for his assiduity, the acuteness of his wit, and for some other talents which are of importance, when a man is once permitted to display them'. Montagu was eager to become Secretary of State in place of Henry Coventry, who was retiring, though his real ambition was to replace Danby. Montagu's sister, Lady Harvey, set to work on his behalf. She decided that the quickest way to reach their goal was the time-honoured path of securing the King's goodwill through a new mistress.

For this purpose she chose the sixteen-year-old Jane, or Jenny, Myddelton, whose mother – another Jane – had been one of Montagu's mistresses and who was only too willing to assist in the scheme. (Indeed, it was alleged by some that Jenny Myddelton was Montagu's bastard daughter.) Because she herself didn't have direct access to the King, Elizabeth Harvey seized upon Nell Gwyn as the best channel of communication. The merry gang followed events closely. As the exiled Henry Savile wrote to Rochester in the country,

Your friend and sometimes (especially now) mine, has a part in it that makes her now laughed att and may one day turne to her infinite disadvantage. The case stands thus if I am rightly informed: My Lady Hervey who allwayes loves one civil plott more, is working body and soule to bring Mrs Jenny Middleton into play. How dangerous a new one is to all old ones I need not tell you, but her Ladyship, having little opportunity of seeing Charlemayne [King Charles] upon her owne account, wheadles poor Mrs Nelly into supping twice or thrice a week at W C's [Chiffinch's] and carryeing her with her; soe that in good earnest this poor creature is betrayed by her Ladyship to pimp against herselfe, for there her Ladyship whispers and contrives all matters to her owne ends, as the other might easily perceive if shee were not too giddy to mistrust a false friend. This I thought it good for you to know, for though your Lordship and I have different friends at court, yet the friendship betwixt us ought to make mee have an observing eye upon any accident that wound any friend of yours as this in the end may possibly doe her, who is so much your friend and who speakes obliging and charitable things of mee in my present disgrace.

The letter speaks eloquently of Nell's naivety and uncalculating loyalty. Even though she'd already joined a cabal with Coventry, Buckingham, Hyde and Savile to promote her friend Hyde for the secretaryship, it appears not to have occurred to her that the sister of the other principal contender might be up to something! In her letter of August 1678 to Lory Hyde, she writes, '. . . we are a goeing to supe with the king at whithall & my lady Harvie. the King remembers his sarvis to you. now lets talke of state affairs, for we [i.e., the Country Party] never caried things so cunningly as now, for we dont know whether we shall have pesce or war, but I am for war, and for no other reason but that you may come home.' Danby, whose voice in the matter could prove crucial, favoured his old friend Sir William Temple who, like himself, was an admirer of the Dutch system of government. As for Jenny Myddelton's suit, it came to nothing, mainly through the efforts of Louise, who realized the danger posed by Montagu. Nor was Charles pursuing female bait with his old zest.

Meanwhile in Paris Montagu was having an affair with the Duchess of Cleveland to try to wind her into his practices. Unfortunately, he was insufficiently discreet about his plans, and when jealousy and mistrust swallowed up the affair, dangerous confidences were spilled. Montagu forwarded to the King letters that Barbara had written to another of her lovers, the Marquis de Châtillon, just as Barbara herself was setting out for London. To add insult to injury he had an affair with Lady Sussex, her daughter by the King, while she was away. In retaliation Barbara wrote a long and impassioned letter to Charles in which she detailed the ambassador's misconduct and his grandiose plans for running the government of England. Aspersions upon the royal family that in her infatuation had been savoured for their humour were now urgently reported, as if the security of the state depended upon it: 'For he [Montagu] has neither conscience nor honour, and has several times told me that in his heart he despised you and your brother; and that for his part he wished with all his heart that the Parliament would send you both to travel; for you were a dull governable fool and the Duke a wilful fool.'

Montagu had also been to Louis XIV requesting him to forbid Châtillon from seeing Barbara at pain of Charles's displeasure. According to Barbara in her letter to Charles, Louis declined, saying, 'that all the world knew that now *all things of gallantry* were at an end with you and I; that being so, and so public, he did not see why you should be offended at my loving anybody. That it was a thing so common nowadays to have a gallantry that he did not wonder at anything of this nature.'

When Montagu, horrified with the turn that events had taken, returned to London without the King's leave, he was summarily dismissed from his post, while his affair with the King's married daughter was more than sufficient to see him banished from court. Here matters might have ended had not Montagu retained an ace of terrible power up his sleeve. Two years previously he had drawn Danby into a compromising correspondence in which the latter suggested that the time was ripe to demand further sums from Louis for England's continued neutrality in his continental wars. Whether or not Montagu knew the full details of the Secret Treaty, this was a none too subtle variation on the theme. Montagu now intended to produce these letters to ruin the Lord Treasurer, and in this piece of knavery he decided to enlist the strongest support possible – that of Louis XIV himself.

Louis had become increasingly frustrated with Charles over the course of the previous year. He resented the pro-Dutch policy of Danby, which in his view had been responsible for continual breaches of the Secret Treaty on the part of England, and was nettled by the marriage of Charles's elder niece, Princess Mary, whom he had wanted for his own son the Dauphin, to William of Orange. It strengthened the hand of the Dutch and tied the King of England to their Prince by bonds of both policy and family. Having approached Barrillon in London, who received his instructions in this matter directly from the King of France, Montagu struck a devil's bargain: to bring down Danby within six months in return for 100,000 crowns (i.e., £25,000, or in today's money nearly £1,925,000). The French may well have instigated the plan, though they were happy for Montagu to think that it was all his own.

Next he had to secure a seat in the Commons, both to set the scene for his coup de théâtre and to win immunity from arrest. He was duly elected at a by-election for the borough of Northampton, his campaign against the Government candidate funded with gold from Versailles. Louis was up to his old policy of divide and rule, funding both Charles and members of the opposing Country Party. As he wrote to Barrillon, 'I leave to your zeal and to your address to make use of the good intentions and the authority of the King of England against the Parliament, and of the Parliament likewise to render of no effect the resolutions which that prince might take against me.'[4]

Charles and Danby had Montagu's papers seized, but he gloatingly informed the Commons that he had given the really juicy letters into the safekeeping of friends. The cabinet in which the letters were concealed was ordered to be brought into the chamber and a locksmith sent for to break the lock. When it was opened Montagu took out a bundle of papers and handed them to the Speaker, who read out a letter of March 1678 from Danby to Montagu in which the latter was instructed to request the sum of 6,000,000 livres from Louis for not convening Parliament and for securing the peace that France wanted with the Dutch. Beside Danby's signature the King had written, 'This letter is writ by my order. C.R.'

The King could not be touched, as it was his prerogative to treat of war and peace with other nations, but Danby was not protected by such a privilege. The Commons moved to impeach him for high treason, and Charles had no option but to dissolve the Parliament that had sat for eighteen years to save his minister. His life spared, Danby resigned his post and was committed to the Tower, where he stayed almost until the end of Charles's reign.

It was ironic that the pro-Dutch Danby, hated by Louis XIV as the architect of the marriage of William and Mary, should have been hounded out of office for colluding with the French, especially when the agent of his fall was being aided and abetted by the French King. It gives one an indication of the unprincipled confusion into which English politics had sunk. It was Danby's affair with Louise de Kéroualle, whether real or merely rumoured, that marked him out for destruction in the hearts of the Country Party. No matter how much his policy was opposed to French interests, he was perceived to be under the influence of the Duchess of Portsmouth, whose unpopularity waxed as Louis's giant war machine advanced across Europe.

Now that Danby had gone, only two men saw their way clearly through the fog: the King and Shaftesbury. In a sense, however, the struggle that these two men were destined to wage over the coming four years was a sideshow, for Danby and his circle (men such as Temple, Halifax and Essex) had already paved a way for the future through the marriage of William and Mary. This had been no mere marriage, but a contract of succession to secure a Protestant constitutional monarchy in Britain, which may even have allowed for William to become Protector of the Kingdom during the reign of the Catholic James. After William's accession, Danby once again became a sort of first minister and was rewarded in 1694 with the Dukedom of Leeds.

Charles had fallen in with the marriage plans because anti-French feeling was running so high. It was a sop to Parliament, which wanted him to send troops to succour the Dutch. Yet he wasn't in the mood to play the poodle to Louis either. A decade of war had depleted France's treasury, and the French King had found excuses not to pay Charles his stipend. Then on 10 August 1678 came the Peace of Nijmegen, which put an end to the Dutch War (albeit to France's advantage). After the fall of Ghent to the French, Charles, spurred on by a fractious Parliament, had begun preparations for an expeditionary force to relieve the Dutch, a move that had forced Louis back to the negotiating table. The English representative at the negotiations had been Nell's friend Lory Hyde.

But, money aside, another factor had intervened to cloud Parliament's judgement in the matter of Danby's fate: the political hysteria created by the Popish Plot. On 13 August 1678 Charles was taking his

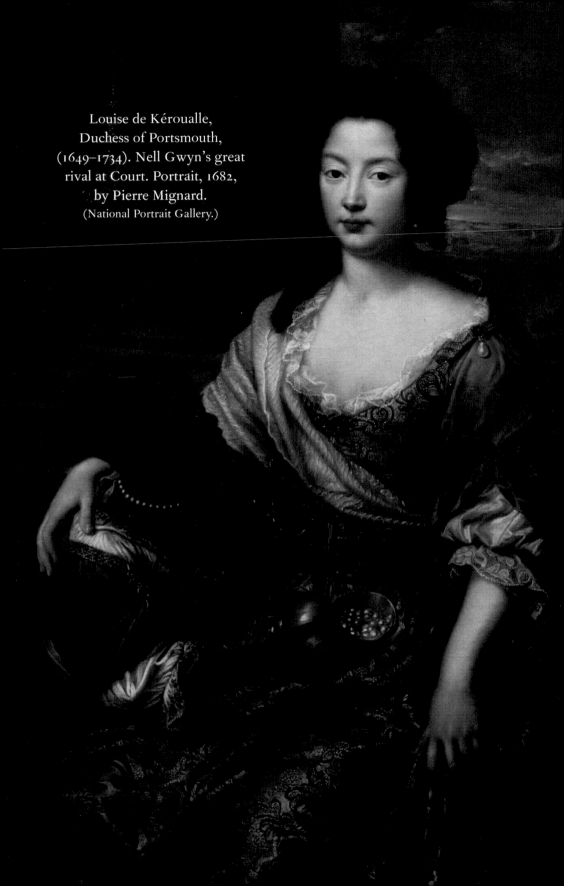

Louise de Kéroualle,
Duchess of Portsmouth,
(1649–1734). Nell Gwyn's great
rival at Court. Portrait, 1682,
by Pierre Mignard.
(National Portrait Gallery.)

Hortense Mancini (1646–99),
Duchesse Mazarin, the Italian
adventuress who became
Charles's mistress for a brief
period in 1675/6. Portrait by
Jacob Ferdinand Voet, c.1675.
(National Portrait Gallery.)

Mary 'Moll' Davis, dancer and
comedienne, who also became
mistress to Charles II and rival
to Nell. From the studio of
Sir Peter Lely. (Bridgeman.)

Opposite.
George Villiers (1628–87),
2nd Duke of Buckingham,
Nell's friend and erstwhile
'manager', c.1675. Portrait by
Sir Peter Lely.
(National Portrait Gallery.)

Henrietta Anne,
Duchesse d'Orléans (1644–70),
known to her family as
'Minette', the King's favourite
sister. Portrait after Pierre
Mignard, c.1665–70.
(National Portrait Gallery.)

James, Duke of Monmouth
(1649–85), Charles II's beloved
son by Lucy Walter, c.1683.
Covetous of his father's throne,
he was dubbed 'Prince Perkin'
by Nell Gwyn.
Portrait after William Wissing.
(National Portrait Gallery.)

Opposite.
James, Duke of York (1633–1701),
later King James II, who was
given the sobriquet 'dismal
Jimmy' by Nell Gwyn.
(Bridgeman Art Library.)

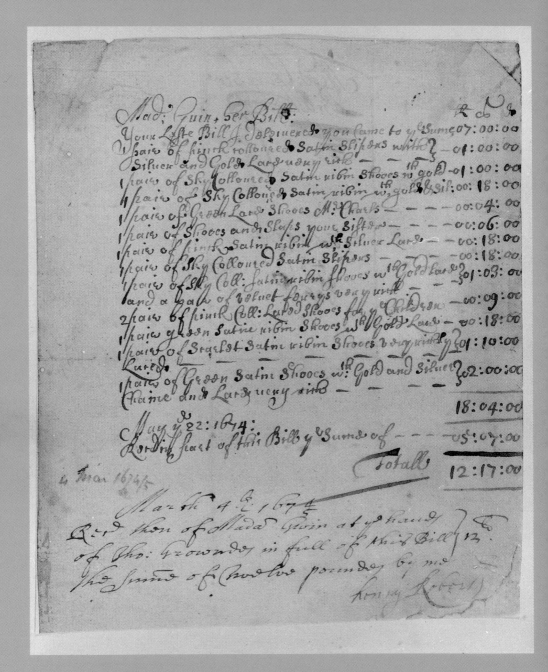

A bill dated 4 March 1674/5 for shoes and slippers
ordered by Nell Gwyn from Henry Roberts.
(From the Crofton Croker album, by kind permission of the Duke of St Albans.)

Top left. Gold ring with cornelian cameo portrait of King Charles I, wearing armour and wreathed like a Roman emperor, a gift to his confessor, Bishop Juxon, at point of execution.
Top right. Reverse of Juxon ring.
Above. Diamond ring given by Charles II to Nell Gwyn.
(Photos by kind permission of the Duke of St Albans.)

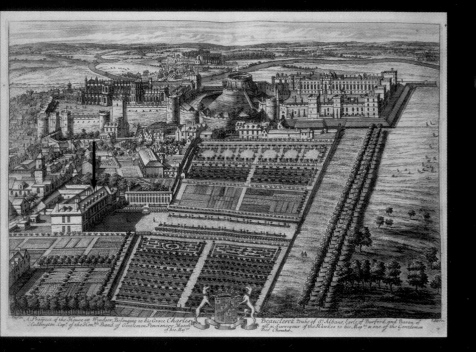

Burford House, Nell Gwyn's Windsor home. Engraved by Jan Kip c.1690 from a drawing by Leender Knyff.
(By kind permission of the Duke of St Albans.)

The wax effigy of Charles II, made after his death, gives a very good idea of what the King must have looked like.
(By kind permission of the Dean and Chapter of Westminster.)

morning walk in St James's Park when he was approached by one Christopher Kirkby, a laboratory assistant at the Royal Society, who warned him not to walk abroad as his life was in danger. The King showed his usual unconcern with matters of personal safety and, telling Kirkby to recount his story to Chiffinch, continued his walkabout. That night he heard through Chiffinch a lurid tale of a Jesuit plot to depose him, massacre leading Protestants and install his brother James as a puppet king under the Pope. The next day he set off for Windsor, as planned, having asked Danby to investigate matters in his absence, and that evening 'was at supper with Mrs. Nelly', who had gone on ahead.

When Danby asked Kirkby to reveal his sources, he produced two very unusual clergymen: Dr Israel Tonge, an educationalist and rector of St Michael's, Wood Street, and one Titus Oates, former Protestant chaplain in the household of the Duke of Norfolk.

Though Shaftesbury later denied cooking up the Popish Plot, he claimed to know who the true author was and fully conceded that he himself had 'had the full hunting of it'. Nevertheless, it is more than probable that Oates was working as an agent for Shaftesbury.

A native of Oakham in Rutland, Oates was a grotesque, even monstrous figure, with broad face, deep-set piggy eyes, bull neck, 'vast wobbling chins' and a high rasping voice. His mouth, we are told, was in the centre of his face, and he was built like an orc, with short bandy legs and long lifeless arms. As with his master, Shaftesbury, his deformity was seen by opponents as evidence of an evil nature. Even as a child, his mother wrote, 'his nose always ran and he slabber'd at the mouth, and his Father could not endure him and . . . would cry "take away this snotty Fool and jumble him about" . . .' At school and university, Oates was a misfit, being expelled from both, and when he became a chaplain on one of the King's ships he was dismissed for homosexuality. It was then that he had courted the Jesuits, most likely as a spy for Shaftesbury, and in late 1677 managed to get himself admitted to the Jesuits' English College at St-Omer in France. As he later revealed, his job was to find out who the Jesuit priests in England were and to whom they ministered. It was fresh from St-Omer that Oates arrived at the end of August 1678. A month later he and Tonge were standing before Danby in the Lord Treasurer's apartments at Whitehall.

Despite his loathsome appearance, Oates was strangely charismatic. Florid, voluble, demonic, he managed to impress Danby and other members of the Privy Council with his quasi-prophetic pronouncements. Danby urged the King to return from Windsor to hear Oates in person. Charles came, and saw through the pulpit rhetoric in an instant, whistling derisively at tales of his imminent assassination, whether by the Queen's physician or by silver bullets fired from a pistol in St James's Park. Indeed, he caught Oates in a number of palpable lies, yet the cleric seemed unabashed.

Had Oates been acting alone, his theories would have collapsed under the King's scrutiny, but he was the mouthpiece of well-organized and powerful conspirators, who had done much of his work for him by cranking up the rumour machine in the capital and lending him a veneer of credibility by feeding him privileged information. Moreover, things had reached such a pitch that the truth of his claims was irrelevent: the people now believed in a Popish plot and were prepared to make a hero of a shameless villain. Leading politicians saw the plot as an opportunity to cause trouble and destroy the Catholics.

With the appearance of Oates, the most monstrous fraud of all, Rochester's description of the age as one 'where virtue is so frequently exactly counterfeited, and hypocrisie so generally taken notice of, that every one armed with suspicion stands upon his guard against it [i.e., virtue]' was exposed for the truth. Restoration society was ready to welcome the ultimate trickster as its saviour. When he stood at the bar of the House of Lords and drawled, 'Aye, Taitus Oates, accause Catherine, Queen of England, of Haigh Traison', peers of the realm, who should have hooted him from the chamber, nodded their solemn assent. Edward Cooke referred to 'the easy credulity of this uncharitable age' and remarked that Jesus himself would have been branded a Papist had he cared to take a stroll through the streets of London during the Popish Plot. Nor were witnesses required, for 'where the witness fail'd, the Prophet [i.e., Oates] Spoke'.

The crisis put the King in a profoundly difficult position, not least because if anyone was guilty of a Popish plot it was Charles himself. After all, through the Secret Treaty of Dover, which he had signed in 1670, Charles had declared himself a Catholic and moreover one who would work towards the conversion of England to Catholicism in return for French gold. His moral dilemma was thus obvious, especially when innocent Catholics began to go to the scaffold (judicial murders on the nod of Chief Justice Scroggs). Yet Charles did not speak out against these atrocities, still less attempt to prevent them. Oates was protected by his government, paid a princely salary for producing false witnesses and given lodgings in Whitehall. Charles knowingly signed the death warrants of innocent Catholics; not to have done so would have cost him his throne. 'Let the blood lie on them that condemn them,' he said, 'for God knows I sign with tears in my eyes.'

Charles's great opponent was Shaftesbury. In 1678 he was fifty-seven years old and badly crippled in the hip from a childhood accident with a carriage pole. He walked with the aid of sticks and was in constant pain. He was in many ways the shadow of the tall, athletic Charles. Ruthless, choleric, embittered, his was 'A fiery Soul, which working out its way, / Fretted the Pigmy Body to decay'. Only too aware of the drama that he was directing from his headquarters in the City, Shaftesbury was as cynical as Charles about its credibility ('the more nonsensical the better', he was said to have quipped). Suborning witnesses to testify against his chosen victims, Shaftesbury created a McCarthyite culture of fear and paranoia. No one dared speak out against the insanity.

With the drama of the Popish Plot in full swing he played his trump card by promoting the Duke of Monmouth as the Protestant heir to the throne. Shaftesbury knew that an anti-Catholic platform was not enough in itself; the people needed a figure to rally behind. Monmouth was brave, charismatic, and *malleable*. Unlike William of Orange, who was wily and self-serving, Monmouth would act as a puppet monarch for Shaftesbury the kingmaker, maybe even a stepping stone to a republic with Shaftesbury as president. Monmouth's bastardy, which he now did his best to sweep aside through rumours of a 'black box' which was said to contain the marriage contract of Charles and Lucy Walter, could be used to discredit him later on if need be. 'He who hath the worst title ever makes the best King' was a slogan frequently heard in Exclusionist circles.

The Duke of York, on the other hand, was unpopular with the

people. Like his father, he was bigoted and idealistic in outlook; proud, humourless and vindictive in his dealings with people. His judgement was also suspect. His father-in-law Clarendon, comparing James with the King, wrote, 'If the duke seemed to be more firm and fixed in his resolutions, it was rather from an obstinacy in his will, which he defended by aversion from the debate, than by the constancy of his judgement, which was more subject to persons than to arguments, and so as changeable at least as the king's . . .' Nor did he possess the skills of a politician, lacking both charm and objectivity. Had he been content to follow his brother's example and keep his faith to himself, the Exclusion crisis would never have happened. But sadly for the nation, James had never emerged from the shadow of his mother's violent dogmatism. Nell's nickname for him, 'dismal Jimmy', was spot on, for James shared the evil luck of his Stuart forebears.

With theatre becoming increasingly political and more and more a tool of the Court Party, the merry gang, aided and abetted by Killigrew, made several attempts during 1677 to lure Nell back to the stage. Aware of her great popularity with the people, they were hoping to make her their mouthpiece in the King's House. But Nell was too wise to be drawn. She knew the danger of making such a conspicuous target of herself; more to the point, she was temperamentally incapable of taking politics seriously and of being anyone's mouthpiece but her own. Not for the first time the merry gang had mistaken her friendship for political allegiance. As ever, her politics could be summed up in a single line: to serve the King with all her heart. It was Charles's motto too.

As the years of political crisis loomed towards the end of the 1670s, Nell's life, so fêted publicly, was buffeted by a series of personal losses. The tone was set in January 1678, on Twelfth Night, when her London home was burgled. A good deal of her treasured silver plate, which she had had made shortly after moving to 79 Pall Mall, was stolen. Engraved ornately with her initials, it had symbolized her arrival in the haut monde. She immediately placed a notice in the *London Gazette*: 'All goldsmiths and others to whom our silver plate may be sold, marked with the cypher E.G., flourished, weighing about eighteen ounces, are desired to apprehend the bearer thereof, till they give notice to Mr. Robert Johnson, in Heathcock Alley, Strand, over against Durham Yard, or to Mrs. Gwin's porter in the Pell Mell, by whom they shall be rewarded.'

While blithely conniving at Lady Harvey's attempts to supplant her in the affections of the King, Nell, as her letter of June 1678 to Lory Hyde makes clear, was preparing to send her younger son, James, to be schooled in Paris. 'My Lord Bauclaire is goeing into France', she announces proudly, but gives no further details. We don't know whom he travelled with, where he stayed in Paris or what school he attended. Though he was the King's son and his mother was a popular icon, nothing is recorded of his two-year stay in the French capital. Even Henry Savile, sent to Paris as envoy extraordinary to replace Ralph Montagu, is silent on the matter. Moreover, the boy was only six years old, a very young age to be sent away even in those days, and it's difficult to imagine Nell letting go of him willingly. Whose idea it was and why, we don't know. We don't even know whether Nell accompanied her son to the coast or whether she said her farewells at home, but it must have been a bitter parting for both of them. Little did they know that it was to be the last time they would see each other.

But Nell's spirits were never dampened for long. She spent the summer at Windsor, where she and Charles could relax in sylvan solitude, far from the stresses and intrigues of London, and joke about the canting solemnity of Titus Oates. The King possessed the remarkable ability of setting aside his anxieties to focus on the enjoyment of the moment. It was an ability that Nell shared, and for a month at least she and Charles, in the words of Dasent, 'enacted . . . the roles of forest lovers'.

Windsor Forest was a magical place that inspired both hunters and poets. In 1704 Pope, whose father lived nine miles west of Windsor, at Binfield, wrote his poem 'Windsor Forest', which begins,

> Thy forests, Windsor! and thy green retreats,
> At once the Monarch's and the Muse's seats,
> Invite my lays. Be present, sylvan maids!
> Unlock your springs, and open all your shades . . .

There were the usual field sports of deer hunting, beagling and hawking. Nell enjoyed hawking for larks with a small bird, usually a merlin or a hobby; indeed, such was her passion for this sport that the King in due course created their son Master of the King's Hawks and Hereditary Grand Falconer of England. The King's hawks wore varvels of solid silver (the rings attached to the 'jesses' or leather straps that went round the bird's legs) engraved with the royal crest and so were easily recognizable if they flew astray and failed to return. Nell also enjoyed sitting on the river bank and chatting with the King as they fished for carp, perch, trout, pike and eel, all of which bred plentifully in the Thames at Windsor. But, for hunting, which was perhaps Charles's greatest passion in the field, she had to content herself with going on ahead to one of the lodges in the forest where he stopped to rest and have a bite of lunch.

There was no council chamber at Windsor Castle, so the King would ride or even walk to Hampton Court for council meetings during his Windsor vacation. While he was away, Nell enjoyed the company of her elder son, Charles, who may have been at Eton, which took boys as young as eight. As summer gave way to autumn, the King was kept informed of the unfolding drama of the Popish Plot. Despite the harbingers of doom who fed a credulous capital with rumour and prophecy, preying on people's fears of another civil war, Charles exhibited the sort of sang froid that the merman spotted that autumn in the river Severn might have applauded. He made his customary trip to Newmarket with Nell and several of his sons, including the Duke of Monmouth. Accompanying the court was Samuel Pepys, who without knowing it was providing himself with an alibi for Godfrey's murder. Shaftesbury would later try to incriminate him through false witnesses and managed to have him committed to the Tower. Happily his stay there was a short one, not least because of Nell's intercession.

Charles still raced, even at the age of forty-eight, and that autumn beat Monmouth and Messrs Elliot and Thynne to win a silver flagon. Though Nell herself was no horsewoman, she made sure that her son Charles became an accomplished equestrian early in life. The boy spent some of his most enjoyable times with his father at Newmarket, for of all places it was the one where Charles most delighted in 'putting off the king'. As John Reresby wrote of Charles there, 'The King was . . . so great a lover of the diversions which that place did afford, that he let himself down from Majesty to the very degree of a country gentleman. He mixed himself amongst the crowd, allowed every man to speak to him that pleased; went a-hawking in the mornings, to cock-matches in the afternoons (if there were no horse-races), and to plays in the evenings, acted in a barn, and by very ordinary Bartholomew fair comedians.'

One anecdote from the King's visit at the time of the Popish Plot nicely illustrates the informal atmosphere that he created around himself at Newmarket. A deputation of puritanical Whigs from Oxford, chief among them one Alderman Wright, had come to town to present a petition to His Majesty, requesting that he confirm the nomination of one of Shaftesbury's henchmen to the office of town clerk. They spent several days circling unsuccessfully about the King, until one morning in their desperation they decided to try to catch him on his walk across the fields outside the town. The King as was his wont took their petition on the hoof, and they were just struggling after him when who should appear but Nell Gwyn, who called out in her loud, ringing voice, 'Charles, I hope I shall have your company at night, shall I not?' This greatly scandalized the deputation and when they returned to Oxford, their petition having been denied, Alderman Wright never tired of enlarging upon the King's vices. He said that he had heard bad things of him, but that now he had seen the evidence with his own eyes.[5]

When the King and court returned to London on 16 October, Nell did not follow. Accompanied by her son and her steward, Sir Fleetwood Sheppard, she travelled to Cambridge where there was an official welcome from the vice-chancellor and scholars, who presented her with some verses. It was perhaps a sign of the growing factionalism of the times that Puritan Cambridge should have wished to honour the Protestant Whore in public. For her part, Nell realized that her presence on the streets could help to reassure the people that they had a voice at court and that the King was committed to safeguarding the Anglican faith. According to Roy MacGregor-Hastie, Nell's political role was less vague. He claims that she was paid £10,000 a year out of secret service funds to win support for the King among members of the Green Ribbon Club.

The day after the King's return from Newmarket, news broke of the murder of Sir Edmund Bury Godfrey, the magistrate who had taken Oates's deposition that September. He was found in a ditch at the foot of Greenberry Hill (now Primrose Hill), run through with his own sword. A post-mortem revealed that he had been strangled to death. The tortuous mania of the times necessitated the careful dissection of the victim's name, which immediately revealed two deeply significant anagrams: 'By dogs in fury murdered' and 'Dy'd by Rome's reveng'd fury', while the location where his body was discovered spelt out the names of the three men eventually hanged for his murder: Green, Berry and Hill! As for the souvenir merchants, they couldn't shift their goods fast enough: mugs and daggers bearing the injunction 'Remember Godfrey' and packs of cards that illustrated scenes from the unfolding plot sold like hot cakes.

Despite the hype, Godfrey's murder proved to be the smoking gun. Overnight the plot had become irrefutable, and the popular mind envisaged London in flames once more, with French warships sailing up the Thames. No man left his house unarmed and even the ladies, following the example of Lady Shaftesbury, carried loaded pistols in their muffs. Now the contrivers of the plot had their fox out in the open, and were free to implement the next stage of their plan: exclusion of Catholics from Parliament, followed by exclusion of the Duke of York from the throne. But though the King went to the House of Lords to make certain theoretical concessions to protect the Church of England in the event of James's accession, he stood firm against the principle of Parliament interfering with the royal succession. He was too wily not to realize that the precedent could be used to topple his own throne.

Charles thought it best too to send the Duke of York abroad to the Low Countries, thereby removing one of the chief objects of popular fury. Monmouth, meanwhile, was dispatched to Scotland. This game of musical heirs went on for several years, and before long it was James's turn to spend his rustication in Scotland, where the hunting was better, while Monmouth rubbed elbows with non-conformist exiles in Holland and searched desperately for an obscure Dutchman who was rumoured to have witnessed the marriage of his mother to the King (Monmouth had been born in Rotterdam).

Parliament having been dissolved at the beginning of the year, the

General Election of March 1679 returned an even more menacing House of Commons from the King's point of view. Danby's old guard, the Court Party he had recruited to support the royal interest, had been slashed from one hundred and fifty to little more than thirty! And no sooner had honourable members taken their seats than they were baying for Exclusion. In April the Duke of York was for the first time openly attacked in the Commons, as if he were an ordinary citizen, and one MP, Thomas Bennett, went so far as to state that the Popish Plot had been planned with the Duke's approval. The same month the King formed an expanded Privy Council of thirty, not least in order to keep his enemies close, especially Shaftesbury, whom he made its president. As for the counsellors themselves, Charles remarked characteristically to a friend, 'They shall know nothing'.

The King was determined not to allow Parliament to sit for long. As a result there were three Exclusion parliaments between the first elections in March 1679 and the dissolution of the final parliament of Charles's reign in March 1681. The elections were for the first time in English history fought along clearly determined party lines. Adherents of the Country Party were now known as 'Whiggamores' or 'Whigs', a term applied to the sour-faced fanatical Covenanters (Presbyterians) of the south-western counties of Scotland, who frequently lived as outlaws. The court faction, on the other hand, became 'Tories', an Irish term describing the Papist bandits who raided English estates in Ireland. Both were terms of abuse pinned on the respective parties by their opponents but subsequently worn as badges of honour.

The Whigs under Shaftesbury were better organized and made use of a sophisticated party machine that scored nearly all the propaganda victories. They commandeered priests to electioneer from the pulpit, held large-scale rallies in the City and stirred up popular fears by mass-producing pamphlets such as *An Appeal from the Country to the City*, which kept the Popish Plot running long after its sell-by date. A typical extract reads, 'Imagine that you see the whole town in a flame, occasioned this second time by the same Popish malice which set it on before. At the same instant fancy that amongst the distracted crowd you behold troops of Papists ravishing your wives and daughters, dashing your little children's brains out against the walls, plundering your houses and cutting your own throats.' Lord Halifax, disillusioned with Shaftesbury's revolutionary tactics, conceded that he would rather sleep in a wasps' nest than in London, as the former would afford him more peace.

Not only was the gallant court of the past eighteen years gone for ever, but the King, supplied neither by Parliament nor by Louis, was forced to make radical economies. The days of his exile must have seemed an apt training as he cut back his household, withheld salaries, sold the royal mews and ate sparingly. Falling into considerable debt, the government just managed to function. It meant of course that the mistresses too had to tighten their belts. In spite of this, a royal warrant dated 11 June 1679 reaffirmed Nell's pension:

> Charles the Second by the grace of God King of England Scotland France and Ireland Defender of the Faith &c. To the Commissioners of Our Treasury now being, and to the Treasurer Undertreasurer and Commissioners of Our Treasury for the time being, Greeting. Our will and pleasure is, And wee doe hereby Authorise and require you, Out of Our Treasure now or hereafter being or remaineing in the Receipt of Our Exchequer, to pay or cause to be paid unto Eleanor Gwyn or her Assignes the Annuity or yearly Summe of Five thousand pounds, Dureing Our pleasure, for and towards the Support and maintenance of herselfe and Charles Earle of Burford, To be received by her the said Eleanor Gwyn quarterly, Att the foure most usuall feasts in the yeare by equall porcions . . .

Not surprisingly, the payments came in dribs and drabs (mostly instalments of £250), rather than in quarterly payments of £1,250, making it little wonder that she wrote frantic letters to Sir Robert Howard urging him to squeeze some money out of her Irish properties. Also at this time Nell appointed a new agent, one James Frazier, and granted him power of attorney to receive the pension on her behalf. It was his job to do battle with the Treasury, pursue those who owed her money and satisfy her creditors. One of the signatories to the power of attorney is the playwright Thomas Otway, whom Nell had hired as tutor to her son Charles. Frazier and Otway between them were replacing Fleetwood Sheppard, who had been dismissed for seducing one of Nell's maids. But she was to fare no better with

Otway, who succumbed to the same temptation. Nell seems to have chosen her sons' tutors principally for their wit; morality came a poor second. Otway, a fine writer, was unfairly denigrated in 'An Essay of Scandall':

> Then for that Cubb her [Nell's] Son and Heire
> Lett him remaine in Otway's care
> To make him (if that's possible to be)
> A viler Poet, and more dull than he.

He was in fact one of the most skilful playwrights of the day, a passionate, deeply sensitive man, who was not cut out for the literary rat race of Restoration England. After leaving Nell's service, he wrote his masterpiece, *Venice Preserv'd* (1682), which delves into the psychology of the revolutionary mind. His dedication of the work to Louise de Kéroualle, Duchess of Portsmouth, 'so good a mistress, and so noble a patroness', was guaranteed to irk his former employer and benefactress, as was his description of himself as her Grace's 'entirely devoted creature'.

Louise, on the other hand, tended to be more resourceful financially and got the King to grant her the forfeited estates of suicides and those executed by the state. Barbara too made one last audacious raid on the Treasury when she returned from France in the autumn of 1679, managing to plunder an astonishing £25,000. When the acting Lord Treasurer, the Earl of Essex, refused to pay the money Charles dismissed him from his post. He was prepared to pay heavily for a quiet life.

Even so, the King's health began to show signs of weakening, and at the end of August 1679 he fell ill at Windsor, having caught a chill by the river after a long, hot game of tennis. The next day he had an intense malarial fever known as the ague, which worsened so dramatically that by the following morning his life was despaired of. It immediately became apparent that the King was still as popular with the people as he had been on the day of his Restoration and that the prospect of his death filled all moderate men and women with dread. He commanded their affection to a degree that only Elizabeth before him had managed. He was a figure of great romantic power, a popular hero, and therein lies a clue to the strange momentum of the Popish

Plot. The nation was desperate for this popular king to produce an heir, and when it became obvious that it wasn't going to happen it forced itself to believe that that heir already existed in the shape of the Duke of Monmouth, in whom the King seemed miraculously renewed. This national fantasy did as much to fuel the Popish Plot as fear of a Catholic coup.

York's supporters sent messages for him to return from Brussels. Meanwhile Nell, who was with the King at Windsor, suffered the agony of being denied access to him when he most needed her. It was one of the cruel hazards of courtesanship. When the monarch's life was in the balance, strict protocol was enforced: physicians, priests, and family alone were allowed around the sickbed. Nell kept to her castle rooms, sending young Burford in her stead to ask after the King.

Charles's oft-tested resilience won through, and by the time James arrived the King was sitting up in bed, tucking into mutton and partridges and talking of going to Newmarket. Sir Robert Howard wrote from Windsor to the Duke of Ormonde, 'The King has contributed much to his recovery by that extraordinary calm temper that he has showed in all his sickness; and in those fits, which are of great pain and uneasiness, he never changed from that calmness he had in health.' The other major factor had been quinine. It was known at the time as 'the Jesuits' powder', an irony that would not have been lost on Charles. Shaftesbury, on the other hand, had been in a state of intolerable nervous tension. Holed up at his City headquarters in Aldersgate Street, he was putting the final touches to his plans for a coup d'état in the event of the King's death. With the King and court at Windsor, London was his. Monmouth was behind him, so was Buckingham, both high on dreams of glory.

Nell, for one, breathed a deep sigh of relief at the King's recovery, for she knew what little charity she could expect at Shaftesbury's hands. 'What meaneth the bleating of the cattle?' he was to ask savagely in the Lords during one of his many attacks on the mistresses. With Barbara in France and Hortense happy to live a bohemian life outside the court, public attention focused on the twin poles of Charles's love life, Louise and Nell. The polarity extended to religion and politics too, with the Popish Plot marking a surge in Nell's already considerable popularity while Louise, a French Catholic, was almost hounded from the country.

Louise's great fear was that Charles would not be able to protect her if the crisis worsened, and towards the end of 1678 she seriously considered retiring to France. But the King, who met almost daily in her rooms with the French ambassador Barrillon, would no more dream of sacrificing her to popular prejudice than he would the Queen. Whenever the subject came up he refused point blank to discuss it. Louise, however, did not repay the King's loyalty, but embarked on a dangerous and highly calculated dance of accommodation with every identifiable interest: York, Monmouth, Orange. Even Shaftesbury was courted in her determination to survive and continue serving her master Louis XIV, for if he was to install a puppet king after Charles's death, she saw no reason why it shouldn't be her son, the Duke of Richmond. And to signal her new Whig credentials she dismissed her Catholic servants. Clearly some of Charles's political guile had rubbed off on her.

But Shaftesbury was a venomous ally at the best of times and stung Louise furiously as she struggled to hold him down. In the summer of 1680, for instance, he attempted to indict her as a common prostitute before a Middlesex jury, but the indictment was quashed at the instigation of Lord Chief Justice Scroggs. Had it gone through and Louise been found guilty, she would have been clapped in the stocks with other, less refined members of her profession and pelted with fruit. Shaftesbury's campaign of intimidation worked, for Louise went so far as to declare her support for the Exclusionists, which greatly angered the King. Just as she had dreamt of being Queen herself in the early days of Charles's infatuation, so now she clung to the desperate image of her infant son as sovereign. If only it would come to pass, she could tolerate Shaftesbury as Lord Protector.

Though nettled by Louise's treachery, Charles kept his indignation to himself. He had grown fond of his Fubbs, and her uses still outweighed the cost of keeping her, both financially and politically. She was crucial when it came to negotiating his subsidies with Louis and generally maintaining the goodwill of the French King. Charles also enjoyed the cultural climate she created around her, in particular her

patronage of foreign musicians and artists. Politically, she was a med-
dler, just as Barbara had been, and made sure that the new generation
of ministers, known as the 'Chits' because of their youth and inexperi-
ence, were at her beck and call. In particular she controlled the career
of Robert Spencer, Earl of Sunderland, who became Secretary of State.
His wife detested Louise, describing her as 'so damned a jade' that 'she
will certainly sell us whenever she can for five hundred pounds'. Louise's apartments at Whitehall, buzzing with diplomats and visiting dignitaries, constituted a foreign office of sorts which Charles still found
an invaluable source of political intelligence. And for the duration of
the Plot they were Louise's entire universe, for she didn't dare leave
the precincts of Whitehall for fear of a lynching.

Nell, on the other hand, wasn't given to making political calculations or declarations of allegiance. Buoyed by Whig tributes and the
adoration of the people, it would have been easy for her to have made
capital out of the Popish Plot and courted the goodwill of those who
might one day govern the country. After all, she was in her way as
popular as Monmouth. As one wag put it, she was 'A saint to be
admir'd the more, / Because a Church of England's whore . . .'⁶ But
dark clouds were gathering over her private life. The King's illness of
August 1679 had come at a particularly sensitive time, following as it
did within weeks of her mother's death, which was reported in the
Domestic Intelligencer, a Whig publication run by Benjamin Harris, for
5 August 1679: 'We hear that Madam Ellen Gwyn's mother, sitting
lately by the water-side at her house by the Neat-Houses, near
Chelsea, fell accidentally into the water and was drowned.' She was
fifty-five years old. The Neat-Houses do not refer to cattle-sheds as
one would expect, but to a famous market garden near Chelsea
Bridge. Narcissus Luttrell was less circumspect, stating simply that Mrs
Gwyn had been 'in drink' at the time of her accident. Anthony à
Wood, writing in Oxford on 20 July, was still more explicit: 'Elen
Gwynn, commonly called old Madam Gwynne, being drunk with
brandy, fell in a ditch neare the Neathouses, London, and was stifled.
Mother to Nell Quin. Lived sometimes in Oxford.'

There followed a number of highly coloured lampoons that stressed
the old dame's bawdy life, drunkenness and gargantuan bulk in sarcas-
tically grandiloquent terms. One mock elegy commiserated with the

brandy merchants, whose trade was sure to decay, 'for none is left behind / That in one day could twenty quarts consume'; others lamented the fact that she was too fat to be washed ashore. In 'A True Account of the late most doleful and lamentable tragedy of Old Maddam Gwinn, mother of Eleanor Gwinn, who was unfortunately drowned in a fish-pond at her own mansion-house, near the Neat-Houses, with an account how that much to be deplored accident came to pass and what is expected to be the sequel of the same', the author, having expressed the 'universal grief' that her death has occasioned among the 'bucksom *Bona-Robas*', proceeds to talk about her estate:

> . . . it is generally believed, that upon so Tragical occasion, the Pallace and the Fish-pond will be forfeited to her most vertuous Daughter Madam Ellen Gwin, as Lady of the Soil, and chief of all the *Bona-Robas* that the Suburban Schools of Venus late have fitted for the Game. And now in Gratitude to this good Matron's Memory, to be imposed upon her Tomb-Stone at the approaching Solemnisation we have composed this Epitaph as followest:
>
> > 'Here lies the Victim of a cruel Fate,
> > Whom too much Element did Ruinate;
> > 'Tis something strange, but yet most wondrous true,
> > That what we live by, should our Lives undo.
> > She that so oft had powerful Waters try'd,
> > At last with silence, in a Fish-pond dy'd.
> > Fate was unjust, for had he prov'd but kind,
> > To make it Brandy, he had pleas'd her Mind.'

It's difficult to know how to take 'the Pallace and the Fish-pond'. It could be a reference to Sandford Manor House with its little river, a property Nell seems to have rented for her mother. But, like many alcoholics, old Madam Gwyn probably found a way of abandoning decent surroundings for a life of misery somewhere. In such a context 'the Pallace and the Fish-pond' could be slang for a hovel with a large puddle outside. We simply don't know. Some of the Tory libellers, such as the author of 'Satyr Unmuzzled', used the mother's tragicomic death to taunt Nell:

Now for a she-buffoon, who, as 'tis said,
Crawled into the world without a maidenhead.
It is most sure 'twas never had by man,
Nor can she say where it was lost, or when;
We must conclude she never had one then.
Her mother grieved in muddy ale and sack
To think her child would ever prove a crack [i.e., prostitute];
When she was drunk she always fell asleep,
And when full maudlin then the whore would weep.
Her tears were brandy, mundungus her breath,
Bawd was her life, and common-shore her death.
To see her daughter mourn for such a beast,
'Tis like her life which maketh up one feast;
Of all her jokes this mourning is the best. [my italics]

But if the scribblers thought they could use the mother to shame the daughter, they didn't know their subject as well as they thought. For returning to London from Windsor, where she received the news of her mother's fatal accident, Nell decided to defy the grim-faced wariness of the capital, besieged as it was by 'the bloody stratagems of busy heads', by staging a flamboyant mock-solemn funeral procession through the streets of London, of a kind her mother would surely have savoured. It was her chance to cock a snook at both Whig and Tory; their solemn posturing, full of hatred, was not for her. She would affirm her enjoyment of life even in the teeth of death. As the author of *A Panegyrick* wrote,

> No cost, no velvet did the daughter spare;
> Fine gilded 'scutcheons did the hearse enrich
> To celebrate this martyr of the ditch;
> Burnt brandy did in flaming brimmers flow,
> Drunk at her funeral, while her well-pleased shade
> Rejoiced, even in the sober Fields below,
> At all the drunkenness her death had made.

It is not hard to imagine the scene. Buckingham, the mastermind of many a Pope-burning parade, was called on to orchestrate the procession. (There were ten days between the death and the funeral, plenty of time to prepare some magnificent props.) The hearse and carriages were decorated with the blue lion of the Gwyns of Llansanor on a field of gold and silver, the horses richly caparisoned, while Nell's entire household appeared in livery, some bearing trumpets, others holding torches burning with brandy, and the merry gang (Buckingham, Rochester, Sheppard, Buckhurst, Sedley, Killigrew and company), meeting together for the last time, marched in front dressed up as bishops, intoning words of consolation from *The Book of Common Prayer*. There may even have been an effigy of the old soak, borne aloft in a chair of gold. From Coal Yard Alley they marched down Drury Lane, stopping at the Theatre Royal, where they were joined by the acting fraternity (including Hart and Lacy), Orange Moll and a phalanx of legendary London bawds (Page, Ross, Cresswell et al.) and then wound their way through the streets of Covent Garden to the Church of St Martin's. Free beer was provided for the crowds who came to watch and cheer, jolted for an afternoon out of their fearful thoughts by the outrageous spectacle. As the satirist wrote, 'Of all her jokes this mourning is the best.'

Nell and her sister Rose were the chief mourners and travelled in the comfort of Nell's coach, which was stopped dozens of times on its circuitous journey so that the crowd could drink her health. Little James could not be there, for he was still in Paris, while the King, envisaging wild scenes on the streets, had insisted that nine-year-old Charles remain at Windsor with him. Nevertheless, it was a memorable occasion for Nell. So many of her dear friends and supporters were there, those who had helped her to the life she now led. Not only all her old friends from the theatre, but both her Charles I and her Charles II, Hart and Buckhurst, were there. The occasion was a fitting end to the most exciting chapter of her life, in which she had played the part of the wild mistress to perfection. There were new challenges lying in wait for her, and though nothing could overshadow her wholehearted celebration of her mother's joyful obsequies, her feelings towards the end of the day may have become somewhat rueful.

Old Mrs Gwyn was laid to rest in the south aisle of St Martin's and Nell had a monument erected to her, which was destroyed when the old church was rebuilt in 1721. The inscription read, 'Here lyes interred the body of Helena Gwynn, born in this parish, who departed this life ye 20th of July MDCLXXIX in the lvi yeare of her age.' Nell returned to Windsor and entertained the King with her account of the funeral. It was probably as well that little Charles had remained with his father; even at the tender age of nine he was beginning to identify strongly with his paternal inheritance and might have been embarrassed by his mother's antics. In November Charles took the boy to Portsmouth with him to see a warship, the *Burford*, launched in his honour, while Nell remained in London. The boy's parents were a difficult duo to reconcile, to say the least.

For Nell, the sense of foreboding remained, even after the King had recovered from his tussle with death, as the familiar world of the past ten years began to unravel. In October she fell off her horse at Newmarket, then in December she was shaken by an ugly incident in Hyde Park, when her lead coach-horse brushed one Henry Wharton as she was driving past. Wharton, a young hothead in the Guards, drew, running the horse through with a single lunge of his sword, for which he was banished. Word got around, however, that it was Nell herself who had been skewered, and on 17 December the editor of the *Mercurius Domesticus* felt called upon to reassure his readers: 'Several false and ridiculous reports being spread abroad concerning Madam Ellen Gwyn, as to her death or absence from her house, we are assured that there is no ground for such a report, the said Madam Gwyn being now at her own house in health, and has not been absent from it.' A public outcry had no doubt made such an announcement necessary.

Then in January the following year (1680) she was sitting in her box at the Duke's Playhouse when a man approached from the pit and called her 'whore' to her face. Though she herself thought little of such insults, her guest on this occasion, George Herbert, younger brother of the Earl of Pembroke, rose to defend her honour, with the result that 'there were many swords drawn and a great hubbub in the house'.

For the first time, too, libels had begun to appear that denigrated her looks and made disparaging comments about her age, and this may have undermined her confidence. She was 'that hairbrain'd wrinkl'd stop'd up whore', 'old Nelly', 'ugly fac'd Nelly', the 'nauceous, false, and wither'd Whore', and the 'lass with rivell'd [i.e., wrinkled] Belly'.

One satire entitled 'Ignis Ignibus Extinguitur' exhorts the King to drop her:

> O Sacred Sir protect this Drabb no more,
> If you must have one use a handsome Whore.
> Of such foul Haggs there ne're can be a Dearth,
> O send her to her Dunghill Mother Earth.
> Old, wrinkled, ugly, loathsome as a Grave,
> Shee'd turn the stomach of your meanest Slave . . .

At thirty, Nell was no longer considered young, but by all unbiased accounts she retained that spirited beauty which impressed all who met her, and which Churchill was to describe as 'transcendent'. Her wit was still reflected in the quick mischief of her face, and her copious red and gold hair retained its power to enmesh men's hearts. The wisdom that had descended upon her was not grave, but sprightly, and the new generation of court debutantes regarded her as they might a figure from a vanished world of glamour and fable. To them she was the stuff of legend, the girl from the slums who had won the heart of a king.

As if all this wasn't enough to deal with, her relationship with the King was put under strain from an unexpected quarter: the Duke of Monmouth. In June 1679 Monmouth had routed the rebellious Scottish Covenanters at Bothwell Brig and proved himself a merciful victor. He returned to a hero's welcome, his growing hopes and ambitions weaving themselves into Shaftesbury's design for an armed uprising. But having recovered from his illness, Charles decided the time had come to discipline his reckless and disloyal son. Stripping him of his offices, he packed Monmouth off to Holland, where the unrepentant Duke tried to win the support of William of Orange. But William was playing his own, far subtler game. Charles's brother, who could hear the cries of 'No York! No Papist!' in the streets of London, was sent to Scotland.

After a month of biding his time at The Hague, Monmouth suddenly returned to London without the King's permission. The whole city was awoken in the early hours of 28 November by the tolling of bells. Bonfires were lit and street criers announced the joyful news. As the capital began to fill with people, coaches were stopped and their occupants forced to drink the Duke's health. The air of celebration lasted weeks. There were riotous scenes in the theatre, where shouts of 'God bless his Highness the Duke of Monmouth' rang from the pit, and a broadside entitled 'Joyful News to England, ye Duke of Monmouth return'd' sold by the thousands. The King was in a rage; the court had never seen him so angry. Monmouth, having spent his first day in consultation with Shaftesbury, sought asylum at Nell's house in Pall Mall. It was an inspired choice.

What better place for the Protestant Duke to stay than at the home of the Protestant Whore? It could only lead to demonstrations of loyalty outside Nell's house and cast a further veil of glamour over the people's idol. Nell too was Monmouth's best line to the King. If anyone could persuade Charles to see his son, it was Nell. Emotionally, too, it was the right place to be. Monmouth had always valued Nell's common-sense advice and felt able to let down his guard in her company. Nell welcomed him with open arms and immediately agreed to see the King on his behalf, not because she sympathized with his political cause (indeed she mocked his pretensions and dubbed him 'Prince Perkin' after another famous pretender, Perkin Warbeck), but because she saw a son's grief at being estranged from his father. We are told that she pleaded with the King, saying that his disfavour had made Monmouth grow 'pale, wan, lean and long-visag'd'. But the father was in no mood for forgiveness; he considered the Exclusionist agenda all but treasonable and Monmouth principal accessory to that treason. On the day after Monmouth's return, Robert Southwell wrote to Ormonde, informing him that the Duke 'supped the last night with Mrs Gwynne, who was this day at her utmost endeavours of reconciliation, but received a very flat and angry denial, and by all appearances His Majesty is incensed to a high degree'. Nell had to relay the King's order that Monmouth return to Holland immediately.

It seems that the King was at first unaware that Monmouth was actually staying at Nell's house, for he continued to dine there during December. Henry Sidney reported one such occasion in a letter to Lady Sunderland, saying that Monmouth was 'shut up in [Nell's] closet' when the King came round. The French ambassador Barrillon was astonished by the situation and wrote to inform Louis that Monmouth was having supper every night 'with Nelly, the courtesan who has borne the king two children, and whom he daily visits.' The situation could not last. When Monmouth insisted that he intended to stay and pursue the cause of Exclusion in rank defiance of the King's orders, Nell was forced to order him out. *A Panegyrick* has these lines:

> True to the Protestant Interest and cause,
> True to th'establish'd Government and Laws,
> The Chief delight of the whole Mobile [*mobile vulgus* – the rabble],
> Scarce Monmouth's self is more belov'd than shee.
> Was this the cause that did their quarell move,
> That both are Rivalls in the Peoples Love?
> No, 'twas her Matchless loyaltie alone
> That bid Prince Perkin pack up and be gone.

Despite their ties of deep affection, Nell was relieved to see Monmouth go, as his presence in her house, together with that of his supporters, who had waltzed in and out at all hours of the day and night, had put her relationship with the King under enormous stress. On the advice of Shaftesbury, the prodigal Duke now made a series of progresses among the people, accompanied by agents who spread rumours of the mysterious black box. He was greeted ecstatically wherever he went, most especially in the West Country. He even touched for the king's evil, and reports of his healing powers bolstered belief in his legitimacy. As Shaftesbury well knew, it was all about creating a personality cult strong enough to sweep Monmouth onto the throne in the event of the King's death.

Another erstwhile house guest and chronic intriguer, the Duke of Buckingham, was once again plotting to oust Louise as *maîtresse en titre*. This time he had seized on one of his sister's nieces, Jane Lawson, a member of the Howard clan. As was his wont, Buckingham created a cabal to manage the affair. It consisted of his sister the Duchess of Richmond, Lady Mary Howard (another aunt of Miss Lawson's), Lory Hyde and Nell. It's difficult to believe that this was a serious endeavour; certainly Nell had little to gain except the pleasure of seeing Louise's nose out of joint. A satire entitled 'The Angler' warned Jane Lawson not to fall in with the designs of the cabal:

O yet consider e're it be too late
How near you stand upon the brink of fate.
Think who they are who would for you procure
This great preferment to be made a whore:
Two reverend aunts, renowned in British story
For lust and drunkenness with Nell and Lory.
These, these are they your fame will sacrifice,
Your honour sell, and you shall hear the price:
My Lady Mary nothing can design,
But to feed her lust with what she gets for thine;
Old Richmond making thee a glorious punk,
Shall twice a day with brandy now be drunk;
Her brother Buckingham shall be restored;
Nelly a countess, Lory be a lord.

This has all the flavour of an intrigue from the 1660s or early 1670s and shows the extent to which Buckingham was caught in the time warp of his own ambition. He still nurtured the vain hope that he could one day reign supreme in the counsels of the King. He was also forgetting the exhausted state of the royal libido. The King's intrigues were now political rather than amorous. In the event, Jane herself behaved with commendable modesty and proved that she could not easily be won, even by a King. When the game had been played out, she retired to a nunnery at York with her four sisters.

In May 1680, succumbing to the stress perhaps of the previous nine months, Nell herself fell seriously ill and was unable to accompany the King to Newmarket. Roy MacGregor-Hastie speculates that she had caught the clap from Charles. We don't know, though he too was unwell, suffering another attack of the ague. Nell had barely recovered the following month when a much greater grief struck her down. News came from Paris that her eight-year-old son James had died 'of a sore leg', which may point to an accident or perhaps even poison. His death must have been sudden, for Nell had not been informed of a lingering illness and made no plans to hasten over to Paris. The circumstances of the boy's life in the French capital are utterly unknown, and no record of his burial has been found. It is unlikely that the body was brought back to England.

Parting with little James must have been grievous enough, but now Nell had to cope with all the demons of remorse and self-reproach as she contemplated the death of a child she had last seen when he was six. He had been born on Christmas Day and she thought back to all the Christmas parties she had thrown in honour of his birthday. The King and his brother had always attended. Those days had seemed so safe and carefree. Now nothing seemed certain. She had lost a parent and a child within the space of a year. James, who unlike Charles had always been a mother's child, would not be there for her when the King was gone. Any dreams that she could set her rest on his kind nursery were gone. Wherever she looked, her prospects were rapidly closing.

The King too was grieved, more for Nell than for his own loss in a well-loved son. Realizing that she needed a project to help her over her sorrow, Charles, who earlier that year had made her the splendid gift of Burford House, Windsor, which had been built on an old vineyard adjacent to the castle, now encouraged her to move in and work on the property. In fact, he had used a grant of £5,000 earmarked for repairs to the royal apartments in the castle itself to build Nell's house, as well as a new tennis court nearby for himself. Although just outside the castle walls, Burford House was very much part of the King's estate and its gardens abutted the royal park. As with 79 Pall Mall, an initial lease was followed three years later (on 7 February 1683) by a warrant granting her the freehold 'for and during her life and after her decease in trust for Charles Earl of Burford and the heirs male of his body'. Her old lover Charles Buckhurst, Earl of Dorset, was appointed one of the trustees of the property, as was William Chiffinch, her early go-between.

Nell, who found more interest and delight in the country as she grew older, readily yielded to the King's friendly prodding. There was much work to be done both inside and out, such as the installation of plumbing and a water supply, and repairs to the garden wall, for which she hired the 'bricklere' Francis Brookes. Charles, who was a keen horticulturist, advised her on the planting of trees. The house had extensive grounds of approximately forty acres, which included formal gardens, orchards, bowling alleys, stables, outhouses and, delight of delights, an orangery – an ornate glass house full of citrus trees. No expense was spared on interior decoration. Charles instructed Antonio Verrio and Grinling Gibbons, who were working at the castle for him, to divert their energies into Burford House. Verrio, a Neapolitan who had settled in England and whose ceiling in St George's Hall at the castle was described by Evelyn as 'stupendous', painted the main staircase with scenes from Ovid's *Metamorphoses*, a work that recounts the amorous adventures of the gods. Sadly they don't survive. Gibbons, whom Walpole would describe as 'a citizen of nature', carved one of the chimney pieces. Meanwhile, Nell's upholsterer and co-signatory to the power of attorney cited earlier, John Potevin, scurried back and forth between London and Windsor with various items of furniture, including a bed for her son Charles.

A house wasn't a house for Nell unless it rang with the laughter of friends, and with London resounding to the bitter slogans of the mob she took particular delight in luring her cronies away from the capital for a weekend's conviviality. Now too she could accommodate members of the court who had come to wait upon the King. Writers and poets came, such as Waller, Lee, Otway, Behn and Wycherley (who had just married the widowed Countess of Drogheda), the usual zany theatre folk, civil servants such as Pepys, a new generation of aspiring fops and a fistful of Whig or Whiggish grandees, including Sidney, Cavendish, Buckingham and Monmouth. According to Lady Rachel Russell in a letter to her husband, the King grew impatient with Nell's hospitality towards men that he now considered dangerous rebels. Maybe the Whigs' advanced social ideas appealed to Nell more than the rigid, hierarchical principles of the Tories.

One old friend who never made it down to Burford House was Rochester, whose death had been falsely reported as far back as April 1678. Having recovered, he wrote to Savile, 'The King, who knows me to be a very ill-natur'd man, will not think it an easy matter for me to die, now I live chiefly out of spite'. And indeed he spewed his venom at all and sundry once more, not neglecting those who held him dear: 'Who'd be a monarch to endure the prating / Of Nell and saucy Oglethorpe in waiting?' he ranted. His fatal error was to abandon the green peace of Adderbury and return to London, for by April 1680 he was sick again. His mind turned to his Creator and he began a series of illuminating conversations with the fashionable confessor Dr

Gilbert Burnet. His mind struggled desperately to find a path through the fog of doubt and self-contempt. But Rochester's real testimony of the spirit comes in his masterpiece 'A Satyr against Reason and Mankind'. His keen appreciation that dogma and all the mental paraphernalia of the Church are obstacles to man's direct experience of the divine reveals a philosophical outlook closely allied to the King's, as does his belief that philosophy should encourage and facilitate the enjoyment of life.

Rochester's introspection in the months before his death was widely reported and stories of his luminous insights made an almost saintly figure of him. To Francis Fane he was that 'seraphic lord', whose wanton days had been a charade to beguile the devil. He died on 26 July 1680 at the age of thirty-three. Nell received the news at Windsor, where she was busy on her new house. In his death she lost not only a friend, but a wise counsellor, for no one had known the pitfalls of court life better than he.

The King and Nell remained at Windsor throughout the summer, where the King's peace was interrupted by a flood of Whig petitions from the shires calling upon him to exclude his brother from the throne. Shaftesbury had not been idle during Parliament's enforced recess. The King was barely courteous to the bearers, who had 'crept upon his troubled hours', and most of the time left others to convey the response that His Majesty had gone fishing. Indeed, his doctors noted with dismay that he could not be dissuaded from fishing on days 'when a dog would not be abroad'. He had, however, put himself on a milk diet to guard against an attack of bile. Bile had no place in statecraft, nor did hastiness, and the patience he now displayed on the river bank was more than matched by his forbearance in the political field. A lesser man would have been provoked by Shaftesbury's bold affronts both to his dignity and his sovereignty, but not Charles. When he struck, he meant to strike for good. He was rewarded that summer by a series of acquittals in the show trials managed by the Whigs, which turned the tide of anti-Papist hysteria. The witnesses 'for the Crown' were properly cross-examined this time and found to be as hollow as their suborner, the preposterous Oates. In addition, his own supporters had not been idle, and he began to receive a very different sort of petition, this time abhorring the demands of the Exclusionists.

Charles knew how important appearances are in politics, and though Louise and Sunderland allowed themselves to be intimidated, he himself intended to show the people that his routine remained undisturbed. Accordingly Windsor was followed by the usual autumn meeting at Newmarket, to which his brother James was invited, and where the King's horse, Corke, beat the field. While there, Charles dictated to Pepys the story of his escape from the Battle of Worcester, maybe to remind himself in the current climate of rebellion just how good he was at getting out of tight situations.

On 21 October 1680 the Parliament that had been elected over a year before with an even greater Whig majority was finally convened. In his speech to Parliament, Charles held his station above the party fray and made an eloquent plea for unity:

> That which I value above all the treasure in the world . . . is a perfect union among ourselves. Nothing but this can restore the kingdom to that strength and vigour which it seems to have lost and raise us again to that consideration which England hath usually had. All Europe have their eyes upon this assembly, and think their own happiness and misery, as well as ours, will depend upon it . . . Let us therefore take care that we do not gratify our enemies and discourage our friends by any unseasonable disputes. If any such do happen, the world will see it was no fault of mine; for I have done all that was possible for me to do to keep you in peace while I live and to leave you so when I die.

But the Commons would not be coaxed and lost no time in passing a new Exclusion Bill, which was carried to the Lords with much acclaim. Charles himself looked on from his casual chair by the fireplace as Shaftesbury tried to browbeat the House and Monmouth pranced nervously about with his tribe of sycophants. In the end, it was the dogged rhetoric of Halifax ('the trimmer') which saved the day for the Crown. After twelve hours of debate, the bill was put to the vote shortly before midnight and defeated by thirty-three votes. The fury of the thwarted Exclusionists was not matched by the mood on the streets, which was subdued. Nevertheless, Charles had doubled the guard in the City just in case.

But Shaftesbury was determined to keep the pressure up. Having secured the election of two Republican sheriffs for the capital, he now had the London juries in his pocket. Many still envisaged an inevitable slide into civil war. On 12 December Evelyn looked out of his window at night and saw 'a meteor of an obscure bright colour, very much in shape like the blade of a sword, the rest of the skie very serene and cleare. What this may portend God onely knows: but such another phenomenon I remember to have seene in 1640, aboute the Triall of the greate Earle of Strafford, preceding our bloudy Rebellion.'

Charles's minor victory had been duly noted by Paris, and Barrillon was instructed to open talks about the possibility of renewing Louis's subsidies to the English Crown in return for guarantees on foreign policy. But Charles, still smarting from Louis's treachery, decided to make his own terms this time. A deal was struck, and Louise for once was kept out of the negotiations, which were conducted in absolute secrecy between the bed and the wall in the Queen's *chambre de lit*. Charles had not forgotten his mistress's unholy alliance with Shaftesbury, even if it had been dictated by fear rather than conviction.

The deal strengthened Charles's hand no end. Now that he had the money to govern for two years without Parliament, he could take the fight to the Whigs. So on 10 January 1681 the King duly prorogued, then dissolved, Parliament. Next he announced that the new Parliament, which he summoned for 21 March, would be convened not at Westminster, but at the old Royalist capital of Oxford. It was a master stroke. This would be the crucial Parliament of his reign, the final showdown, and it was vital that the Whigs be divorced from their power base in the City. More than that, the King knew that the choice of Oxford itself would stir memories of the Civil War, for it had been his father's headquarters during that bloody conflict. In 1641 men had not known the cost they would have to pay; in 1681 they knew only too well and, bar a small group of fanatics, would do anything to avoid paying it again. Above all, the King was setting the agenda and had wrong-footed his opponents. When Shaftesbury and Essex appeared before him at the head of a deputation from the Lords to complain of his decision, Charles felt able to dismiss their petition as 'the opinion of so many men'. It seemed the heavens were on his side as well: several folk near Abingdon saw a crown of light above the rising sun.

Having taken precautions to secure the capital in case of a rearguard action, the King made his way to Oxford via Windsor with all flags flying. People flocked to the roadside to cheer his coach. As soon as he rode through the gates of the city, Charles knew that he had made the correct calculation, such was the universal acclamation of his welcome. In the eyes of the people of Oxford he had lost none of the mystique that had accompanied his return from exile in 1660. Anthony à Wood wrote of his entry into Oxford,

> But that which is most to be noted is that all the way the king passed were such shoutings, acclamations, and ringing of bells, made by loyall hearts and smart lads of the layetie of Oxon, that the aire was so much peirced that the clouds seemed to divide. The generall cry was 'Long live King Charles', and many drawing up to the very coach window cryed 'Let the king live, and the devill hang up all roundheads': at which his majestie smiled and seemed well pleased. – The throng and violence of people to express their affections were such that the coach was scarse able to pass.[7]

With Shaftesbury's arrival the town assumed a more combative air and the streets were filled with armed partisans, some bearing the red ribbon of the Tories, others the blue of the Whigs and shouting, 'No Popery! No slavery!' Men jostled their opponents and scuffles broke out. The air was thick with aggression. According to Dalrymple, 'it seemed more like a meeting of the county militia than the assembly of Parliament'. Monmouth, who was staying with the priggish Alderman Wright, was carried about in a sedan surrounded by a bunch of powdered thugs wielding leaden flails, while Shaftesbury, who had entered Oxford in great state, remained closeted at Balliol, devising how best to steer the Exclusion Bill through Parliament.

Never one to bow to public prejudice, Charles had brought both Nell and Louise to Oxford with him, as well as the Queen. The satirists and ballad-mongers, in tune with the popular imagination, were determined that the tabloid-style rivalry between the two mis-tresses should continue. After all, the two women provided a vivid, albeit crude illustration of the political contest being fought. One Whiggish wag even wrote an imaginary war of words between 'Tutty' and 'Snapshort', two lapdogs belonging to Nell and Louise. Unsurpris-ingly, Tutty, who gives a bold defence of his mistress as 'a good commonwealth's woman', worsts his French counterpart, who never-theless doggedly upholds his mistress as 'a whore of the greater magnitude'. As for Nell, she warns Louise to keep her distance, since Tutty has a keen nose for 'a Popish Miss'. But it is the two dogs who end up fighting, with Nell putting a guinea on Tutty.

Nell enjoyed being back in the (likely) town of her birth, and her refuge during the plague. During the day she took rides through the streets to visit some of her old haunts. It was on one such occasion that her coach was mistaken for Louise's and surrounded by an angry mob of Whig sympathizers, who banged on the sides and poured forth their curses. Nell signalled the driver to halt and, sticking her head out of the window, cried out good-humouredly, 'Pray, good people, be civil, I am the *Protestant* whore!' Immediately, the curses turned to cheers, caps were tossed in the air, and a path cleared for her coach. Waving and smiling, she passed on.

Having received the town dignitaries and finalized his plans for the Parliament, Charles was determined to enjoy his two weeks in Oxford. He and Nell went to Burford in the Cotswolds, the town from which their son took his title and where Rochester had attended the grammar school, and dined at the priory. The next day, despite the frost and snow, they went hawking on Burford Downs and watched the horse-racing. The King's Plate for that year had been transferred from New-market to Burford. The *Protestant Oxford Intelligence* reported proudly, 'From Burford we have advise, that most of his Majesty's race-horses are brought thither, and that several gentlemen from the adjacent parts are sending theirs, haveing taken stables at very dear rates, so that 'tis thought if His Majesty's horses continue there, horses will be sent thither from all parts of England, and raceing will be established, to the great joy of the inhabitants of that burrough.' The Theatre Royal players came up to Oxford as members of the King's household and put on a performance of *Tamerlane the Great* at Christ Church by a new playwright called Charles Saunders. The King attended with Louise on one arm and Nell on the other, and was no doubt gratified by the theme of an absolute monarch in command of an expanding empire.

But the real coup de théâtre was Charles's to deliver. When he opened Parliament on 21 March the King was apparently conciliatory, taking pains to reassure the Commons that significant safeguards and limitations would be placed upon a Popish successor, who would be King only in name. Charles made these extravagant concessions, not because he believed in them, but because he knew it was safe to offer them to opponents who were blinded by their own fanaticism. Being the subtler psychologist, Charles knew that he could have his cake and eat it by speaking reasonably and acting ruthlessly. He was not, however, prepared to alter the legitimate succession in principle, even by way of a bluff. He reminded members that the legitimacy of the Crown was their only guarantee of freedom, and no doubt he had Cromwell in mind when he said, 'I, who will never use any arbitrary government myself, am resolved not to suffer it in others . . .' Shaftesbury, however, wasn't interested in concessions; he wanted to humiliate the King. The Commons, who were convened in the Geometry School, once more raised their belligerent cries of 'No Papist! No York!'. But for all their shouting they could not square the circle of Monmouth's illegitimacy.

On the following Monday, the twenty-eighth, the day appointed for the introduction of the third Exclusion Bill, furtively, swiftly, Charles put his plan into action. Walking down to the Lords, which was sitting in Christ Church Hall, he had his robes and crown conveyed separately in a sedan chair and covered with a cloak. Changing quickly and in secret, he gave orders for the Commons to be summoned. The latter, believing that the King was going to announce his surrender, hurried over with bated breath. When they arrived, they were amazed to see the King in full regalia, sitting on his throne, and even more astonished when, with very little ado, he forthwith ordered the Lord Chamberlain to dissolve Parliament, then left the chamber with great dispatch. The crestfallen Commons stared blankly at the throne; Shaftesbury spat with rage. One eyewitness spoke of their 'loud sighs' and 'dreadful faces'. They were never to meet again during Charles's reign.

The King was in buoyant mood as he disrobed, telling one young Parliamentarian to be of good cheer, for 'you had better have one King than five hundred'. Outside, the spring that had been so late in coming finally began to burgeon. Charles hastened back to Whitehall via Windsor. It was time to settle accounts.

~ 15 ~

The Last Reckoning

FROM THE DISSOLUTION OF THE Oxford Parliament to the King's death there would be but four years, not even that, for Nell to enjoy the companionship of the man she loved. Charles's health had grown erratic, and with modern medicine still in its infancy (going to bed with a live sheep was still considered a sensible remedy for measles) she knew only too well that the next serious chill or bout of ague could be his last. Even now there was a feeling of quiet contraction to the King's daily round, and the rhythm of his life was marked by a single clear notation: rallentando. As Charles aged he grew more paternal in his concern for Nell; for her part, she finally had a chance to care for the father who had eluded her.

Nell found herself outside the limelight. The King's love life no longer made headline news, and peace and prosperity did not provide fertile ground for the jester's art. Ever the faithful fool, she followed her master about in his annual progresses between Whitehall, Windsor, Newmarket and eventually Winchester, but life didn't have that old edge of bravura. The danger and the hilarity had gone. Now a seasoned hostess, Nell took pleasure in entertaining the King and his friends, decorating Burford House and generally living the life of a country lady. Gambling too still had its charms, and still she staked too high, losing £1,400 to Hortense in a single night. It was a mad sum to lose when she should have been laying down stores for life without Charles, but Nell had never been one to plan ahead. In Tom Brown's *Letters from the Dead to the Living* (1702), there is a facetious letter from

Nell to Peg Hughes, Prince Rupert's mistress, in which she scolds her for having lost on cards all the money acquired through whoring. 'I am ashamed to think,' she writes, 'that a woman who had wit enough to tickle a prince out of so fine an estate, should at last prove such a fool as to be bubbled of it by a little spotted ivory and painted paper.'[1]

Having wrongfooted the Whigs with his sudden dissolution of the Oxford Parliament, Charles lost no time in pursuing his advantage. Intelligence reports indicated that King Shaftesbury and his six 'privy counsellors' (Monmouth, Russell, Sidney, Essex, Howard and Hampden) were plotting the violent overthrow of the government. Their desperate conspiracy encouraged Charles to keep to the high ground, and he fired the first shot in the ensuing propaganda war by publishing a *Declaration to All His Loving Subjects* to be read in churches, in which he explained his reasons for dissolving the last two Parliaments. When it came to Shaftesbury and his cronies, Charles refrained from naming his tormentors, but no one could doubt the target of his blows: 'Let not the restless Malice of ill Men, who are labouring to poyson Our People, some out of fondness of their Old Beloved Commonwealth Principles, and some out of anger at their being disappointed in the particular Designs they had for the accomplishment of their own Ambition and Greatness, perswade any of Our Good Subjects, that We intend to lay aside the use of Parliaments.'

No one did more than Dryden to release men from the spell of the Popish Plot. As David Ogg writes in his *England in the Reign of Charles II*, 'There are times when national sanity can be restored only by sarcasm . . . It was so in England when, after three years of madness, men read *Absalom and Achitophel* and laughed themselves out of their own follies. It was the triumph of native common sense.' Dryden's masterpiece was published in November 1681, its final lines giving the glad tidings of a second Restoration ('Once more the God-like *David* was Restor'd').

Now the hunter became the hunted, and Shaftesbury was given little room for manoeuvre. In July 1681 he was arrested on a charge of high treason − for suborning witnesses during the Popish Plot and planning a coup d'état − and sent to the Tower. In poor health, he petitioned the King to be allowed to retire to his plantation in the Carolinas, where no doubt he could have taken up the title of 'new sovereign' that Dryden sneeringly conferred on him in his *Epistle to the Whigs*, but was refused. Charles did not trust him and freely admitted that he would have granted the request had it come from anybody else.[2]

Shaftesbury's Old Bailey trial was awaited with trepidation. Many loyal to the Crown believed that they had 'gott a bear by the tooth' and that a conviction would provoke anarchy in the streets of the City. In the event the jury of City magnates returned a neutral verdict of '*Ignoramus*' ('we do not know'), and Shaftesbury walked free. The City erupted with bonfires, fireworks and all manner of rejoicing, and a medal was struck with Little Sincerity's garlanded head upon it. On Charles's suggestion Dryden wrote a satire against sedition entitled 'The Medal', in which he described Shaftesbury as,

> A Vermin wriggling in th'Usurper's ear,
> Bart'ring his venal wit for sums of gold,
> He cast himself into the Saint-like mould;
> Groan'd, sigh'd, and pray'd, while Godliness was gain,
> The lowdest Bag-pipe of the Squeaking train.

The sums of gold came from those City magnates who financed Shaftesbury's political campaigns in the belief that he could deliver their dream of a commercial city state along the lines of Venice. Otway in his play *Venice Preserv'd* (1682) points up the dangers of the City's political freedom, seeing within its walls a hotbed of sedition. Like the banking community in Amsterdam, with which it had close links and whose unfettered financial power it coveted, the City was also a Masonic enclave, which saw both Church and Crown as obstacles to its dream of a single world government. Little wonder that Charles moved to secure the election of Tory officers for the City and called in its ancient charter.

Otway's portrait of Shaftesbury as the perverted old senator Antonio presented a face of the elder statesman that must have shocked a good many of his admirers. Antonio is revealed as a man whose private life contradicts the public image he so sedulously cultivates. The grave senator is a kinky whoremonger, who pays the courtesan Aquilina (or 'Nicky Nacky', as he calls her) bags of gold so that he can act out his fantasies on her. One moment he is a bellowing bull, the next a dog who barks about his mistress's ankles from under a table and is kicked for his pains. Then, when she starts to whip him, he cries, 'Nay, prithee Nacky, now thou art too loving . . .'

Shaftesbury's furtive sexual life impaired his integrity, and it infuriated him that Charles, who was so nonchalantly frank about his own sins, should have seen through his mask. One morning during the year of Shaftesbury's chancellorship (1672), as he entered the Presence Chamber in full ceremonial garb, preceded by sergeant-at-arms and purse-bearer, Charles had nodded and said, 'Here comes the greatest whoremaster in England'. Shaftesbury, it seems, wasn't as different from the King as he would like to think. When some of Charles's supporters remonstrated with him for pursuing his former minister with a ruthlessness worthy of his opponent, Charles replied, 'At Doomsday we shall see whose arse is blackest'.

After his release Shaftesbury made one last-ditch attempt to overthrow the Crown. Together with Russell he planned to take the City with his 10,000 'brisk boys' from Wapping, while his other lieutenants, including Monmouth, were to start risings across the country. The government had full intelligence of Shaftesbury's plans, and he was forced to hide out in the City. Crucially, though, he had lost touch with the country and failed to recognize the tide of abhorrence against Whig extremism; nor did he understand the old feudal principles that still governed country life. Shaftesbury's other misperception concerned Monmouth. Though wildly popular among the Whig gentry, the Protestant Duke was despised as a lightweight by the old-school Puritans and Dissenters who were vital to the revolutionary cause.

In imminent danger of his life, Shaftesbury eventually fled to Holland disguised as a Presbyterian minister. There he went by the name of Johnson (Charles himself had been Jackson following his flight from Worcester) and deposited £30,000 – almost £2.5 million in today's money – in an Amsterdam bank under the aegis of the Jewish merchant Abraham Keck. But the rebel leader's health was giving out. He died in January 1683 and lay in state in Amsterdam before his body was shipped home to Dorset. According to witnesses, he lay 'with a very smileing countenance'. Perhaps he knew that the forces he had set in motion were ultimately unstoppable.

But for now peace and prosperity spread their banners in the land,

and the English busied themselves with that thing that Charles had once told Minette was nearest to their hearts – trade. Europe was at war, but England stood aloof and self-absorbed. According to Arthur Bryant, 'the very force and treasure which England poured out so lavishly in the wars of Marlborough, she drew from these quiet years when King Charles was leading her through green pastures. Everywhere men were laying up for themselves and their children treasure for the future. On every sea the adventurous ships of England sailed, coming home with treasure in their holds to enhance the wealth of a little island of squires, yeomen and homely merchants, and bringing silks and scents and delicate cloths for their ladies'.[3] Bryant rightly emphasizes the word 'treasure', though the greatest treasure the English found in these years was of no pecuniary value, being a creative sense of their own nationhood.

Now that he was secure financially, and the monarchy was safe for as long as he lived, Charles felt truly restored. The climate in 1660 had been euphoric but uncertain; now, in the spring of 1681, there was no room for doubt: the throne was his for keeps. Charles looked for some way of expressing this new sense of permanence and splendour and found it on the old castle hill above Winchester. Here he decided to build a palace that would set the seal upon his reign and be a symbol of the values he had restored. After detailed consultations with Wren, Charles began to visit Winchester regularly to lay out his plans, as well as to enjoy the excellent hawking and hunting provided by its proximity to the New Forest. The palace would be an English Versailles, able to accommodate the entire court. The town responded with great enthusiasm to the King's plans, for the benefits to business were obvious. Indeed, the town corporation went so far as to place a notice in the *London Gazette* for July 1682 announcing their intention of establishing a plate in the King's honour for a race to be run on the downs at the end of August. The invitation was duly accepted, and the King and Queen and court, among them Nell, travelled down to Winchester for the race.

One of the King's harbingers had gone on ahead to prepare lodgings for the bigwigs. It was arranged that the King would stay at the deanery, while rooms were found for Nell at the house of the Revd Thomas Ken, prebendary of Winchester Cathedral and recently appointed court chaplain. Only Ken was having none of it: he categorically refused to have 'a woman of ill repute' staying at his house. According to one tradition, Ken was given no warning and so Nell had already moved in before he could protest, whereupon he had the roof removed bit by bit until she agreed to go. Either way, Nell declined to take offence and reported the matter to Charles with good humour and ungrudging admiration for the doughty Ken. Meanwhile she herself was transferred to the deanery, a much more congenial arrangement from her point of view. Two years later when the bishopric of Bath and Wells fell vacant, the King, who had shared Nell's admiration for the swarthy little priest, declared, ''Od's fish! who shall have Bath and Wells but the little black fellow who would not give Nelly a lodging?' Years later, during the reign of George II, the playwright and poet Edward Young tried to persuade the Duchess of Portland to help him to a mitre with the words ''Tis certain Nell Gwyn made Dr. Ken a bishop'. Later on during the visit she stayed at Avington, an estate belonging to the Countess of Shrewsbury, a salty gal whose affair with the Duke of Buckingham had caused a social scandal in the late 1660s.

The whole town turned out to greet the King and court. Charles walked the streets, chatting gaily to its inhabitants, and touched over sixty people for the king's evil. Winchester had suffered many depredations during the Civil War for its loyalty to Charles I, and now it seemed that restitution was at hand. Nell accompanied the King up onto the downs for hawking, cantering beside him as they followed the hawks, flanked by the royal falconers in their gold-trimmed crimson coats. They also travelled the twelve miles to Southampton for a day's yachting, and Charles got to inspect his beloved warships. Messing about on boats was another passion that the King and his mistress shared. Once his palace was completed, Charles would be able to keep tabs on the navy without leaving its walls, for with the aid of a telescope he could view the movements of his fleet from the cupola. The King reviewed Wren's plans constantly and exhorted him to lose no time in seeing the work through. 'If it be possible to be done in one year,' he chivvied him, 'I will have it so, for a year is a great deal in my life.' The devastating fire at Newmarket in the spring of 1683 meant that the King laid even more store by Winchester, for it would be the destination for his spring and autumn sporting excursions. Evelyn considered the new venue 'infinitely . . . preferable to Newmarket for prospects, air, pleasure, and provisions'.

It was clear, too, that Charles intended Winchester to be his twilight home, the place where he could enjoy his final years. In so doing, he would be restoring the ancient seat of the Kings of Wessex, for Winchester had been Alfred the Great's capital. He was also breaking with two hundred years of Tudor and Stuart tradition by building his principal country residence outside the Thames valley. It was very much a medieval gesture. Alfred of course was the King who had codified the laws that became the basis of the English Common Law, and it was to the ancient Common Law above all that Charles had restored his subjects after the dictatorship of Cromwell. More than this, Winchester was connected in the popular imagination with Camelot and King Arthur, and the legendary Round Table, which hung on the wall of the great hall of the Norman castle. Charles was thus allying the monarchy with the chivalric capital of the nation, as opposed to its commercial and political centre, London. Shrewd realist that he was, Charles was also a romantic who understood the importance of tapping the wellsprings of the nation's mythology.

Having been something of a prodigy who peaked early, Nell was finding the pillars of her formative years folding one by one. It was certainly a bad time for the theatres, for politics had appropriated all the plots and audiences were dwindling. Drury Lane in particular had severe administrative and financial problems. Tom Killigrew had retired in February 1677 and was succeeded rather haphazardly by his sons Charles and Henry, a pair of wrangling debauchees. There was friction too between the remaining old-timers like Hart, Kynaston and gout-ridden Mohun, and the younger generation, which included the arch-rogue Cardonell ('Scum') Goodman, who had been sent down from Cambridge for slashing a portrait of the Duke of Monmouth. Salaries were pitifully low, when paid, and Hart and Kynaston entered into secret talks with the rival company at Dorset Garden about a possible union.

They managed to come to a deal, and in November 1682 the

United Company, as it was known, began performing at Drury Lane under the management of its principal actor, Thomas Betterton. Charles Hart, to whom Nell in large part owed the success of her career both as actress and royal mistress, retired with the demise of the King's Company. Sadly, his retirement lasted but nine months. He had been suffering from gallstones, and died at his house in Middlesex in August 1683. Nell's other early mentor, John Lacy, had died in September of the previous year in his rooms in Drury Lane, while Tom Killigrew himself passed away in March 1683. The Theatre Royal as Nell had known it – and it had been her home – was no more.

But for Nell it was easy to put aside thoughts of loss, for Charles was in generous mood after scattering the Whigs at Oxford. In April 1681 he granted her the leasehold on Bestwood Lodge outside Nottingham, later converted to freehold. Situated on the edge of Sherwood Forest, Bestwood had been a royal hunting lodge since the reign of Edward III, who issued letters patent from his 'Park of Bestwood' in 1364. Aptly enough, the first monarch to be associated with Bestwood was Henry I (b. 1068), known as 'Beauclerk' for his learning, who kept the territory as a royal domain 'wherein no man commons'. According to Thoroton in 1677, 'Bestwood hath a very fair Lodge in it, and in respect to the pleasant situation of the place, and conveniency of hunting and pleasure, the Park and Lodge have for these many years been the desire and achievement of great men.' He also mentions the abundance of red deer there before the Civil War.

In his gift Charles was clearly thinking of securing property for the line that he and Nell had founded together, and Bestwood Lodge was destined to remain in the Beauclerk family until it was sold by the 12th Duke of St Albans in 1940. Sherwood is rich in legends, and the story has it that Charles and Nell used Bestwood as a woodland hideaway, where they could live the simple life, a couple of amorous outlaws beneath the greenwood tree, where the immemorial rite of hand-fasting bound hearts more securely than ink and parchment.

Nell eagerly assumed the role of country mistress left vacant by her more sophisticated rivals, and it is poetically just that the title Charles wanted to confer on her at the time of his death was Countess of

Greenwich – i.e., of the green abode. Whether at Windsor, Newmarket or Burford, in the pastoral realm her power went unchallenged. At court and in public the original spark of their combined presence frequently turned to friction and misunderstanding, for the court now dominated by James had become more formal, but when they were alone there was peace, a very special, hard-won peace.

Charles, we are told, promised Nell that she should have as broad an acreage at Bestwood as she could ride around before breakfast. Nell's horsemanship was mediocre at best, which might explain why the estate comprised little more than 3,700 acres at the time of the grant; or perhaps she just didn't get up in good time. Whatever the case, Nell was more comfortable acting out the role of Mad Merry on a hobby-horse, which is what she did on Twelfth Night 1682, when she joined the law students of the Inner Temple at their Yuletide festivities. They knew whom to invite for a fun evening, even if meant an extra outlay on 'sweetmeats for Madam Gwyn'.

Other gifts of property were made in the next few years. A grant of 10 December 1684 by 'the Dean and Canons of the King's Free Chapel of St. George within the Castle of Windsor' licenses William Chiffinch of Whitehall 'to assign to Elenor Gwinne the tenement, garden and orchard of 2 acres in the parish of New Windsor called the Old Hawes'. The same month she was granted another Windsor property, this time in Priest Street – now St Albans street – which included stables and a garden. Yet Nell still found it remarkably easy to fall into debt. There were the clothes and furnishings she loved to display, the bills for sumptuous parties at Burford House and Pall Mall, the gambling, the wild impulsive purchases, such as the pearls she bought from Prince Rupert's estate, not to mention her many acts of personal and civic charity. When there was a great fire in Shaftesbury's recruiting ground of Wapping in November 1682 Nell gave £100 for the relief of those made homeless. She also helped her neighbourhood priest, Dr Tenison, with the settlement of Huguenot refugees in London.

On the Bestwood lease Nell is described as 'Lady Elinor Gwynne', which has a fine ring to it. Nor would Nell have been in a hurry to correct such mistakes, for she still coveted a title. It would be a way of cocking a snook at all her backbiters and detractors over the years and would help her feel less excluded from the aristocratic world in which her son moved. For though she had plenty of aristocratic well-wishers, both men and women, she was still vulnerable to the jibe of 'gutter-snipe' when civilities broke down. But Charles, for once, was restrained by the mores of the nobility, which would have regarded Nell's elevation to its ranks as a scandalous affront. It could tolerate her at court as a joker in the pack, but never as one of the titled cards. For once its snobbery was justified, as a title would surely have robbed Nell of her popular appeal.

Even at the age of twelve it seems that Charles Beauclerk was being primed for a career in the military, just as his elder half-brother Monmouth had been, doubtless in the hope that he wouldn't meddle in politics, a minefield for the royal bastard. Charles enjoyed taking the boy with him when he reviewed his guards or inspected the fleet at Chatham or Portsmouth. And the boy himself had been inspired from an early age by Monmouth's tales of heroism at Bothwell Brig and the Siege of Maastricht. Prince Rupert, whose war record had made him a living legend, also took an interest in the young Charles Beauclerk. He admired Nell's outspoken humour and was a keen patron of the theatre, as his own mother, Princess Elizabeth, had been. His plan to marry his daughter Ruperta (whose mother had also been an actress) to Lord Burford, as he was then known, was scotched by his own death in November 1682. Ruperta was only nine, and if her father is to be believed both feisty and extremely pretty. While Rupert lay dying, he sent his Garter to the King, 'desiring Lord Burford might have it'. But, like the proposed marriage, it was not to be. The match may well have proved a dynamic one; certainly Burford was to evince an hereditary predilection for actresses when he came of age.

The King shared Rupert's interest in the boy and managed to convince Nell to allow him to go to Paris to continue his education. Given little James's fate, the mother's reluctance is understandable. The boy was to be placed under the care of Lord Preston, who was Charles's Envoy Extraordinary to Paris. Preston was a Catholic, who was raised to Secretary of State by James in 1688 and who almost lost his life in attempting to restore that unhappy monarch. In a letter to

Preston from George Legge, a trusted companion of the King's, Charles's concern for what he perhaps considered his most vulnerable son is apparent:

> His Majesty is extremely fond of my Lord Burforde, and seems much concerned in his education, and he being now of an age fit to be bred in the world hath resolved to trust him wholly in your hands; no impertinent body shall be troublesome to you, nor anybody but whom you approve of to wait on him. I am to be your solicitor for providing money and all things necessary for him . . . I told his Majesty you would be forced to take a larger house [to accommodate Burford and his servants], and your expense must needs be much increased by this; he acknowledged it, and bid me take care that my Lord Burforde should have an appointment ready provided by you in your own house . . . masters must be provided for him, the best can be got of all sorts, but more particularly the King would have him study mathematics, and in that fortification, and that when the King of France moves in any progresses he constantly go with you to view all places in France, etc. . . .

Mathematics and fortification were two of the King's passions and were a necessary concomitant to the general military training that Burford would have received in France. Writing two months later, Legge had to explain why Burford hadn't yet crossed the Channel. 'Nelly,' he wrote, 'desir[ed] he should be delayed for a little time in the hopes of some settlement being made upon him.' Whether this referred to a title or a marriage settlement we don't know, but to make up for her stalling she engaged Peter de Launé, who had been tutor to the two Stuart princesses, to teach him French. What is certain is that Burford spent 1683 in Paris, first at Preston's house and then with one Jean de Gachon, his principal tutor, who lived a few miles outside the capital on the Sceaux Road. Sadly we have no record of his travels in France, and don't know whether he was presented at court or met Louis XIV, though Sceaux itself, being in the possession of Louis's chief minister Jean-Baptiste Colbert, was the scene of many a royal banquet.

Another reason for Nell's hesitation may have been news of M.

Faubert's application to set up a military academy in London for the sons of gentlemen and noblemen. The plan was put before the Royal Society in August 1682, which duly agreed to supervise the project and help raise the necessary funds from subscriptions. Evelyn was enthusiastic, for he saw the new academy as a way 'to lessen the vast expence the Nation is at yearly by sending children into France to be taught military exercises'. Faubert was a Protestant from Paris who had decided to settle in London for reasons of conscience. The academy was certainly up and running by the end of 1684, as Evelyn witnessed a demonstration by certain young gallants, 'Mr. Faubert having newly rail'd in a manage' (probably in St James's Park), in which they executed a series of four exercises all performed at full speed: '1. running at the ring; 2. flinging a javelin at a Moor's head; 3.discharging a pistol at a mark; lastly, taking up a gauntlet with the point of a sword.'

But England at least was at peace with the world, and London, the centre of a burgeoning empire, was a place of pilgrimage for exotic ambassadors from around the globe. In January 1682 it was the turn of the Moroccan ambassador Named Achmet, who came to discuss the troublesome English colony of Tangier, which had been part of the Queen's dowry. He was received by the King and Queen at the Banqueting House at Whitehall and garnered favourable reports for his modesty and civility. Evelyn commented that the Russian ambassador, who was still at court after an extended embassy, 'behav'd himselfe like a clowne, compar'd to this civil heathen'. Among other things, Achmet presented Charles with two lions and thirty ostriches. The King joked that all he could think to give in return was a flock of geese.

After the official reception, it was Louise de Kéroualle who took upon herself much of the responsibility of entertaining the honoured guest. The silks, jewels and spices that he had brought with him held many attractions for her, as did the person of the ambassador himself if the gossips of the time are to be believed. Nor did she spare any expense in her effort to impress him. Evelyn wrote,

This evening, I was at the entertainement of the Morocco Ambassador at the Dutchesse of Portsmouth's glorious apartments at Whitehall, where was a greate banquet of sweetmeates and musiq, but at which both the Ambassador and his retinue behav'd themselves with extraordinary moderation and modesty, tho' plac'd about a long table a lady betweene two moores, and amongst these were the King's natural children, *viz.* Lady Lichfield and Sussex [Barbara's daughters], the Dutchess of Portsmouth, Nelly, &c. concubines, and cattell of that sort, as splendid as jewells and excesse of bravery could make them.

Sitting at the banquet, sandwiched between two Moors and bedecked in tokens of the King's love, Nell was able to hold her own with as much aplomb as the most brazen courtier. She may not have travelled beyond the shores of England, but her salon had been frequented by those who had visited the furthest corners of the globe, and she herself had played many a Moorish princess at Drury Lane. There on the stage, playing the wild mistress, she had transformed others' perceptions of their world, while apprenticing herself to the high life. And now that the high life was hers, she had the wit to see that the play was still afoot, for the play was life itself. Actors and actresses came and went, and her own role was constantly changing, but the play – whether at court, at home, on the streets or in the theatre itself – was the same.

Charles didn't make an appearance until the ambassador had already risen to leave and was thanking the Dutchess of Portsmouth with the compliment that God would bless her 'and the Prince her sonn', meaning the nine-year-old Duke of Richmond. From Charles's point of view, it was useful to have young and beautiful mistresses to share the burden of hosting foreign visitors. Louise above all relished such duties. With the Popish Plot over, she now entered upon her glory days; socially, politically and by dint of her wealth she was queen in all but name. She enjoyed the support and gratitude of the two most powerful monarchs in Europe, and the darts of her enemies made no dent in the gilded panoply of her state. When the real queen, Catherine, commented that 'the mistresses govern all', her words conveyed no malice, and no one paid the slightest attention to them. Where Louise was concerned, Charles had grown fond, and was heard to mutter, 'my dearest Fubbs', as he contemplated her spreading form.

She must have wondered whether she was still capable of rousing his jealousy.

Unsurprisingly for such a fastidious and strenuously respectable woman, Louise had a penchant for sordid relationships. Though emotionally phlegmatic, she was prey to sudden compulsive desires that could sweep away years of politically expedient fidelity. Caving in to her lustful yearning for degenerate young men could cost her everything: wealth, status, influence. But having perforce restrained her cupidity to breaking point, Louise would suddenly be consumed by feelings of overwhelming depravity. In 1681 one of these 'eruptions' coincided with a visit to London from Philippe de Vendôme, Grand Prior of France and a great-grandson of Henri IV. He had come to visit his aunt Hortense Mancini; at least that was his pretext for running amok among the ladies of the court. Vendôme was a coarse, drunken womanizer with the charm and high birth to seduce almost anyone who caught his eye. He was instantly drawn to Louise, both because of the challenge that her cool facade presented and for the erotic charge he sensed behind it. He wanted to know how reckless this most calculating of women could be. As for Louise, as a young girl she had never enjoyed a passionate love life. Charles had in a sense deprived her of her youth, and now that the opportunity to retrieve it had arrived she threw caution to the winds.

Louise found it hard to hide her infatuation, and it wasn't long before the King grew irritated with the young man's presence at court. Old and largely impotent himself, Charles would not tolerate such trespasses. When Vendôme returned to France, he and Louise parted as lovers, and she made him promise to return before long. He possessed great wealth and status in his native land, and it may well be that Louise was thinking ahead to life after Charles. Her affair, then, was a calculated risk: offending Charles was a price worth paying if it meant securing a comfortable retirement in France and a place at the court of Louis XIV. In fact, Louise had been thinking for some time of paying a visit home, both in preparation for the day when she would be forced to return permanently and in order to show herself at Versailles as the great lady she now was. For in her own country she had in her youth felt something of the scorn that she had once heaped upon Nell Gwyn for her low birth and unsophisticated ways. Now she sought to be redeemed. When she finally set out in March 1682, as Nell and the King were preparing to go to Newmarket for the spring meeting, the scandalmongers were not slow in taking up their pens. Her trip, they sensed, had been prompted by a desire to be reunited with her young lover.[4]

The trip exceeded Louise's expectations, becoming one long triumphal progress. She was received with honour at the court, where she was granted the coveted *tabouret* (the right to be seated in the King's presence), and invited to all the balls and fêtes at Paris, Versailles and Saint-Cloud. Louis, primed by Barrillon, was ostentatious in his gratitude. The ambassador had written ahead from London, 'The truth about her [Louise] is, that she has shown great, constant, and intelligent zeal for Your Majesty's interests, and given me numberless useful hints and pieces of information.' She also took the opportunity of visiting the domain of Aubigny, which she coveted for her son. Wherever she went, she made her presence felt and took care to flatter the right people, laying the ground for her eventual return. In Paris she invested a great sum of money extorted from the English Treasury. (In due course Louis made her son a French subject so that he could inherit such monies.) All in all it was four months well spent.

Nell caused no trouble at home while Louise was away, though the satirists found a ready market for reams of fictional invective between the two mistresses, whose great rivalry, a pale shadow of what it was, still bulked large in the public mind as a metaphor for Anglo-French enmity. The people rejoiced to hear of Nell's victories at court, for they felt she was striking a blow for them, and for England. The following exchange in 'A Dialogue between The Dutchess of Portsmouth and Madam Gwin at Parting' was typical:

Gwin

Let Fame that never yet Spoke well of Woman,
Give out I was a Stroling Whore, and Common,
Yet have I been to him [i.e., the King] since the first hour,
As Constant as the Needle to the flower;
Whilst you to your Eternal Praise and Fame
To Forreign Scents betray'd the Royal-Game:
Witness the *Prior* on your Bosom lay,

And in that posture did your Lust betray,
For which now with a Pox you're sent away.

> *Port.*
> I'le find a way in Spight of injur'd Fame
> To make thy Race obscure as is thy Name,
> Who like the Serpent made thy Lord to sin
> For a Dry Orange, or a Russetin
> Which greedily the Monarch did Devour,
> Tho it nourish'd fatal seeds within the Core.

Nell goes on to maintain she doesn't mind whether Louise stays in France or returns to England, but reckons she will end up rotting in her native land. She admits that Louise was wise to make her hay while the sun shone, for now she can 'uphold [her] splendor in the *Gallick* Court' with her ill-gotten gains. She ends her broadside with an interesting jibe at Louise's exotic sexual appetite:

> But *France* is for thy Lust too kind a Clime
> In *Africk* with some Wolf or Tyger Lime [i.e., copulate]:
> Or in the *Indies* make a new Plantation
> And ease us of the *Grievance of the Nation*.

There followed a purported exchange of lewd letters between the mistresses, one from Louise to Nell 'on her landing in France', the other 'Madam Gwins Answer'. In the first Louise is made to brag of Neptune's love for her during her Channel crossing. The sea god, we are told, compared her to Venus and expressed his desire to get upon her 'a Generation of Maremaids'. But she declined, recommending Nell instead, as being more to his taste, for she had been born in a ditch and 'wriggled through the Mud to the Throne'. Having made further scurrilous reflections on Nell's ancestry, the Duchess launches a fierce attack on the lewd lives and indiscriminate appetites of court ladies in England, who rule their husbands, making cuckolds of them with their own servants. The writer clearly knew his subject, for such ranting does little to conceal the Duchess's envy of the sordid affairs of her freer colleagues. Indeed, she tells Nell plainly that without husbands 'you and I lie under the Censure of every Cobler and

Tinker, that will take upon him to Order and Regulate affairs of State . . .' Finally, she urges Nell to find herself a husband before it's too late, whether he be 'some honest Tapster' or a 'lusty Jocky at *Newmarket*'. The explanation for this friendly counsel is simple enough: 'The best Gennet, when she is past Service, is thrown to the Dogs. It may be your Fate, since Wrinckles, Age and Ugliness, the Tyrants of Loves Empire, have already Usurpt the Throne of Beauty, and have a care you fall not a Fee to the Grooms of the Stable, when you are no longer fit for the Royal Game. This (*Madam*) if you mind in time, is the last and best Advice can be given from Your Friend PORTSMOUTH.'

Because in her letter Louise had boasted that she expected her son, who was already Master of the Horse, to be given the office of Admiral (he was nine), the author has Nell retort that she had 'a little Lord that crep out of my cranny that may for ought I know prick your Bladder and let out that ambitious wind. Both sprung from one Branch and why should not he hope for some thing, as well as yours gape for all . . .?' She then proceeds to denigrate Louise's family, before comparing her to the King of Morocco's ostriches in St James's Park, birds famed for their capacity to eat anything. Finally, Nell gives a lengthy and spirited defence of the wild mistress. There is no way that she would give up her life of freedom to be burdened with a husband ('now I can go to *Newmarket*, anon to *Windsor*, and from thence to *London*, and who dare say to *Nelly* where goest thou?'). She ends her missive with a defiant ditty:

I am not so old but I can Skip to *Newmarket* as nimbly as the youngest lass in *Town* and whilst any Royal sport is stirring hope to come in for a snack.

> *Whilst any thing is stirring for the Belly,*
> *The best I'th Land will give a piece to Nelly*
> *And comfort her old age with Royal jelly.*

If truth be told, there wasn't much royal jelly to go around by the spring of 1682, but this in no whit diminished the intimacy between Nell and the King. With Louise abroad, the King dined frequently at 79 Pall Mall, where he took his afternoon nap, falling asleep to Nell's halting recitations from the *London Gazette*. (She was quite relieved to be interrupted by his snoring.) Sometimes there were guests for lunch, as when Sir Christopher Wren came to discuss the plans for the Royal Hospital, Chelsea, a project close to the heart of both monarch and mistress. Although Sir Stephen Fox was brought in by the King to help fund and organize the project, he cannot take credit for the idea, nor did he dig deep into his own vast fortune, which had been amassed as Paymaster General of the Army. The true begetters of the Hospital, apart from the King, seem to have been Nell herself and the Duke of Monmouth.

As far back as 1677 Monmouth had written to Louvois, Louis XIV's Minister for War, asking for the plan of the Hôtel des Invalides in Paris, drawn to scale and to include all the façades, 'car le Roy sera bien aise de le voir' (in other words Charles had asked to see it). Monmouth was famous for the care he took of his men, showing a compassion towards sick and wounded soldiers that was rare for the times. He also had a family interest in seeing the many Civil War veterans who were sick or destitute properly cared for. Having visited the military hospital in Paris, it's only natural that he should have suggested a similar set-up for London. Nell's own father was a Civil War veteran who had fallen on hard times, and she may well have known of the Coningsby Hospital for 'worn out' soldiers in Hereford, which was after all Gwyn territory. No doubt she and Monmouth discussed the project while he took refuge at her house during the winter of 1679/80. Intriguingly we know from a letter written by John Verney on 1 December 1679 that the previous Saturday, which would have been a couple of days or so after Monmouth's sudden return from Holland, both Nell and Sir Stephen Fox went to visit the Duke. Then there was the meeting with Wren and Charles at which Nell is supposed to have torn her handkerchief into strips and placed them in a square over Sir Christopher's plan to recommend a larger building. One can see her cajoling the King into a more ambitious frame of mind with the idea that no finer monument to his greatness could be imagined.

Although it was a bit early to be thinking of his own monument, the King did suffer another fit of the ague that May. His quick recovery (the patient would sit covered with blankets in a bath of hot milk) was a comfort to his supporters, for whom the King's health seemed the only promise of peace and prosperity in the country. But in truth, behind his nonchalant façade, Charles was suffering from nervous exhaustion. The news recently received of Monmouth's latest treacheries had bitten deep – his own rebellious flesh at work in the land – and where emotional pain was concerned, Charles tended to imitate the large flightless birds then sojourning in St James's Park; he buried his head in the sand. Nell was one of the rose-tinted crew; for her, the King's death was unthinkable. Catherine, on the other hand, vainly urged a proper convalescence.

Towards the end of May, James returned for good from Scotland, where he had proved an able administrator. The London mob who had so recently demonized the Duke gave him a hero's welcome in the capital, singing 'The glory of the British line, / Old Jimmy's come again'. Only yesterday fickle 'young *Jemmy*', their beloved Monmouth, had been all their song, but the Popish Plot was old hat now and they yearned for the stability of the established order. The King was happy to leave much of the day-to-day business of government to his brother, who formed a rather awkward triumvirate with Louise and her placeman, the Earl of Sunderland. Nell too was not without influential friends at the top. Her old buddy Lory Hyde, now First Lord of the Treasury, was Charles's closest adviser, as his father had once been. Ennobled in 1682, he was granted Wilmot's old title, Earl of Roches-ter, which hardly sat well with such a conscientious minister. But not even Hyde, for all his subtlety, could prevail upon the King to ennoble Nell.

Much to her chagrin, Louise was still in France when the Javanese, or East India, ambassadors arrived in London to add to the diplomatic logjam. Evelyn found them quite outside his ken and recoiled from their alien looks and habits, though he acknowledged their sobriety and granted them a certain cunning. 'They sate cross-legg'd like Turks,' he tutted, 'and sometimes in the posture of apes and monkeys; their nailes and teeth black as jet, and shining, which being the effect, as to their teeth, of perpetually chewing betel to preserve them from the tooth-ache, much raging in their country, is esteem'd beautifull . . . Their meate was cook'd, carried up, and they attended by several fat slaves, who had no covering save drawers, which appear'd very uncouth and loathsome.' The only thing that seemed to astonish the guests was the thought that their English hosts were property owners, which to them meant that they must all be kings, for in their land only the king could own property, his subjects having the status of slaves.

Louise returned at the end of July glowing with pride and was received with a new respect at court. Barrillon commented that the 'homage paid her by Louis XIV' had worked like 'sunshine, gilding and glorifying an insignificant object'. All the years of patient dissembling and all the humiliations at the hands of Nell Gwyn had been miraculously redeemed: Louise was now the biggest cheese in the larder. Even Charles seemed dazzled, and the City nibs were not slow to send out a warning to the duchess's old antagonist:

> Now Nelly you must be content,
> Her grace begins to reign;
> For all your brat you may be sent
> To Dorset [i.e., Buckhurst] back again.

But there was no need for such admonishments. Though she still sent up her old rival in private, Nell no longer feared her own position or Louise's political influence over the King. Shaftesbury might be skulking in the City, but revolution had been averted, and it would have been churlish to continue fighting the battles of the previous decade.

Whitehall had a distinctly altered feel under James's officious eye, and Nell now preferred the freedom of the country. The summer saw her at her beloved Windsor with a house full of guests. There were the usual lazy afternoons by the river, fishing and boating, followed by candlelit picnics under the stately oaks of the Great Park. On cooler days they made day trips to some of the outlying forest towns, or organized hawking parties. At the castle itself, there were amateur theatricals, concerts and masquerades. Charles also invited travelling companies from France and Italy to perform the witty continental comedies he so admired. Puppet shows were also a great favourite with the royal family. Nell loved to invite some of her favourite acting friends down from London. Together they arranged little impromptu shows at Burford House – skits and parodies of scenes from well-known plays – to entertain themselves and on occasion the King. One such friend was the comedian Joe Haines, who reminded the King in one of his verse epistles that he had moved him to laughter 'at Dame Ellen Gwyn's'.

Nell also enjoyed the attentions of amorous young courtiers, for it comforted her to know that she could still move hearts. There were many ungenerous spirits at court who would have liked to see her brought down by a passing infatuation and were quick to interpret her coquetry in venal terms. One of Nell's Windsor guests that summer was her Pall Mall neighbour Mall (or Maria) Knight, and the two of them appear to have conducted a series of flirtations with a number of young officers attached to the Court Party, chief among them William Dutton Colt, Charles Granville (Lord Lansdowne) and Stint Duncombe, a lieutenant in the King's Foot Guards. These intrigues were dramatized by George Etherege, who doubtless had them second or third hand, in his satire 'Mrs. Nelly's Complaint' (1682). In it the summer is over and Nell is made to complain that she is haunted at night by the chilling spectre of Mall Knight, now in France, who accuses her of having poached her lover, William Colt. Colt, who was the same age as Nell, was Gentleman of the Horse to Prince Rupert. Mall inveighs against Nell as a shameless whore:

> Blushing's a thing thou'st conquered long ago,
> And modesty has always been thy foe.
> If e'er thou affect it, 'tis with awkward grace,
> For bawd is always opened in thy face;
> Bawd is thy art, thy accomplishment and trade,
> For that, not love, thou wert a mistress made.

But Nell is ready with an ingenious excuse for her behaviour. Mall, she says, was deceived not by her, but by Colt himself, whose squint deceived her — Mall — into thinking that she was the object of his ogling!

> Colt, who for close intrigues was doubtless made,
> Whose love was never by his looks betrayed;
> For while his melting eyes did mine survey,
> They craftily still seemed another way,
> Which when fond Knight, our confidante, did see,
> She claimed the homage that was paid to me . . .

Most unlikely of all, Nell tells us that she complained to the King, who upheld her right to 'that Adonis', Colt. The only thing that rings true is that she and Mall ended up having a swearing contest, from which she, Nell, emerged victorious.

The notion that Charles would deliver Nell up to the caresses of the panting Colt is absurd. Indeed, the following spring when Vendôme returned to woo her, Louise would be reminded abruptly that there were limits, superannuated though he was, that Charles would not see transgressed. Bolder in his advances the second time, Vendôme's ardent courtship and continual presence in Louise's apartments spurred the King's anger and set tongues wagging. Using Barrillon as his herald, Charles ordered the young gallant to leave the country without delay, but Vendôme refused. He wanted to hear it from the King himself. Yet when he was finally granted an interview by the exasperated Charles, the Grand Prior dug in his heels. The court was aghast at this act of insolence. Charles sent his Lieutenant of the Guard to serve notice of expulsion with the threat of force if compliance wasn't forthcoming. Louise grew alarmed at what looked set to become a damaging show-down. Vendôme had a bundle of love letters penned by her at the height of her infatuation which could cause her the utmost embarrass-ment. After a number of frantic interviews with Barrillon, it was the authority of Louis himself that finally did the trick, and the Young Turk was advised in no uncertain terms to forget that he'd ever been involved with the Duchess. This gagging order proved effective.

There can be no doubt that Nell, like Louise, had sexual feelings for other men and was probably sorely tempted on occasion, but, unlike Louise, she had lived a full, sexual life as a teenager; far from sacrificing her youth to the King, she had in a sense been saved by him from further degradation. She owed him everything, including her emotional well-being, and knew the sterile aftermath of sexual infatuation better than most. She wasn't going to gamble the lasting love of a King on a few nights of passion. Nell was a convert to the monogamous life and, like a typical convert, proved more zealous than those to the manner born.

But if Charles now imagined that he could retire comfortably to the arms of his well-fed mistresses, he was sadly mistaken. The fruit of his promiscuity was suddenly bitter in the mouth. Monmouth, who like Shaftesbury was being tracked by the intelligence service, was arrested for disturbing the peace following one of his famous 'progresses' in the north. Wherever he had gone there had been bells, bonfires and shouts of 'A Monmouth! A Monmouth!' (with a seditious aside or two). For his part Monmouth had charmed the people as only he knew how. He had again touched for the king's evil, a rite superstitiously reserved for the sovereign, and flirted with the daughters of the gentry. Shaftesbury had in fact sent him up to the north-west to gauge support for a rising and when he learnt of his arrest sent a message, urging him to escape his captors, return to Chester and raise the standard of revolt.

But Monmouth knew that the time was not ripe. He returned to London and was bailed pending an appearance before the King's Bench. Once again he fell into the company of plotters and malcontents, men caught up in Shaftesbury's disastrous web. But the web was badly tangled now, and nobody was sure who had signed up to what plan, and the plans themselves were sketchy. One hardcore Republican group was talking of murdering the King and the Duke of York by ambushing them on the way back from Newmarket. Others, like Monmouth, favoured risings in the City and across the country in order to secure a Protestant succession through Parliament, but the time had to be right. In his desperation Shaftesbury had lost all sense of timing. He and Monmouth no longer trusted each other, and anyway he was soon to be out of the picture. Monmouth always expressed horror at the idea of murdering his father or uncle, yet it must have fascinated him too. At the very least, Monmouth was guilty of misprision of treason, for he had been privy to treasonable talk and not reported it. He was consorting with known traitors. The King received reports of his son's treachery with a sinking heart. Monmouth had to be brought to heel, yet he was determined to protect him as far as he could from the wrath of his brother.

The rebels met secretly in obscure corners of the City. They planned to organize a rising in London on 19 November 1682 and another in the west under John Trenchard, President of the Green Ribbon Club. The settlement of Carolina, Shaftesbury's great overseas interest, was used as a pretext for meetings as well as for the movement of key supporters into the capital. With Shaftesbury himself gone, his old Council of Six now held the reins. Letters were sent in cipher. The King was known as 'Mr. Ker' and Monmouth aptly enough 'Mr. White', linking him once again for the purposes of our story with Nell, whose surname meant 'white'. Trenchard, however, was unable to ready things in the west for lack of funds. The London rising was postponed, then put off altogether.

Monmouth, as usual, found it impossible to keep still. Having been discharged by the King's Bench, he went horse racing at Burford, where he won the plate, and then in the early spring of 1683 slipped off to Paris to take part in the international race at Achères. There, too, before Louis himself and the entire French court, he won the magnificent plate worth a thousand pistoles. One wonders whether Nell's son Charles, in Paris at the time, was there to see his brother's triumph. Even in an age when the sons of the nobility virtually grew up in the saddle, Monmouth stood out as a superbly gifted horseman. The image of the centaur comes to mind, not just for his equestrian skill, but because of his tendency to let passion sway his judgement. When Monmouth did something, he did it at full tilt.

Both brothers, Monmouth and Burford, made the mistake of identifying almost exclusively with their father (in Monmouth's case, to the point of coveting his throne). The mother's inheritance was kept firmly in the cupboard marked 'skeletons'. But, as often happens in such cases, the discarded element festered, acting subversively from within. Monmouth in effect became a political whore, susceptible to flattery and manipulation, his great need for approval feeding his lack of discrimination and disrupting his sense of purpose. For all his high ideals, a certain baseness kept creeping in. This was less true of Burford, who had no pretension to the throne and who cherished his mother's finer qualities.

Monmouth was vociferous that he had never been privy to the plot to murder Charles and James as their coach passed the Rye House on their way back to London from Newmarket. Whatever the truth of the matter, it is doubtful whether the plotters would have had everything in place by the end of March 1683 to make their ambush. Moreover, it seems likely that the Duke of York was using government agents to help foment the plot in the hope that it would bring him Monmouth's scalp. Either way, a devastating fire at Newmarket on 22 March meant that the King and his brother left a week early, and so unwittingly foiled the plot. As details of the scheme emerged, arrests were made, with James in charge of the round-up. The men arrested met with the same parody of justice to which they had appealed during the Popish Plot. Sidney and Russell were executed, and Essex committed suicide in the Tower. (When Charles heard of Essex's death, he claimed that he would have granted him a reprieve, for his father had died for the Royalist cause. 'I owed him a life,' he quipped.) Most people were too relieved that the King was safe to foresee that James's vengeance might have even freer scope when he came to the throne.

As for Monmouth, he remained at large, though a Grand Jury had found him implicated in the plot. The King feared that his son's fate would pass beyond his control were he to order his arrest. Instead, he sent messengers to encourage him to confess his part in the conspiracy and beg for the Duke of York's intercession. In the end, a reconciliation took place at Whitehall, and Monmouth, having received the King's pardon in advance, made a written confession in which he maintained that he had not known of the design upon the King's life. A few days later, however, he retracted his confession and asked for it back. The King was furious and returned the statement, consigning his son to hell. No longer under the King's protection, Monmouth fled to Holland.

Nell's son, meanwhile, seems to have returned from France sometime over Christmas, intending to go back later in the year. Paris, it seemed, had done him a power of good. With the court having now been transferred permanently from the Louvre to Versailles, Paris, famed for its playhouses, opera and university, was a place of undreamt of freedom and excitement for a young aristocrat with the theatre in his blood. An unfamiliar London greeted him on his return, one carved in ice, for the Thames had frozen solid and the life of the city had to all appearances been transferred in its entirety to the river, which was covered with hundreds of pavilions, their brightly coloured pennons glittering in the frost. Even the ocean was locked in ice and the trees, hung with icicles, made strange music in the wind. 'I went crosse the Thames on the ice, now become so thick,' wrote Evelyn, 'as to beare not onely streetes of boothes, in which they roasted meate, and had divers shops of wares, quite acrosse as in a towne, but coaches, carts, and horses, passed over.' Children skated and whizzed around in sledges, there were coach races, bull-baiting, puppet shows and the usual drunken carousing. The stranded boats, their sails stiff with frost, were used as camps by rival gangs of kids.

On 2 January 1684 Henry Jermyn, Earl of St Albans, died without issue, rendering the earldom extinct. Eight days later, on 10 January, the King created the final dukedom of his reign by making his and Nell's surviving son Charles Duke of St Albans. The St Albans title seems to have had royal associations in Charles's mind. Francis Bacon, the eminent philosopher who was created Viscount St Albans in 1621, is thought by some to have been the illegitimate son of Queen Elizabeth by her lover the Earl of Leicester; while Henry Jermyn himself was said to have contracted a secret marriage with Charles's widowed mother, Queen Henrietta Maria. Certainly he was granted the earldom of St Albans at her behest.

The symbolism of the title, derived from St Alban, who suffered a martyr's death in the late third century, is fascinating. Alban came from a wealthy and cultured Roman family which had been living in Verulamium for some generations. A generous and hospitable man, Alban, or Albanus, received many visitors and travellers into his home on the banks of the river Ver. One day he took in a Christian priest, who was being pursued by the authorities. Impressed by his piety, Alban questioned him about his faith. That night he had a powerful vision of the crucifixion and resurrection of Jesus and the next day was baptized by his guest. With the Roman soldiers now hot on the heels of the priest, Alban exchanged clothes with him and was tried and executed in his stead. His death was accompanied by several miracles, a well springing up on the wooded hill where he was beheaded. He was the first British martyr, and according to some the founder of freemasonry.

The name Alban, or Albanus, is derived from the Latin 'albus' meaning 'white' or 'bright', making another immediate connection with Nell's surname. And the story of Alban's martyrdom, which is the story of a man who finds himself by disguising himself, reflects an important dynamic in the Beauclerk inheritance as well as framing an apt description of the actor's art, Nell's early profession. (It was through her fooling that her son was originally ennobled.)

The young St Albans, who was still thirteen, had rooms at Whitehall with his fellow royal bastards. The half-brothers, known as 'the fraternity', certainly seem to have spent time together accompanying the King both privately and in public. On 30 March 1684, Easter Day, Evelyn went to the chapel at Whitehall where the Bishop of Rochester preached before the King, 'after which his Majestie, accompanied with 3 of his natural Sonns (viz. the Dukes of Northumb: Richmond and St Albans, base sonns of Portsmouth, Cleaveland, Nelly – prostitute creatures) went up to the Altar . . .' Two days earlier in Covent Garden six or seven people had been killed in the huge crush of bodies at the door of the King's surgeon, Mr Knight. They had been pressing for tickets to be touched for the king's evil, a ceremony performed on Wednesdays and Fridays. The King's Register of Healing records that he touched no fewer than 8,577 of his subjects between May 1682 and April 1683.

Later that year Evelyn dined at Sir Stephen Fox's with the Duke of Northumberland (Barbara's third son, George Fitzroy, born at Merton College during the plague year), who had been abroad and seen action at the Siege of Luxembourg that May. Evelyn admits to a grudging admiration for Northumberland and goes on to say, 'what the Dukes of Richmond and St Albans, base sonns of the Dutchesse of Portsmouth a French lasse, and of Nelly, the Comedian and Applewoman's daughter, will prove their youth does not discover, farther than they are both very pretty boys and seeme to have more Witt than the rest.'

An undated portrait by Kneller of the teenage St Albans shows a slightly built young man with delicate, almost feminine features. He has a round, rather dreamy face with the eyes cast downwards, giving a self-absorbed look. There seems to be a tension in both countenance and posture between the man of action and the contemplative. His lips are full and crimson, his complexion flushed and his fair, classical features framed by a full head of dark hair. Yet there is a natural alertness to his stance and expression that bespeaks a quick wit, and a slight haughtiness that perhaps gives warning of a sharp tongue. His dress – white chemise, sea-green tunic and red satin cloak – is delightfully fresh and informal. Despite the strong resemblance to his mother, St Albans's picture is very close to some of the early portraits of his half-brother Monmouth. One could be forgiven for sensing a rather spoilt young man, who is perhaps a little defensive.[5]

A later portrait of him also by Kneller in battle dress shows a striking likeness to Charles II, and though there is more of an effort to appear the man of action, a certain glamour and artistic sensitivity shine through, silent testimony to his Gwyn blood. John Macky, a secret agent in the service of William III, described St Albans at the time of the later portrait as 'a gentleman every way *de bon naturel*, well-bred . . . of a black complexion, not so tall as the Duke of Northumberland, yet very like King Charles'. He also mentioned the young man's dislike of business, a trait he inherited from both parents!

As Evelyn noted, St Albans was certainly an attractive figure, and must have been the object of many a young lady's desire. The brothels of Paris probably provided his first sexual experiences, as there are references in the satires of the mid to late 1680s of his predilection for the bawdy sisterhood. It was, after all, in his blood. There may even have been some sort of scandal while he was abroad. In the second part of 'The Vindication' (1686), a laborious libel full of obscure jokes about contemporary figures, occurs the following stanza:

> St Albans return'd
> From his Travels is scorn'd
> By the Ladies at Court, & o'th'City.
> That such a great Duke
> Shou'd of all be forsook
> Provokes not my Pen, but my Pity.

His name was being mentioned at that time in connection with Margaret Cavendish, one of the daughters of the 2nd Duke of Newcastle (whose stepmother had been the eccentric philosopher and scientist of the same name), but for whatever reason the liaison proved unenduring and, if the satires are to be believed, St Albans, who was in any case an unwilling suitor, was subjected to the familiar taunt of being the son of a whore. For no matter how exalted the blood on his father's side, his mother's background would always be a hotbed for new humiliations. The author of 'Madam Le Croy' (1686) turned the knife with the usual glee:

> St Alban's Duke, who never sought her,
> By th'Bargain, gets Newcastles Daughter:
> So says Le Croy; but juster Fate
> Dooms him a Match at Belin's gate;
> Nor will Newcastle his hopes place
> In a base Bastard Pippin Race.[6]

'Belin's gate' is Billingsgate, a district of London notorious for fish-wives and whores. There is doubtless a cut here too at Nell's early trade of hawking oysters. A true bargain was, however, struck a little later, though this time the father-in-law was Aubrey de Vere, 20th and last Earl of Oxford, who was known as the noblest subject in Europe, for the Earls of Oxford had been peers of the realm for over 550 years. Something of the mystique that the name of de Vere had accrued over the centuries is revealed in the figure of Tennyson's Lady Clara Vere de Vere, 'the daughter of a hundred earls'. Oxford's daughter and co-heiress Diana de Vere, only eleven or so at the time, is thought to have been betrothed to St Albans in 1687. King Charles's strategy had been to establish his sons by marrying them off to wealthy heiresses and this certainly happened in the case of Barbara's children. St Albans, however, proved less fortunate. Though his wife was an heiress, and a noble and beautiful one at that, there was no money or land to inherit, for the 17th Earl, Edward de Vere (1550–1604) had dissipated the family estates in funding the Elizabethan theatre and supporting hard-up writers such as Thomas Nashe.[7] Money or no money, Charles and Diana married in April 1694 and had nine sons and three daughters over the course of an outwardly happy marriage. Their descendants took the surname de Vere Beauclerk.

Diana's father, Aubrey, privy counsellor and colonel of the Royal Regiment of Horse Guards or 'the Oxford Blues', also had a connection, albeit an infamous one, with the theatre. In 1662 he contracted a notorious mock marriage with the actress Hester Davenport, known as 'Roxalana' for her genius in the role in Davenant's *Siege of Rhodes*. Having at first been rejected by the decorous Miss Davenport, who had no wish to leave her profession to become the mistress of a gallant, Oxford turned up at her lodgings one morning with clergyman and witness in tow. The wedding ceremony was conducted with all due gravity, the impromptu bride presenting a fellow actress as her witness, and the happy pair were pronounced man and wife. Roxalana duly left the stage, only to find that the clergyman that married them had been one of the Earl's trumpeters and the witness his kettle-drummer. Highly distraught, the mock countess appealed directly to the King, but Charles preferred not to get involved. The pair ended up living together for some years and had a son, Aubrey de Vere, in 1664. The Earl's second marriage took place in April 1673 to Diana, daughter of George Kirke, an impoverished court official. A noted beauty, it was she who gave birth to St Albans's future wife, Diana de Vere, in whom that noble line expired:

> The line of Vere so long renowned in arms,
> Concludes with lustre in St. Alban's charms;
> Her conquering eyes have made their race complete,
> They rose in valour, and in beauty set.

An anecdote from 1695, the year after St Albans's marriage, strongly indicates that the Duke had not been able to shake his penchant for young actresses. He went backstage at Drury Lane after a performance of Thomas Southerne's stage adaptation of Aphra Behn's *Oroonoko*, no doubt intending to invite one of the leading ladies out to dinner. His eye lit upon Susanna Mountfort, whose previous actor-husband William had been run through by a jealous suitor. She was now married to Oroonoko himself, a large, rough-looking actor by the name of Jack Verbruggen. Though he knew that he was an illegitimate son of Charles II, Verbruggen struck the Duke and called him the son of a whore. The next day he was warned that only a public apology could salvage his career, so when he came on stage that evening, dressed as the royal slave, he admitted his fault and expressed his regret, but in doing so deliberately repeated the insult.[8] It is extraordinary that the story of *Oroonoko* should have been the background to this fracas, since it appears to have dramatized the tragic dimension of Charles and Nell's relationship. One wonders how many other unreported incidents of this nature coloured the Duke's early life as he sought a relationship with his mother's ghost.

. Nell herself (the fully incarnated version) was thrilled by her son's elevation, for it was among other things an expression of the King's respect and affection for her. Though untitled herself, it put her on a par with Louise and Barbara, whose sons had all been raised to dukedoms. To be able to refer to her son as 'my Lord Duke', as she now repeatedly did, was heady stuff for a former orange girl, yet her feelings of jubilation were modified by an increasing sense of alienation from the world into which her son had now been absorbed. Her real association with that world had been confined to the King, now ailing, and the merry gang, who were no more. Wit had been her passport, and Charles's court had been the scene of many a triumph of wit, but it had never been her natural sphere; nor had its creatures, alarmed by her frankness, been her close companions.

Now, as she grew older, her sense of disaffection from that realm loomed larger, and she only felt truly comfortable in the company of her sister, the acting fraternity or the King himself. Burford House at Windsor was now her favoured retreat, for that was where she found the King at his most relaxed and affectionate. But her debts were mounting once again, her health was suffering and in her bones she knew that soon the King would not be there to protect her from the gathering storm. The following letter, addressed to her dressmaker Mrs Jennings (mother to Frances and Sarah, the future Duchess of Marlborough), is eloquent of her chaotic state of mind:

These for Madam Jennings over against the
Tub Tavern in Jermyn Street, London.

WINDSOR, BURFORD HOUSE
April 14, 1684

MADAM,
I have receiv'd yr. Letter, & I desire yu would speake to my Ladie Williams to send me the gold Stuffe, & a Note with it, because I must sign it, then she shall have her Money ye next Day of Mr Trant; pray tell her Ladieship, that I will send her a note of what Quantity of Things I'le have bought, if her Ladieship will put herselfe to ye Trouble to buy them; when they are bought I will sign a Note for her to be payd. Pray Madam, let ye Man goe on with my Sedan, and send Potvin

[her London upholsterer] and Mr Coker [silversmith John Coques?] down to me, for I want them both. The Bill is very dear to boyle the Plate; but Necessity hath noe Law. I am afraid Mm. you have forgott my Mantle, which you were to line with Musk Colour Sattin, & all my other Things, for you send me noe Patterns nor Answer. Monsieur Lainey [her son's tutor] is going away. Pray send Word about your Son Griffin [her son-in-law Edward Griffith], for his Majestie is mighty well pleasd that he will goe along [i.e., to France] with my Lord Duke [of St Albans]. I am afraid that you are so much taken up with your owne House, that you forgett my Businesse. My service to dear Lord Kildare, & tell him I love him with all my Heart. Pray Mm. see that Potvin brings now all my things with him: My Lord Duke's Bed &c. if he hath not made them all up, he may doe that here for if I doe not get my Things out of his Hands now, I shall not have them until this Time Twelve-month. The Duke brought me down with him my Crochet of Diamonds, & I love it the better because he brought it. Mr Lumley, & everie Body else will tell you that it is the finest Thing that ever was seen. Good Mm. speake to Mr Beaver to come down too, that I may bespeake a Ring for the Duke of Grafton before he goes into France.

I have continued extream ill ever since you Leaft me, & I am soe still. I have sent to London for a Dr. I believe I shall die. My service to the Dutchesse of Norfolk [Nell's friend Mary Mordaunt], & tell her I am as sick as her Grace, but do not know of what I ayle, although she does, which I am overjoyed that shee goes on with her great Belly.
Pray tell my Ladie Williams, that the King's Mistresses are accounted ill-pay-Masters, but shee shall have her Money the next Day after I have the Stuffe. Here is sad Slaughter at Windsor, the young Men's taking ye. Leaves & going to France, & although they are none of my Lovers, yet I am loath to part with the Men. Mrs Jennings I love you with all my Heart, & soe good by.

E.G.

Let me have an Answer to this Letter.

Lady Williams was a former mistress of the Duke of York and one of Nell's London neighbours. Nell had clearly seen some gold ornaments that took her fancy at a house sale and wanted her friend to secure them, despite the fact that she was having to melt down some of her silver plate to pay for them! The silver plate celebrated the enchantment of her early love for the King; now she was trading it for the false glitter of gold. Maybe the early vision of love had been supplanted by the desire for status and material comforts. 'Necessity hath noe Law,' she says, meaning *desire* hath no law. As a mistress of the King she had lived outside the ordinary financial laws that bound others. Certainly the letter reveals the commanding style in which Nell had grown accustomed to living. Her word, the word of a royal mistress, was still sufficient credit in itself, and at her behest was a whole legion of craftsmen and tradesmen.

There is a rather desperate feeling in the letter that things are slipping beyond her grasp: ornaments, clothes, people, her own son, her own body and above all the vast unspoken apparition of the slowly disappearing King. She is anxious to have everything now, for 'this Time Twelve-month', though she doesn't know it, the King will be dead and buried. Then there is the desire to have everything to impress her son, who has been elevated beyond her reach and is about to return to Europe to complete his grand tour. She must look her best for him and that means wearing her mantle lined with musk-coloured satin. Everything he touches now turns to gold and becomes treasure to his doting mother. (In his absence she will treasure the objects that he has touched.) Thinking of sons and jewels, her unfailing generosity is prompted by the thought that the Duke of Grafton, the son of her rival Barbara, is going off to war. He must have a ring as a mark of her affection. Her ardent nature is also to the fore, for when she loves she loves with all her heart.

She herself is so ill that she thinks she's going to die. But her real illness lies in her sense of dread that Charles's reign is coming to an end and with it all the glamours and consolations of her life. With Dismal Jimmy's accession her world will collapse, and the dawning age will have no place for her. Thus even the Duchess of Norfolk's 'great Belly' is seen as an illness, for the future holds no promise. Finally, the leave-taking of the young men off to war[9] is described as a sad *Slaughter*, a strongly incongruous word in the context. But the concepts of death and departure are so tightly knit together in Nell's panic-stricken mind that to say farewell is to raise the spectre of death. Throughout the letter death overshadows the busy colours of everyday life.

Evidently Nell dictated the letter as things came into her head, yet there is a clear association of thoughts. Her preoccupation with money and debt is linked to concern about clothes (i.e., her personal and social standing), which in turn is bound up with her fear of losing her son (for his prestige elevates her in the eyes of the world). Her worries about her son's bed, which move her to picture him as a boy again, are connected to thoughts about the swift passage of time. Next her mind skips to objects that are not subject to time's vagaries (i.e., jewels) and these in turn are associated with the King's sons (her own son and Barbara's son, Grafton), for they are true jewels. But they are going abroad, so her thoughts return to loss, illness, death and the new, alien age that is dawning. (She also thinks of payment again, death being the ultimate debt). As it turned out, the Duchess of Norfolk was labouring under the delusion of a phantom pregnancy, and the new age did in the end prove to be a sad slaughter, an age of strife and war, with England drawn into the great European conflicts of the 1690s. Danby, who would be a major player in this new era, had finally been released from the Tower two months earlier in February 1684.

Nell was nursed back to health by Dr Richard Lower, a Whig physician and fellow of the Royal Society, who was soon to attend the King on his deathbed. He loved to draw out her memories of court life as well as all the current gossip, and became as much a companion as a doctor. Her debts, however, were less easy to cure. Despite her annual income of roughly £10,000, which included revenues from the Bestwood estate, the tax on logwood and fitful Irish rents, Nell owed large sums to both Child's Bank and to various private creditors. But it wasn't just her love of the high life that wiped out her income, though the London party circuit was a heavy drain, as was maintaining two sizeable establishments, one at 79 Pall Mall, the other at Burford House, Windsor; acts of charity, for both individuals and causes, continued to play a vital role in her life. The beggar woman at her door never went away empty-handed, and Dr Tenison was always brimming with new projects to inspire her philanthropy, such as the public library he established to keep young priests out of the taverns and coffee houses of Covent Garden, and the free schools for poor children of the parish.[10]

Perhaps sensing that the King's days were numbered, Barbara had returned from France in March and was living once again at Cleveland House, opposite St James's Palace. Her live-in lover was Cardonell 'Scum' Goodman, now an actor at the Theatre Royal. When the King's Company was in crisis in the early 1680s Goodman had supplemented his income by becoming a highwayman, though by all accounts he overplayed his part and met with limited success. Even after setting up with Barbara and returning to the stage, he persisted in playing the brigand and managed to secure a pardon each time he was caught (about 200 occasions in all). Not content with robbery, he hired a cook to poison two of Barbara's sons, the Dukes of Grafton and Northumberland. He stood trial when the plot was discovered and was fined £1,000. Barbara, of course, forgave him immediately. He was handsome and devoted to her, and that's all that mattered in her book. Besides, he had an endearing habit of keeping the whole audience at Drury Lane waiting, including the Queen once, while he scanned the boxes to make sure that Barbara was in her place. 'What! Is my Duchess come?' he would roar from the front of the stage, and if she hadn't he would refuse to act. They even had a child together, her seventh, dubbed 'Goodman Cleveland' by the scandal sheets.

It was fitting that Barbara should have come full circle into the arms of an actor, for as a professional trickster the actor was, in a sense, the idol of Restoration society, the hero with a thousand faces, from quack to pimp to gallant to king. Restoration man was protean man, and none more protean than the King who had raised Barbara above the other ladies of the court. It's fitting too that Goodman, like her erstwhile lover Charles Hart, was famed for his portrayal of kings and emperors, in particular Alexander the Great, for being a king and playing a king amounted to much the same thing, at least where the erotic sensibilities of Barbara Cleveland were concerned.

Charles himself completed the daily round with his typical enthusiasm, but at a statelier pace. He rose later and gave up those perilous early morning constitutionals in the river or on the tennis court. He still took two walks a day, but no longer left a train of puffing ministers in his wake. His collection of rare birds on the canal in St James's Park still afforded him hours of fascination, and he continued to enjoy the casual and affectionate attentions of his subjects, something that fear of assassination denied his brother James. He spent a good deal of time in the laboratory, both at Whitehall and Windsor, conferring with his chemist, Dr Williams. And then there was the new palace at Winchester, his retirement home, to look forward to. Each day brought news of its progress.

Politically Charles still had his eye very much on the ball. The common notion that his Catholic brother and mistress, James and Louise, were co-regents in all but name is false and comes from Barrillon's letters to Louis XIV. For instance, when Louise fell ill in November 1684 Barrillon declared to his master that public business in England had come to a standstill. But he was by no means an unbiased observer. Softened by Louise's charms and her air of cosy luxury, Barrillon took upon himself the task of reminding Louis almost daily of de Kéroualle's vital influence in English government. It's true that the King spent many hours tending his mistress in her illness, but it's equally true that he was aware of the nature of such carefully timed maladies. In this case Louise used her indisposition to extort assurances of further honours for her son.

The King's political problems had not disappeared altogether. Troubled by his brother James's extremism and his lack of grace and subtlety, Charles's thoughts turned more and more towards Holland and his beloved Monmouth. He had written to his son and sent money, but had not made public his desire for the return of the prodigal, lest he should excite James's wrath. James, like his mother before him, was violently principled and subject to fits of speechless fury. He had never stood up to Henrietta Maria; as a result, her bigoted rage lived unabated in him. Yet Charles was not one to be intimidated, and he had pretty well made up his mind to summon another Parliament and use the occasion to recall Monmouth. At a pinch James might be sent to govern Scotland again, for his presence at the heart of government could only provoke fresh divisions with MPs. Charles worked behind the scenes with a few close advisers, applying his old determination. He had one ambition above all others before he died: to restore the lost sheep to his fold.

Also high on his list of priorities were Nell and their son Charles St Albans, for of all his family they were the most vulnerable to the blows of fortune. He wanted to make Nell Countess of Greenwich but, as with Monmouth's return, knew that he had to proceed furtively and wait for fate to provide an opening. In a letter to King James three months after Charles's death, Nell was to write, 'had hee lived hee tould me before hee dyed that the world shuld see by what hee did for me that hee had both love and value for me . . .' As for their son, his living expenses were provided by the King. In addition he had an income of some £1,500 a year, which was increased as further honours were conferred upon him. Having visited Winchester with the King in September 1684, father and son proceeded to Portsmouth, where St Albans embarked for France. When he returned in January 1685 he was appointed to the title of Hereditary Grand Falconer of England (in reversion), which when he came to enjoy it was worth almost £1,400 a year. There were, however, duties to undertake and expenses to be paid, including salaries for the one sergeant, ten falconers and twenty-two feeders under his command. He was responsible for acquiring and training the hawks for hunting in the royal parks and forests and seeing to the upkeep of the royal mews. The Registrarship of the High Court of Chancery, another hereditary title granted to Nell in reversion in 1676, was not his to enjoy until 1698. Both titles are still held by the Dukes of St Albans.

Towards the end of January 1685 the King seemed slower and weaker. He had a sore on his heel which prevented exercise, and his attendants detected a slightly troubled air. On the evening of Sunday, 1 February, after dinner, the King made his way over to Louise's apartments, which echoed to the high, clear note of a boyish treble. By the time Evelyn arrived an hour or so later, Charles had settled down to enjoy himself, as the diarist's agitated account makes clear:

> I can never forget the inexpressible luxury and prophanenesse, gaming and all disoluteness, and as it were total forgetfullnesse of God (it being Sunday evening) which . . . I was witnesse of, the King sitting and toying with his concubines, Portsmouth,

Cleaveland, and Mazarine, &c. a French boy singing love songs, in that glorious gallery, whilst about 20 of the greate courtiers and other dissolute persons were at Basset round a large table, a bank of at least 2000 in gold before them . . . Six days after was all in the dust!

Evelyn mentions the three Duchesses, but can't bring himself to include Nell by name, but his '&c.' is eloquent enough. It was the eve of her thirty-fifth birthday.

If Evelyn had been able to put aside his prejudice for a moment, he might have seen the spectacle that night in a more positive light, and as a fitting image of the King's last active day on earth. For there before him were symbols of three of the most important things that Charles had cultivated in his reign: culture, commerce and female companionship. It's difficult to see how the loyalty, friendship and support that he had given the mistresses that surrounded him that night could be construed negatively. A lesser man would have cast off his concubines when they became troublesome and expensive, but disloyalty was not one of Charles's traits. As for the cost of the mistresses, better to have suffered their vanity than that of the vastly more expensive and troublesome male favourites that were the curse of previous monarchs.

Retiring around nine as was his custom of late, Charles proceeded to his Bedchamber to undress for the night. All agreed that he had been in a particularly genial mood that evening. He was accompanied by his grooms, Lord Bruce and Harry Killigrew, Rose Gwyn's early lover. At the door the candle that Bruce was holding to light the King's way suddenly went out, which made him uneasy, for there had been no draught. As the King sat on his close-stool and chatted merrily to his servants his thoughts turned to Winchester and his new palace. 'I shall be so happy this week,' he exclaimed, 'as to have my house covered in lead.' (Bruce's father Lord Ailesbury later commented, 'And God knows the Saturday following he was put into his coffin.') That night the King, who usually slept deeply and without stirring, in defiance of loud clocks and fidgety spaniels, was somewhat restless. In the morning his agitation had grown, and he was found pacing distractedly in his Closet. His face was ashen and he seemed unable or unwilling to speak. When he eventually sat down facing the Thames to be shaved, he fell back with an inhuman shriek, mouth foaming, eyes staring in abstract horror.

The surgeon who had come to dress the King's heel, fearing for his life, bled him without waiting for the proper sanctions; the Duke of York was sent for, and a whole tribe of physicians (more than enough cooks to spoil the broth). Charles himself, once restored to consciousness and back in his bed, called weakly for his wife, but she was too distressed to remain long in the room. This was just as well, for over the next four days at the behest of no less than sixteen physicians Charles was laid on the rack of contemporary medical ignorance. He was dosed, bled, cupped, purged, clystered, scarified, cauterized, shaved and blistered. Myriad emetics, tonics and emulsions, drawn with bizarre precision and authority from nature's vast storehouse, were poured down his throat, including 'spirit of human skull', 'pearl julep' and 'oriental bezoar stone' (filched from the stomach of a Persian goat). The doctors swung giddily between hope and despair as further convulsions gave way to comparative peace and lucidity, only to return once more to overwhelm the gains of a few hours. The King bore everything with astonishing stoicism, and flashes of his old humour challenged the general grief. When forbidden to talk by the doctors, he joked that such an injunction would have killed Harry Killigrew. Towards the end he apologized to everyone present for taking so long to die.

In his long funeral poem in praise of Charles, Dryden used the image of war to describe the assault of the physicians:

> Th'impregnable Disease their vain attempts did mock;
> They min'd it near, they batter'd from a far
> With all the Cannon of the Med'cinal War;
> No gentle means could be essay'd,
> 'Twas beyond parly when the siege was laid:
> The extreamest ways they first ordain,
> Prescribing such intolerable pain
> As none but *Casear* could sustain;
> Undaunted *Caesar* underwent
> The malice of their Art, nor bent

Beneath what e're their pious rigour cou'd invent.
In five such days he suffer'd more
Than any suffer'd in his reign before . . .

When news of the King's condition was published in the *London Gazette* crowds gathered outside the palace gates in gloomy silence. Those that went about their business did so with tears in their eyes, shaking their heads in disbelief. The King had been in danger before and had always rallied, but this time people seemed to sense the worst. In Charles's Bedchamber, claustrophobic with doctors, priests and ministers, clocks ticking in maddening disharmony, coal fire blazing, spaniels panting, the patient stretched upon the rack, the Duke of York broke down and sobbed like a child. All who witnessed his grief, friend and foe alike, attested to its depth and authenticity. James had never mourned his father's death. He had been a youth of fifteen at the time, exiled from his homeland and too caught up in the adventures of the moment to stop and take stock. Now, as he kept watch by the bedside of the dying Charles, all the dammed-up grief of thirty-six years burst its banks and came spilling out onto his brother's deathbed. The Queen too was prostrate with grief, and each time she made the traumatic pilgrimage to her husband's bedside she had to be carried out again in a swoon. Towards the end she sent to the King to ask his pardon if she had ever offended him, to which Charles, much moved, replied, 'Alas! poor woman! She ask my pardon? I beg hers with all my heart: take her back that answer.'

Around midnight on the Thursday, Charles's final night of suffering, the Queen, the Duke of York and all his sons, save the exiled Monmouth, came to take their leave and receive a final blessing, for the doctors were not sure that he would live to see the morning. Each of his sons knelt in turn beside the bed and Charles drew their heads down with trembling hand. When he came to Nell's son Burford (as the King still called him), he motioned to James to take the boy's hand and besought him to take a particular care of his education, 'for he will be spoiled else'. He also gave the boy the gold ring which his father had given to Bishop Juxon on the scaffold. On it the old King's head, wreathed like the emperors of Rome, was carved in carnelian. It was the last thing that Charles I had touched, and if any object symbolized the tragic kingship of the Stuarts, it was the Juxon ring. To James himself he entrusted his keys and his breeches and wished him a long and happy reign. Finally, he asked his brother 'to be kind to the Dutchesse of Cleaveland, and especially Portsmouth' and to 'not let poor Nelly starve'. (Even at the very end he still thought of her as a waif.) At dawn Charles asked that the curtains be drawn and the window opened so that he could see the sun rise over his beloved Thames one last time and breathe the cool air of the river. At ten o'clock he fell into a coma, and by noon he was dead. He died on Friday, Venus's day, in the thirty-seventh year of his reign, and was buried eight days later on Saturday, 14 February, St Valentine's Day.

~ 16 ~

In the Shadows

THE KING'S DEATH FELL HEAVIEST on Louise and Nell (Barbara had a partner and a life apart from Charles), for as mistresses they were excluded from the King's Bedchamber and thus unable to say their goodbyes. Nell was particularly vulnerable, exposed by the depth of her love and her lack of provision for the future. From the accounts that we have, it is clear that she rushed to Whitehall as soon as she heard of the King's fit that morning, hoping against hope to be admitted to his bedside. But it was not to be. The bureaucrats had already taken over management of the King's death and she got no further than the antechamber, where 'she roared to a disturbance and was led out and lay roaring behind the door'. They were to have celebrated her thirty-fifth birthday that evening. Returning to Pall Mall, Nell spent the whole week in a state of the most awful dread and grief, relieved only by the visits of her son, who as a de facto member of the royal family had unrestricted access to Charles and could provide her with eyewitness accounts of his condition. As the King's life ebbed away, the loneliness of her position bore down upon her with crushing clarity. As she had so often been the voice of the people at court, so now her sentiment that she had lost a father in the King was echoed by men and women up and down the country.

As for Louise, she shut herself up in her apartments, where Barrillon found her distraught, yet mindful of all she needed to do to protect her interests and those of her son. She had already begun to pack up her treasures and spoke of returning to France. There was one thing, however, that was of vital importance to the King that she alone had remembered, and taking Barrillon aside she urged him to go to the Duke of York and arrange for Charles to be received into the Catholic Church before it was too late. In this she rendered great service to the King, though as always with Louise her actions can be seen in a self-serving light. Certainly, she knew that her suggestion could only be received with the sincerest gratitude by both James and Queen Catherine, as well as with plaudits from across the Channel. Luck too was on her side, for it so happened that Father Huddlestone, the priest who had given succour to Charles after the Battle of Worcester, was in the palace that day. Having gained Charles's assent to Louise's scheme, James managed to clear the Bedchamber and prepare for Huddlestone to administer the communion and last rites of the Catholic Church. When he saw the familiar figure enter, Charles with a supreme effort raised himself in bed and greeted the old priest with the words, 'You who saved my life are come now to save my soul!'

There was no mourning contest now between Nell and Louise, no division of far-flung kingdoms; the grief was real. According to the protocol of the time, Nell and Louise, as ladies-in-waiting to the Queen, could don mourning weeds for the departed King, but were forbidden to put their servants in mourning, drape their rooms in black (as the Queen did) or 'to use any varnish'd or bullion nails to be seen on their coaches or [sedan] chairs'. There was no state funeral, as there had been for old King Noll; the Stuarts didn't go in for expensive obsequies. Charles was buried at night, with his nephew Prince George of Denmark as chief mourner. His tomb had no inscription and remained anonymous for more than 200 years. It's difficult not to accept Professor MacGregor-Hastie's statement that Nell 'swathed in a black cloak . . . stood in a corner of the abbey while [the King] was buried, and when the official mourners had gone was allowed by the guards to put flowers on the tomb'. It certainly rings true. Barred by officialdom from saying her goodbyes in person, Nell would not have permitted anyone to deny her a final farewell with flowers.[1]

For all the mistresses it was as if midnight had struck in the middle of the prince's ball and they had been sent scurrying for their gilded coaches, only to find that they had turned into pumpkins and that their own gorgeous dresses, interlaced with tissue of gold and silver, were nothing but rags. The pensions, the gifts of jewellery, the grace-and-favour mansions all vanished in an instant. Moll Davis faded away, dying in obscurity, no one knows quite when, or indeed where. Hortense, whose extravagance was, if anything, stimulated by debt, moved to a small house in Chelsea, where her dedicated and irrelevant little court still congregated. She became overfond of spirits and, though she didn't fall into a ditch like another famous Chelsea soak, brandy did play its part in her demise. She died in June 1699, so hopelessly in debt that the bailiffs made a bid to have her corpse included among the household chattels! She had once been the wealthiest heiress in Europe. Barbara, though she managed to salvage her income from the Post Office, fell heavily into debt and beyond into the half-lit world of sharpers, pimps and bawds. A nymphomaniac almost to the very end, she found herself in some degrading and abusive partnerships. Her second marriage, to Robert – better known as 'Beau' – Fielding, was a classic Restoration fable: farcical, ironic, cruel and with no discernible moral. Even Etherege would have been hard put to devise a more intricate plot.

Barbara was sixty-four when she fell in love with Beau, a handsome cad who had made a fortune by prostituting himself to rich women. They married in November 1705. He lived for extravagant gestures, dressing his footmen in the livery of what he claimed were his Hapsburg ancestors and hiring a drummer to drum in his morning tea. He made no secret to Barbara that he was eager to enjoy the body that had satisfied a king. But beneath the bravura lurked a vicious cheat, who used blackmail and violence to get his way. Barbara, to her horror, soon discovered that Beau had married another woman two weeks before their marriage, one Mrs Deleau, an heiress worth £60,000. Only it turned out that he hadn't married Mrs Deleau but a penniless girl by the name of Mary Wadsworth, whom he dubbed the Countess of Fielding! He had been duped by his go-between, who had pocketed a large bribe. Tried and convicted for bigamy, but pardoned by Queen Anne, Fielding vented his fury on Barbara, beating her and stealing her money. When her grandson the Duke of Grafton intervened, Beau was sent to Newgate Prison. On his release, he took up with Mary Wadsworth, the woman he had married by mistake! Barbara, however, contracted dropsy and, swelling to a huge bulk that swallowed up the last vestiges of her beauty, died at Chiswick in October 1709, aged sixty-eight.

As for Louise, she fled to the French ambassador's house in London, but James insisted she return to Whitehall to put her affairs in order and pay her debts. Eager to keep in with her master, Louis XIV, James nevertheless maintained her pension of £19,000 a year, which greatly assisted her social life in Paris, where she took up residence in August 1685. But in 1689, when William and Mary came to the throne, all monies from England were stopped. No longer on the books of the Sun King, Louise retired to the country, where she lived in the sort of genteel poverty she had known as a girl, only now she was alone. She died on 14 November (the same date as Nell Gwyn, whom she outlived by forty-seven years) in the year 1734, at the ripe old age of eighty-five.

Nell had no royal spymaster to protect her; her world came crashing down about her ears, socially, financially, emotionally. The King had been father, friend and nation to her: the pillars upon which her world rested. And never having been one to sprinkle court holy water, she had neither the guile nor the motive to claw her way back up the ladder of preferment. She had got where she had by being herself; now that very self seemed threatened. Her word had once coined gold; now it provoked scorn and pity. The City fathers who had once toasted her in champagne outlawed her for debt, wiping out her credit overnight. The vultures were at her door. But she still had her trustees, highly placed men whose affection she had won in sunnier days, and with their help she was able to raise £10,500 to keep her most importunate creditors at bay by mortgaging the Bestwood Lodge estate for £3,500 and depositing plate and jewels at Child's Bank for a further £6,000. The remaining thousand was advanced by the Treasury through the influence of her old friend Lory Hyde, now Earl of Rochester.

In a brief, distraught letter to King James written in May 1685, Nell wrote,

> had I suferd for my God as I have don for yr brother and you I
> shuld not have needed ether of yr Kindnes or iustis to me
> I beseech you not to doe any thing to the setling of my

buisines till I speake wth you and a poynt me by Mr Grahams [Richard Graham, Keeper of the Privy Purse] wher I may speake wth you privetly God make you as happy as my soule prays you may be, yrs . . .

James did not grant Nell an interview. She was a ghost from the past, and he had other more pressing concerns. But with Charles's injunction to 'not let poor Nelly starve' still ringing in his ears, the pious King sent her some money via Graham together with assurances of his support in the future. Nell wrote back the same month to express her gratitude:

Sir,

   This world is not capable of giving me a greater ioy and happyness then yr Majesties favour not as you are King and soe have it in yr power to doe me good having never loved yr brother and yr selfe upon that account but as to yr persons

   had hee lived hee tould me before hee dyed that the world shuld see by what hee did for me that hee had both love and value for me and that hee did not doe for me, as my mad Lady Woster, hee was my frind and alowed me to tell him all my grifes and did like a frind advise me and tould me who was my frind and who was not

   Sir the honour yr Ma:tie had don me by Mr Grahams has given me great comfort not by the present you sent me to releeve me out of the last extremety, but by the Kind expressions hee mad me from you, of yr Kindnes to me wch to me is above all things in this world having God Knows never loved yr brother or yr selfe interestedly, all you doe for me shall be yours it being my resolution never to have any interest but yrs, and as long as I live to serve you and when I dye to dye praying for you.

The letter confirms what generations of admirers have instinctively known about Nell Gwyn: that she loved the King for himself, not for the wealth and status he could confer, and that the two had enjoyed a friendship unique in the annals of royal love affairs. There was no longer anyone in whom she could confide her grief; in fact the only man who might have come close to filling Charles's shoes as a friend was about to play out his final fitful scene on life's stage.

In June 1685, egged on by Shaftesbury's old cronies in Holland and a previous generation of exiles, Monmouth sailed for England with about one hundred and fifty men and a shipload of arms, hoping to raise the West Country. He landed at Lyme Regis and was accorded all the old adulation. The peasantry flocked to his standard, and he was proclaimed king at Taunton. Foolishly, Monmouth declared James a traitor and, what was worse, a fratricide. These sensational charges were to cost him his head. Confusion, ill discipline and the pitch dark all conspired to rout Monmouth's rabble army at Sedgemoor on 6 July 1685. After the battle he fled towards the coast. Having stumbled across his father's old escape route from Worcester, he was found several days later in a ditch on Cranborne Chase in Dorset, a known hideout for outlaws. Bearded, disguised as a shepherd, wracked with fatigue and hunger, Monmouth was identified by the Order of St George found in his pocket. Like another more recent high-profile captive, he trembled and seemed lost for speech. The cruellest irony was that his discoverer was a man by the name of Perkin! Back in London Monmouth begged for his life on his knees, but James did not trust his nephew's assurances of loyalty. Having recovered the courage that he had so often displayed on the battlefield, Monmouth was executed with brutal incompetence on 15 July, attended by the vicar of St Martin's, Thomas Tenison.[2]

The Queen Dowager Catherine had interceded for him, but to no avail. She knew that Charles would never have sanctioned the execution of his son. As for Nell, her voice was now worthless. She could only grieve from afar as her dear friend and the brother of her son was hacked to death on Tower Hill. The world that she had known was cut adrift by the strokes of Jack Ketch's axe. She was at Windsor when she received the news of his death, and without her son to comfort her.

Though still numb from the King's death, she made an effort to jolly herself up for the summer season. She was even persuaded to take part in a little intrigue, but nothing could alter the profound indifference she felt to the life around her. Her old friend Mary Mordaunt, Duchess of Norfolk, she of the phantom pregnancy, was looking to bed John Germaine, a handsome Anglo-Dutch fortune-hunter reputed to be the bastard son of William II of Orange. (Evelyn, however, described him as 'a Dutch gamester of mean extraction'.) Nell was invited by the Duchess to make up a foursome at cards at Windsor Castle as a cover for the intended seduction. At least she felt she could look on with amused objectivity, for she had already rebuffed Germaine's advances by kindly informing him that she was 'no such sportsman as to lay the dog where the deer had lain'. At all events, the Duchess bedded her man, but her luck soon ran out, and with it her marriage. During the divorce trial, which ended in 1700, one of the witnesses related Nell's part in the saga, including her witty digs at the Duchess the morning after.

Everywhere Nell turned in Windsor that summer the King's shadow seemed to beckon to her. The forest, like the river bank, had been their special retreat, where they could say with Duke Senior,

> Hath not old custom made this life more sweet
> Than that of painted pomp? Are not these woods
> More free from peril than the envious court?[3]

She remembered the candlelit picnics in the Great Park, and could hear Charles's laughter above the general chatter, while the castle itself and her own Burford House begot endless memories: voices, faces, toasts, merry speeches, theatricals, wild parties that had spilled out into the night and outfaced the dawn, and quiet moments snatched from the ever-present throng of courtiers, guests and servants, when she and the King had been alone.

James's court was very different from his brother's: if not po-faced, then decidedly sanctimonious. There were no mistresses, no jesters and no French love songs. (The best image for James that Dryden could conjure in his opening poem of the reign was Hercules!) As for the Restoration wits who had made the court their playground and crowned the King with cap and bells, they were now either reformed or dead, or like Buckingham living in rural obscurity, which for him was the same as being dead. Only Harry Killigrew, a true aficionado of folly, remained in place. But even had it not been so, it is doubtful that Nell would have joined in. Her health was not good. After long years of the clap,[4] her circulation was poor, her blood pressure climbing. And pervading everything were grief and the stress of indebtedness.

In September that year, however, James made good his promises to Nell. He deputed the task of dealing with her finances to Richard Graham, who immediately paid the £729 for which she had been outlawed. New trustees were appointed to handle her affairs, and a yearly pension of £1,500 was granted. James also paid off the mortgage on Bestwood, which came to £3,774, and ensured that the freehold would pass to her son and his descendants. He also made her two bounty payments of £500 each. The following year Burford House was leased to the King's son-in-law Prince George of Denmark for £260 a year. There was no question now but that Nell would be able to live comfortably while James was on the throne.

The King's largesse did not come without a price, however. Through Graham he informed Nell that life would be a lot smoother for her if she and her son became Catholics. (James himself, having initially vowed to uphold the Church of England, had been attending Mass in public and was already placing Catholics in positions of power.) Within months there were rumours of her conversion. On 19 January 1686 Evelyn wrote, 'Dryden the famous playwriter, and his two sonns, and Mrs. Nelly (Misse to the late King) were said to go to masse; such proselytes were no greate losse to the church.' Dryden did convert, but not the Protestant Whore. Her appearance at Mass had been no more than a gesture of goodwill, or an attempt to divert attention from her son who was still travelling in Europe. As Charles had played the Scottish Covenanters, so Nell wasn't above putting on a show to keep things sweet with the new Catholic King.

But when St Albans returned from the Continent, James began to tighten the screw and apply the sort of emotional blackmail that comes so easily to the bigoted mind. The King sent for Nell – their first meeting since Charles's death – and insisted that she now dismiss her son's French Protestant tutor and replace him with a Catholic, who according to Harry Killigrew would syllogize the Duke to death, being 'a very fierce, active, discursive Papist'. James reminded her that Charles had died a Catholic and that he had entrusted St Albans's education to him, his beloved brother, fearing that the boy would be spoiled else. To James's narrow mind, this could only mean one thing:

Charles had intended that his son should be converted to the Church of Rome.

But Nell was not about to bully her son into an alien faith. She agreed with Dryden that 'conscience is the royalty and prerogative of every private man' and that 'he is absolute in his own breast and accountable to no earthly power for that which passes only betwixt God and him'. Moreover, she knew the English hatred of Papism and had taken to heart Charles's gloomy prediction that it wouldn't be long before his brother was forced to go on his travels again. It would be folly to bind her son's heart in this way, and besides St Albans himself had no intention of yielding to his uncle's tyranny. When James saw that he was getting nowhere, he began to make threats about his nephew's inheritance. The strain seems to have been too much for Nell and in March 1687 she suffered the first of two apoplectic strokes, which left her paralysed down one side of her body. Rumours of her death abounded. That same month, Alice Hatton, daughter of Sir Christopher Hatton, 1st Lord Kirby, wrote to her brother Christopher, by then Viscount Hatton, in the belief that Nell was dead: 'Ye King has seazed on hir estate and jewles for hir son, but unless he will change his religion, he's not to have anything, wch he is yet very unwilling to.'

There was probably no malice in James's campaign against St Albans; rather, it was his cack-handed way of showing his concern for his nephew. Nevertheless, there does seem to have been some sort of deep-rooted aversion at work, which is possibly explained by the boy's resemblance to James's old nemesis, the Duke of Monmouth. Both had the same sort of mother, or at least mothers that would have been classified together in James's mind, and had St Albans possessed his older brother's charismatic nature he may well have commanded the same degree of popular appeal. James despised popular appeal, and recoiled from the prospect of another populist Protestant prince swanning about the country.

Meanwhile, St Albans had more important things to think about: his mother was clearly dying. In May Nell suffered a second stroke, and was thenceforth confined to her silver bed, which had caused such a sensation when it was made. But what had once been a bower of enchantment was now a ship of death. The eagles were her creditors, the cherubs reminded her of her lost son, James, and the crowns were crowns of thorns. Sir Charles Lyttelton wrote, 'Mrs. Nelly has bine dying of an apoplexie. She is now come to her sense on one side, for ye other is dead of a palsey. She is thought to be worth 100,000li; 2000li in revenue, and ye rest jewells and plate.' She was attended by two full-time nurses, and four of the physicians who had taken the King in hand during his last illness: Doctors Lower, Lister and Harrell and the distinguished chemist M. Lefebure.

In addition to visits from her son, her sister and various friends and neighbours, Nell found a constant companion in Dr Thomas Tenison, the saintly rector of St Martin's, a blond giant who had directed some of her charitable impulses in the past. He had also ministered to Monmouth in his last hours. He was known to relish tough cases and had no doubt fortified himself against Nell's legendary retorts. But it seems that the pupil was ready for the master, for by all accounts he now guided her to a true repentance, which moved him sufficiently to agree to preach her funeral sermon. It is debatable, however, whether Nell had much to repent of in any formal moral sense, for she had lived her life in unselfish enjoyment and bestowed many blessings on her fellow creatures, most notably the gift of laughter. Like Charles, she had found it impossible to get worked up about religion and had always avoided factionalism in matters of the spirit. Indeed, her Protestantism may have been little more than an instinctive expression of her patriotism.

On 9 July 1687 Nell made her will, beginning,

> In the name of God, Amen. I, Ellen Gwynne, of the parish of St. Martin-in-the-fields, and county of Middlesex, spinster, this 9th day of July, anno Domini 1687, do make this my last will and testament, and do revoke all former wills. First, in hopes of a joyful resurrection, I do recommend myself whence I came, my soul into the hands of Almighty God, and my body unto the earth . . .

She appointed four distinguished executors, all former friends, and paid them £100 each for their pains, plus expenses. They were Laurence Hyde, Earl of Rochester, Thomas, Earl of Pembroke (who had defended her honour at the theatre), the Attorney-General, Sir

Robert Sawyer, and the Hon. Henry Sidney (who once complained that Charles did nothing but fish all day). Her lands, tenements, chattels and hereditaments all went to her 'dear natural son, his Grace the Duke of St Albans'. Her individual and charitable bequests followed in the two codicils that she drew up in the autumn, but by that time she was almost completely paralysed. She who a decade before had been described as 'the wildest and indiscreetest creature' ever to grace a royal court could now barely speak, much less sign a document – hence both codicils are described as 'attested and acknowledged' by Nell.

In addition to the financial bequests made to her sister, friends, doctors, nurses and household servants, Nell stipulated the following:

- I desire I may be buried in the chancel of St Martin-in-the-Fields.
- That Dr Tenison may preach my funeral sermon.
- That there may be a decent pulpit-cloth and cushion given to St. Martin-in-the-Fields.
- That he [her son] would give one hundred pounds for the use of the poor, of the said St Martin's and St James's Westminster, to be given into the hands of the said Dr Tenison, to be disposed of at his discretion, for taking any poor debtors of the said parish out of prison, and for cloathes this winter, and other necessaries, as he shall find most fit.
- That for showing my charity to those who differ from me in religion, I desire that fifty pounds may be put into the hands of Dr Tenison and Mr Warner, who, taking to them any two persons of the Roman Religion, may dispose of it for the use of the poor of that religion inhabiting the parish of St James's aforesaid.
- That His Grace would please lay out twenty pounds yearly for the releasing of poor debtors out of prison every Christmas-day.
- That the Lady Hollyman [identity unknown] may have the pension of ten shillings per week continued to her during the said lady's life.

Nell had known real poverty in her early life, and her father was said to have died in a debtors' prison. As a result, her will reflects a genuine sympathy with the poor. These are no mere generic bequests, but deeply felt gifts of a practical nature. As Chesterton remarked, 'Nell was not only sorry for people whose shoes pinched them; she knew *where* the shoe pinched.'[5] A Mr Wigmore wrote of her to her old friend George (now Sir George) Etherege, 'She is said to have died piously and penitently, and as she dispensed several charities in her lifetime, so she left several legacies at her death.' Though her death had been predicted and announced with great regularity over the summer, Nell's battered body held on longer than she might have wished. For thirty months now her only real ambition had been to join Charles in the Land of Promise. In its own brutal fashion, 'The Lady of Pleasure' had it about right:

> Nor wou'd Nelly long be his [the King's] Surviver.
> Alas! who now was good enough to Swive her
> She was too Generous, to let Subjects dabble
> Where she so oft had soak'd the Royal Bauble.
> A mother by a King, and be so base
> To let a Mortimer to take his Place!
> So she gave way to her consuming Grief
> Which brought her past all Gally-pot relief,
> Tho some report her Brains were quite exhaust
> By the Caresses of her Pamper'd Lust.
> However twere as the old Women say
> Her time was come and then there's no delay,
> So down into the Stygian Lake She dropt
> To meet the Prince She had so often topt.

It was a horribly lingering death for one who had been so bright and stirring, but at least when the end came, on 14 November 1687, at ten at night, she died in the knowledge that her son would remain a Protestant and that any possible parsimony on James's part would be more than compensated by the pension of £2,000 per annum that the Queen Dowager Catherine had decided to bestow upon St Albans. He had told his mother during one of their whispered conversations towards the end that he was privy to the secret correspondence of leading nobles with William of Orange and that plans were already afoot to make William and Mary regents, with James remaining non-executive head of state. Nell did not live to hear of her son's heroic deeds on the battlefield or his support for the Whigs, nor did she ever meet his wife or any of her twelve grandchildren, yet she must have died a proud mother, who never failed to delight at seeing the King miraculously resurrected in her own flesh and blood. Queen Catherine's pension had been a treasured tribute and said as much about her affection for Nell as it did for her son, Charles, for of all the principal mistresses she was the only one not to have antagonized Catherine (quite a feat for the only non-Catholic among them), as well as being – in Catherine's eyes – the only one who loved the King for himself.

Nell's funeral took place on 17 November in a packed St Martin's, with well-wishers lining the streets outside. They were saying good-bye, not just to a friend and benefactress, but to the age that she had come to embody. The sheer variety of people at her funeral, from the highest to the lowest, reflected her universal appeal. Few there had known her personally, though Dorset – her Charles the Second – now very fat and troubled with the spleen, was observed easing himself into a pew. It was to those for whom the myth of Nell Gwyn was real and vital, the London apprentices and serving girls and their parents, that the funeral spoke most deeply. For Nell had been one of them, and the love and respect which the King had shown her kindled a corresponding warmth in their own hearts.

Tenison, who spoke 'much to her praise', took as his text the parable of the lost sheep from Luke 15:

> What man of you, having an hundred sheep, if he lose one of them, doth not leave the ninety and nine in the wilderness, and go after that which is lost, until he find it? And when he hath found it, he layeth it on his shoulders, rejoicing. And when he cometh home, he calleth together his friends and neighbours, saying unto them, Rejoice with me; for I have found my sheep which was lost. I say unto you, that likewise joy shall be in heaven over one sinner that repenteth, more than over ninety and nine just persons, which need no repentance.

The text of Tenison's address doesn't survive, though we know it caused a stir among polite society and made him the subject of considerable censure. Bastard versions of the address, purporting to be genuine transcripts, circulated on the streets and Tenison was forced to issue a notice of denial: 'Whereas there has been a Paper cry'd by some Hawkers, as a sermon preached by D.T. [Dr Tenison] at the funeral of *M.* E Gwynn, this may Certify, that that Paper is the Forgery of some Mercinary people.' The sermon was also used against him much later, in 1691, when he was appointed to the see of Lincoln. Lord Villiers, whose father-in-law was the former whoremonger royal William Chiffinch, intervened with Queen Mary to oppose a candidate of his own. In his submission he reminded Her Majesty that Tenison had preached 'a notable funeral sermon in praise of Ellen Gwyn', clearly grounds for disqualification in his mind. The Queen disagreed. 'I have heard as much,' quoth she, 'and this is a sign that the poor unfortunate woman died penitent; for, if I have read a man's heart through his looks, had she not made a truly pious end, the Doctor could never have been induced to speak well of her.'

The one political idea that Nell could be said to have enshrined was that of the King as the father or shepherd of his people. If she was the lost sheep, then Charles was the shepherd who lifted her up and brought her home rejoicing. By going astray in childhood Nell discovered those qualities that brought her success as an adult. And in finding the lost child, Charles redeemed something vital in his own nature: trust. The lost sheep is also the chosen sheep of the hundred, and in the context of Nell's life marks her out as someone special or fated: someone who brought an erring King back to the covenant with his people.

For once, the poetasters put aside their cynicism to elegize the departed Nell and protested that this was no mere convention. As the anonymous author of 'An Elegy in Commemoration of Madam Eleanor Gwyn' wrote,

> . . . some may cast objections in and say
> These scattered praises that we seek to lay
> Upon her hearse are but the formal way.
> Yet when we tell them she was free from strife,
> Courteous even to the poor, no pride of life,
> E'er entertaining, but did much abound

In charity, and for it was renowned;
Not seeking praises, but did vain praise despise,
And at her alms was heard no trumpet noise;
And how again we let them further see
That she refused and hated flattery,
And far from her dissemblers did command,
We may have hopes her fame for this will stand.

The recurring images in the other elegies are those of the light and brightness cast by her smiling looks ('Her smiles made summer and she always smil'd'),[6] her laughter and the laughter she inspired in others and, above all, her lack of pretension. Fine tools with which to capture the heart of a king, and of a nation too.

> Our Lady of Laughter, invoked in no psalter,
> Praise be with thee yet . . . !

Epilogue

The House of Nell Gwyn

THE CIVIL WAR SHOOK THE family tree of England like a great storm, undermining the old social dispensation. Nell Gwyn was very much the product of this storm. Her father lost himself in the war and never recovered; her mother survived, but in a demoralized state. Nell herself belonged to the new generation, that strange and wonderful fruit put forth by the battered tree, and her wit and confidence equipped her to take advantage of the new uncertainty at the heart of the nation.

Nell was both a catalyst for and a product of the new zeitgeist. It both devoured and spawned her. She was like the alchemical mercury in her dynamic effect upon the society of her time. Like the fool, whose volatile nature kept him clear of established roles and definitions, Nell revelled in the ambiguities and contradictions of her life. Whether skipping barefoot through the alleys of St Giles, serving firewater in a bawdy house, entertaining audiences at Drury Lane or playing the wild mistress at Epsom or the fool at Whitehall, she transformed herself with as much delight as she transformed others.

Our story has told of the ways in which Nell forced the King to change on a personal level, and these changes had social and political ramifications. She herself didn't so much leap across the social divide as completely ignore it! She *walked through* the thousand social barriers that had been erected over the centuries by the ruling elite without uttering a single password. All the social frippery of the court, its decorous defences and well-guarded shibboleths, came clattering to the ground in the face of the jester's frank impudence. The veil was rent and the court flung open to the scrutiny of the people. Artistic, capricious, childish, bold, funny and frank, Nell has played the joker in the family pack ever since her death 320 years ago, discomfiting her complacent descendants with a hearty dose of puckish mischief.

The great majority of her male descendants in the house of Beauclerk have perhaps rejected Nell's gifts, albeit unconsciously, while identifying with their royal inheritance. In doing so they have rejected a vital element in their own natures, which left unexpressed has returned furtively to embroil them in licentious scandal or emotional dependence on women. There has also been the taint of bastardy, which in royal and noble families was projected onto the mother, who was of humbler birth and a convenient scapegoat for her child's feelings of inferiority.

Indeed, it is said that the family title was originally granted because Nell Gwyn insisted on addressing her son as 'you little bastard' in the King's presence. Crucially, not only had the King not granted the child a title, he hadn't given him a surname. This feeling of anonymity has remained with the family, though the threadbare sense of identity it has engendered has provided a welcome asylum from the eyes of the world. The dukedom, unsupported as it was by the trappings of an exalted title, appeared almost fictional. That said, the Beauclerks' poverty and diminished standing stem from something fine and decent in the soul of Nell Gwyn. Because she lacked the greed and rapacity of her fellow royal mistresses, Nell failed to secure the huge prizes for her sons that fell into the laps of Barbara's brats and Louise's infant prince.

The Dukes of St Albans have always been considered eccentric and something of an embarrassment to the upper classes; certainly they have stood outside the charmed circle of the aristocracy. Because their common ancestor, Nell Gwyn, was a low-born public figure who could not be kept in the cupboard like the anonymous housemaids and washerwomen that have mothered countless aristocrats, there has been a strong sense of resentment towards the Beauclerks, as if they've somehow let the cat out of the bag, a feeling reinforced by the 9th Duke of St Albans's marriage to the former actress Harriot Mellon in 1827.

Torn between the opposing poles of whore and king (or king and jester), at the heart of the Beauclerk psyche is a crisis of identity. Insiders by birth, they have remained outsiders by temperament, mistrusting the establishment that demands the sort of clear definition of social status that they so conspicuously lack. On the whole they have shied away from public office, preferring a life of privacy and simplicity. And though there have been some distinguished exceptions, it somehow seems appropriate that the two things that have been named for the family over the years are a mock orange – *Philadelphus* 'Beauclerk' – and a rare type of flea.

There is a sense of lingering shame in Nell's descendants that so prestigious a title could spring from a king's love for a street-seller and actress, rather than from outstanding service to one's country, a shame that no amount of bawdy banter about Nell's oranges can hide. To an extent, then, the bar sinister has acted as a bar to self-belief. Unsurprisingly perhaps, the title has been open to a good deal of imposture and impersonation, most recently in 1996 when one Eugene Riggs, an Indian gentleman living on the Peabody Estate and calling himself the 15th Duke of St Albans, made a number of rental demands on the residents of Westminster and contacted the real Duke's stockbrokers with the intention of selling his shares.

This frail sense of identity has fostered another form of invasion, more destructive than impersonation – mental instability and even outright madness. Three of the 8th Duke's children and two of the 10th Duke's, including the 11th Duke himself, lived and died in asylums, while apoplexy and epilepsy between them have accounted for several deaths. Other holders of the title, including the 3rd and 9th Dukes, were described, quite kindly one feels, as simpletons. When introduced to a famous pair of Siamese twins in the 1820s, the 9th Duke asked the man who was showing them whether or not they were brothers. (Presumably he could see that they were closely related.)

All of which is to say that the union of king and whore has caused considerable tension in the Beauclerk soul, and not always in a creative fashion. Indeed, the consequences have at times been so unfortunate that one is tempted to see in the original union of Charles and Nell a violation of the social order, from which a curse has fallen on the family. Despite the validity and success of their relationship, it was clearly not the basis for a viable ducal house. The result has been a ducal family in name alone, whose title holders, trapped between two worlds, have led strange half-lives on the fringes of the aristocracy.

Looking back over the history of the family, the dominant themes to emerge are literature, theatre, religion, travel, horsemanship and the sea. There have been thirteen published authors among the Beauclerks, several of them descended from the noted aesthete and bibliophile Topham Beauclerk (1739–80), who was a grandson of the 1st Duke of St Albans, while the theatre has always intruded on the family's life, both through art and marriage. Life has frequently been more palatable for the Beauclerks overseas, where their nebulous status has mattered less. They have ended up in most corners of the earth, whether as wanderers, diplomats or, more recently, aid workers. The Church, too, has provided a haven for the family's many unworldly souls, though, apart from Nell's grandson Lord James Beauclerk, who rose to become Bishop of Hereford (1746–87), they have been happy to potter about their country parishes. One of them, Charles Sidney Beauclerk (a great-grandson of Topham), became a Jesuit and the rector of Holywell in Flintshire, where he helped restore St Winefride's Well as a shrine, instituting a daily service at the well-side in the 1890s, a ritual which continues to this day.

Horsemanship was inherited through Charles II, whose governor as a boy, the Earl of Newcastle, himself a noted equestrian, wrote, 'No man makes a horse go better than I have seen some go under His Majesty the first time ever he came upon their backs, which is the quintessence of the art.' His son the 1st Duke of St Albans possessed a similar talent and won the very first race at Royal Ascot in the summer of 1711, riding a chestnut horse called Doctor, at the tender age of forty-one. In the reign of George II the 1st Duke's eldest son, another Charles Beauclerk, was involved as warden of Windsor Forest in recreating Ascot as it is today. Another of Nell's grandsons, Lord Henry Beauclerk (1701–61) won the twenty pound plate there in 1724 on a horse called Puppet. The 5th Duke's youngest son, the Revd Lord Frederick Beauclerk, won the St Albans steeplechase in 1834 when over sixty, though he rode under an alias to avoid offending his bishop. He also had a saddle fitted in his pulpit to bolster his confidence as a preacher. Further down the line still, in January 1893, the 11th Duke of St Albans (1870–1934) accepted a wager of £500 to ride across rough terrain from Napier to Auckland (New Zealand) inside sixty-six hours, a distance of some 300 miles. He won the wager, completing the distance in sixty-one hours and riding 132 miles on the final day.

Having inherited Charles II's love of seafaring, many Beauclerks have displayed competence on the high seas. The family has produced two admirals: Lord Vere Beauclerk (1699–1781), one of Nell's grand-sons, and Lord Amelius Beauclerk (1771–1846), the third son of the 5th Duke. Her youngest grandson, Lord Aubrey Beauclerk (1711–40), was a naval captain and died a hero's death at the Battle of Cartagena in the West Indies. Having had both legs shot off, he refused all medical attention until he had communicated his last orders to his first lieutenant. The 8th Duke (1766–1825) was also in the navy as a young man, and two of his sons, Lords Frederick and Charles Beauclerk, were decorated for gallantry at sea.

Returning to Nell's son, the 1st Duke was only seventeen at his mother's death, which effectively left him orphaned. Unable as he was to inherit his father's status, name or substance, life must have seemed something of a fiction at times. After a few months in London to settle his affairs (principally the debts he had inherited from Nell), he set off for Hungary, where he joined the army of the Holy Roman Emperor Leopold I, commanded by Prince Charles of Lorraine, which was attempting to drive the Turks back from the Danube.[1] St Albans distinguished himself at the Siege of Belgrade in August 1688, and a report in the *London Gazette* that September declared that he had 'had a great share in the glory of [the] Action'.

Rather conveniently, he was still abroad when William of Orange landed at Torbay in November and his uncle James fled to France. Nevertheless, his regiment was one of the first to declare for William, and St Albans, having clearly inherited his mother's democratic instincts, remained a staunch Whig throughout his life. Indeed, one of his most common nicknames in the satires of the time was 'Prince Orange', a jibe at Nell's early trade of orange girl. A satire entitled 'The Heroe', having discoursed of Barbara's sons the Dukes of Grafton and Northumberland, praises Nell's for his military prowess:

Mighty *St. Albans* must not be the last
This Quixot has been going these three years past.
Who tho' the third in Court to follow on
In feats of arms, is second unto none.
When these great Princes shall divide the spoyl
To their eternal fame i'th' Brittish Isle,
For sure the Hollanders must go to pot
Orange of course falls to *St. Albans* lot.
Besides by the Father being near ally'd,
He has a Title by the Mother's side.

When St Albans returned to England he brought with him two seven-year-old Turkish boys captured at the siege, who were brought up in his household. They were baptized at Windsor parish church in June 1704 as 'Geo: & Charles Mustapha, aged about 23'. The witnesses were the Duke of Northumberland and the Duke and Duchess of St Albans. George returned to his homeland, but Charles remained in England, was christened 'Charles Wise' and created a Poor Knight of Windsor by patent of King George II in June 1742. The Duchess of St Albans, who died later that year, left him twenty pounds per annum in her will. A portrait of the children with a Mrs Loftus, presumably their nurse, hung in Burford House.

St Albans remained in the army until the Peace of Ryswick in September 1697, at which Louis XIV finally recognized William as King of England. In 1693 he fought against the French in Flanders and was reported dead at the Battle of Neerwinden. That same year William created him Captain of the Band of Gentlemen Pensioners.[2] In December 1697 he was sent as Ambassador Extraordinary to France to congratulate Louis XIV on the marriage of his grandson the Duke of Burgundy, for which William presented him with a set of coach horses 'finely spotted like leopards'. The mission seems to have been a political success, marking as it did the resumption of diplomatic relations between France and England. Socially, the young Duke made a favourable impression and bore out St Evremond's observation that he had 'the art of pleasing all the ladies'. Not everyone was contented, however. Lord Portland, who had been sent as ambassador in the wake of St Albans's mission complained to the King about his behaviour: 'I am annoyed to have to tell your Majesty that the Duke of St. Albans left this place without making the usual present to the introducers, which has made a very bad impression, even as regards your Majesty. He has left debts unpaid in the shops, and borrowed £150 from Lord Paston to avoid having his luggage seized. He promised to pay when he got home, and has forgotten both.'

The Duke was forced to sell 79 Pall Mall the year he married in order to pay off his remaining debts. He and his wife made Windsor their base, and most of their thirteen children were born at Burford House, Nell's old home beside the castle. He was made Lord Lieutenant and Custos Rotulorum of Berkshire and seems to have enjoyed a life of relative retirement. He got on with George I as well as anyone could, though the new parsimonious, clockwork court was a far cry from his father's witty and indulgent salon. Gallantry was a dead word, and it was no longer considered monstrous to live contentedly with one's wife and family. He was elected a fellow of the Royal Society in 1722 and died four years later at Bath, where he was taking the waters for a lingering illness. He was fifty-six.

The 1st Duke's children (Nell's grandchildren) were born between 1696 and 1716. Of his eight surviving sons, six were MPs at one time or another (no fewer than four of them for Windsor, which was something of a pocket borough for the Beauclerks), two were in the army, two in the navy, one in the Church, one was a rogue and one very nearly destitute. Four of them went to nearby Eton. The eldest son, who became the 2nd Duke, was a favourite of George II, and carried the Queen's crown at the coronation of 1727. In addition to his father's old posts of Lord Lieutenant and Custos Rotulorum of Berkshire, the King made him High Steward of Windsor, Captain and Constable of Windsor Castle and Warden of Windsor Forest. Like the 1st Duke, he largely absented himself from public affairs, and he could not claim his father's military prowess. Lord Hervey described him as 'one of the weakest men either of the legitimate or spurious blood of the Stuarts'. He did, however, manage to marry an heiress, Lucy, daughter of Sir John Werden, who brought much-needed estates into the family. His brother, Lord William Beauclerk, married Lucy's sister Charlotte on the same day, as a sort of insurance policy. As ever, though, the properties managed to slip through the family net.

William, who was the grandfather of the 4th Duke, seems to have been unstable or even mad. His health broke down and he and his family lived in great poverty. Lady Huntingdon, who came across him in Bath, wrote that 'of all the objects of pity, I never saw one equal him. He goes about but appears in his looks to have lost the greatest share of his senses'. He died in his early thirties. His daughter Charlotte, who eventually inherited many of the Werden estates, married John Drummond, son of the founder of Drummonds Bank. The third son of the 1st Duke, Vere Beauclerk, had a distinguished career in the navy, rising to become Admiral of the Blue and receiving a peerage from George II. He married an heiress, Mary Chamber, whose exotic lineage (she had a half-caste grandmother) set Horace Walpole buzzing. A fanatical admirer of the de Veres, he was aghast that Lady Mary should have 'blackened the true stream' of that noble blood. The marriage brought Hanworth Palace in Middlesex into the family, and Lord Vere of Hanworth (to give Vere Beauclerk his title) became the ancestor of the 5th and all subsequent Dukes of St Albans.

Lord Sidney Beauclerk, the fifth son, was the sort of charming, slightly vicious rogue that peoples the pages of Restoration comedy. Lady Mary Wortley Montagu described him as 'Nell Gwyn in person with the sex altered', adding that he occasioned 'such fracas amongst the ladies of gallantry that it passes belief'. He was a notorious fortune hunter, who managed to persuade Mr Richard Topham MP to leave him his estates at Windsor and Clewer Brocas, on top of which he married a Lancashire heiress, Mary Norris of Speke Hall, near Liverpool. Their son, Topham Beauclerk, was a famous aesthete and bibliophile, immensely learned and eloquent, who amassed a collection of over 30,000 volumes, which he housed in a specially built wing of his home in Great Russell Street. He was a good friend of Samuel Johnson, who, after Topham's death at the age of forty, declared that 'Beauclerk's talents were those that he had felt himself more disposed to envy than those of any whom he had known'. He also spoke of the 'wonderful ease' with which his young friend 'uttered what was highly excellent'.

But for all his gifts Topham was an idler, who was as fond of dissipation as disputation. His aversion to business of any kind was well known, as was his inattention to matters of hygiene. Lady Louisa

Stuart described him as 'what the French call *cynique* in personal habits beyond what one could have thought possible in any one but a beggar or a gypsy'. At a Christmas party at Blenheim Palace, attended by him and his wife Lady Diana Beauclerk, the eldest daughter of the 3rd Duke of Marlborough, an outbreak of itching among the guests, which greatly inconvenienced the ladies, was traced back to Topham. When one of the guests remonstrated with him, he expressed disbelief that people should be concerned about such a trifle and declared that he had enough lice under his wig to stock a parish.

A clear virtue that emerges from Topham's letters is his dedication to the classical ideal of friendship. In a letter to his dear friend Lord Charlemont in Ireland, he wrote urging him to 'leave your parliament and your nation to shift for itself, and consecrate that time to your friends, which you spend in endeavouring to promote the interest of half a million scoundrels'. 'Do not let us lose that moment that we have,' he continued, 'but let us enjoy all that can be enjoyed in this world; the pleasures of a true uninterrupted friendship.' This innocent devotion to his friends inspired the love and loyalty of the grave and pious Dr Johnson. The good doctor was even beguiled from time to time to play the libertine with his young friend. On one famous occasion, related by Boswell, Beauclerk and his Oxford friend Bennet Langton decided to knock up Johnson at three in the morning and try to persuade him to join their revels. They beat violently upon the door of his chambers until he finally emerged in his nightshirt, brandishing a poker. When he realized who they were, he cried, 'What, is it you, you dogs! I'll have a frisk with you.' They drank sweet spiced wine in a local tavern, then rowed down to Billingsgate to continue their debauch. Langton had a breakfast engagement, but Johnson and Beauclerk 'were so well pleased with their amusement, that they resolved to persevere in dissipation for the rest of the day'.

Though he talked endlessly of literature and was a founder member of the famous literary club that boasted Johnson, Burke, Goldsmith, Reynolds and Hawkins among its number, Topham was not a writer himself. Several of his descendants have been authors, however, among them – though not without a twist – Helen de Vere Beauclerk (d. 1969), whose novels include *The Green Lacquer Pavilion* and *The Love of the*

Foolish Angel. She was the adopted daughter of Captain Ferdinand Beauclerk, a great-grandson of Topham.

The 2nd Duke was succeeded in the title by his only son, George (1730–86), who had the unsettling experience of being a Restoration fop in the England of George II. In him appeared all the vices of Charles II, without the brilliance and compassion to redeem them. A scapegrace on a fabulous scale, he seemed to conjure up a world of fantastical exploits, only they – and the mayhem they left in their wake – were startlingly real. Like a number of the other Dukes of St Albans, he embodied the archetype of the *puer aeternus*, which manifested as a pathological refusal to take responsibility for his life, nowhere more strikingly than in his prolific production of bastards. (He opened his innings by fathering an illegitimate son while still at Eton.) As with his father and grandfather, Windsor, where he was High Steward, was his base of operations, and he too was granted the office of Lord Lieutenant of Berkshire. With his profligate lifestyle he quickly encumbered himself with debts. Escaping to the Continent, he found new sources of credit in Brussels, which quickly became his home from home. Returning to England in 1752 he married a considerable heiress, Jane Roberts of Glassenbury in Kent, said to be worth £125,000, but the couple were soon living apart.

Next he took up with a Windsor dairymaid called Molly, with whom he eloped to Paris. They had a son called George, but Molly proved no match for the actresses and operatic divas of Paris, who quickly engrossed the Duke's attention as well as his remaining credit. Paris was followed by Venice, and finally Brussels again, where St Albans fell into the hands of dupes and card sharps and was arrested for debt. There were a string of mistresses and illegitimate children, as well as more fleeting sexual encounters. In a letter to Sir Horace Mann in February 1758, Walpole wrote, 'The simple Duke of St Albans who is retired to Brussels for debt, has made a most sumptuous funeral in public for a dab of five months old that he had by his cook-maid.'

Though he tried living in England for periods of time, it didn't work out. England meant responsibilities, married life and insufficient credit. At least nothing was expected of him in Brussels, and he could act the part of an English Duke with some plausibility. Unalloyed reality held few charms for George Beauclerk, but the salons of Brussels, which were riddled with impostors and allowed him to recreate himself on a nightly basis, suited his quixotic temperament. Besides, he was now holding court at the Château d'Indevelde outside the city and had had a great many of his family chattels shipped over from England. Believing that bandits were lying in wait for him in the grounds of the chateau, he wrote endless letters to Count Cobenzl, the Prime Minister of the Austrian Netherlands, requesting his protection. His delusions extended to his wife, whom he transplanted to Brussels in the belief that she would live happily *à trois* with his mistress, Marie Petit. When things didn't work out, he took Marie to England instead, but not before he'd done another spell in prison for debt. Having sold Burford House to the King, thus ending the Beauclerks' happy association with Windsor, he returned to Brussels for good in 1780. His final act of folly was to build a palace at Laeken, north of the city, which remained unfinished at his death. Those goods that hadn't already been seized by the government were auctioned off in June 1786, some four months after he died.

His successor, another George, and grandson of the Lord William Beauclerk who died out of his wits, had his agent bid for family chattels at the Brussels auction, while the future 5th Duke, Lord Aubrey Vere, was probably there in person. After joining his father's regiment, the 3rd Foot Guards, the 4th Duke fought in the American War of Independence. He was promoted lieutenant colonel in March 1786, just after succeeding to the title, but less than a year later died of a mysterious illness, aged twenty-eight. He was succeeded by his cousin Aubrey, the son of Admiral Lord Vere. In his portrait by Romney Aubrey St Albans gives the impression of a stolid, ruddy-nosed country squire in his green shooting jacket and buff waistcoat. The truth is he led a very private life and was best known as an art collector, a passion he shared with his father-in-law, Lord Bessborough. Like all the previous dukes he spent no time at Bestwood, which he leased to a local farmer for £1,500 per annum, making his principal seat at Hanworth Palace, which he had inherited from his mother.

On his death in 1802 the 5th Duke left four sons. Aubrey, the eldest and least interesting, who succeeded as 6th Duke, joined the army as a young man, serving in North America and Canada and rising to the rank of lieutenant colonel. He married twice, advantageously both times, but money and property did their usual vanishing trick. He died of apoplexy aged forty-nine, his adult life having been dogged by ill health. Lady Harriet Cavendish described him as 'the most hideous, disagreeable little animal that I have ever met with'. A son and heir was born to him and his second wife Louisa Manners four months before he died, though the Duke's brothers were disposed to think that the father had been one George Sinclair. With the succession to the dukedom at stake, recriminations were rife. Fortunately for all concerned, however, the duchess and her infant son (Aubrey, the 7th Duke) died suddenly of 'a hectic disease' within three hours of each other on 19 February 1816. The title passed to the 6th Duke's younger brother Lord William Beauclerk (1766–1825).

William, who succeeded as 8th Duke, had begun life in the navy, but left to make his way in the world, which in his case meant fortune-hunting. Described as a good-for-nothing roué by Sir Charles Anderson, he possessed the sort of ruthless charm that had secured an inheritance for Topham's father, Lord Sidney. Through his two marriages, both to Lincolnshire heiresses, substantial properties came into the family. Well before he inherited the dukedom he made his principal seat at Redbourne near Brigg in Lincolnshire, an estate he had clinched for the family by destroying his first wife's second will. There had also been much bullying when she was alive, and the imputation of mental cruelty rings true. His rapaciousness appears to have been a necessity, however, as his brother the 6th Duke had left all his landed property as well as his chattels to his second wife, who in turn left everything to her favourite sister. So if the 8th Duke hadn't established himself in Lincolnshire, he would have been left with nothing but the dukedom, the Bestwood estate in Nottinghamshire, a few works of art and the hereditary offices of Grand Falconer of England and Registrar of the Court of Chancery. He would, in effect, have been reduced to living on the income of a squire.

William St Albans had a large family of six sons and six daughters, certainly enough to justify an enthusiasm for amateur theatricals. Redbourne was the scene of artistic soirées, and there is a painting of one such occasion, in which the Duke himself is pictured playing the flute among his guests. His penchant for theatrical display extended to public life, and at the coronation of George IV in 1821 he appeared as Hereditary Grand Falconer in full hawking costume of green velvet trimmed with apricot silk, with a large velvet hawking glove, plumed hat and suede boots. Life in the Beauclerk family was further spiced by the Duke's two younger brothers, Lords Amelius (1771–1846) and Frederick (1773–1850), who took an active interest in their many nieces and nephews. Amelius joined the navy as a boy and rose to become Admiral of the White and principal Naval ADC to William IV. The King, an old sea dog himself, had a fondness for Beauclerk and danced a country dance with him at Brighton Pavilion during the New Year celebrations of 1833. He also presented him with a jewelled sword. Amelius had no legitimate offspring, but fathered a bastard son at the age of sixty-five.[3]

Lord Frederick, who became the vicar of St Michael's in St Albans, apart from his steeple-chasing prowess was a demon cricketer, scoring eight centuries at Lord's and becoming President of the MCC in 1826. Formidable sportsman though he was, Lord Frederick used every trick in the book to stay at the crease, win the game and make a considerable sum of money from it. He used to boast of making six hundred guineas a year by bribing players and scorers, as well as rigging matches. He would put off opposing bowlers by pretending to be injured or disabled, often limping grotesquely out to the crease at the start of his innings, though no one was quicker between the wickets. If he was already known to the bowlers he would provoke them by hanging his gold watch on middle stump, then taunt them with their inability to hit it. As with his racing, he frequently played under an assumed name, such as Mr Williams, for he had a vile temper and liked to use the 'most unparsonical language'.

Lord Frederick's daughters, Caroline and Henrietta, were writers and co-authored a volume of stories entitled *Tales of Fashion and Reality* (1836). Two of the 8th Duke's children, Lord Charles and Lady Maria, were accomplished artists. The former published a book of lithographs of battle scenes during the rebellions of Papineau and MacKenzie in Canada, where he was serving under Sir John Colborne, and wrote an accompanying narrative. The whole was published in London in 1840 under the title *Lithographic Views of Military Operations in Canada*. The

8th Duke's second surviving son, Lord Frederick Beauclerk (1808–65), was the grandfather of Violet Mary Beauclerk, the author, who won the James Tait Black Memorial Prize in 1933 for *The Book of Talbot*. She also wrote mystical poetry and in 1950, at the age of sixty-six, became a Poor Clare nun under the name Sister Mary Seraphim.

Three of the 8th Duke's children, Lord Henry and Ladies Maria and Charlotte Beauclerk, were certified insane and died in asylums. Maria and Henry were admitted to Ticehurst House in Sussex in 1851 and 1852 respectively; she was fifty-three and he was thirty-nine, but both had suffered bouts of insanity since their early twenties. Both were committed by the 9th Duke's second wife, Elizabeth Gubbins, Duchess of St Albans. Maria's mental disorder is given as 'dementia', its cause, 'disappointment of the affections'; she spent twenty years at the asylum, dying of epilepsy aged seventy-three. Henry suffered from 'imbecility', and the cause was given as 'hereditary', which suggests acknowledged incidences of madness in earlier generations of the family (the 1st Duke's second son, William, springs to mind). Henry's sole delight was to drive about the grounds of the asylum in a donkey carriage, and it was during one of these jaunts that he suffered an apoplectic seizure, dying a few days later at the age of forty-three. Charlotte, another spinster, died of 'atrophy' at a Highgate institution, aged forty. She too suffered from frustrated affections.

When Willie Burford, the future 9th Duke, was courting Fanny Gascoyne, or rather when his family were courting her on his behalf, it was his sister Charlotte (above) who described him with unironic zeal as 'this eighth wonder of the world'. Other observers were less admiring. When he did become engaged in 1823 – to Lady Elizabeth Conyngham – a betrothal that lasted a matter of days, Lord Holland noted in his journal that the young lady had 'consented to marry the idiot Lord Burford'. In the end, after two false starts, he made one of the most talked-about marriages of the entire nineteenth century, and one which scandalized the aristocracy, confirming them in their view that the Beauclerks were quite beyond the pale. His bride was a low-born former actress, twenty-four years his senior, who happened to be the richest woman in England.

The lady in question was born in 1777 to an Irishwoman of peasant stock called Sarah, who appears to have worked as wardrobe keeper to a theatrical company. Her father was said by one account to have been a Lieutenant Matthew Mellon of the Madras Native Infantry, who met Sarah while on leave, then disappeared back to his regiment, never to be seen again. Another account has the father an actor by the name of John Kinnear, who had had to leave Ireland for political reasons and assumed the name 'Malone', which was adapted to 'Mellon' by the daughter when she began her career in London. Either way, Harriot Mellon, as the girl became known, spent her childhood attached to her mother's travelling troupe, acting children's parts and gaining a stepfather at the age of five when her mother married one of the company's musicians, Thomas Entwhistle. They led a nomadic life with few luxuries. Later in life Harriot used to recall how her 'poor mother' used to make tea 'out of a kettle under the hedge'.

A chance meeting with Sheridan, who saw Harriot act in Stafford when she was seventeen, emboldened Mrs Entwhistle to move to London with her daughter so that she could pursue her career in earnest. Harriot duly made her first appearance at Drury Lane in October 1795 in the role of Lydia Languish in *The Rivals*. She remained a member of the company for twenty years and was for a time the understudy of Dorothea Jordan, who bore the Duke of Clarence, later William IV, no fewer than ten children. With her sensuous good looks and soft, provincial manner, Harriot was known more for her pleasant nature and good humour than her acting ability, and certainly never had the charisma to become a star. Her most celebrated role was Mrs Candour in *A School for Scandal*, and Sheridan's comedies, which would have appealed to Nell Gwyn as the nearest thing to Restoration comedy at the end of the eighteenth century, seemed to have played to Harriot's strengths.

Harriot's next chance meeting transformed her life even more dramatically and occurred once again at the initiative of her mother. It was 1805 and Harriot was in Cheltenham performing at the town theatre when Mrs Entwhistle, who lived at the spa town with her husband, discovered that Thomas Coutts, the banker, was visiting to take the waters. Described as 'an old, pallid, sickly, thin gentleman in a shabby coat and brown scratch wig', Coutts duly received a note from Mrs E. requesting that he purchase a subscription to Harriot's benefit performance. He sent five guineas for a box, and fell deeply in love. The rumour mill worked overtime. Not only was Coutts almost seventy to Harriot's twenty-eight, but he was a married man. No matter, he lavished her with gifts of jewellery and property that excited the envy of society, on one occasion writing a cheque for £15,000 for some diamonds that had taken her fancy. It is unclear to this day whether he and Harriot were lovers, or simply soulmates, but their illicit friendship lasted almost ten years, until his elderly wife gave up the ghost in January 1815. A mere two weeks later, the eighty-year-old Coutts, eager to secure Harriot's prospects, led her to the altar at St James's, Westminster, for a secret ceremony. When he died in 1822, he left Harriot his entire fortune of £900,000.

This then was the fifty-year-old former actress that the 9th Duke of St Albans, William Aubrey de Vere Beauclerk, married in 1827. He was a bachelor of twenty-six with no experience of women. Harriot's wedding present to the Duke was a cheque for £30,000 and an estate in Essex worth £26,000. For his part, no doubt to maintain his self-respect, he settled upon her an annuity of £1,000. They divided their lives between Piccadilly, Brighton and Redbourne in Lincolnshire. They had been drawn together by their love of Shakespeare, of whom Harriot was 'so much an idolater that she scarcely accorded any merit to modern poetry'. As for St Albans, he liked nothing better than to step before a group of assembled guests and launch into a soliloquy from one of the tragedies.

If Harriot's marriage to Coutts had aroused resentment in society and the gibes of the columnists, her union with the youthful Duke of St Albans called forth a flood of angry ridicule. She was Dollalolla, Queen of the Giants, he Lord Noodle or the mighty Tom Thumb. She was 'Mother Malone', 'Melons' and 'her Grease', while he was mocked as 'Dukey' and 'pet Mr. Duke'. This was 1827, and the great industrial fortunes of the Victorian age had yet to be made. Wealth and high birth were still synonymous. It was profoundly disturbing to the aristocracy that the richest woman in the kingdom should be an Irish peasant. Even more galling was the fact that one of the most senior noblemen in the land should have lent this monstrous parvenue a respectable face through the sacred institution of matrimony. The fact that the Duke was considered a simpleton somewhat mitigated the disaster in their eyes and encouraged them in their disparagement of his mental powers. For them, the equation was simple: Harriot had married the Duke for status, and he had married her for money. One lampoon entitled 'A Beau-Clerk for a Banking Concern' has Harriot reminding the Duke that she expects him to work for 'the concern'. Handing him a cheque for £100,000, she says, 'I will make you a sleeping partner, and here's a trifle for you to buy a pair of gloves.'

Harriot was naturally the principal target of social obloquy, which was particularly unjust, as she was a decent warm-hearted dame who was candid about her origins; and though she could be pompous in her later years, she was never pretentious. Sir Walter Scott, a friend of hers, wrote, 'It is the fashion to attend Mrs. Coutts' parties and to abuse her. I have always found her a kind, friendly woman, without either affectation or insolence in the display of her wealth, and most willing to do good if the means be shown to her. She can be very entertaining too, as she speaks without scruple of her stage life.' And when she and her husband were invited out as a couple, many a noble commentator was forced to admit, albeit grudgingly, that Harriot was better value. Lord Holland, who was at a dinner with them in Brighton in December 1829, wrote in his journal, 'The Duke is a sad spectacle [he was twenty-eight at the time]; but yet he seems partly to understand what is said to him, at least the sense of what he has heard an hour ago sometimes flashes across his mind. The Duchess though vulgar and purseproud does not want for a sort of frank good humour and hearty gaiety, which alone makes her sufferable.'

When her social rank compelled an invitation to some civic reception or other, it was not uncommon for Harriot to be given the place of honour by dint of her newly acquired rank and then to be strenuously ignored by her fellow guests. It was a bitter pill to swallow. At other times, the snub was more direct, as when her name was omitted from the guest list of a ball at the Royal Pavilion in January 1831 despite being the highest-ranked inhabitant of Brighton. Months later her husband and two of his sisters, Ladies Louise and Mary Beauclerk, were invited to a Court ball, while Harriot herself was deliberately excluded. But Dukey leapt to her defence. At the inauguration dinner for the Mayor of Lincoln in 1828, St Albans, in his speech in response to the toast drunk in honour of Harriot, declared, 'I am proud of my wife and I love her — the Duchess and myself despise the miscreants who assail her.' She was, however, eventually presented to Queen Adelaide, and took her place behind the Duchess of Richmond at the coronation of William IV in September 1831, a ceremony at which her husband bore the royal sceptre.

Although society was fastidious in keeping Harriot off its own turf, it was only too eager to enjoy her hospitality. The parties she threw at Holly Lodge, Highgate, were the stuff of legend even in her own time, and given that the royal family banked with Coutts, it was quite common for the King's brothers, the Dukes of Sussex and Clarence to attend. At one party, to celebrate the couple's first wedding anniversary, there were Tyrolean minstrels, Russian ballet dancers, a military band and a company of archers, as well as a specially erected ballroom, in which Litolff and Adam's 'much esteemed new French quadrille band' played the dance music. An extravagant 'breakfast' was laid out across eight rooms and, according to the *Morning Post*, 'there was a constant succession of amusements, dispersed in various parts of the grounds'. Indeed, with the Duke's penchant for fancy dress and Shakespearean recitals, the guests never quite knew what to expect. The party lasted from two in the afternoon to eleven at night.

Still, despite the slights, Harriot had led something of a fairy-tale life, and her sense of this is related in a letter to Sir Walter Scott in 1827:

> What a strange eventful life has mine been, from a poor little player child, with just food and clothes to cover me, dependent on a very precarious profession, without a talent or a friend in the world! 'To have seen what I have seen, see what I see.' Is it not wonderful? is it true? can I believe it? – first the wife of the best, the most perfect being that ever breathed, his love and unbounded confidence in me, his immense fortune so honourably acquired by his own industry, all at my command . . . and now the wife of a Duke. You must write my life; the History of Tom Thumb, Jack the Giant Killer, and Goody Two Shoes, will sink compared with my true history written by the Author of *Waverley* . . .

The parallels with the life of Nell Gwyn are obvious, and many a lampoon appeared in the chronicles of the time portraying Harriot as

a sort of fake Nell. A poem in *The Age*, purporting to be written by
Nell Gwyn herself to the editor, savages any notion that she could be
compared with Harriot:

> My King – no, Charles Stuart – the man next I shared,
> With charmers enough to have filled a serai:
> I was *constant* and *satisfied*: think you I cared
> For titles or flatterers? – Marry, not I.
>
> Look first upon that picture, then upon this –
> Say, had I less beauty – less clothes on my back?
> Can *brandy* or brass give HER *my* air of bliss?
> Was I *bloated* and *raddled*, or *bearded* and *black*?

And so on. Whatever the public perception, it is clear that the 9th
Duke's marriage to Harriot Mellon revived the original family para-
digm laid down by the union of Charles and Nell, though the earlier
relationship was based more firmly in reality. What strikes one about
the union of Dukey and Dollalolla are the huge doses of fiction
required to keep the thing going. Both husband and wife were carried
away by the romantic associations of the title and a desire to recreate
the flavour of medieval chivalry in their daily lives. A good illustration
of this are the huge falconry displays that they mounted both at
Brighton and Lincoln, which drew crowds of twenty thousand or
more. The Duke, splendidly attired as Grand Falconer, directed the
spectacle from horseback followed by a page in Lincoln green, while
Harriot looked on from an open barouche. After the display the birds
would be presented to the Duchess, who sat caressing them in her
carriage.

Harriot's miraculous journey in life was not, of course, without its
emotional price. Her insecurities revealed themselves most openly in
her relations with the Duke's family, who were as protective of him as
she was controlling. There were a number of scenes and feuds between
her and the Duke's uncles and siblings. For instance, not long after she
and the Duke were married they were joined at Portsmouth by three
of his brothers, Lords Frederick, Henry and Charles. One morning the
four brothers, anxious to set off on a sailing excursion, breakfasted
early and were chatting gaily over their coffee when the Duchess came

charging into the room and, seeing the table in a mess, 'burst into one of her terrific fits of passion and abused the Duke so grossly, that he indignantly left the room, ordered his carriage and actually ran away from her . . .' When the Duke wrote to his uncle Lord Frederick Beauclerk relating the incident, he expressed his disgust at Harriot's 'person and age'. In her will, Harriot made her bequests to the Duke on condition that his uncle Lord Amelius and his brothers Lords Frederick and Charles were not to reside with him even for one week in the year.

She may also have resented the family sponging on her. In a satirical poem entitled 'Mother Malone's Fete' (1828), an account of one of her famous parties, there occurs the following stanza:

The beggarly Beauclerks will come at a wink,
In her *Grease's* rich larder their lean sides a-pitching;
She won all their hearts by her victuals and drink,
She had faults, they confessed – but then damn it! – her kitchen!
And sure every pin,
She's as good as Nell Gwynn,
The respectable source where their houses begin;
If by one side they trace their breed up to a throne,
Oh! the other can't rank above 'MOTHER MALONE'.

Harriot died in 1837 aged fifty-nine, clutching Mr Coutts's pillow to her breast. The thirty-six-year-old widowed Duke consoled himself by seducing a servant girl, by whom he had a daughter. If he had had any notion of inheriting Harriot's vast fortune, now estimated at £1,800,000, he was to be disappointed. She left it to one of Thomas Coutts's granddaughters, Angela Burdett, who became the famous philanthropist Baroness Burdett-Coutts. Once again for the Beauclerks, the money had vanished like a stash of fairy gold. In May 1839 St Albans married an Irish girl, Elizabeth Gubbins, the youngest daughter of General Joseph Gubbins of Kilfrush, Limerick. The couple had two children, William (b. 1840), who became the 10th Duke, and a daughter, Diana (b. 1842). Elizabeth's brother, Charles Gubbins, was mad, which was convenient for the Beauclerks, as it provided them with an alibi for their own insanity. The 9th Duke died in 1849 at the age of forty-eight after falling from his horse.

William Amelius Aubrey de Vere Beauclerk, the 10th Duke, who was only nine when his father died, was a very different kettle of fish. Described by a contemporary as 'a cheery, sensible, steady, kindhearted man of business', he was the first Duke of St Albans to make Bestwood the family base and turn it into a thriving agricultural estate. In fact he did much more. Not only did he rebuild the mansion itself, creating a Victorian Gothic pile that resembles a smaller version of St Pancras Station and replanting the park with a rich variety of firs, but he also founded the Bestwood Coal & Iron Company, which by 1884 was raising 350,000 tons of coal a year and employing 720 men. He took an active part in local affairs, becoming Honorary Colonel of the 1st Notts. Rifle Volunteers (the Robin Hoods), Captain of the Yeomen of the Guard and Lord Lieutenant and Custos Rotulorum of Nottinghamshire. He also founded the Bestwood Park cricket club and laid out a fine pitch that could be seen from his drawing-room windows. He was consciously creating a conventional ducal stronghold for future generations of the family to enjoy. But it was in defiance of the family dæmon, and he was to be bitterly disappointed in his hopes.

He had already befriended the Prince of Wales as a young man, and his close relationship with the royal family was reinforced by his marriage in June 1867 at St James's Palace – and in the presence of the Queen – to the eighteen-year-old Sybil Grey, eldest daughter of Lt.-Gen. the Hon. Charles Grey, who was the second son of the 2nd Earl Grey, the Reform Bill Prime Minister. He was also Victoria's private secretary and a great favourite of the Queen. Sybil herself had been brought up at Court and was extremely well connected. She was also a direct descendant via her mother of the American Indian Princess Pocahontas. Various members of the royal family were frequent visitors at Bestwood, and when their son was born in March 1870, both the Queen and the Prince of Wales were godparents. He was named Charles Victor Albert Aubrey de Vere Beauclerk in their honour and in time became the 11th Duke of St Albans. There were two daughters as well, Ladies Louise and Sybil. Tragically, their mother died after giving birth to Sybil in September 1871. Remembered as an almost saintly figure at Bestwood, she built Emmanuel Church in the grounds of the estate. The Duke remarried an Irishwoman, Grace Bernal-Osborne of Newtown Anner, Co. Tipperary, and had five further children, including two sons, Osborne (known as 'Obby', b. 1874) and William (b. 1883).

The family presented a charming and cultured face to the outside world. Bestwood was the scene of countless children's theatricals, balls and concerts, in which all the Duke's offspring participated. At Christmas 1883 there was a children's fancy ball. Charles Burford, the heir, went as Mephistopheles, his sister Louise as a 'fishwoman' and Obby as a 'powdered footman'. The thirteen-year-old Mephistopheles danced with the Virgin of the Snow, but who she was is not recorded. A journalist from the *World* invited to lunch in 1892 wrote rapturously of the warm family atmosphere and lively table talk. But a dark undertow was gathering beneath the surface gaiety.

Burford, in particular, had an uneasy relationship with his stepmother and had never forged a bond with the grieving father who had turned his back on his children to plough his energies into creating a profitable estate. The mother who had slipped out of his life when he was eighteen months old was never mentioned. He had no friends at Eton, and his tutor wrote that he was 'a very strange boy who could not be influenced, and on whom no impression could be made'. He left two years early. Later he made a show of joining the army, but was dogged by mysterious fevers and a bad heel. A young man of exceptional vitality, he voyaged out to the northern kingdom of New Zealand in 1893, where his knife-blade horsemanship was admired by the Maoris. Jack Seely, who accompanied Burford on the trip, described him as fearless.[4] Yet, on his return, he lost his nerve in the saddle and grew morose. His youthful fire seemed turned inwards. He accused his father and stepmother of attempting to poison him and suspected the doctors of being in league with them. His father packed him off to India as ADC to Lord Elgin, but he contracted dysentery in the jungle and suffered a nervous breakdown. By the time he returned to England in 1897 he was suffering from quite severe schizophrenia, an illness not understood at the time, and had ceased to believe that he was responsible for his actions.

When the 10th Duke died of cancer in May 1898 at the age of fifty-eight, he was widely mourned not just at Bestwood and Nottingham, but in the county at large. Two months after the funeral Burford, now the 11th Duke, went aboard his father's 305-ton yacht, the *Ceres*, which was moored at Southampton, armed to the gills and in a state of nervous mania. Having shot at the captain, he ordered the crew to arm themselves against a gang of invisible conspirators and locked himself in his cabin with loaded revolvers. He was arrested and taken back to London, where he was examined and certified as insane. One of the medical officers was Henry Maudsley; the other, Dr Savage, wrote, 'He told me he was King of England, that there was a great plot among lawyers against him, and that his relations had tried to poison him.' He spent the next thirty-six years until his death in 1934 at Ticehurst House asylum for the insane in Sussex. The archetype of the *puer aeternus* that had sent the 9th Duke scurrying to the fancy-dress wardrobe had worked an altogether darker alchemy in the soul of his grandson, who found he couldn't make any sort of bargain with reality. The 10th Duke's hopes for the family were in tatters.

The 11th Duke's youngest brother, Willie, was also mad and having set fire to a building at Eton spent the remainder of his life at the Priory, Roehampton, where he died in 1954. The middle brother, Obby, who succeeded 'poor old Bur' as 12th Duke in 1934, was eccentric and prey to fits of melancholy, but not certifiable. For the Queen's coronation in 1953 he applied to the Earl Marshal's office to carry a live falcon at the Abbey and, when told that he would have to make do with a stuffed one, declined to go at all. He was a restless man who travelled the world seeking the pot of gold at the rainbow's end – as when he set up a goldmining venture at Thibert Creek in British Columbia – but he always finished face to face with his own desperate and fantastic nature. Deeply insecure about who he was, he overplayed the part of duke, putting others down with acts of appalling snobbery and as late as the 1960s addressing the hall porter at Brooks's club in London with the words, 'Wind up my watch for me, there's a good fellow'. On the other hand, an electrician arriving at his house in Tipperary to change a light bulb was quite likely to leave with an old master under his arm, having had it forced upon him by the grateful Duke. An abiding sense of worthlessness informed both his cruelty and his inflated generosity. Either way he was an extremist. Even his lack of pretension, when he decided to play that particular card, could be extreme, as when he arrived at a smart house-party in the country walking across the lawn carrying a brown paper bag containing a toothbrush and a pair of pyjamas.

Unlike his father, of whom one obituarist wrote, 'a better man of business never lived', Obby had a dread of all financial matters, unless they were wild get-rich-quick schemes. The family fortune built up by his father rapidly decayed in his hands. His mad brother's trustees had sold Redbourne in 1917, and Obby, who never lived there as Duke, sold Bestwood in 1940. It had been in the family for 260 years. No sooner had the 10th Duke established the Beauclerks as a respected force in the world and given them the stability they had always lacked than the family dæmon reasserted itself. As had been true of the royal Stuarts in the sixteenth, seventeenth and eighteenth centuries, there was something in the Beauclerk soul that resisted success. Where failure and hardship at least made members of the family feel real and plausible, success weighed like death upon their hearts.

The sisters, in particular those from the first marriage, fared better on the level of soul. Lady Louise (1869–1958), known as 'Cuckoo' within the family, was a follower of Rudolf Steiner. In Switzerland, one holiday, she had an experience of 'cosmic consciousness', a profoundly transformative episode in which her whole being was flooded with light and she felt at unity and peace with all creation. She was a strong advocate of women's rights and in 1907 travelled to the United States to study the movement there. She was married to the MP and horticulturalist Gerald Loder, later Lord Wakehurst. Her younger sister, Sybil, never married and, like the mother for whom she was named, died early. On her writing table at her death, aged thirty-nine, was found the following note in her hand: 'God is life and love. I am one with God, his life–love–wisdom and strength flows into me every moment. I am one with God, and nothing can hurt me or make me afraid.'

Obby died in 1964 in his ninetieth year and was succeeded as 13th Duke by his cousin Charles Frederick Aubrey de Vere Beauclerk (1915–88), my grandfather. Charles Beauclerk was the only surviving grandson of Lord Charles Beauclerk (1813–61), a younger son of the 8th Duke. Lord Charles had joined the army as a young man after graduating from Sandhurst and saw service in Ireland, Canada and the

Crimea. He was a talented artist, whose skills as a portraitist got him into hot water with his sister-in-law Harriot Coutts, who came upon him drawing a caricature of her. He was also an inventor with several patents to his name. He died a hero's death at the age of forty-eight, attempting to rescue the crew of the Scarborough lifeboat which had been dashed against the pier on its maiden voyage.[5]

The 13th Duke's father was Lord Charles's third son, Aubrey Topham Beauclerk (1850–1933), a rover like Obby, who was born in Brussels and spent most of his life in the colonies. As a young man he emigrated to South Africa, leaving the suitcase containing all his money in the cab taking him to Southampton. Once there he managed to acquire a goldmine, but lacked the capital to exploit it. It seems, too, that he entered into some sort of tribal marriage with a native girl, by whom he had a daughter who later became a nurse in London, where she committed suicide in the 1960s. The story was told by Gerard Shelley in his novel *The White Villa at Dinard* (1927), only the daughter has metamorphosed into a son whose mother claims that he is the true heir to the dukedom.[6]

After South Africa, Aubrey Beauclerk went to live in Canada, where he managed the Fitzwilliam estates (his sister Laura was married to Lord Milton, the son of the 6th Earl Fitzwilliam). By the time he returned to England in search of a bride, he was already in his sixties. Nevertheless, his quest was successful, and in the autumn of 1913 he married Gwendolen Loftus Hughes, the thirty-three-year-old daughter of Sir Frederick Hughes (1814–95), former High Sheriff of Wexford in Ireland and Knight of the Royal Persian Order of the Lion and the Sun. Their only child, my grandfather, who was born two years later in 1915, used to refer to his Irish relatives as 'the bog fairies'. At his birth his father was sixty-five years old, old enough to be his great-grandfather.

The couple led a nomadic life with 'de Vere' – as they called their son – in tow. During the 1920s they spent five years in France, a year in Belgium and two years in Germany, moving from house to house and sometimes hotel to hotel. Whether this had anything to do with the African scandal I don't know, but it was certainly an unsettling life for a man in his seventies and his young family. My grandfather remembered his father as a courtly, silent old gentleman, out of touch with the modern world, and wrote of him in his introduction to Douglas Sutherland's *The English Gentleman Abroad*, 'his appearance . . . certainly struck an exotic note in the countries he patronized. A Homburg hat, a mustard-coloured cloak with a scarlet lining and a silver-topped cane, combined to arouse in me the maximum reactions of shame and embarrassment!' His mother too was slightly fey, and when she eventually sent him to boys' school, it was 'with long curls, very girlish clothes, and a necklace of blue beads'.

When they finally returned to England, they settled in Aldeburgh in Suffolk. Aubrey knew it well as he had spent much of his childhood at nearby Leiston Hall, the home of his uncle Lord Amelius Beauclerk, who became his guardian when he was orphaned at the age of eleven. They had also lived there during the Great War, when Aubrey, who used to sit in the garden overlooking the sea in the evenings smoking his pipe, was arrested under suspicion of sending smoke signals to the German U-boats. He died in 1933, knowing that he had managed to keep the dukedom going with his belated contribution to the Beau-clerk gene pool. Had he not had a son in 1915, the title would have fizzled out with Obby's death in 1964.

The 12th Duke was already sixty-two when Charles Beauclerk came of age in 1936, so the latter was never quite sure when he might inherit the title. As heir, his education at Eton was paid for by the family trustees, and he received allowances from both Obby and his cousin Billy Fitzwilliam. After Cambridge he worked for a while as a journalist, but his career was cut short by the outbreak of war in 1939. Being trilingual, he joined the Intelligence Corps and worked in the psychological warfare branch in North Africa (Algiers, Tunisia and Libya), as well as Malta, Sicily, Italy and, finally, Austria. After the war, which he ended as the youngest colonel in British Intelligence, he became head of propaganda with the Allied Commission for Austria in Vienna from 1946 to 1950. On his return to London he joined the Central Office of Information, where he became Chief Books Editor and, later, Director of Films and Television. His marriage to Nathalie Chatham Walker in 1938 did not survive the vicissitudes of the war, though it did produce my father, Murray de Vere Beauclerk (b. 1939), the present and 14th Duke of St Albans. In 1947 Charles married as his second wife the painter and author Suzanne Marie Adèle Fesq (b. 1921), who is of French and Australian stock.[7] Together they produced three sons and a daughter.

Having inherited the title, my grandfather sold the last remaining ancestral acres at North Ormsby in Lincolnshire and the family became landless wanderers once more. In the meantime he went into business with the money he had inherited and, according to Brian Masters in *The Dukes*, 'had the acumen to make himself a millionaire'. (A dukedom was then a valued commodity in City boardrooms.) Soon he had recovered a number of family treasures, which he housed in Chelsea, where he and his wife cultivated an artistic salon that included figures such as Terence Kilmartin, translator of Proust, John Davenport, a critic, man of letters and drinking companion of Dylan Thomas who collaborated with Thomas on *The Death of the King's Canary*, and playwright Peter Luke. They also ran the Upper Grosvenor Galleries, where they mounted a number of innovative exhibitions. But the Duke proved an innocent in the cut-throat world of high finance and lost a fortune when he pulled out of a group of companies that were being criminally mismanaged. He sold up in London and went to live in Vence in the south of France, where his wife's family had property.

As with Obby, Charles's ability to put on a show camouflaged a weak sense of identity that was easily exploited. Uncomfortable with ceremony, he never took his seat in the House of Lords and often seemed most at home with the simple folk of Vence, or pottering among his orange trees. What I remember in particular were his marvellous sense of the absurd and his ability to turn our daily excursion to the local market into an adventure. Like so many of his predecessors, he couldn't tolerate large helpings of reality, for the *puer* strain lived strongly in him. He expected life to be bright and congenial; problems, whether practical or emotional, were glossed over or dismissed. Though a keen historian, he never dwelt on the past. He did, however, enjoy what he perceived to be the echoes of Charles II's life in his own: the early 'exile' across Europe, surviving on one meal a day (in his case when his mother cut him off for marrying beneath him), his father dying when he was eighteen, his womanizing, his Continental wife, the mistrust of emotion and so on. Part of him may have consciously modelled itself on the merry monarch. There was even a physical resemblance, commented upon by the *Daily Telegraph* obituarist.

My father, who succeeded him in 1988, has always kept a low profile; indeed, according to Brian Masters in *The Dukes*, the phrase might have been invented for him. It is not my place to blow his cover. His great love is music, in particular opera, and he is president of the Beaufort Opera Company. When he made his maiden speech in the House of Lords in January 1994, the first time a Duke of St Albans had spoken there in 127 years, he spoke on arts funding. To his delight, his fellow maiden that day was the violinist Yehudi Menuhin.

His half-siblings, the children of my grandfather's second marriage, Peter, James, John and Caroline, have all set aside their courtesy titles. Peter practises traditional Chinese medicine and acupuncture in California and is a licensed captain of the US Coast Guard; he has also been a practising alchemist. James, a quixotic character, has wandered beyond the family ken and lives under various aliases in the north of England. John has worked all over the world for Oxfam and Save the Children, including six years in Peru and five in Mongolia. He also spent many years working in Africa and is the author of *Hunters and Gatherers in Central Africa* (2002). Caroline, after several years as a social worker, founded the charity Albaction, which helps Albanian refugees settling in England. Through their work they have been able to give expression to the family mythos in a practical and devotional manner, which is quite inspiring.

Having used the Woolsack in the House of Lords as an impromptu soapbox to defend the golden principle of sovereignty, I too set aside my courtesy title. And as the Beauclerk family begins a new cycle, it seems that the genius of Nell Gwyn is strongly reasserting itself. The ultimate torch-bearer, and a sure pledge of better times, is my nine-year-old son, James, in whom the mischievous spirit of his ancestress lives on!

Notes

Prologue: Shining White

1. Clifford Bax, *Pretty Witty Nell: an Account of Nell Gwyn and Her Environment*, Chapman & Hall, London, 1932, p. 1.
2. Jeanine Delpech (trans. Ann Lindsay), *The Life and Times of the Duchess of Portsmouth*, Elek Books, London, 1953, p. 49.
3. Aphra Behn, Epistle Dedicatory to *The Feign'd Courtesans*, 1679.

1. Humble Beginnings

1. W. B. Yeats, 'The Curse of Cromwell' from *New Poems*, Cuala Press, Dublin, 1938.
2. According to Antonia Fraser in *King Charles II* (Weidenfeld & Nicolson, London, 1979 p. 19), the royal oak became Charles's badge at the age of eight when he was made Prince of Wales.
3. 'For the remainder of her life [after the King's death] she lived in retirement, under the title of Lady Simcock, and performed many acts of charity, some of which are kept up to this day – Lady Simcock's gift of bread to the unfortunate debtors in Ludgate Prison is one of them.' John Fairburn, *Fairburn's Edition of the Life, Amours and Exploits of Nell Gwinn, etc.*, J. Fairburn, London, 1820, p. 26.
4. 'Orange Moll' was the nickname of one Mary Meggs, widow, who was in charge of selling fruit at the King's Playhouse.
5. William Blake, 'The Little Girl Found' from *Songs of Experience*, 1794.

2. *Restoration*

1. Maintaining his alias of John Clarke, Richard Cromwell lived at Cheshunt in Hertfordshire and was described as 'a little and very neat old man with a most placid countenance'. He died in 1712.
2. Winston S. Churchill, *A History of the English-Speaking Peoples*, vol. 2, Cassell & Co., London 1956, p. 272.
3. John Dryden, 'Threnodia Augustalis', London, 1685.
4. Hesketh Pearson, *Charles II: His Life and Likeness*, Heinemann, London, 1961, p. 129.
5. *A Supplement to Burnet's History of My Own Time*, ed. H. C. Foxcroft, Clarendon Press, Oxford, 1902, p. 50.
6. Cecil Chesterton (brother of G. K.), *The Story of Nell Gwyn*, T. N. Foulis, London and Edinburgh, 1911, p. 66.

3. *Rising from the Ashes*

1. Samuel Pepys, *Diary*, 25 February 1665.
2. Cited on p. 28 of Arthur Bryant's *Restoration England*, Collins, London, 1960.
3. According to Professor Roy MacGregor-Hastie in *Nell Gwyn*, Robert Hale, London, 1987, p. 32. Source not cited.
4. Tom Brown, 'From worthy Mrs Behn the Poetress to the famous Virgin Actress', *Letters from the Dead to the Living*, first published in *Works of Mr Thomas Brown*, 5 vols, 1720, vol. 2, p. 303.

4. *A King of Love*

1. Henri IV, the first Bourbon King of France, was stabbed to death by a religious fanatic, François Ravaillac, on 14 May 1610.
2. BM Stowe MS 1055, folio 15. The account of Barbara's exploit is given by antiquary Lord Coleraine. The bishop in question was Robert Braybrooke, who had died in 1404. His mummified body had fallen out of its tomb in St Paul's during the Fire of London and had become something of a tourist attraction. Barbara visited it at night and 'dismembered as much of the privity as [she] could get into her mouth'. Coleraine ended his account in jocular vein: 'Though some ladies of late

have got Bishopricks for others, yet I have not heard of any but this that got one for herself.'

3. Having retired to the bedroom, followed by all the guests, the bride, having got into bed, would fling her stocking, rather like a bride today throwing her bouquet, and the person who caught it was next to be married.

4. Virginia Woolf, *A Room of One's Own*, Grafton, 1987, p. 61 (originally published by the Hogarth Press, 1929).

5. Stepping Up

1. Cecil Chesterton, *The Story of Nell Gwyn*, T. N. Foulis, London, 1911, p. 136. Source not cited.

2. Obliterated in the last century to make way for the Stalinesque Bush House, home of the BBC.

3. From the Nell Gwyn Album compiled in 1843 by Thomas Crofton Croker, owned by the Duke of St Albans.

4. Richard Ames, from his poem *The Female Fire-Ships, A Satyr against Whoring*, London, 1691.

5. John Harold Wilson, *All the King's Ladies: Actresses of the Restoration*, University of Chicago Press, Chicago, 1958, p. 10.

6. Colley Cibber, *An Apology for the Life of Mr. Colley Cibber, Comedian* (1740), ed. R. W. Lowe, 2 vols, London, 1889, vol. 2, p. 222.

6. Stars in her Eyes

1. Related by Capt. Alexander Smith in *The History of the Lives of the Most Noted Highwaymen, Foot-Pads, Shop-Lifts and Cheats of Both Sexes, in and about London and Other Places . . . for Fifty Years Last Past*, 2 vols, London, 1714, vol. 1, pp. 89–92.

2. In August 1665, at the start of the Second Dutch War, the English made an unsuccessful raid on Dutch shipping off Bergen.

3. The Infanta Marie-Thérèse of Habsburg was the daughter of Philip IV of Spain. Louis, whose mother, Anne of Austria, was Philip's sister, was thus married to his own first cousin.

4. Margaret Cavendish, *The Description of a New World, called the Blazing World* (1666) from *The Blazing World and Other Writings*, ed. Kate Lilley, Penguin, London, 1992, p. 185.

7. The Wild Mistress

1. Related by Professor Roy MacGregor-Hastie in *Nell Gwyn*, Robert Hale, London, 1987, pp. 61–2.
2. As King, James created her Countess of Dorchester. She followed him into exile in France.

8. Her Charles the Third

1. Even serious ministers were trashed. Clarendon said of Secretary of State Sir Henry Bennet, later Earl of Arlington, that he 'knew no more of the constitution and laws of England than he did of China'.
2. Mary, the elder, became Queen in 1689 when her father James fled to France. She ruled jointly with her husband, William of Orange, and died in 1694. Anne, the younger, became Queen in 1702 on the death of her brother-in-law.
3. John Wildman, 1621–93, a lawyer and businessman, was one of Buckingham's closest Republican friends and, as his executor, sold off the Duke's estates after his death to pay his debts.
4. Sir Orlando Bridgeman was made Keeper of the Great Seal instead.
5. Astraea was a virgin goddess associated with the astrological sign of Virgo, the maiden harvester. The Elizabethans applied the name to their Queen and thought of Astraea as the herald of a new golden age.
6. Aphra Behn, from her poem 'A Paraphrase on the Eleventh Ode out of the First Book of Horace'.
7. The story is told, with variations, in a number of the anonymous 'satyrs' of the time.
8. When the then Prince of Wales (the future Edward VII) lost his virginity to the bouncy actress Nellie Clifden in 1861, the London hacks began referring to her as the Princess of Wales. Queen Victoria was not amused.

9. A Bastard Grace

1. This was probably a blessing in disguise, as the offended party usually hired a gang of toughs to beat up the actor or actress as they left the theatre. Such was Edward Kynaston's fate when he impersonated Sir Charles Sedley.

2. In describing Oroonoko Behn writes, 'His nose was rising and *Roman*, instead of *African* and flat. His mouth the finest shaped that could be seen; far from those great-turn'd lips, which are so natural to the rest of the negroes . . . His hair came down to his shoulders, by the aids of art, which was by pulling it out with a quill, and keeping it comb'd; of which he took particular care.' From *Shorter Novels: Seventeenth Century*, ed. Philip Henderson, Dent, London, 1967, p. 154. Behn also condemns his black complexion as a fault, an absurd thing to do in the case of a negro. Also, like Charles, Oroonoko is passionate about mathematics and fortification, and rejects the hypocritical formulations of dogmatic Christianity.

3. John Evelyn, on a visit to Newmarket, wrote in his *Diary* for 22 July 1670, 'We went to see the stables and fine horses, of which many were here kept at a vast expense, with all the art and tendernesse imaginable.'

4. Jonathan Richardson the younger, *Richardsoniana: or occasional reflections on the moral nature of man . . . with several anecdotes interspersed*, London, 1776, pp. 90–1.

5. Andrew Marvell, from his poem 'Upon the Cutting of Sir John Coventry's Nose'.

6. The Popish Plot was a fictitious Jesuit plot, most likely fabricated by the Earl of Shaftesbury and his supporters, and promoted by Titus Oates. The Jesuits were supposedly planning to assassinate Charles II and place his brother James on the throne.

7. The Chiffinches were also in charge of the King's dogs and arranged the roster of walkers. The *London Gazette* of 16–19 July 1673 has the following advertisement in the lost-and-found column: 'A small liver-coloured bitch lost from the King's lodgings, on the 14th instant, with a little white on her breast and a little white on the tops of her hind feet. Whoever brings her to Mr. Chiffinch's lodgings at the King's Back Stairs . . . shall be rewarded for their pains.'

8. It is fascinating to note how certain myths weave themselves into the fabric of Nell's life. Here the 'little slipper' leads us back into the tale of Cinderella. It is by means of the lost slipper that Cinderella is found by the prince, and it seems eerily fitting that this image should herald the beginning of real intimacy between Charles and Nell.

9. Professor Roy MacGregor-Hastie paints an attractive picture of the couple's domestic life in his *Nell Gwyn*, Robert Hale, London, 1987.

10. Colbert de Croissy's letters to the French foreign secretary Hugues de

Lionne provide a good deal of anecdotal material on Nell Gwyn and the other royal mistresses at this time.

10. Final Curtain

1. In a private letter to the author.
2. The term applied today to those who believe that the lost ten tribes of Israel found their way to the British Isles in the seventh century BC, and that their present-day descendants are God's Covenant people and their throne the throne of David.
3. The ultimate secrets of Freemasonry seem bound up with the sacred architecture of the Temple of Jerusalem built by Solomon. Laurence Gardner in *Bloodline of the Holy Grail* (Element, Shaftesbury, 1996) p. 324 writes,

> the Stuart kings were at the very forefront of Scottish Rite Freemasonry, which was founded on the most ancient of all arcane knowledge and Universal Law. Their Breton heritage was closely allied to the noble families of Boulogne and Jerusalem, and their background was largely Templar-inspired. It should come as no surprise, therefore, that it was under Charles I and Charles II ... that the *Invisible College* of the Royal Society emerged – a college that within a brief period of Stuart patronage revealed some of the greatest scientific discoveries of all time.

4. John Heneage Jesse, *Memoirs of the Court of England during the Reign of the Stuarts, including the Protectorate*, 6 vols, Richard Bentley, London, 1901, vol 5, p. 231.
5. From an undated cutting in the Nell Gwyn album compiled by Francis Hopkinson during the latter half of the nineteenth century.
6. Final proof, if it were needed, of Charles's sense of humour can be found in the motto that he appended to Barbara's new crest. It read, '*Et decus et pretium recti*' (Decency and the price of virtue).
7. The 'other house' was the Duke's Company, which had originally presented the jest at Dover in May.
8. Of all Charles II's children, Prince Rupert held his son by Nell Gwyn in particular esteem and affection.
9. Anecdote related by Professor Roy MacGregor-Hastie in *Nell Gwyn*, Robert Hale, London, 1987, p. 103.

11. A Chargeable Lady

1. Folklore has it there was a physician at the court of Charles II by the name of Dr Condom, or Conton, who developed a prophylactic sheath to help combat venereal disease. The device itself has been around for thousands of years, and the name 'condom' probably comes from the Latin verb 'condere', meaning 'to conceal'.

2. Colley Cibber, *An Apology for the Life of Mr. Colley Cibber, Comedian,* London, 1740, p. 448.

3. Count Lorenzo Magalotti (ed. J. Mawman), *Travels of Cosmo the Third Grand Duke of Tuscany Through England During the Reign of King Charles II* trans. from the Italian, London, 1821, pp. 319–20.

4. Principal sources used by the author: Crofton-Croker and Francis Hopkinson Nell Gwyn albums (privately owned), and the collections of household accounts and other receipts at the Army and Navy Club, London, and the Brotherton Library, Leeds University.

5. Graham Hopkins, *Nell Gwyn: A Passionate Life*, Robson Books, 2000, p. 147; the most thorough and scholarly account of Nell's life to date.

6. The poet and journalist Samuel Laman Blanchard (1804–45), who was a friend of Dickens and Thackeray, wrote a charming poem entitled 'Nell Gwyn's Looking Glass'. It begins,

> Glass antique, 'twixt thee and Nell
> Draw we here a parallel.
> She, like thee, was forced to bear
> All reflections, foul or fair;
> Thou art deep and bright within,
> Depths as bright belonged to Gwynne;
> Thou art very frail as well,
> Frail as flesh is – so was Nell.

7. The pearls that Nell bought from Prince Rupert's mistress had once belonged to his mother, Princess Elizabeth, daughter of James I, at whose wedding festivities in December 1612 *The Tempest* was played. Elizabeth was known as 'the Pearl of Britain' and 'Queen of Hearts'.

12. Foreign Honours

1. Cecil Chesterton, *The Story of Nell Gwyn*, T. N. Foulis, London, 1911, pp. 116–17.

2. In his introduction to the masque, Crowne wrote about the pitfalls of his theme:

> And as men who do things in haste, have commonly ill fortune, as well as ill conduct, I resolving to choose the first tolerable story I could meet with, unhappily encountered this, where, by my own rashness, and the malice of fortune, I involved myself, before I was aware, in a difficulty greater than the invention of the Philosopher's Stone, that only endeavours to extract gold out of the coarsest metals, but I employed myself to draw one contrary out of another; to write a clean, decent, and inoffensive play on the story of a rape, so that I was engaged in this dilemma, either wholly to deviate from my story, and so my story would be no story, or by keeping to it, write what would be unfit for Princesses and Ladies to speak, and a Court to hear. That which tempted me into so great a labyrinth, was the fair and beautiful image that stood at the portal, I mean the exact and perfect character of Chastity in the person of *Calisto*, which I thought a very proper character for the princess [Mary] to represent; nor was I mistaken in my judgment, the difficulty lay in the other part of the story, to defend chastity was easy, the danger was in assaulting it . . .

   The Dramatic Works of John Crowne, eds James Maidment and W. H. Logan, vol. 1, p. 237, Edinburgh and London, 1873.

3. The core of both this and the following anecdote are related by Baroness d'Aulnoy in her *Memoirs of the Court of England in 1675*, pp. 287–90 and pp. 314–16, and have since been embellished by a number of Nell's biographers.

4. H. Noel Williams, *Rival Sultanas: Nell Gwyn, Louise de Kéroualle and Hortense Mancini*, Hutchinson, London, 1915. No source cited.

13. The Court Jester

1. *Diary* of Samuel Pepys, 8 December 1666.
2. A term of endearment used by Prospero to Ariel in *The Tempest*, V, i, 226.
3. *Sir Francis Fane's Commonplace Book*, Shakespeare Library, Stratford-upon-Avon, f.169v.
4. Ibid., f.180r.
5. Having fallen into disrepute at the French Court, he had sought revenge by holding secret talks with France's sworn enemy, the Dutch. When his treason was discovered, he was arrested and brought to trial and shortly thereafter executed at the Bastille on 27 November 1674. Louise's public display of grief was hardly designed to go down well with Louis XIV.
6. Captain Alexander Smith, *The History of the Lives of the Most Noted Highwaymen, Foot-Pads, Shop-Lifts and Cheats of Both Sexes, in and about London and Other Places . . . for Fifty Years Last Past*, 2 vols, London 1714, vol. 2, pp. 52–3.
7. Henry Savile in a letter to the Earl of Rochester, 1 November 1677; *The Rochester–Savile Letters, 1671–80*, ed. John Harold Wilson, Ohio State University Press, Columbus, 1941, p. 48.
8. J. Granger, *A Biographical History of England*, 4 vols, London, 1775; vol. iii, p. 211.
9. Henri Forneron, *The Court of Charles II 1649–1734* (Compiled from State Papers), Sonnenschein & Co., London, 1897, p. 178.

14. Politics – A Deadly Pursuit

1. Heroes of Restoration comedy.
2. *Londons Defiance to Rome, a Perfect Narrative of the Magnificent Procession, and solemn Burning of the Pope at Temple Barr, Nov 17th, 1679. (Being the Coronation-Day of that Never-to-be-forgotten Princess, Queen Elizabeth.) With a Description of the Order, Rich Habits, Extraordinary Fire-works, Songs, and General Tryumphs attending that Illustrious Ceremony,* London, 1679.
3. Godfrey was the magistrate who took Titus Oates's original depositions concerning the alleged plot in September 1678. He went missing on 12 October 1678 and was found murdered five days later.
4. Paul Barrillon had been appointed French ambassador to London in

place of de Courtin in May 1677, as the latter had shown himself rather too squeamish about bribing MPs. Barrillon, who held his post until the end of Charles's reign, had no such scruples.

5. Reported in the news-sheet *Loyal Protestant Intelligencer*, 20 September 1681.

6. From 'The Ladies March', Harleian MS 7317, p. 30.

7. *The Life and Times of Anthony Wood, abridged from Andrew Clark's edition and with an introduction by Llewelyn Powys*, Oxford University Press, Oxford, 1961, pp. 252–3.

15. The Last Reckoning

1. Tom Brown, 1663–1704, was a satirist and hack writer who used the device of fictional letters from the dead to the living to ridicule writers, actors and other public figures.

2. Charles in fact greatly encouraged life in the colonies. It was a good place to send political radicals, and had he not been king one senses that he would have been in the vanguard of the new constitutional forms that were being discussed in America and which would one day be implemented to the benefit of the English-speaking peoples.

3. Arthur Bryant, *King Charles II*, Longmans, Green & Co., London, 1931, p. 345.

4. An anonymous ballad, 'The Duchess of Portsmouth's Garland', drove the point home:

> When Portsmouth did from England fly, to follow her
>   Vendôme,
> Thus all along the Gallery the monarch made his moan,
> O Châtillon, for charity, send me my Cleaveland home!
> Go, Nymph, so foolish and unkind, your wandering Knight
>   pursue,
> And leave a love-sick King behind, so faithful and so true,
> You Gods, when you made Love so blind, you should have
>   lam'd him too.

5. When I showed a copy of the portrait 'cold' to my son, then eight years old, and asked him to tell me what this man was like, he replied without hesitation, 'Bossy, kind, and thinks he's posh'.

6. It seems that Madam Le Croy was a palm-reader and fortune-teller.

7. The Earls of Oxford had been patrons of acting companies for several generations. The 17th Earl is today recognized by an increasing number of scholars as the poet and dramatist who wrote under the pseudonym 'William Shake-speare'.

8. Richard Ryan, *Dramatic Table Talk*, 3 vols, J. Knight & H. Lacey, London, 1825; vol. 2, p. 122.

9. The men were most likely being sent to keep Louis XIV out of Luxembourg. If so, they failed, for at the end of May 1684 Evelyn records the surrender of the duchy and makes the gloomy prediction that the Netherlands and Germany will follow, and that the French King now has a clear road to 'universal monarchy', i.e., a European empire à la Charlemagne.

10. Evelyn, a great admirer of Tenison, praises the good doctor for using his own money to fund many of his charitable projects. The public library in St Martin's was designed by Wren.

16. In the Shadows

1. Roy MacGregor-Hastie, *Nell Gwyn*, Robert Hale, London, 1987, p. 182.

2. Jack Ketch, the executioner, tried four strokes of the axe but could only partially sever the head. In the end, he lost his nerve and, throwing down the axe, took out a knife and finished the job like a butcher. Evelyn wrote of it in his *Diary* for 15 July 1685, 'the wretch made five chopps before he had his head off; which so incens'd the people, that had he not been guarded and got away, they would have torn him to pieces'.

3. William Shakespeare, *As You Like It*, II, i, 2–4.

4. Both syphilis and gonorrhoea were treated at the dreaded sweat houses of Leather Lane, where the patient would be subjected to a steam bath in mercury vapour. Mercury cures were as likely as the diseases themselves to produce high blood pressure.

5. Cecil Chesterton, *The Story of Nell Gwyn*, T. N. Foulis, London, 1911, p. 134.

6. From 'Laurinda: A Pastoral on the Lamented Death of the Incomparable Madam Guin', Harleian MS 7319, p. 532.

Epilogue: The House of Nell Gwyn

1. The Turks had originally been brought in by Louis XIV as a diversion while he finished the job of conquering Flanders.
2. This was the sovereign's personal bodyguard, created by Henry VIII. Today the Gentlemen Pensioners are more accurately known as Gentlemen at Arms.
3. His granddaughter, Diana de Vere, who lived to be a hundred, died in 1968, nearly 200 years after the birth of the admiral!
4. Major-General the Rt. Hon. J. E. B. Seely, *Adventure*, Frederick A. Stokes, New York, and William Heinemann, London, 1930, p. 16.
5. An account of the tragedy appeared in the RNLI journal, the *Life-Boat*, 1 January 1862 vol. v, no. 43, pp. 1–2. Lord Charles was posthumously awarded the Institution's silver medal for gallantry.
6. In the novel Aubrey Beauclerk, who is given the name Pontifex Fitzroy, is blackmailed by a former business partner from South Africa, who brings his African wife and son over to Brittany, where the Fitzroys are spending the summer. In the end, Pontifex's wife Hermione manages to destroy the incriminating marriage licence, thus protecting her son's inheritance of the title, but not before her husband has killed himself. High melodrama!
7. Her many books, written under the name Suzanne St Albans, include a childhood autobiography, *The Mimosa and the Mango*, a study of Oman, *Where Time Stood Still*, and a biography of Padre Pio entitled *Magic of a Mystic*.

Bibliography

Acton, Lord, 'Secret History of Charles II', *Home and Foreign Review*, July 1862 vol. 1, pp. 146–74.

Adamson, Donald, and Beauclerk-Dewar, Peter, *The House of Nell Gwyn: The Fortunes of the Beauclerk Family 1670–1974*, William Kimber, London, 1974.

Airy, Osmund, *Charles II*, Longman & Co., London, 1904.

Andrews, Allen, *The Royal Whore: Barbara Villiers, Countess of Castlemaine*, Hutchinson, London, 1971.

Anonymous, *Memoirs of the Life of Eleanor Gwinn, a Celebrated Courtesan in the Reign of Charles II and Mistress to That Monarch*, London, 1752.

Ashley, Maurice, *Charles II: The Man and the Statesman*, Weidenfeld & Nicolson, London, 1971.

d'Aulnoy, Marie Catherine, Baroness, *Memoirs of the Court of England in 1675*, trans. Mrs W. H. Arthur, John Lane, London, 1913.

Bax, Clifford, *Pretty, Witty Nell: An Account of Nell Gwyn and Her Environment*, Chapman & Hall, London, 1932.

Beauclerk Family Papers, London Metropolitan Archives.

Bedford, John, *London's Burning*, Abelard-Schuman, London, 1966.

Behn, Aphra, *The Works of Aphra Behn*, ed. Montague Summers, 6 vols, Phaeton, 1967.

Betterton, Thomas, *History of the English Stage from the Restoration to the Present Times*, ed. Edmund Curll, London, 1741.

Bevan, Bryan, *Nell Gwyn*, Robert Hale, London, 1969.

Bevan, Ian, *Royal Performance: The Story of Royal Theatregoing*, Hutchinson, London, 1954.

Bolitho, Hector, *The Romance of Windsor Castle*, Evans Brothers, London, 1946.

Boswell, Eleanor, *The Restoration Court Stage*, London, 1932.

Bowle, John, *John Evelyn and his World*, Routledge & Kegan Paul, London, 1981.

Brown, Louise Fargo, *The First Earl of Shaftesbury*, D. Appleton-Century Co., New York and London, 1933.

Brown, Thomas, *The Works of Mr Thomas Brown*, 5 vols, London, 1719.

Bryant, Arthur, *King Charles II*, Longmans, Green & Co., London, 1931.

——, *Restoration England*, Collins, London, 1960.

——, (ed.), *The Letters, Speeches and Declarations of King Charles II*, London, 1935.

Burghclere, Lady Winifred, *George Villiers, Second Duke of Buckingham*, John Murray, 1903.

Burnet, Gilbert, *History of My Own Time*, ed. Osmund Airy, 2 vols, Clarendon Press, Oxford, 1897, 1900.

Burney Collection of Newspapers, British Library.

Butler, Samuel, *Hudibras*, ed. John Wilders, Clarendon Press, Oxford, 1967.

Calendar of State Papers (Dom.), British Library.

Cartwright, Julia, *Madame. A Life of Henrietta, Daughter of Charles I and Duchess of Orleans*, Seeley, London, 1894.

Cavendish, Margaret, *The Blazing World and Other Writings*, ed. Kate Lilley, Penguin, London, 1992.

Chancellor, E. Beresford, *The Annals of Covent Garden and Its Neighbourhood*, Hutchinson, London, 1930.

Chapman, Hester W, *Great Villiers: A Study of George Villiers, Second Duke of Buckingham 1628–1687*, Secker & Warburg, London, 1949.

Chesterton, Cecil, *The Story of Nell Gwyn*, T. N. Foulis, London, 1911.

Churchill, Winston S., *A History of the English-Speaking Peoples*, vol 2, Cassell & Co., London, 1956.

Cibber, Colley, *An Apology for the Life of Mr. Colley Cibber, Comedian*, London, 1740.

Clarendon, Edward Earl of, *The History of the Rebellion and Civil Wars in England*, ed. W. Dunn Macray, 6 vols, Clarendon Press, Oxford, 1888.

Cook, Aurelian, *Titus Britannicus: an Essay of history royal: in the life & reign of*

His late Sacred Majesty, Charles II, of ever blessed and immortal memory, James
Partridge, London, 1685.

Crawfurd, Raymond, *Last Days of Charles II*, Clarendon Press, Oxford, 1909.

Croker, Thomas Crofton, Memorials of Nell Gwynn, 1843; MS property of
the Duke of St Albans, held at Child & Co., No. 1 Fleet Street, London.

Cruickshanks, Eveline (ed.), *The Stuart Courts*, Sutton Publishing, Stroud,
2000.

Cunningham, Peter, *The Story of Nell Gwyn*, ed. Gordon Goodwin, London,
1903.

Dasent, Arthur Irwin, *Nell Gwynne, 1650–1687*, Macmillan, London, 1924.

Defoe, Daniel, *A Journal of the Plague Year*, J. M. Dent & Co., London, and
E. P. Dutton & Co., New York, 1908.

Delpech, Jeanine, *The Life and Times of the Duchess of Portsmouth*, trans. Ann
Lindsay, Elek Books, London, 1953.

Drinkwater, John, *Mr Charles, King of England*, Hodder & Stoughton,
London, 1926.

Dryden, John, *John Dryden, the Major Works*, ed. Keith Walker, Oxford
University Press, Oxford, 2003.

Duffett, Thomas, *The Spanish Rogue*, London, 1674.

Etherege, George, *The Dramatic Works of Sir George Etherege*, ed. H. F. E.
Brett-Smith, 2 vols, Blackwell, Oxford, 1927.

Evelyn, John, *The Diary of John Evelyn*, ed. E. S. de Beer, Oxford University
Press, Oxford, 1959.

Evelyn, Mary, *Mundus Muliebris, or the Ladies dressing-room unlock'd, and her
toilette spread*, printed for R. Bentley, London, 1690.

Fane, Francis, Commonplace Book, MS held at Shakespeare Library, Strat-
ford-on-Avon.

Fanshawe, Sir Richard (attrib.), *Eikon Basilike: The Advice and Instructions given
by our Soveraign Lord King Charls the First, to his renowned son and successor
Charls the Second*, printed for Thomas James, London, 1660.

Fea, Allan, *King Monmouth: Being a history of the career of James Scott 'The
Protestant Duke,' 1649–1685*, John Lane, London and New York, 1902.

Forneron, Henri, *The Court of Charles II 1649–1734*, (Compiled from State
Papers), Sonnenschein & Co., London, 1897.

Foxcroft H. C. (ed.), *A Supplement to Burnet's History of My Own Time*, Clarendon Press, Oxford, 1902.

Fraser, Antonia, *King Charles II*, Weidenfeld & Nicolson, London, 1979.

——, *The Weaker Vessel: Woman's Lot in Seventeenth-Century England*, Phoenix Press, London, 2002.

Furley, O. W., 'The Whig Exclusionists: Pamphlet Literature in the Exclusion Campaign, 1679–81', *Cambridge Historical Journal*, 1957, vol. 8, pp. 19–36.

Genest, John, *Some Account of the English Stage, 1660–1830*, 10 vols, printed by H. E. Carrington, Bath, 1832.

Gilden, Charles, *Lives and Characters of the English Dramatic Poets*, London, 1790.

Glasheen, Joan, *The Secret People of the Palaces: The Royal Household from the Plantagenets to Queen Victoria*, Batsford, London, 1998.

Grammont, Count de, *Memoirs of the Court of Charles II*, ed. Sir Walter Scott, London, 1864.

Granger, J., *A Biographical History of England*, 4 vols, London, 1775.

Greene, Graham, *Lord Rochester's Monkey, being the life of John Wilmot, second Earl of Rochester*, Bodley Head, London, 1974.

Haley, K. D. H., *William of Orange and the English Opposition, 1672–74*, Clarendon Press, Oxford, 1953.

Hamilton, Elizabeth, *Henrietta Maria*, Hamish Hamilton, London, 1976.

Hammond, Paul, *John Dryden: A Literary Life*, Macmillan, London, 1991.

Hardy, Alan, *The King's Mistresses*, Evans Brothers, London, 1980.

Harleian Manuscripts, British Library.

Hart, William Henry, *A Memorial of Nell Gwynne, the Actress, and Thomas Otway, the Dramatist*, J. R. Smith, London, 1868.

Hartmann, Cyril H., *The Vagabond Duchess: The Life of Hortense Mancini Duchesse Mazarin*, G. Routledge & Sons, London, 1926.

Henderson, Philip (ed.), *Shorter Novels of the 17th Century*, J. M. Dent, London, 1930.

Hibbert, Christopher, *The Court at Windsor: A Domestic History*, Longmans, London, 1964.

Hobbes, Thomas, *Leviathan*, Penguin, London, 1982 (originally published in 1651).

Hopkins, Graham, *Nell Gwyn: A Passionate Life*, Robson Books, London, 2000.

Hopkinson, Francis, Nell Gwyn Album, MS compiled 1850s and 1860s.

Imbert-Terry, H. M., *A Misjudged Monarch: Charles Stuart*, William Heinemann, London, 1917.

Jameson, Storm, *The Decline of Merry England*, Cassell & Co., London, 1930.

Jesse, John Heneage, *Memoirs of the Court of England during the Reign of the Stuarts, including the Protectorate*, 6 vols, Richard Bentley, London, 1901.

Jones, J. R., *The First Whigs*, Oxford University Press, Oxford, 1961.

Jusserand, J. J., *A French Ambassador at the Court of Charles II: le comte de Cominges, from his unpublished correspondence*, Fisher Unwin, London, 1892.

Kenyon, John Philipps, *The Stuarts: A Study in English Kingship*, B. T. Batsford, London, 1958.

Love, Harold (ed.), *The Penguin Book of Restoration Verse*, Penguin, London, 1968.

Luttrell, Narcissus, *A Brief Historical Relation of State Affairs from September 1678 to April 1714*, 6 vols, Oxford University Press, Oxford, 1857.

MacGregor-Hastie, Roy, *Nell Gwyn*, Robert Hale, London, 1987.

MacQueen-Pope, W. J., *Theatre Royal Drury Lane*, W. H. Allen, London, 1945.

Macky, John, *Memoirs of the Secret Services of John M. esq.*, London, 1733.

Magalotti, Count Lorenzo, *Travels of Cosmo the Third Grand Duke of Tuscany through England during the Reign of King Charles II* (1669), trans. from the Italian, ed. J. Mawman, London, 1821.

Margoliouth, H. M. (ed.), *The Poems and Letters of Andrew Marvell*, 3rd edn, 2 vols, Clarendon Press, Oxford, 1971.

Mason, Lady Anne, 'Account of the Death of Charles II by a Wife of a Person about the Court at Whitehall', *Household Words*, London, 1954, vol. 9, pp. 277–8.

Masters, Anthony, *The Play of Personality in the Restoration Theatre*, ed. Simon Trussler, Boydell Press, Woodbridge, Suffolk, 1992.

Masters, Brian, *The Mistresses of Charles II*, Constable, London, 1997.

Masters, Brian, *The Dukes: The Origins, Ennoblement and History of Twenty-Six Families*, Pimlico, London, 2001.

Melville, Lewis, *Nell Gwyn: the Story of her Life*, Hutchinson, London, 1923.

——, *The Windsor Beauties*, Hutchinson, London, 1928.

Memorials of Nell Gwyn, Brotherton Library, University of Leeds.

Mitford, Nancy, *The Sun King*, Hamish Hamilton, London, 1966.

Norrington, Ruth (ed.), *My Dearest Minette: the letters between Charles II and his sister Henrietta, Duchesse d'Orléans*, Peter Owen, London, 1996.

Ogg, David, *England in the Reign of Charles II*, 2nd edn, 2 vols, Clarendon Press, Oxford, 1963.

Oldys, W., *The History of the English Stage, from the Restauration to the Present Time. Including the lives, characters and amours, of the most eminent actors and actresses. With instructions for public speaking*, compiled by William Oldys and Edmund Curll from the papers of T. Betterton, 2 vols, E. Curll, London, 1741.

Ollard, Richard, *The Escape of Charles II after the Battle of Worcester*, Hodder & Stoughton, London, 1966.

——, (ed.), *Clarendon's Four Portraits: George Digby: John Berkeley: Henry Jermyn: Henry Bennet*, Hamish Hamilton, London, 1989.

Osborn Collection, Yale University.

Palmer, Tony, *Charles II: Portrait of an Age*, Cassell, London, 1979.

Parker, Derek, *Nell Gwyn*, Sutton Publishing, Stroud, 2000.

Pearson, Hesketh, *Charles II: His Life and Likeness*, Heinemann, London, 1961.

Pepys, Samuel, *The Diary of Samuel Pepys: A New and Complete Transcription*, ed. Robert Latham & William Matthews, 9 vols, Bell, London, 1970–76.

Picard, Liza, *Restoration London*, Phoenix, London, 1998.

Prinz, Johannes, *John Wilmot Earl of Rochester: His Life and Writings*, Mayer & Müller, Leipzig, 1927.

Rochester, Earl of, *The Complete Poems of John Wilmot, Earl of Rochester*, ed. David M. Vieth, Yale University Press, New Haven, Connecticut, and London, 1968.

——, *A Genuine Letter from the Earl of Rochester to Nell Gwyn. Copied from an* original manuscript in the French King's Library, National Art Library, Victoria & Albert Museum, London.

Rowse, A. L., *Oxford in the History of the Nation*, Weidenfeld & Nicolson, London, 1975.

Ryan, Richard, *Dramatic Table Talk, or, scenes, situations and adventures, serious and comic in theatrical history and biography*, 3 vols, H. Knight & H. Lacey, London, 1825.

Sackville-West, Vita, *Aphra Behn, the Incomparable Astrea*, Gerald Howe, London, 1927.

Settle, Elkanah, *The Empress of Morocco*, London, 1673.

Smith, Capt. Alexander, *The History of the Lives of the Most Noted Highwaymen, Foot-Pads, Shop-Lifts and Cheats of Both Sexes in and about London and Other Places . . . for Fifty Years Last Past*, 2 vols. London, 1714.

Southworth, John, *Fools and Jesters at the English Court*, Sutton Publishing, Stroud, 1998.

Summers, Montague, *The Restoration Theatre*, Macmillan, London, 1934.

——, *The Playhouse of Pepys*, Macmillan, London, 1935.

Sydney, William Connor, *Social Life in England from the Restoration to the Revolution*, Ward & Dawney, London, 1892.

Thomas, Keith, *Religion and the Decline of Magic*, Weidenfeld & Nicolson, London, 1971.

Thomson, Gladys Scott, *Life in a Noble Household, 1641–1700*, Jonathan Cape, London, 1937.

Trease, Geoffrey, *Samuel Pepys and His World*, Thames & Hudson, London, 1972.

Van Bassen, Frederick, *The Royal Cedar*, 1688, p. 129, La.III.222 at Edinburgh University Library Special Collections.

Vincent, Samuel, *The Young Gallant's Academy, or, Directions How He Should Behave Himself in All Places*, London, 1674.

Wakehurst, Lord, *The Book of Beauclerk*, 1920, Essex Record Office, Chelmsford, MS A5344.

Welsford, Enid, *The Fool, His Social and Literary History*, Faber and Faber, London, 1935.

Wewitzer, R., *Dramatic Reminiscences*, London, Thomas Hailes Lacy, 1891.

Wheatley, Dennis, *Old Rowley: A Private Life of Charles II*, Hutchinson, London, 1933.

Whitcombe, Robert, *Janua Divorum: or Lives & Histories of the Heathen Gods, Goddesses & Demi-Gods*, for Francis Kirkman, London, 1678.

Williams, H. Noel, *Rival Sultanas: Nell Gwyn, Louise de Kéroualle and Hortense Mancini*, Hutchinson, London, 1915.

Wilson, John Harold, *All the King's Ladies: Actresses of the Restoration*, University of Chicago Press, Chicago, 1958.

——, *Nell Gwyn: Royal Mistress*, Frederick Muller, London, 1952.

——, *The Court Wits of the Restoration*, Princeton University Press, Princeton, 1948.

——, (ed.), *The Rochester–Savile Letters, 1671–80*, Ohio State University Press, Columbus, 1941.

Wood, Anthony, *The Life and Times of Anthony Wood, antiquary of Oxford, 1632–95*, ed. Andrew Clark, 5 vols, Oxford University Press, Oxford, 1891–1900.

Wright, James, *Historia Histrionica: an historical account of the English-Stage, shewing the ancient use, improvement, and perfection of dramatick representations in this nation*, W. Haws, London, 1699.

Wyld, H. C. *A Short History of English*, John Murray, London, 1914.

Index

NELL GWYN'S LOOKING GLASS,

In the Collection of Sir Page Dicks of Port Hall